Ted Simon was raised in London and studied chemical engineering, but he went to Paris where he fell into journalism. He is the author of several books, including the classic *Jupiter's Travels*. He now lives in northern California.

Dreaming
of Jupiter

TED SIMON

Little, Brown

LITTLE, BROWN

First published in Great Britain in 2007 by Little, Brown
Reprinted 2007 (four times)

A CIP catalogue record for this book
is available from the British Library.

ISBN 978-0-316-73227-7

Typeset in Baskerville by M Rules
Printed and bound in Great Britain by
Clays Ltd, St Ives plc

Little, Brown
An imprint of
Little, Brown Book Group
100 Victoria Embankment
London EC4Y 0DY

An Hachette Livre UK Company

www.littlebrown.co.uk

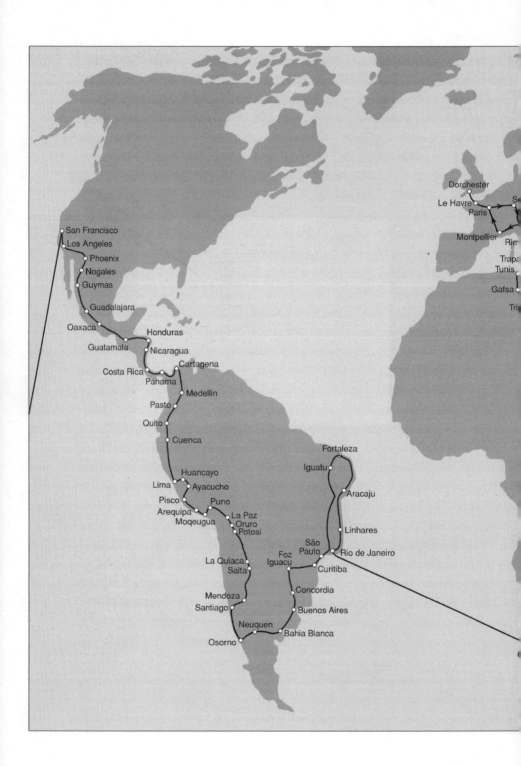

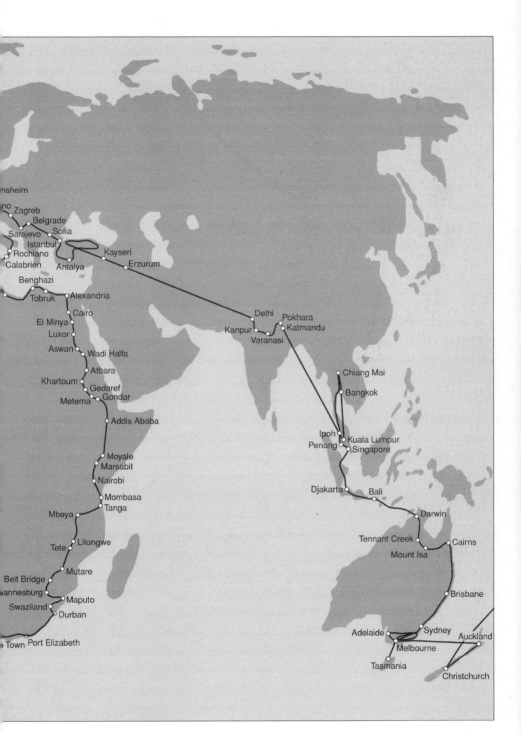

PROLOGUE

In March of 1973 I decided to travel around the world on a motor-cycle. The idea came, you could say, out of the blue, although it was a rather grey day on the south coast of England. I chose the motor-cycle for two main reasons. First, it seemed like the most versatile vehicle to use. Second, because I didn't think anyone had ever done it on a bike, and being the first to do it would make for a good book.

I was a writer, not a rider. Although I had admired motorcycles since childhood, I knew nothing about them, but that didn't bother me. Millions rode them, why shouldn't I? I was forty-two years old. Some people said, 'Surely you're too old for this kind of thing!' But that didn't bother me either, and in fact it turned out to be a good age.

The journey took four years. It was very hard, very exciting, and out of it came *Jupiter's Travels*, a book which many people have read.

If I had been told that I would do it again at the age of seventy I would have said that was ridiculous. Seventy would be much too old for that kind of thing.

In fact, twenty-four years later, when I was sixty-nine, I thought, Why not? I can still ride a bike. Wouldn't it be fascinating to find out what had happened along that 78,000 mile trail that I invented for myself in the seventies, and to see if I could recapture, in some way, the person I was then – this man who acquired briefly the rather lofty nickname of Jupiter, and who became for some an almost mythical figure.

There are thousands, I know, who dream of doing what that Jupiter did. Why shouldn't I?

1

The future is not what it used to be.

Paul Valéry

He appears in my memory like a wraith, tantalising me, a figure with no outline, just a presence that fades as I try to focus, and revives as I avert my mind. At the time we met, thirty years ago, he was merely a curiosity and not important to me, but now, swimming up from some cranny of the unconscious, he has taken hold.

He was a deckhand on the *Zoë. G*, the only ship I could find to carry me and my Triumph from Africa to South America. She was just a small tramp steamer, destined soon to be beached and broken up on some distant Indian shore, but she took me safely through a horrifying storm to Brazil, and for me she was a ship of dreams. I was already loaded with my own freight of memories from the journey through Africa and I was deep in thought, sifting through them and making discoveries about myself and my experiences. Perhaps I wasn't available to see him as more than a passing phenomenon. Today I see him as a presentiment. Had I paid more attention, perhaps I would have better foreseen the shape of things to come.

We were often alone together on the narrow metal deck where my bike also stood, lashed to a rail and bundled up under a canvas shroud, looking sad and inconsequential. His principal job was to repaint the ship's bubbling ironwork in a valiant effort to make the old lady presentable. His face was a discordant jumble of features, a mixture of many races. This I remember only because it's what I told myself at the time, and not because I can see him now. In the apartheid South Africa of the time he would have been classified as 'coloured'. There was some Chinese in the mix, I thought, along with Indian and maybe Malay, but he was predominantly black African. He was young, barely twenty, lean, muscular, with a liking for colourful tank-tops and for conversation. We had plenty of time to talk.

Why I remember him, what struck me most particularly, was his point of view. On my way from London to Cape Town I had been collecting opinions. What did newly independent black Kenyans think? Or Tunisian Arabs? Or Afrikaaners? Or Egyptians? Or white Rhodesians? Or Sudanese Christians? Or Turkana tribesmen? Or young unemployed Libyan Muslims?

But this man – I must have known his name but it's lost to me – saw things quite outside categories. A vivid intelligence shone through his ill-assorted features, unhampered by too much education, nourished on innumerable encounters in ports around the world. He was the Third World embodied, yet somehow he transcended it. He was a great optimist, mischievous, full of humour and insight. He stood outside the attitudes of deprivation, but he asked sharp questions. There was no chip on his shoulder, no fear in his eyes, no violence in his heart, only a clear awareness of possibilities. He had an intuitive grasp of the forces at work in the world, and seemed contemptuous of them.

I can't remember the words he used but they made a big impact on me. I had never expected to meet a man so able to liberate himself from his circumstances. However, I realise now that his true meaning escaped me. At the time I couldn't see beyond what I had only just absorbed for myself, which was a view of people throughout a continent locked into their own tribal, national and religious beliefs, and profoundly suspicious of their neighbours.

After two weeks the ship docked in Fortaleza to offload a cargo of cashew nuts. This was a steamy tropical port I had never heard of, and though I had paid to go on to Rio, I decided on a whim to take advantage of this surprise landfall and disembark with the nuts. The bike was spirited away into customs limbo and while I waited for the bureaucratic process to unravel I made contact with some Irish priests and stayed at their parish house. They were wonderful men who embraced liberation theology and had the quaint idea that they should actually give material help to the destitute peasants of the region. This did not endear them to the authorities.

It was May 1974 and Brazil was ruled by a ruthless military dictatorship. Puzzled by my unexpected appearance (in both senses of the word) the police decided quite soon to lock me up, thinking I was there to foment revolution. For a while I was in fear of my life which, as Dr Johnson observed, 'concentrates the mind wonderfully' and gave me more urgent things to think about, so the memory of the deckhand slipped away into the distant recesses of my brain.

When I was finally released I put all my energy into recovering from that frightening and miserable experience, and rode my 500cc Triumph south to Rio, gaining strength as I went, until a month later I made my triumphal entry into the city.

Friends in London had given me an introduction to Baby, and it was Baby who first pronounced me 'fantastic' and gave me the key to the city; Baby Bocayuva, the Brazilian millionaire, whose incongruous name connected me to my austere youth, when I would gaze at newsreel clips of Latin American playboys with over-ripe features and names like Porfirio Rubirosa, twirling polo sticks and escorting heiresses at Ascot. Bocayuva was not a polo player, but the irreverent 'Baby' attached to a plump middle-aged businessman expressed well the light touch of Rio, and his wife Dalal was a match for all Porfirio's heiresses.

Having anointed me, as I stood in my motorcycle boots on a priceless rug in his Ipanema apartment, Baby handed me over to Dalal to make arrangements for my forthcoming reign over the city, and as a result I found myself in the hands of four women whom I thought of as the Arab, the Portuguese, the German and the Slav.

Dalal was from the upper classes of Lebanon and a ballet dancer. With the help of Baby's money, she had made it her life's work to raise the standard of dance in Rio from mere tripping around in tutus to the level of international performance. To assist her she had enlisted the help of Marcia Kubitschek, daughter of the former President of Brazil who was still, in those days of dire dictatorship, the most admired man in the country.

Together they formed a dance company, the Ballet Dalal Ashcar, and found two other women to help. Esmeralda, a reserved blonde, took care of the administration. Another dancer, Maria Luisa, born into an old Portuguese family, occupied herself with the teaching programme.

All of them were very attractive. My most vivid memory of Dalal, who had stopped performing but still practised hard, was after a session at the barre, when she was wrapped in towels with sweat streaming down her aquiline, intelligent and aristocratic features. Marcia had the polished beauty of a jet-setting celebrity. Esmeralda was tremendously pretty and cool behind her desk, but with a smouldering jealousy ready to incinerate any woman who came near her husband, Tito. And finally Maria Luisa, who was Lulu to her friends, with the luxuriant black hair, the great dancer's body, and mobile features that reflected every emotion from deepest misery to unrestrained joy.

Because Lulu was the only unmarried one among them it was decided that I should be in her care, a responsibility she took very seriously. She installed me in a spare studio apartment. We had countless lunches and dinners together. We went to parties, attended concerts and performances, always with complimentary tickets, and mingled with the high and mighty of Brazilian society.

In 1974 I felt as though Rio de Janeiro belonged to me. I owned the beaches from Gloria to Gavea, the mountain peaks that overlooked them, and everything in between, including the palatial residences on the grand boulevards and the precipitous slums in their muddy ravines, the *churrascarias* and the juice bars, the opulent French apartments, the villas, the clubs and, above all, the Opera House. I conquered Rio by virtue of my motorcycle exploits and the added lustre of my imprisonment by the dreaded Polícia Federal.

I have no doubt that I could have had access to any person or place I desired. People regarded me with admiration and, I daresay, a degree of longing. There was no doubting the aphrodisiac effect of my recent adventures, my motorcycling persona, and above all my ordeal at the hands of the dictatorship which granted me a seal of authenticity. Although I was careful not to let myself be swept away by all this adulation, it certainly occurred to me to wonder whether I could convert it into some kind of permanent place in Brazilian society, but it was never a serious thought. I knew I would have to go on, and eventually I did.

Meanwhile the memory of the deckhand slipped away into oblivion, and didn't surface again until I started writing this book thirty years later. I know better now what he was saying. He was in a perfectly natural sense a prophet. He represented a future in which countless millions of others, too, would refuse to be categorised, and would claim the world as their own.,

If I had paid more attention, perhaps I would also have seen that there was a dark side to the future he symbolised. Because if those countless millions began to see the possibilities he saw and were then frustrated, there might be hell to pay. And they have been frustrated. And there probably will be hell to pay. It has taken all these years for the message to come through.

2

The deckhand on the *Zoë. G* was not the only prognosticator I met on my first journey. In Africa there was the man who predicted accurately the birth of Zimbabwe, a joyful independence which has now sunk into ruin. In South America an obnoxious Swiss gave me a shocking glimpse of where my personality might lead me if I weren't careful. But the most important by far was the clairvoyant in India who gave me the title of my book.

When he said, 'You are Jupiter', I chose to misinterpret him, of course. He meant that I was under the influence of the planet Jupiter, though what *that* meant was never very clear to me.

'You owe everything to your mother,' he added (which was true enough, since my father had disappeared from my life when I was five), and he predicted two accidents of a particular kind which did in fact materialise much later. But there was one other thing he told me at the time which made me quite uncomfortable. He said, 'You have a weak hold on the affections of women.'

After leaving him I spent many of my solitary hours on the bike wondering what he meant. I naturally resented the suggestion that women didn't care for me much; that they would just lose interest and drift away. To test the truth of this unpleasant observation I combed mentally through all the romantic attachments I could remember. Some of my recollections made me squirm. It struck me that I had probably not been a very nice person to be involved with in my early days, but if there was a problem with attachments, it seemed to me to have been more usually the opposite. Fed on romantic nonsense in my youth, as we all were, it was I who had always been inclined to lose interest when my adored ones turned out to be real women.

But that was earlier. As I rode home from India there were two spectacular women in my life, and I had no doubt about the affections of either. I loved Carol, whom I had left behind on the border of Bangladesh and whom I was confidently expecting to marry. At the same time I was very reluctant to lose the respect of Jo, whom I also loved, if in a different way now, and who was certainly expecting me to return to her in France.

In the end I lost them both, but it was not through any lack of affection. It was partly fate and partly my own pusillanimous and confused behaviour that wrecked our relationships. As a result, after a rather turbulent time, I found myself on forty acres in California, instead of in a stone house in France. I had a new and equally spectacular wife and a baby son, and spent the next fifteen or so years in multifarious activities having nothing much to do with motorcycles.

Even so, it was the success of *Jupiter's Travels* that had 'bought the ranch'. *Jupiter's Travels* was still the book with which I was most often identified, and in the mid-nineties it again became a positive factor in my life. In America, where it was out of print, I discovered almost by accident that people were taking to motorcycle travel in large numbers, and that my book had become a cult classic. As an experiment, I went to a BMW bikers' rally in North Carolina with a few boxes of books I had brought over from England and gave a slide show. To my amazement people rushed up to shake my hand. They quoted passages of my own book at me. Everybody wanted to buy me beer and fill me with barbecue and pizza. It seemed I could do no wrong and I must admit I revelled in it.

I began to think the book was more than just entertainment. It transported people. I learned that many had made similar journeys because of it. I became attached to the hundreds of pictures I was now showing for the first time, and wished that more readers could see them.

*

Early the following year I was on a plane with Jacques. Who's Jacques? Let me explain. When I was young and trains were the best way to get around I heard about the Gold Pass. If you were extremely important to a railway company, it was said, you were given one of these and you could travel anywhere you wanted, at any time, for nothing. I used to have fantasies about rescuing some bewhiskered old man from under the wheels of a locomotive, only to discover that he was the Chairman of the Board of the Great Western Railway Company.

'What can I possibly do for you, my boy?' he would quaver effusively. And I would claim my Gold Pass.

It took another forty years or so, but in the end I got my Gold Pass, or something like it. Jacques, you see, has an Air Pass worth a million times its weight in gold. He bought it many years ago for what was then a huge amount of money. With it he can fly first-class anywhere, any time, on this particular airline, free, and *with a friend*. Who would not want to be Jacques's friend? And how lucky for me that I became his friend before I even knew about the miraculous ticket.

It seems that Jacques read *Jupiter's Travels* long ago, at a time when life had become difficult for him, and he credits the book with having given him the strength and confidence to turn things around. Much later, when I was visiting Dallas, he sought me out and we became friends. It was a few years on that he mentioned, rather diffidently, that he possessed these supernatural flying powers, in case I might care to accompany him somewhere. So I persuaded him to take me to a meeting of long-distance motorcycle travellers held every year at the end of winter in a deliberately muddy, sometimes semi-frozen, field on the eastern edge of Belgium.

The promoter of this event was a pipe-smoking German biker, Bernd Tesch, an old Africa hand, big, burly, bearded and bald like a German Asterix soaked in nicotine. He had found me in California years earlier and entreated me ever since to come to his meeting. Jacques liked bikes too. He had a Ducati in his garage. He thought it would be fun to go and play in the mud, so we flew to Frankfurt and borrowed a couple of bikes.

I put on a slide show which received unwarranted applause, given the poor state of my German. I was again struck by the significance that the book and the pictures seemed to have for people. I wished I could find a way to publish the book with all those pictures. And *that* was the costly, and some might say self-indulgent, idea I mentioned to Jacques on our way home. He had another idea: 'My thought would be that you could do the whole thing again, but this time you would be going round with a professional photographer.'

I looked at him across the celery sticks and dip, the half-finished glasses of champagne, the warmed nuts and the unopened dinner menus. He seemed quite serious, though his gravity was hedged as always with hints of humour and self-deprecation.

'You mean with two bikes, I hope?'

I was intrigued and alarmed by the extravagance of the proposal. Still, in the first-class cabin of a Boeing 747 there's only a fine line between ambitious fantasies and realistic projects.

'Absolutely,' he said. 'Triumph ought to jump at the idea.'

So it was Jacques who first put into words the notion that I might repeat that unrepeatable journey. Do it again.

We went so far as to visit the new Triumph factory together, where we met with the marketing manager, Bruno Tagliaferi. Jacques has an endearing and persuasive manner, and his speech is cultivated East Coast, but he is a big man. He looms several inches above my six feet, and is physically big in every respect. I don't know whether he moved to Dallas because he is big, or whether he became big because he moved to Dallas. He certainly looks like everybody's notion of a big Texan.

Bruno was a small man in a shiny brown suit. He seemed to me to be readying himself against a physical onslaught as Jacques outlined our grand scheme. 'We were thinking that the whole thing could probably be accomplished for about thirty thousand dollars,' he said winningly.

Bruno was shocked. 'We simply wouldn't have anything like that in the budget. Our marketing budget is quite restricted. We are a production-driven company.'

Production-driven? What could that mean? I could see this going nowhere. I wanted to throw Bruno a lifebelt.

'Well, would you give us a couple of bikes?' I asked.

'Yes,' he said, but that was it. No support, no money, and without that Jacques's idea couldn't fly. Still, the memory of the offer stayed with me and somewhere the seed of a new journey took root.

By the year 2000 I was seriously considering it. How fascinating it would be to go back over the same track, to follow again that slender thread on which so many remarkable experiences had been strung. How much, or how little, had the world changed in a quarter of a century? What had become of the cast of characters that danced through the pages of *Jupiter's Travels*? And how would I handle that journey now?

What made the idea so surprising, even to me, was that I actually thought myself capable of doing it. I was approaching seventy years of age. Put like that, baldly, objectively, the idea seemed absurd, and yet the question of age never really entered into my own calculations. I had no sense that my powers had particularly diminished, at least not in any way that would prevent me from riding a motorcycle in difficult conditions. After all, I was never a very gifted or daring rider, having come very late to the game. Essentially what I had done in the seventies was to muddle through, depending much more on my wit and my attitude than on strength or athletic ability. Wit and attitude I still seemed to have enough of.

Unfortunately I couldn't make myself believe that others would see it the same way. Though my age didn't worry me, I couldn't help imagining the reactions of people who didn't know me, especially people in the motorcycle trade.

''Ere mate! Reckon I've 'eard it all now. There's this geezer who thinks we'll send 'im round the world on one of our bikes! Pushing seventy too. What a nutter!'

So whenever I thought about the project and having to sell myself to get support a great weariness came over me. It was all so different from those heady days in 1973 when it seemed nothing could stop me. Then I was energised by the extraordinary challenge of attempting something I thought had never been done before, but in the last two decades all that had changed. So many had followed me round the world that, among motorcycle travellers, the journey had been reduced to an acronym: RTW. At the same time I could now see how difficult it is for most people to break with their lives and follow their dreams. I had a son growing up. I had some land I loved that needed caring for, and a mortgage that needed servicing. I was publishing my own books and could not afford to lose the small income they produced.

All of this changed suddenly one millennial morning in California, towards the end of June. I was just raising my bowl of breakfast coffee to my lips when the phone on the wall by my right ear rang, and the coffee spilled over. Perhaps a bowl is not the safest container for hot coffee, but you get more into a bowl and every-body knows that the second cup is never so good.

The call came from Geneva. A man speaking British English with a very faint trace of some kind of accent introduced himself as Stephen Kinloch. He worked at the United Nations office which organised UN volunteers all over the world. He was very polite and formal, and hoped he wasn't disturbing me. I decided not to men-tion the coffee.

'The Secretary General, Kofi Annan,' he said, 'has decreed that the year 2001 will be the Year of the Volunteer.'

I said this was news to me.

'Well, some of the volunteers have made a plan to ride motor-cycles around the world, to win support for volunteerism. They have read your book and they are very excited about it. It has been an inspiration to them, and they would like to know if you will give them a message of support.'

'Of course,' I replied, and asked a lot of questions to find out just how serious this was. I discovered that Honda had promised them bikes, and that Toyota would probably help with support vehicles, which they would need because they wanted to do the whole jour-ney in one year. There were about six of them, young men and women, and most of them were working in Kosovo. Some had never ridden bikes before. My kind of people. So without any hesi-tation I said, 'Of course they have my blessing. I am flattered that it matters to them. But wouldn't it be even better if I went with them?'

And as I said it, a huge wave of relief swept over me.

Even if I had known then that the volunteer effort would eventually come to nothing, I think that phone call would still have fired me up. In some way that I can't explain, it flicked a switch. Instead of seeing the project shrouded in an impenetrable fog of difficulties, I could begin to identify the problems, one by one, and find ways to solve them.

It is truly wonderful how a single all-consuming ambition can energise and transform a life, and it is an experience I would wish for everyone. All the minor irritations of day-to-day living become insignificant. So what, if you're stuck in the wrong check-out line, if the cat poops on your carpet, if your neighbour gives you a dirty look, if the egg you crack is rotten, if it rains on your birthday? You're soaring on a quite different level. Somehow or other it all gets taken care of, and soon all of it will be forgotten.

Nothing will ever rival the electric excitement that charged me up as I was planning my first big journey, and in my own mind it still remains the crowning achievement of my life, but there have been other projects that come close. And of course whichever one it is, when it's happening it is always the most important thing you could ever do. You are not making comparisons. If there *is* a drawback, I'd have to say that it's not great for relationships. There are couples who can raise themselves to an equal pitch of intensity – I have met some on the road – but that's rare. I am not a hermit. There was someone I would have to leave. We had known I was going when we met, but even so it is never easy . . .

It may seem pretentious to call a journey a great achievement. It can easily be seen as mere escapism. Or as a self-indulgent folly. So I am always astonished by the eagerness that people have shown to help me get on the road, but finally I do understand it. There is so much in life that is restrictive. There are so many good reasons for not breaking out into the world, and yet most of us dream of other lives, where we might run barefoot and feed off the ocean, or build cabins in the mountains and live off the forest, or run a bar in Bangkok or a hostel in Nairobi or a pub in the Outback.

Because I am willing to do without the things that tie people to their homes and hearths, I stand in as their proxy, and sometimes as much more than that, because a good many have already followed in my footsteps. And, once on the road, I fulfil another function that has earned pennies and suppers and a bed throughout history, as a wandering storyteller, bringing news from the other side of the mountain.

In true bureaucratic fashion the UN bosses never said yea or nay, but by September it became obvious that time had run out, and the volunteers were forced to abandon their project. I felt sorry for them but by then I was quite ready to make the journey on my own, and more than happy to do so.

The UN connection did not end there, though. I told Stephen that I was going ahead alone. He talked it over with the others and they asked me to represent them as a goodwill ambassador. I said I would feel privileged. I could call in at various UN offices along the way and help them to get publicity, and Stephen suggested that it might also be useful to me. I had no idea then just how useful it would turn out to be.

I was left with one major uncertainty: what bike to ride and where to find it.

There was a big philosophical difference between the two journeys. In 1973 I was a relatively young man heading out into the unknown, quite unaware of how the world would receive me, and how I would respond to it. As it turned out, people were a great deal more welcoming and generous than I expected, and surviving was a good deal easier than I had imagined. I took four years over that journey but I could have continued on far longer. I had left nothing behind me but an uncertain relationship and an ancient stone building which would stand quite happily without me for a hundred years.

What drew me back was the promise I had made, to myself and to others, to write a book. The travelling for its own sake was not enough. The ultimate excitement for me was to give the journey some meaning that I could convey to others. I travel as a writer. Towards the end I knew that I simply could not contain the full experience unless it ended soon. Twenty-eight years later, the need to give meaning to the exercise was just as strong, but the kind of meaning would be entirely different, and so were my circumstances.

Ironically, I was much better equipped now to wander out into the world without a care. I knew the essential secret of survival was pace. The slower you travel the easier it is to make connections and to receive the help and the comfort that people everywhere are only too ready to offer. The slower you travel, too, the better you are able to adapt to changes in food, in climate and in custom; the easier it is to learn a language. The more slowly you travel the cheaper everything becomes, and the better you are able to profit from unexpected opportunities.

But I was not willing, any more, to leave my life behind and forget about it. I was quite clear about my objective, which was to see what had happened to the world I had once known, and to report on it. So I resolved to make this journey the opposite of the first one. Instead of seeking to lose myself in the world, I would take advantage of all the communication technology that had sprung into existence since the seventies. I would carry a computer, a CD burner, a digital camera. I would use email, and I would run a website. I would be in constant touch with everyone. It would be a mobile electronic extravaganza. And of course this would have to affect the choice of motorcycle.

Since the journey would begin in England, that was the obvious place to meet these criteria, and I arrived in London in mid-October on a bike I'd borrowed in Germany.

About that time I got an email from a man I didn't know saying that he wanted to support my journey with a little money, and if I was coming to Britain he would like to invite me to dinner. His name was Stephen Burgess. I thought he just wanted to shake my hand. I rang the mobile number he'd given me, and got a cheerful, matter-of-fact voice at the other end. I explained that I was staying with a friend in Battersea, and that there was a restaurant we could go to on the corner called Fish in a Tie. He said 'Righto' and we fixed a time for him to come to the house. He sounded relaxed but busy.

He arrived in a moderately expensive car, wearing a business suit, white shirt, dark tie. He was medium height, strongly built with a good head, clean-shaven, auburn hair brushed down flat, a broad, alert and cheerful face with a touch of pugnacity about it, quick to laugh and, I guessed, with a quick mind behind the laughter. I still had no idea what he did or what he wanted.

We walked into the Fish in a Tie and sat at a small table. He passed over the £80 he'd promised me while we ordered. I thought I'd have the duck and asked the waitress if it was good. She said, 'It's terrible.'

Startled, I asked her if she'd tried it herself, and she made a face and said, 'No. I'm vegetarian', and laughed. So we laughed too, and I had the duck.

Stephen didn't take long to get to the point. 'I've read your books. I like what you do,' he said, 'and I'd like you to use my bike.'

I didn't know how to respond. He explained that he'd bought this bike and set it up to make a long journey of his own, but then he was prevented from making it. He didn't tell me how or why, but I gathered later that it was an illness of some sort.

The bike was a BMW, an R80 GS, and I knew enough to know that it would be a very likely candidate for what I wanted to do. He said he'd had it fixed up for himself, but – 'I'll put anything on it you want. It's entirely up to you.'

I told him of the arguments I'd been having with myself – that I was still keen to see whether a smaller bike would work, but of course I thought it was a very generous offer. He said he wanted to help me in any way he could, and I should think about it. The bike was at a dealership in Dorchester, and the dealer was a friend of his and would be happy to do anything to it I wanted.

I asked him what kind of business he was in, and he said it had to do with ports and shipping cars across the Channel. He was very offhand about it.

'By the way, when do you think you'll start the trip?'

'In January,' I told him. 'It's really important to get through Sudan and Ethiopia before the rains start. That means I ought to be there before the end of March. I've no idea what that road's like now, but it was terrible then even in the dry. In the wet it would be impossible. 'So yes, if I leave by the end of January I should be able to get through all right.'

'How are you getting around now?' he asked.

I told him I was on a bike and he said he could fix me up with a car if I liked.

'We've always got cars. Maybe when you come back in January. We might even ship you across the Channel. Are you going to write a book?'

'Yes, of course. It's what I do. Why?'

'Oh, I'm not looking for anything like that.' Brusquely: 'You can leave me out of it. I'm not looking for recognition. Just interested.'

He was being deliberately mild, even diffident, restraining an ego which I imagined, in other circumstances, could be a force to reckon with.

We talked more about my plans, what I hoped to achieve, how long I thought the journey would take, and so on. I found myself enjoying his company, even though he had little to say about himself. Usually I find it easy to prompt others, particularly strangers, into telling me about themselves. It spares me from having to talk about myself too much. Still, he was paying, and besides it was interesting to try out my ideas on an intelligent listener. The duck was good too.

I told him I'd decide soon about his BMW. Clearly I needed to get the matter of the bike settled. The main factors were weight, reliability, comfort, ease of maintenance, and some kind of support with spare parts in case of breakdowns or accidents. I was going to be sitting on this bike for at least two years, and carrying quite a lot of stuff. A heavier bike is more comfortable, more strongly built, and probably more dependable. The R80 GS was certainly reliable. The technology was older, simpler, and manageable by me. On most of the sixty thousand miles I was planning to ride it would be ideal, and it looked as if Steve and his pal in Dorchester could be counted on for back-up support. But . . .

There were about a thousand miles in Africa and maybe as many again in South America, where the weight of the GS could cause me real problems. I have never been a powerful man, and coming up for seventy I wasn't getting any stronger. I would barely be able to lift it unloaded and I knew, absolutely, that I would drop it, probably many times. So I kept turning back in my mind to lighter single-cylinder bikes like the Kawasaki KLR, or the Yamaha XT that is so much liked by some European travellers. Obviously they would be cheaper to transport over water, cheaper on fuel and easier for me to handle on the really rough bits.

On the other hand, when I thought about all that electronic stuff I wanted to carry I wondered whether it could survive on a smaller machine. I had to put it to the test, and I made an arrangement to ride the Yamaha for a few miles. It was raining when I took it out, and though I was well protected it was still awkward, riding around wet suburban streets with a foggy visor on this unfamiliar bike. The machine felt very small and a bit bumpy and uncomfortable. Before long I had convinced myself it wouldn't do, and with that I more or less decided that Stephen's offer was too good to turn down.

I was introduced to the GS the next day. Stephen invited me to spend the night at his house in Hampshire. In the morning he took me over to Dorchester on the back of his own bike to meet David Wyndham. The dealership was tucked into a trading estate on the south side of town. Of course I had no idea then how big a part CW Motorcycles would play in my adventure. Dave was a tall, comfortable-looking man with dark hair and a closely cropped beard, whom I judged to be in his late forties. He spoke carefully, in a deep, almost caressing voice, appearing to be the very soul of benevolence, and nothing I experienced later belied that impression. He said he was delighted that Stephen had brought him into this, and said his mechanics were enthusiastic about it too. He contrived to make me believe, without embarrassing me, that it would give him great personal satisfaction to be part of my adventure, well beyond any public-relations benefit it might bring for his company.

Naturally, we talked a good deal about the bike. All the improvements that had been made to it, I took for granted. I knew nothing about the relative qualities of various front forks, and shocks and bars. I was interested that it had three electrical accessory outlets, and we discussed all my electronic fantasies for a while. Stephen had

had an optional kick-start fitted, which impressed me at the time. The most important thing about the new bike, from my point of view, was that it was sturdy and fairly easy to work on.

So the choice of bike was settled, but there was always more to do. I felt I still needed more financial support so I went the rounds. *Classic Bike* offered to publish a column from me. Reiner Nitschke, in Germany, came to my aid offering a monthly page in his magazine *Touren-Fahrer*. Then, quite unexpectedly, another friend in Germany, a documentary film director who worked generally on rather highbrow musical subjects, became excited by the idea of filming my journey. I knew Manfred Waffender very well, and I trusted him completely. Although I was surprised by his interest, I knew that anything he did would be of very high quality.

His plan was to fly in and out at different places along the journey through Africa with a crew. He picked up some financing from Arte, a European TV channel, and a little of it came my way. Then I got one more big break. An old friend had become editor of the *Independent on Sunday*. She offered to run a monthly column from me, and pay me a decent amount of money for it. Almost as good as the money was the fact that with a newspaper behind me I had no trouble getting a second passport, and that was a tremendous help with visas. Getting visas for Libya, Sudan and Ethiopia could be difficult and slow, and with two passports there was a much better chance of getting them in time.

Feeling much more confident, I rode back to Germany and spent a few days with Manfred. We decided to film in Italy, Tunisia, Sudan, Kenya, Zimbabwe and, finally, Cape Town. He would fly in with a cameraman and a sound man and spend a few days in each place. I would take a mobile phone with me so that we could find each other, if necessary. And of course he would be there for the grand departure and the ride to Southampton docks.

Then I returned to California.

There was still so much to figure. My decision to run a website as I travelled involved a great deal of work and learning on the computer. I needed help to set it up and run it, and I was up late at nights trying to get a grip on the complexities of it. Handing over a small business was not easy either. At times it seemed I was drowning in details and complications. I felt more like Gulliver than Jupiter, pinned down by a thousand threads of obligation, but I could hardly complain. It was entirely my own doing. Nobody imposed these bothersome restrictions on me. I accepted them for the benefits they offered, and because they were there.

When I came back to England in January Dave Wyndham put me up in his thatched house outside Dorchester, and Stephen Burgess found a car for me, which gave me great freedom. He couldn't do enough for me. Saying, flippantly, how much he was enjoying this 'RTW by chequebook', he took me to a camping store in Southampton and, waving his hand vaguely, said, 'See if there's anything here you need.'

I tried to be conservative, but all the same I came out with a tent, perhaps a bigger tent than I needed, an ultra-light set of cookware, a collapsible bag to carry water, and a groundsheet. I also got a neat little folding seat because I am uncomfortable sitting on the ground, something that has always disqualified me for the New Age.

In America I was offered electrically heated clothing and gloves, and remembering how I had almost frozen to death in 1977 coming back through eastern Turkey, I accepted them gladly. Besides, I knew that this time I would have to cross northern Europe in the depths of winter.

The digital camera called for batteries, so I needed a charger. There was now a lightweight inverter available to recharge my laptop, so I took it. And an equally lightweight pump to blow up a flat tyre, not to mention metal capsules of compressed air. The computer and its accessories had to be protected from vibration and dust, so I accepted a rubber Pelican case which filled half of one of the big alloy boxes I got from Bernd Tesch. I took inner tubes in case the tubeless tyres failed, a repair manual and spare parts, and pretty soon the rest of that box was full.

All these things had to be carried, but when it came to thinking about the load on the bike my mind was absurdly split. On the one hand I knew that the less I carried the better.

'Oh Ted,' exclaimed Dave, 'weight is of the essence.'

'How right you are, O Dave,' I nodded.

And yet, I remembered so well that I had once come all the way from Afghanistan carrying not only a full load of clothes, camping equipment, tools, parts and other necessities, but also a bolt of Indian cloth, a carpet and a samovar. And all that on a smaller, less powerful bike than the GS.

So I let Dave show me the latest wonders in weatherproof bags by Ortlieb, bags with almost impenetrable waterproof skins and hermetic zips that slide on silicone . . . and I took two of them and filled them up. I knew of course that these decisions would have a great bearing later on, might even be crucial, but I couldn't guess in which way, and said a mental To hell with it.

The BMW was prepared with meticulous attention. From the sump guard to the hardwired GPS, from the headlamp shield to the adjustable Ohlins shock absorber, every detail had been considered and, where possible, improved. Dave, his partner Wally, and their mechanics made my bike their priority. It had a very fancy windshield. All the cables were doubled. I had heated grips. And they'd even gone so far as to install a gadget on the handlebars to hold my umbrella, which has become a trademark eccentricity over the years. I felt tremendously in their debt.

Of course, publicity surrounding my departure would certainly help CW, and I agreed to set a firm date so that we could tell the motorcycle world. We settled on Saturday 27 January because Dave thought some fans would want to ride with me to the Channel port. Then, a week before I was due to leave, two things happened. I caught a bad case of the flu and, quite unexpectedly, the media broke into a frenzy.

How it started I'm not sure, but I think it was through a fan I'd never met called Peter Bradfield. He talked about me to his girlfriend Georgie, who worked on the *Daily Express*. She sent a feature writer to interview me. The *Mail* and the *Standard* picked it up. BBC radio had me twice, Southern TV and radio wanted me too. So in the last week, instead of concentrating on preparing the bike, I was rushing about with my temperature hovering between 100 and 102.

By Friday night Dave knew that something like a hundred bikers were going to turn up next day to escort me. He was sure that most of them would either want to buy *Jupiter's Travels*, or have me sign their copies. Then Manfred turned up with his crew, wanting a picture of all my stuff laid out on a studio floor. All of this, first setting up the picture, then the repacking of everything on the bike, then all the talking and signing of books, more interviews and finally the ride to Southampton, would have to be fitted in next day before midday. I realised that I couldn't do all this and have flu at the same time, so I let the flu go, and it went.

The scene in the showroom was chaotic. Bikers in heavy waterproofs were swarming around, wanting signatures. Dave shouted from the office, 'I've got Johnnie Walker on. Can you do the radio now!' This is how it went:

'Hi Johnnie. Thanks for having me. Yes, I'm taking the same route I took last time – trying to check out how things have changed in twenty-five years. Well, it goes down Africa to Cape Town, then around Latin America – from Brazil south, and up the Pacific side to California, then around Australia and back overland – Singapore, Malaysia, India, you know. If I can go through Afghanistan of course I will. . . . Yes, I know, but if you're being too careful there's probably no point in doing it at all.

Should be about two years . . . Yeah if you'd like that, by all means keep in touch with the CW blokes here – they're my interface with the practical world . . . no Johnnie I'm a Londoner, though I haven't lived there for twenty years . . . My son is twenty now and doesn't really need me, and that's about it. Yeah, I'm completely free again . . . my website will tell you everything . . . Jupitalia . . . yeah, dot com. OK, thanks. Bye-bye.

Being the centre of attention has an invigorating effect at first, like a massive dose of vitamins. Everything happened pretty much as it was supposed to. Even the sun cooperated. My radio shtick, banal as it sounded to me, apparently went down well. I must have signed close to a hundred books. Everybody beamed at me. The cavalcade of bikers who were going to ride behind me was apparently being marshalled somewhere along the route. Two of Dorset's finest motorcycle police were going to make sure we arrived in Southampton without getting split up.

Outside the shop a big crowd waited to see me off and the bike was standing there in the middle of them all, packed like a furniture lorry. Not a huge improvement on the unwieldy beast I had set off with twenty-eight years earlier, I thought, remembering that black and rainy night in 1973 when I slipped away with not a single soul to wave me on. Standing there now, the focus of so much expectation, I couldn't help longing for an anonymous departure.

When I eventually hoisted my leg over the saddle, cameras flashed and there was a lot of cheering. I felt rather stupid, as though they were surprised I could even get my leg up that far. Luckily I remembered to kick the side-stand back before I trundled off. I think it was Dave, on his own bike, who led me out of the parking area and on to the route, although Stephen must have been there too. Eventually we met up with the police, and they swung out in front of me with a thumbs-up sign, and then I saw a column of riders come in from behind. It was a bit embarrassing, even though I knew it was a tribute. I tried to think about the pleasure it was giving those who were supporting me, but I knew that I would never have been one of them, and felt like an ungracious curmudgeon at the thought. I wished I could have dived off into a side road, and just watched them all go by.

It was the first time I'd ridden the bike with a full load, and when I got close to seventy on the motorway I noticed the beginnings of a wobble. Before I could back off Dave came rushing up alongside me and waggled his finger in what struck me as an officious manner. I felt a sharp stab of annoyance. Is he telling me how to ride a bike? I thought, and then immediately realised how strung out I must be. Of course his concern was natural and obvious. Just imagine, if I'd crashed there . . .

It was interesting to see how effortlessly the two cops managed the procession. When we came to a junction, one of them would peel off and block traffic while we went through. At the next junction the other one would stop, while the first cop caught up and went ahead. I enjoyed their professionalism. When we got to the edge of town, they each gave me a very serious and prolonged salute before leaving us. That touched me, and revived a memory of three police sergeants who had taught me a few tricks back in 1973. For the first time I really felt as though I might be doing something worthy of all this attention.

We arrived safely at the docks, the crowd milled around me once more, and at last I felt a powerful surge of warmth and affection welling up inside me for all these people who had given up their time to cheer me on. Still, it was only when the last of them had rumbled out of the parking area into the dusk that I felt the journey had begun.

But it was so different from that first departure, and there was one other big difference that didn't strike me until later. On 6 October 1973, the day I rode off, Egypt attacked Israel and the Middle East was plunged into the Yom Kippur war. But in January 2001 the world was more or less at peace. Nobody knew then what was in store for us.

3

I rumbled off the boat at Le Havre into a cold, grey dawn, which turned into an even colder grey day. The flu was making a last-ditch attempt to get me, and the night on the boat had not been hilarious. It would be better to take it easy, and I remembered that the daughter of a friend, who lived south of Paris, had offered a bed. Now that the journey had begun I was half immersed in memories of the previous one; to be able to pull out my mobile and dial a number in Paris seemed both miraculous and deflating. What kind of a phoney adventure would this be, I thought, if I could always get on the phone?

Lane Whitney was as good as her word, and helped me whip the last remnants of flu into submission. After a hot meal and a long, warm sleep in her home on the banks of the Seine, I set off more comfortably next day with my electric jacket and gloves plugged in, on my way to Germany. I was still, in a sense, faking it. The past week had gone by in such a delirium of fever and photo ops that some quite essential matters had never been addressed. For one thing, I was loaded with equipment I still didn't understand and, for all I knew, might not even work. For another, the packing was a disgrace. I knew I would have to start again from scratch. Finally, I needed to get well again, and the obvious place to do this was at Manfred's home, near Frankfurt. Manfred and I could talk about the film. Reiner Nitschke had his *Touren-Fahrer* office in a castle not too far away, in Euskirchen, and the United Nations was nearby too, in Bonn. I could visit them all.

From Fontainebleau I found my way up through Melun to La Ferté, and then I took a long back road across the champagne country to Châlons. The weather was getting steadily colder, wetter and windier. The flat landscape was bleak and impoverished. The very idea that this stark, miserable ground could produce bottles of luxurious, bubbling conviviality seemed quite surreal. My visor fogged up persistently, but at least the jacket was keeping me warm. Then on the edge of Châlons, in the middle of a busy crossing, the bike stopped dead. The battery was exhausted.

Headlights are obligatory in France. I had to assume that the combination of lights, electric jacket and gloves was too much for the alternator. I was very unhappy. I unplugged everything, and paddled my way to the side of the road.

One of the many things to be said in favour of that old Triumph was the kick-start. It worked, with or without a battery. I remember thinking then that an electric starter would be great, but I would never have traded it for that kick-start. When I first heard that Stephen's bike had an optional kick-start fitted I was delighted. Then one day in Dorchester I had tried to use it. Obviously, it had been designed intentionally to expose me as an incompetent fool. I challenged Dave's mechanics to make it work. They didn't seem keen. Wally, they said, could do it. So Wally came out, and with the bike up on the stand he stood astride it and thrashed at it. It was a great display of vigour and determination, and in the end it worked, but then the sun was shining, and Wally was wearing light clothes.

Now it was raining, I was wearing heavy rainproofs, and feeling anything but vigorous or determined. Still, I tried until the sweat poured from my brow, but sweat was the only fruit of my labours. So, under the gaze of two suspicious gendarmes across the road, I sat on the bike for a while to recover and ponder my fate. It may seem strange and irrational, but I find it more dispiriting to get stuck in the middle of civilisation than in some barren desert. I could not imagine how this 'interruption' could lead to anything better than an uncomfortable and expensive episode with a *garagiste*.

As a final futile gesture before giving up I pressed the starter button one last time . . . and the battery reached down and found life in some lost leaden crevice, and the bike fired up. I was enormously relieved to be going again, but clearly something would have to be done about the alternator. I rode for a while without heat or lights, but then it got too cold and I turned up the heat, and as I approached a bigger town I switched my lights on again, and again the battery failed, but this time, thank goodness, I was at the top of a hill.

I learned my lesson, quickly found a hotel and next day, wearing heavier clothing, I got to Manfred's place unelectrified. With a bit of time on the phone I discovered that there was one older model of BMW, the R90/6, with a more powerful 20 amp alternator and the part was still available. So I rode up the autobahn through snow to a BMW service place near Reiner Nitschke's office. He arranged for it to be installed at his own expense, which was very generous of him, and I never had battery problems again throughout the entire journey.

I visited Reiner in his castle, his photographer took pictures of the bike, and we spent some pleasant time together over dinner. We had never met, although I knew he had done a lot to promote my book in German when it first appeared. Very blond, very forthright, very German, he was at pains to tell me that my book had been influential for him. He was anxious that when I wrote for his magazine it would be 'the real Ted Simon', and I promised to do my best.

He put me up for the night in a sort of guest-house for academics in Bonn. The people there weren't really old, they just looked it. I went out to meet with some of the UN volunteers and talked about ways of carrying their message and spreading their word, but although they were pleasant people I found their culture difficult to penetrate. That evening they took me to a party in the small top-floor flat of one of the big bourgeois buildings of the staid city that is Bonn. The space was crammed with young people, flushed and excited, holding beakers of wine and bottles of beer and bobbing up and down to the beat. There was no room to move, the music was deafening, and conversation was pretty much impossible.

There's only one good reason to be here, I thought, and that's to get laid. But since this was very unlikely to happen to me I left early feeling old and sorry for myself and went back to my own kind.

Luckily my days with Manfred and his family more than compensated for my minor life crisis. I made a much better job of distributing stuff around the bike. I found out how most things worked. Manfred got a bit of air time on the local TV. I shook off the last traces of sickness, and by the time I was ready to go the snow had melted away.

We planned to begin the serious business of filming in the south of Italy, in Calabria, where I had met Giuseppe Zanfini in 1973. He was the first of the truly remarkable people I encountered on that journey. Large, rotund, bewhiskered, operatic, he was saved from pomposity by a burning passion for educating the people of this poor and underprivileged area of Italy. Back then he had established an institute to combat illiteracy in a small town in Calabria called Roggiano, but his projects were grandiose. Sadly I had already heard from an Italian friend who had searched the web that Zanfini had died just two years earlier. At least his name was known and remembered. I was eager to see what, if anything, he had achieved in twenty-six years.

This Italian friend of mine, Franco Panzanini, had come across my own website in 1997. The discovery, he told me in an email, had rendered him ecstatic. He claimed that he had read my book twenty times in both languages. In fact he had the two versions glued together, and used it as an English primer. We met when I passed through Milan in 1998. Far from being the nut I half feared to find, Franco is a seriously industrious fellow with a good sense of humour, a fine family he cares for deeply, and a factory that makes lift doors. The only criticism I could make of him is that he rides and loves a Harley Sportster, but in Italy I find that forgivably eccentric.

'Franco,' I said to him one day, 'why do you only make lift doors? Why don't you make the whole lift?'

He gazed at me with patient tolerance through his faintly tinted glasses. 'Listen to me, Ted,' he said. 'Nobody make the whole lift.

Some make doors, some floors, and so on. But the biggest names, they make only the brass plate with their name on it.'

Franco planned to take some time off from his factory in Milan to travel down to Roggiano with me and help to interpret for us. 'Ted,' he said, 'you must come first to Milan. I 'ave booked a restaurant close to my 'ouse. Tomorrow we will go south together. But I must tell you something. I am coming in the car.'

'But Franco,' I exclaimed, 'what about the Harley?'

'Listen to me, Ted. I am not coming with the 'arley-Davidson. For one thing we will 'ave to stop every 'undred kilometres for petrol. Moreover, my wife Livia is not 'appy. She say nothing but I see it in her eyes. So I will come with the car.'

I knew how keen Franco was to ride with me, and that the only thing that could trump his enthusiasm for biking was his love for his family. Franco's wife Livia first began to worry as winter closed in on the Italian Alps, but then, when she realised that after leaving me in Roggiano he would have to ride home alone she worried even more. It's a two-day ride. She didn't doubt his ability as a rider; it was the Calabrians that bothered her. Calabria, next to Sicily, is riddled with mafiosi, and people with funny ideas about honour and wounded pride. She thought he might get into trouble.

'You know, Ted, I spend a thousand dollars to prepare the bike. But never mind. We will talk about this tonight when you come to dinner.'

I was looking forward to it. The ride to Milan would not be difficult. Through Switzerland, and then the Gotthard Tunnel into Italy. Less than a day's journey.

It started well, in bright sunshine. After I'd been riding for several hours I peeled off the autobahn somewhere in Switzerland to take a short rest, but found myself instead on another series of similar roads with nowhere to stop, so five minutes later I got back to the main road and went on. That detour cost me a dinner, and could have cost a lot more.

The Gotthard is ten miles long, the longest of the alpine tunnels. The shorter ones are dual-bored, each tunnel carrying traffic one way only, but the Gotthard, like the Mont Blanc, was so long and so expensive to build that they made just one bigger tunnel that carries vehicles going both ways. It is a major artery, and the traffic streams are solid, with a high proportion of heavy trucks. Some of them make the journey three times a day. Some drivers get sleepy.

On a motorcycle the din in the tunnel was already quite alarming but I was halfway through when an even louder crash rose above the steady roar. Suddenly the left lane was empty. Then the traffic in front of me stopped just as suddenly. I saw flickering light on the walls ahead of me. When I was sure nothing was coming the other way, I rode up past the stalled vehicles.

Three large trucks had collided and blocked the tunnel with a heap of flaming wreckage. If I'd been a few seconds earlier I could have been caught in the disaster. The thought was very unpleasant. I tucked in alongside a car. There was some smoke, but not enough to indicate danger to me. Still it was a relief to know that I could easily turn and leave the tunnel, unlike most of the traffic. I heard the seesaw sirens of approaching emergency vehicles, and waited long enough to watch ambulancemen load one blood-spattered driver on to a stretcher. When I learned that it would be at least six hours before the tunnel could be cleared, I rode the five miles back to the sunlight.

Six hours was too long to wait, I would never make it in time; but I was reluctant to miss dinner with Franco, who knows about food. I tried to find another way over the top to Milan, but of course, in midwinter, all the passes were closed – and not just with signs, but with huge barriers of snow piled up by snowploughs. Reluctantly I gave in, found a small, inexpensive hotel not too far from the tunnel, and consoled myself with a decent meal and red wine.

Two thoughts occurred to me above all others: first, how fortunate I was to be able to make myself so comfortable in an emergency. It wouldn't be like that, once I was out of Europe. And second, how little interest people showed in my bike, compared with 1973. Back then everyone was curious; today a heavily laden motorcycle was commonplace, and I received little attention. With some chagrin I reflected that this was as much my own doing as anyone's, having written the book. Not that I craved the attention for its own sake, but I remembered how it had helped me in the past to feel that I was doing something extraordinary, and how that feeling had given me an edge which made everything seem more significant.

If what I was doing now was extraordinary, I would have to create that feeling for myself. To others I would be just another long-distance motorcyclist.

4

When Franco and I met next morning I had already come more than a hundred miles in freezing fog and rain. We went into a roadside rest-stop for a coffee before going on, but there was not much time. We had two days to get to Roggiano, and Italy is a long country. I followed his saloon car east from Milan so that we could go down the Adriatic coast and avoid the heavy traffic around Rome and Naples. The fog persisted almost as far as Venice but then it lifted, and at last I felt I could pack the electric Gerber jacket away. It was a lifesaver when I needed it, but I couldn't imagine wanting it again for a very long time. Africa was already in my mind.

The autostrada wound through sunlit farmland beneath reclusive stone and tile villages visible on the hills as we passed, but we were going too quickly for any single thing to fix itself in my memory. My 43-litre tank was more than equal to Franco's big car. We stopped twice in three hundred miles, but I need not have stopped at all. His target was Pescara, a city about halfway down the Adriatic coast. He knew it because he'd been there on his honeymoon.

Pescara has the dubious distinction of being Mussolini's birthplace, and has its share of what used to be called Fascist architecture. He led me down a dark alley to a restaurant where he and Livia had eaten decades ago. It was a cantina called Jozz. He remembered it as a scruffy peasant place where the customer had no rights at all and where they just piled whatever they had on your plate, like it or not. Obviously it had become much more sophisticated and expensive since then but it was just as autocratic, and it was my good fortune that I liked the food very much.

Next day he took me sightseeing, first to a remarkable Norman castle, Castello del Monte, so well restored that it might have been built yesterday, and later to Matera, an impressive town built of blinding white stone. In the early evening we arrived at our hotel at exactly the same time that Manfred and his crew drew up in their van from the airport.

Roggiano is on the edge of a long valley where several rivers join together to empty out into the Gulf of Taranto, just above the toe of Italy, but our hotel was in Altamonte, another village not far away, because according to Manfred's location manager Gilbert, there was no decent hotel in Roggiano. I wasn't surprised to hear this. I remembered Roggiano as a small and primitive village, with just a few buildings around a dusty square where I'd drifted to a standstill one hot afternoon twenty-seven years before, to light a cigarette and to wait for something to happen. I was eager to see the place again. For the first time on this journey I would be putting those memories to the test. Above all I wanted to find out whether Zanfini was really the heroic figure I had portrayed in my book, or whether I had simply encountered a minor bureaucrat and puffed him up to suit my own dramatic needs.

The weather made it difficult. On my first arrival in October 1973, at the end of a long hot summer, the land was parched and brown. Now, in early February, the fields were green after rain and above us clouds were gathering, promising more rain the next day. And indeed, when we set off to Roggiano in the morning, a light drizzle began to fall. I tried to find the same road in that I had taken back then, but nothing was familiar. Instead of the one dusty square I remembered there were many, and Roggiano was more a town than a village, with streets of presentable houses and a structure that made it quite distinct from the surrounding countryside.

Through the mayor of Roggiano, Manfred had already found the address of Zanfini's widow, and the three of us, Manfred, Franco and I, went there first. The house was in a block of traditional middle-class houses. We were ushered into a pleasant but very conservative drawing-room by a young woman who turned out to be a daughter. The widow, a small, reserved figure in black, came and sat down. In half an hour she managed to tell us almost nothing. It was as though she had determined to forget everything about her husband and their life.

Back in '73 there had been a young woman at the institute, dressed in black. I remembered her better than anyone other than Zanfini himself. She was passing through a doorway with an enormous pile of laundry on her head at the time, and she did it with such grace and ease that the image never left me. Who was it? I asked, through Franco. I heard a sharp reply.

'She say "It was not me", and I see a flash in her eye,' said Franco. It was the only time in the interview that she came to life.

We asked about the son who had first greeted me at the institute, but strangely could elicit nothing about him either. Franco was translating, and I watched them carefully, but I got no sense of an explanation from their body language. Finally we just gave up, feeling that we had no right to press her. An air of mystery hung over the whole affair. In fact I wondered whether 'affair' was perhaps the key word. Maybe the family situation had been more complicated than I realised.

'They are a typical proud family of the south,' said Franco. 'Ted, these are funny people down 'ere, you know.'

We went to visit the mayor – it was all about paying respect – but we learned nothing much more than that Zanfini was a famous man in this part of the world and that a school had been named after him. Perhaps the subject of such recent illiteracy was too sensitive to discuss, but it made me very happy to think that Zanfini had apparently made a reality of his vision.

Later, on our way to the institute, with the mayor still in tow and drawn to the camera like a good politician, we passed the school, a good modern building of some size, with children bustling around it. As for the buildings that I had known, we came to them up on a hill in some parkland on the edge of town. Evidently I must have reached them originally by a different road through some outlying village because I had never seen the town we had just been visiting.

When I saw the institute I was shocked to find it empty and derelict. I remembered that the rooms had been built by the voluntary labour of poor farmers from the surrounding lands, and it made me very sad to see them abandoned. Apparently there were no plans to use them; it seemed such a waste.

There was a caretaker living in a house set apart from the rest, whose name was Antonio. He claimed to remember me from 1973, but I was not convinced of it. He took us through the deserted rooms where I had once talked and slept, and I was overcome by melancholy.

I had with me a print of a group picture I had taken in 1973, and Antonio recognised one of the boys in it. He was now a butcher in town, and we went to his shop to meet him, but the meeting produced nothing of much interest. Nevertheless, Manfred filmed it, and then there was more filming on the road, and soon the useful light was gone, and the day was over. I was beginning to appreciate how much time and endless repetition would be involved in making the film, but I was all the more appreciative that someone of Manfred's stature was willing to devote his expertise to my adventure.

The Hotel Barbieri in Altamonte was a great discovery. The food was brilliant, the atmosphere cordial, the rooms good, and the price was a gift. I spent some time on the phone with the *Independent on Sunday* in London, which had suddenly woken up to what I was doing and wanted more. I wrote a piece for them, and emailed it. I slept well that night. In the morning Manfred wanted more film of me riding. He had me going up and down the same long stretch of curving road for a while. Then he wanted to film me arriving at the institute. I was sitting on my bike at the bottom of the access road, waiting for a signal to ride up for his camera, when a small red Fiat screeched to a halt beside me and a ruddy-faced young man leaned out of the window and pointed at me, grinning.

'Jupiter!' he shouted.

He leapt out and talked rapidly in Italian, and I couldn't do more than guess the sense of it. I asked him to follow me to the top of the hill, where Franco informed me that the man's name was Claudio, that he had read my book in Italian, and that he had somehow recognised the logo on the bike. But the most extraordinary revelation was that Claudio was Zanfini's son, who had been there on my first visit. I was flabbergasted: first that he had spotted me, and second, that his mother had said nothing about him. I was full of questions, and prodded Franco to ask them, but he was obviously reluctant, sensing a hint of scandal.

From that moment on the atmosphere became warm and friendly. We filmed, and then went back into town where Claudio ran a small bar. He said he was anxious to try out the effects of a special cocktail that he had invented himself. The narrow bar was crowded. Manfred, Bernd Meiners the cameraman, Pascal the sound man, and Gilbert were filming. Claudio, Antonio, Franco, the mayor, myself and various friends and onlookers were packed in with the rest. The temperature rose, and at last I felt that we were accepted in Roggiano, but I was never able to resolve the mysteries surrounding Zanfini's family. Why would a mother deny the existence of her son? Why did the daughter not make some reference to her brother? Who *was* the woman in black, with the laundry on her head?

The next morning, with a tear in his eye, Franco took his leave of us and drove back to Milan. We set off for Sicily and, eventually, Tunisia. I tried to identify my feelings about the whole episode. In one sense it was a disappointment and a failure. I'd met nobody I recognised. Evidently, on my first arrival I had never actually been in the town itself, so I could say nothing about how it might have changed. But there was no doubting that Zanfini himself had had a considerable effect; that in itself was pleasing. It was also obvious that the people of Calabria were a good deal more sophisticated than they had been then, but for Franco they were still those 'funny people' in the south, and I had had a glimpse of their secretive, mysterious ways.

5

Three sheep's eyes stared up at me blankly from a battered table-top where the heads they belonged to, cooked or pickled to a rosy hue, lay on a sheet of cardboard accompanied by other, unrecognisable, animal parts. Nearby a poultry merchant stood dangling two decapitated chickens over a vat, about to plunge them into scalding water while their uncomprehending mates looked on from a cage. All around me in this busy Tunisian market, crowds of women wrapped in coats and headscarves bustled around stalls piled high with every conceivable kind of foodstuff, the staccato shouts of stallholders punctuating the steady hum of French and Arabic.

There were heaps of all the familiar vegetables – potatoes, carrots, onions, tomatoes, leeks, peas, beans, beetroot, turnips, heads of garlic, lettuce, escarole, endive and so on – accompanied by brilliant displays of multicoloured peppers and aubergines, and other vegetables I couldn't even identify. Pyramids of oranges, lemons, bananas, pumpkins, squashes and melons shone in the sunlight. Carcasses swung from hooks. Calves' heads, gizzards, entrails, hearts, livers and kidneys, hooves and tails, were all spread out for my delectation.

I have never been a squeamish shopper, and the variety and vitality of the market delighted me, but I stood there utterly confused and bewildered. How could all this possibly be happening here, in this street?

I had checked the address very carefully: Mohamad Ben Mansour, Rue 10093, Number 27, Cité Nouvelle el Kabaria, Tunis.

It was there, in my own handwriting, in the notebook I had carried with me in October 1973. With it was a sketch of the place I had stayed in for three days, a primitive compound of small rooms around an equally small yard, protected from the road by a wall, with a door through which I had only barely been able to squeeze the Triumph and a kiosk window from which Mohamad's father sold tobacco. It was one of many similar compounds, made to resemble the rural homes of Tunisian peasants, and I had a photograph of the area from that time.

Now I was in a street of conventional houses, most of them two storeys high. Number 27 was a grocery, with a home above it. The young woman behind the counter seemed quite hostile at first. When I explained what had brought me there she glared at me as though I were laying claim to her property, but she gradually softened. I told her that I was simply trying to rediscover something from my past. She was as mystified as I was. Her family, she said, had been there for twenty-five years. Neither she nor her husband had ever heard of Ben Mansour.

It seemed incredible, but there seemed to be only one explanation. What was in 1973 a quite separate satellite of cheap dwellings had been completely reconstructed and absorbed into the city of Tunis. What was more, the houses looked as though they had been there for ever, used, abused, bits added on, other bits falling down. There was no trace of the original. The scene of my initiation, where I had been so deeply touched by my first experience of Arab hospitality, had vanished, and so had the Mansour family.

Would it be like this wherever I went? I pondered. Was a quarter of a century enough to wipe the slate clean? Would I find myself travelling through a completely unfamiliar landscape, finding nobody from that other time?

Of course, so far as the big old cities were concerned, this could only happen on the impoverished edges. The wealthy centres could not change so fast, but it was sobering to realise how enormously Tunis must have expanded since I last passed this way. Was it all due

to population growth? Even twenty-eight years ago they were flood-
ing in from the countryside. Perhaps the flood had become a
torrent. There would be consequences on the land as well.

Manfred and his crew were still with me and filming as I confronted these prospects. Not that I was alarmed. After all, part of
my purpose was to discover how much had changed, and in any
case, the journey would be its own reward.

We did some filming in the streets, and later in the souk. I was
sorry that we had not found Mohamad, for Manfred's sake. It would
have been good for the film, but he was quite stoical about it.
Obviously the chances of finding him in such a short time were
almost nil. As I said then, if a muezzin had called for Mohamad
from the top of the tallest minaret ten thousand Mohamads would
have come running, but how would I find mine among them?

I had my last dinner with the crew and made the most of it. My
standard of living would plummet as soon as they were gone.
Inevitably the crew had to stay in decent hotels just for the security –
the cost of the equipment was so high that saving on a hotel bill was
not worth the risk. Even so, Gilbert only just caught a passer-by
walking off with one of the camera cases as they were unloading.
Then, at lunchtime the next day, Tuesday 14 February, they left, and
for the first time since leaving Europe I was alone. I was delighted,
but even so I felt a shiver of apprehension. Now I would discover
whether I really still had the right stuff.

With one more night at the hotel paid for I went for a walk through
the city in the evening, looking in an aimless sort of way for a
restaurant where I could sit and write. When the crew was paying
the bill I ate very well. Even in a luxurious restaurant the bill wasn't
big, maybe twenty dollars a head including wine and live music. Not
expensive for them, but I couldn't afford such extravagance.

It was already after dark. I walked a long way through the crowds
hurrying home from work. Most people were dressed in black,
many men in leather jackets, women in neat dresses and coats.
Long, green trams brightly lit and packed with passengers snaked
past through the streets. Barber shops were very busy everywhere, as

were the pastry shops, cafés and 'Taxiphone' shops full of public telephone booths. Most of the shops were open to the street and music burst from them: swirling plangent phrases that hit like shafts of light as I passed by.

This was a life my mother would have recognised, so similar to her own in London when she was working in the forties: the life of a big city, predominantly poor, ruled by work, by the exigencies of public transport, the need to fit all the chores into too few hours, but still not too bad if you could stay healthy, keep up your energy, and believe in better times to come.

Offended by the garishness of the cheapest places, in the end I fell into the trap of going not for the cheapest but for something less expensive than the best, getting bad service, inferior food and an ill-mannered waiter. I should have chosen the two-dollar roast chicken dinner on a plastic tablecloth under a fluorescent tube. It can be hard to make the transition to the local way of life.

In the morning I looked at the map and, on the spur of the moment, decided to change my route and ride some hundreds of miles inland, to an oasis town called Gafsa, trying to recapture the sense of travelling into the unknown. It felt eerie, exciting. Even though there was nothing to be afraid of I had that tingling sensation, waiting for the unexpected to happen. Almost as though I'd just started, although I'd already come well over two thousand miles.

I crossed long stretches of semi-desert on a deteriorating road. Then, just before dark, the road became perfect and an explosion of lush green vegetation made my heart sing. The town itself was rather quiet and private after Tunis. I liked it but saw nothing there to stay for, so I left in the morning and came back to the coast at Gabés, and then to Médenine, where the ghostly remnants of an ancient Arab quarter of the town enchanted me. Then I prepared myself to enter Libya the next day.

I had no qualms coming up to the Libyan frontier. It seemed to me that I had already done all that could be asked of me, and more, in Mr Shelli's small office in the Grand Mosque in London.

Getting a visa to enter Libya had not been easy in 1973. Just after the revolution Colonel Gaddafi was cock-a-hoop and defying all the old colonial powers. I remember a long and elaborate dance through several conversations with a press attaché. When the visa came it filled a page of my passport with questions in Arabic which I was supposed to answer in Arabic. But at least it was cheap. When I got to Tunis, I asked Mohamad to translate the questions for me, and then write in the answers. He could have written 'This man is a British spy', but I guess he didn't, because I got in all right. (Ah, Mohamad, so flamboyant, yet so anxious. 'My skin may be brown, but my heart is lily-white,' he wrote for me, in French.)

This time the visa was no easier, and a lot more expensive. My efforts to get it from the Libyan embassy drew a blank. Unless I could come up with an invitation from one of Colonel Gaddafi's loyal citizens I was not welcome. But at the last minute someone behind the counter mumbled the name of a Dr Shelli – 'Perhaps he can help you . . .' – and a hastily scribbled phone number was tossed towards me.

I called the number. 'Yes you can see me. I will be here. My office is in the mosque.'

The Grand Mosque is on the edge of Regent's Park. Under the eyes of various watchful men I parked the bike, found the building Shelli had mentioned and went up to the second floor, where I met a soulful and harassed man buried under files. Mr Shelli, who was not a doctor, was eager for conversation. He explained that in order to supplement his teaching income he represented Shukra Tours in Tripoli. In exchange for rejoicing with him over his fatherhood of a small boy, and sympathising with his professional frustrations and the burdens of life in general, I was able to reduce the cost from £700 for a full week's tour of Libya to a mere £300 for a three-day visit, including a hotel, a trip to Leptis Magna and the visa. I am not saying the conversation was without interest. Nor was I without sympathy. I daresay with a few more days of conversation we could have got Shukra Tours to pay me to go to Libya, but there was no time, and time is money.

At any rate, on 17 February I rode up to the border with my visa, and the strength of Shukra Tours behind me.

The day before in Gabés I had happened to meet a New Zealand couple called Hird, also on bikes, who had been having trouble. First they had been refused entry into Tunisia and sent back on the ferry to Italy, which surprised me because they both looked so respectable. They had tried again, this time with a visa though it was not supposed to be necessary, and succeeded. Now they had been told that even *with* a visa they couldn't get into Libya without a tour guide to meet them at the border. What did I think?

I said I couldn't believe it. After all I had actually booked a tour – however reluctantly – and been told nothing about any such difficulties. But it got me worried, and on my last night in Tunisia, from the hotel in Médenine, I phoned my contact in Tripoli. He was an Italian called Michele, and he assured me it was nonsense. 'Just come to the hotel in Tripoli and call me when you get there,' he said confidently.

Relaxed, I rode the fifty miles to the frontier in the morning. It was sunny but with a big wind blowing. I stopped to take a picture at a signpost to Cairo. It said I still had 2522 kilometres to go. I passed a line of men flourishing bundles of Libyan money for exchange. There were also mountains of plastic containers full of what I thought at first was orange juice but turned out to be Libyan petrol for sale cheap, but there was no point in my buying it. Petrol in Libya was even cheaper, at about 20p a gallon.

I was looking forward to the ride from the border to Tripoli. When I first came this way the road had run almost entirely through open desert and I had stopped halfway and camped. That was one of the great moments of my first journey. It suddenly struck me then, in a way I hadn't felt before, that I was *really* doing it – that I was out there in the desert, completely alone – with the whole world in front of me. I could still remember the exultation I felt, and I wanted to stop there again, out in the desert, to savour the meaning of all that had happened since then.

There would be plenty of time. I arrived at the border before midday, and found a small queue of cars waiting to go through, including a party of elderly Germans with four-wheel-drive Toyotas. The immigration facilities seemed even more primitive than they had been in '73: a cement building on one floor with a small barred window where an official collected passports, and a converted container on a platform which served as the money-changer's office, where a portrait of Gaddafi hung askew on the plastic wall.

Eventually I arrived at the window and handed in my passport.

'Where is your guide?' asked the official.

'But just yesterday the agents told me no guide was needed.'

'You cannot go without guide. Next please.'

'But I must call them! How can I call them?'

He waved airily in the direction of Tunisia.

'Go back. You will find telephone. Next. . .'

I was furious. Indignant. I didn't know who to hate more, the agent or the official. I reflected on how stupid, pointless, ridiculous, senseless, the whole thing was. As soon as I was in Libya I could send the guide away. I would be riding to the other end of the country anyway without a guide. But none of these angry eruptions was going to solve my problem. Then I remembered my two mobile phones. Neither one of them worked. And I felt like hurling them to the ground.

I went and asked the Germans what they were doing. They were angry too. They were waiting for a guide to come. They had been waiting for hours, and were expecting him at any moment. Perhaps I could go through with their guide.

In fact he arrived almost immediately, and I asked him. Sure, he said, and went to tell the immigration official. Then he came back and said, no, I had to have my own guide. But they had relented a little. They did agree to telephone Shukra Tours and tell them to send a guide. Perhaps I should have insisted on talking to Shukra myself, sounding as outraged as I felt. Maybe then the guide would have arrived sooner, but I doubt it.

It is less than a hundred miles from Tripoli to the border, but I waited six hours. By the time the guide came the sun was close to the horizon, and there was no chance of experiencing anything on the road but chagrin. There was a little paperwork to do first. I had to pay a deposit for an Arabic number plate – forty dollars I didn't expect to see again. I wondered, bitterly, whether the whole business of guides had to do with bribery. Then we drove off.

The road had changed completely. There were buildings, or shacks, or some kind of construction all along it. There was rubbish everywhere too. While the light lasted I could see that just about every protuberance on open ground had a colourful plastic bag caught on it, and in between the bags, bits of discarded metal foil and glass sparkled merrily under the setting sun. No more boring empty desert, I thought. Welcome to civilisation.

Chilled by the night air I arrived at Tripoli's grandest hotel, in time for a dinner of fried fish and grape juice. Alcohol, of course, is forbidden in the Great Socialist People's Libyan Arab Jamahiriya. The restaurant area was enclosed by a wooden lattice fence, part of a huge open lobby, and I showed my room key to get in. There was an abundant self-serve buffet, but in the end the only thing I really liked was the soup. I developed a passion for Libyan soup, a fragrant spicy combination of meat and vegetable juices.

All around me, men ate in pairs discussing esoteric aspects of the oil business. Suddenly a thunderous voice in Arabic blasted down from loudspeakers above my head, and young men in tracksuits raced through the lobby. This happened several times. It was not a restful atmosphere, and I thought there had to be something odd about a society that accepts as normal such Big Brother interruptions of meals and discourse.

In the morning I went to see Shukra Tours to find out what they had to say about my six-hour wait at the frontier. Shukra's managing director was 'Mr Mustafa', an autocratic older Arab with wavy silver hair who wore a blazer and an old school tie. He sat behind a huge desk in a large empty room at one end of a suite of offices and, eschewing intercoms, simply bellowed the name of anyone he wanted to see as though we were all in the same tent.

However, the business was really run by Michele, an engaging young man, who worked in a cluttered office at the other end of the floor behind clouds of cigarette smoke. He was always on the phone, or trying to be. In Tripoli, trying to get through on the phone was a major pastime. Shukra had redial programs on its

computers, and the office muzak was the sound of the same seven
numbers being dialled again and again, the digital equivalent of the
North African music that plays repetitively in all public places, and
a lot less agreeable.

Both men apologised for keeping me at the frontier. Then
Mustafa elaborated on a little scheme he had devised for getting me
to meet with Colonel Gaddafi. In essence, the idea was that I would
make an heroic entrance into Libya on my motorcycle, heralded by
extracts from the London papers extolling my past exploits. This
information would be presented to the government information
officer who, delighted to hear that I held the Libyan people in high
esteem, would have me interviewed on television.

Then Colonel Gaddafi, being an outdoorsy sort of man who
enjoyed sports and approved of adventurous types like me, would
see the programme and have me brought into his presence. Thus I
would secure an interview with the controversial colonel. Even
though my entry had been less than heroic, Mustafa, brushing his
silken whiskers, still felt the plan had a chance. 'But we have to
know first what you would say on TV about the Libyan people.'

So much for journalism, I thought, and replied that the ordinary
people of Libya had been wonderful twenty-seven years before, and
had done nothing yet to change my opinion.

'Then I will let you know before tonight what we can do,'
Mustafa promised.

Meanwhile it was time for my tour of Leptis Magna, about an
hour away from Tripoli, and I have to say that it was a quite extraordinary experience. Until I stumbled on the Greek ruins of Cyrene,
on the east Libyan coast, nearly three decades earlier, I had had no
idea that the remains of ancient cities could be so vast and, in a
sense, so complete. Leptis Magna is Cyrene's Roman equivalent,
and though I found the latter more beautiful (the golden afternoon
light had had something to do with it, I think), Leptis has more
evocative detail. You can see the notches worn into the side of a well
by the ropes, and the knife cuts in the marble of a fishmonger's slab.
And, if you are so minded, you can sit on a Roman latrine and chat
with your neighbour.

Very well satisfied, I returned to the hotel to be shouted at again over dinner, and to look more carefully around the vast lobby. On the walls there were various portraits of the Colonel which I was to see far too often later. They are crudely drawn in comic-book style, the favourite being one in which he gazes sternly towards the heavens through dark glasses, his headcloth streaming. It is meant, I'm sure, to be inspiring, but to me it looks rather silly. One end of the lobby was dominated by a portrait in oils, twice lifesize, propped up on an easel. He gazed straight ahead, a charming guy, with a twinkle in his eye, the sort of likeable fellow you can do business with. It was intended perhaps to impress the delegates to the Organisation of African Nations (which Gaddafi would so dearly have liked to lead), who were due to arrive at that hotel in a day or two.

I bought a copy of his *Little Green Book* in translation, Gaddafi's answer to Mao's *Little Red Book*, I suppose. It offers the 'ultimate solution' to all the world's social, economic and political problems, and I took it to bed with me. There was, of course, no message from Mustafa.

I came out of the hotel on that third day ready to pack and leave, expecting to hear no more from Mustafa. I found a stocky, greying foreigner observing my bike with a dreamy expression. He said he had been looking at it for a long time, touched clearly by some longing in his heart. We talked, eventually, about Libya. He was an Italian businessman who had been coming there every year since 1970, just after the revolution, and I knew he was telling me the truth as he knew it.

'Are things better?' I asked.

'They are worse,' he said. 'Much worse. Look at this.' His gesture embraced the small part of Tripoli on the waterfront where we were standing, spiked with high-rise blocks to look like a modern city. 'This is chickenfeed for a country like this. Where is the money? Nobody knows. And the people are not like they were – so nice. Gaddafi has set them against each other. There are many people who are very poor, who haven't enough to eat. I have a friend, high in the police, and I know. Every day, people are shot, ten, twenty, but nobody knows. It is covered up.'

Just then one of Mustafa's helpers drove up to the hotel. The interview was on after all, and the TV unit was coming to film me at his office at 10.30. I finished my packing, and followed him through the streets. Tripoli was not the same city it had been when I had last been there. It was much larger, the traffic was horrendous, and the people were almost all in Western dress. The most obvious change, though, was in the status of women. In 1973 they had all been shrouded, with no female faces in sight. Now they dressed much like women in London on a cold day, and I was told you might even, occasionally, see a bare shoulder.

The Shukra office was one block behind one of Tripoli's more prosperous streets, but as soon as you turned the corner you were plunged into deep potholes, shifting slabs of concrete and heaps of rubble and waste – the same streetscape that characterised most of the North Africa I had seen. On my first day I thought, What a dump. By the third day I thought nothing of it, and could have fallen easily into the assumption that there was no money for such superficial amenities as clean streets. In the case of Libya, of course, that was nonsense. Libya's oil income over the past thirty years had been phenomenal despite the embargo. There was one question everyone I spoke to in Libya was asking, and couldn't answer. Where had all the money gone?

I performed for the TV, somewhat sobered by everything I had heard, wondering all the time whether I was disgracing my profession, and then set off towards Benghazi and Egypt. The interview was entirely banal, very amateurish, and it had made me late. I decided to go only as far as Zliten, a mere hundred miles, and take pictures along the way. They were not chosen with any particular aesthetic aim, or for any dramatic quality. I just wanted to take an impression, unhyped and unvarnished, of what it was like to be on the road in Libya to put on my website.

The road was dual-carriage all the way to Zliten, and the surface was good. There were long rows of primitive shops with broken earth-and-cement frontages at the approaches to every small town. Isuzu had a firm grip on the pick-up market, and Isuzus were used for every purpose – as buses, to carry extended families, to transport flocks of sheep and other livestock. One pick-up passed me with a camel sitting proud and stately in the back.

I turned off to Zliten, a town of moderate size that sits between the road and the coast, and a motorcycle cop with a filthy collar stopped me at the first junction. His face looked oddly corrupt, in a way that was slightly shocking, and he seemed determined to get me into a hotel immediately. But I talked loud and fast at him in English, which baffled him, and then rode off quickly. I noticed a fancy mosque and one hotel where I eventually spent the night. It looked good, although the things in it, like the lifts and the plumbing, tended not to work.

First I needed an Internet connection to send emails, and found one in the shopfront of Miftah Muman, a courteous gentleman with an imposing head and a limp, who once studied English outside London for a few months and ran a translation business. The connection was very slow and frustrating, as they all were in North Africa at that time, but afterwards Mr Muman insisted on taking me to his home for a late lunch, and introducing me to his family while a number of special dishes were prepared.

He gave me a more moderate version of the state of affairs in Libya than the one I'd heard at the hotel, but like everyone else, he wondered where all the money had gone. I am sure that if I had given him the opportunity he would have invited me to spend the night in his house, and in retrospect I can't think why I didn't, but probably it was because I needed time alone to write and update my website. Already I was learning how much of a burden I had taken on with all those commitments. I had Libyan soup, still wondering why it was so good, and slept well.

Libya is a huge country (only twelve others in the world are larger) with a very small population. Most of them live on the coast where there are a few big cities – Tripoli, Sirte, Benghazi, El Meri, El Bayda, Derna and Tobruk – strung out along the Mediterranean. Deep in the desert are Ghadamés, Sebha and Kufra, but I could not possibly allow myself the weeks it would take to visit any one of them, even supposing I would be allowed there. Sirte was next, about two hundred miles along my route. In 1973 I had approached it after dark, direct from Tripoli, surprised to find myself on an improvised airstrip surrounded by armed soldiers. Respectful but firm, they had bundled me down some dirt roads into a cheap hotel. Only later did I discover that this was Gaddafi's tribal territory.

Since then Gaddafi must have pumped money into the town. No more dirt roads. There was a new hotel, and the lift worked. The main road was dual-carriage with fancy lighting, and lined with shops that all shone brightly although every one, as far as I could tell, sold the same cheap stuff. In a Turkish restaurant I was lucky enough to meet a Kiwi telecommunications engineer called Larry, who told me that he had just been working on Gaddafi's estate where he had done terminal damage to the leader's lawn. That was the high point of my visit to Sirte.

Benghazi is 350 miles beyond Sirte, and here there was still open desert, with occasional herds of camels. It was on that road, I remembered, that the trouble with the Triumph began. Sand had got into the carburettor and the throttle slide had stuck open. At Ben Gawad I had found shelter in a garage where they had let me work on the bike, and fed me with a free meal of spaghetti. I reflected that so far absolutely nothing had gone wrong with the BMW. For a traveller who thrives on interruptions, the BMW was obviously the wrong bike to be riding.

In Benghazi, a major Libyan port, I had great hopes of finding someone who would remember me. I had spent a week there trying to solve the problem of entering Egypt during a war. Kerim el Fighi ran a motorcycle repair shop, and through him I had made friends. He gave me the run of his small place, and it was there that I did my best to camouflage the bike. With its white fibreglass boxes and chrome it looked as bright and garish in those days as a space vehicle, and I painted everything I could green, to tone down my outlandish appearance. There was no such problem now. Even in Libya, not much frequented by tourists, scarcely anyone paid attention.

I found Kerim's street at last. It was not much changed, I thought, but his shop was now occupied by a fabric merchant. The Oilfield Hotel where I had once slept in a dormitory (I can still summon up the outrageous snoring of my roommate) was closed and crumbling away inside, but I did find the old Sudanese cook who owned it and still lived above. Immensely tall, gaunt, aged, and black as coal, Zaid el Rashdi received me with courtesy. He remembered nothing of my visit but told me what had happened to two of the people I'd known.

Kerim, he said, had been dead for some years after a heart attack, and Mustafa, the genial welder whom I used to visit in his yard across the street, had passed away only two months before my arrival. He knew nothing about the others. I was desolate. Apparently Benghazi was to be just another strange city I was passing through. Zaid brought out tea and cakes, and we talked about Libya in general. He was the only person I had met so far who was enthusiastic about Gaddafi.

'I had many Sudanese friends,' he said, 'who used to work for Gaddafi. They all liked him. He treated them with great respect. He is a good man. A very good man. Yes.'

I spent that night in a big modern hotel, with the bike parked up on the steps visible to the receptionist inside, but even so someone tried to wrench off the headlight assembly during the night. Such a thing would never have happened in 1973.

Sometimes I wonder how I ever found my way around the world. I have a surprising talent for losing myself in the simplest situations. The road from Benghazi to Tobruk is very clear on the map: was then, and is now. Because I was sure I would not be allowed into Egypt, my plan in 1973 was to go straight to the border and then, when I was turned away, I would visit the famous Greek ruins on the coast on my way back. But I lost my way, and found myself at the ruins of Cyrene instead of on the road to Tobruk. It was a very fortunate error because they *did* let me into Egypt after all. But for my mistake I would never have seen those ruins, and they were a high point of my journey.

This time I intended to revisit Cyrene, and on the way I was determined to discover where I had made that mistake. I failed, completely. Nowhere on the way did I make a choice to leave the main road, and I still ended up at a ruin. As far as I am concerned, you cannot get to Tobruk from Benghazi without first visiting a ruin. The fact that thousands do leaves me cold.

What's more, it seems impossible to visit the same ruin twice. I wanted to go to Cyrene, but I ended up in Apollonia, a quite different ancient Greek city. I don't want to hear from people about this. I accept that the world seems to have been arranged in a particular way for me personally, and I am glad of it. I found Apollonia behind a building site, and had to worm my way between small mountains of sand and gravel. I parked my bike on the side-stand opposite the ticket office. The ground was bare stone, on a slope. The steel pad on the foot of the stand slid on the stone, the bike rolled backwards and fell over. Why, I asked myself, do I have to learn everything the hard way?

Apollonia was an ancient Greek port that served the city of Cyrene. What is left of it is relatively sparse, but the columns still standing are a triumph of white stone against blue sea. The Greeks really knew about white and blue. No wonder those are the colours of their flag. I spent the night in a hostel in the nearby town of Shahat, and set off in the morning, happy and refreshed, for Tobruk.

The highlands of Cyrenaica are a blessed relief from the desert. There is greenery everywhere. It rains. The road twists, rises and falls, and passes through lovely scenery. After another fifty miles or so I was down at desert level again, with plenty of camels to look at. When I stopped for a break near Tobruk, two brothers in a car drew up and invited me to their home. They introduced me to their family, showered me with food and hospitality, and then with two other male relatives they took me on a sightseeing trip to the war graves and memorials above Tobruk.

Tobruk, of course, was the scene of a huge and critical battle in the Second World War, involving Germans, British, French, Italian and Polish forces. All have their particular style of memorial. Most are laid out in an open landscaped form, but the German one is defiantly different and captured my interest. It is in the form of a fortress, with completely blank walls, as though the Germans were wishing to hide their grief from a world that couldn't be expected to share it.

The brothers fetched the key from a caretaker, and we went inside. The interior was tasteful and cool. Enormous care and expense have been lavished on it. The names of the fallen are set in blue mosaic into the walls, and a huge decorated iron urn stands in the centre. One of the men started clowning around, clambering into the urn and striking comic poses, and I watched with very mixed feelings. It seemed extraordinary that he felt free to engage in such antics, much like dancing on gravestones. I would have liked to stop him, but couldn't bring myself to. How could I explain?

The inscriptions inside made it clear that the builders of this memorial wanted the war in Africa, Rommel's war, to be set apart from the main event. This, they implied, was a war between gentlemen, a war limited to combatants only, fought on classic, chivalrous principles. It should be treated differently from the rest, afforded a special respect. But as I saw it, nothing could erase the fact that Rommel was fighting in the service of a perverse and inhuman ambition. I and my family were all victims of Hitler's megalomania, and we were on both sides of that war.

If you don't quite know where you stand it's best I suppose to get above it all, so I let them clown. It meant nothing to them, and everybody else present was dead.

Later they took me to see some members of their family who, they said, preferred to live a rural life. This had nothing in common with any sentimental European notion of a rural life. It was an arid and impoverished existence on a bare and dusty plateau. They lived in mud-built hovels. The women wore grubby galabiyas, were barefoot, hennaed and clearly subservient. Nothing grew around them. A little way from the houses was a sheepfold made entirely from pieces of rusty scrap metal off roofs and broken vehicles. Yet their relatives, my hosts, wore good-quality Western clothes, lived in a prosperous style and drove a decent car. Unfortunately, their English was very limited – otherwise, I might have tried to penetrate deeper into this family mystery.

At my hotel one of the guests pointed at me with a huge grin. He had seen me on the TV. He was the only person in Libya as far as I know who had been watching that night. There was no word from Gaddafi. I read his *Little Green Book* and had to admit that a lot of work had gone into it, but the idea was purely Utopian. It depended on everybody being a whole lot nicer than they really are; it promulgated one of those you-can't-get-there-from-here political systems. Certainly nothing I had seen in Libya seemed remotely like it.

6

Another day, another border. Sometimes it seemed to be all about crossing borders, one after another. I rode up to the Libyan side good and early, as usual, and was sent back again three miles to hand my number plate in to the police. It didn't even occur to me to complain that I should have been told, that there were no signs, and so on. Why should they care?

It was easier than I expected to find the police. They were behind a blue-painted door in a converted house on the main road in a busy village. I just hadn't noticed on my way through. No reason to. They took the plate, asked me to sign something, and *gave back my forty dollars*. I did mental penance for all the bad-mouthing I had done, and rode again to the frontier.

Libya made it easy to leave. I was stamped out in no time, and found myself passing an Egyptian police checkpoint and into a gated area with a prefabricated office up on a platform. I parked and went up the steps.

Inside the office were two officials at separate tables, and at the back a door into another room where I supposed the boss resided. One of the officials put out his hand for my passport. I could tell immediately that he had no interest in getting me into Egypt any time soon. There was a stack of passports on his table. Mine went to the bottom. He said, 'Wait.'

I went outside and waited on the bike. There was another gate that obviously led to the customs area, but I couldn't see past it. It was guarded. A man came through and went into the office. That was all that happened for an hour or so. It was extremely peaceful. I was wearing jeans and my red riding jacket over a shirt. The sun heated up so I took off the jacket.

Eventually I went into the office so as to be in shade. There was a bench there, and I sat on it, and watched the two officials. The passports were still stacked where they had been. The man sitting in front of them, handsome and in his thirties, apparently thought himself a reincarnation of Rudolph Valentino, very dapper, in expensive leather riding boots which he tapped often with a ruler. He was careful never to turn his supercilious eye in my direction.

After a considerable time, the man I had seen come in emerged from the back office with an armful of passports. Rudolph stamped them in lackadaisical fashion and the man took them away. A while later he came back, and Rudolph handed him his own pile of passports, mine among them, which disappeared into the back office. Perhaps a suitable amount of money might have hastened things along, but it never crossed my mind to offer anything. I had no idea what the going rate might be, and the wrong offer could be worse than none at all. I am very inexperienced in bribery.

After another half-hour or so, the passports re-emerged. Rudolph stamped through them until he came to mine. He looked through it, slowly, disdainfully. Then he showed it to his colleague who also spent a lot of time on it, before handing it back. They giggled and smirked. You might have thought it was pornographic. Rudolph stamped a few more passports, then he gave me mine back with a slip of paper printed in Arabic.

'You can go,' he said.

I rode through the gate and gave a policeman the paper.

'Did they stamp your passport?' he asked.

Of course it was stamped. 'Yes,' I said.

It was like passing from limbo into hell. The other side of the gate was a scene of impenetrable confusion and noise. There was a series of lanes divided by raised stone platforms. Sprawled all over them, and around equally chaotic heaps of bundles, boxes and bags, were crowds of people dressed or draped in every conceivable kind and colour of material. They were debating, arguing, pleading; there were shouts and whistles. Somewhere in this mêlée were customs officers, but at first I couldn't tell them apart, as they wore no uniforms. I parked and tried to understand what was going on.

To the left was a building with an open concourse and counters, like a railway station. I guessed that I had to take my passport to one of them, and a mustachioed man with a long-suffering expression leafed through it with increasing impatience. 'Where is the stamp?' he spluttered. 'There is no stamp. You must go back.' Rudolph had been too busy cultivating his style, or maybe he just wanted to show me. I lost another ten minutes taking care of it. Rudolph's languid self-importance remained undisturbed.

When I came back with the passport I was given a piece of printed paper roughly torn off a pad. It was the first of many. They were all in Arabic, incomprehensible to me. The customs examination was the least bothersome. I managed to identify an officer, because he moved from one knot of humanity to another. He spoke some English. Only very few of the men did, and this was a huge change from the seventies when everyone I met spoke my language.

He didn't much care what I'd brought with me. 'You have a gun?' he asked. 'Drugs?'

I said, 'No.'

Then he pointed me towards an office that had to do with transit. From that time on I was lost. A young man with no English dragged me from building to building. It went on for hours, and it was very hot. I paid out innumerable amounts of money, and each time I got an indecipherable scrap of paper. You could call it a powerful lesson in humility.

Finally I had to get temporary Egyptian licence plates, but there weren't any. We stood at a fence, and the young man hollered at somebody a hundred yards away. It took him a while to raise his opposite number, but finally the plates were brought and tossed over the fence. I had to tape one on the front of the windshield. The other screwed on at the back. They cost more dollars. I got more paper. Altogether I spent one hundred dollars and several pints of sweat. The whole performance, from start to finish, took six hours. At 4.30 p.m. I was on the road and through the frontier town of Salloum.

I looked back wistfully to 1973, when there was a war on and I should not legally have been allowed through at all. Then it had taken half the time, everyone spoke English, I'd been given tea, and it had cost me next to nothing. From the Egyptian point of view I suppose things have improved greatly since then. The other dramatic change was that at some time since the seventies Egypt must have switched sides on the road. Now everybody drove (more or less) on the right. I could only be thankful that I wasn't riding there when they made the change.

I had no map of Egypt as such, only the same very large-scale Michelin map of Africa that I had used in 1973, but updated of course. There appeared to be a new road running east away from the coast, but it came back to rejoin the old road at Mersa Matruh. It was near there at a crossroads that I had spent my first night in Egypt, sleeping on boards at a military checkpoint with ragged soldiers around me chanting, 'Nekesta week, brekfast in Tel Aviv.' For old times' sake Mersa seemed like a good place to sleep. Besides, I had never seen the actual city.

Since both roads went there, I didn't much care which one I was on. I simply wanted to get away from the border, and all that boredom and aggravation. At four-thirty in the afternoon I had an hour or two of daylight left. At around five, I saw the city in the distance. At five-thirty, as it grew dark, I had to face the fact that I was no longer on the road to Mersa, and that somewhere I had either missed an exit or taken a wrong turn. I was on my way to Alexandria instead.

I have always hated to retrace my steps. I would do almost anything to avoid going back the way I came. To cover my embarrassment I have even developed a mini-philosophy that embraces my mistakes as signs from providence leading me into unexpected adventures. So, finding myself on an excellent highway with an unblemished surface I broke my own rule about riding in Egypt after dark (just as I had in 1973). The bike was humming along contentedly, the air was warm, there was no sign of animals or other obstacles. So I rode on looking for somewhere to eat and sleep.

For extra security I looked for another vehicle to nurse me along, and soon found one. A small delivery van passed me travelling at a good speed, and I sat behind its tail-lights for fifty miles or so, scanning the side of the road for any sign of a hotel or a piece of open ground. But the night was black, with no road lights, and nothing showed up. I saw no houses. The road seemed to be lined with either fence or thick vegetation. Eventually the van peeled off on to a road that disappeared into darkness, and I went on more slowly for another hour wondering whether I would have to sleep hungry by the roadside.

A lighted object far ahead resolved itself into a hut in the middle of the road – some sort of police post, I supposed. I rode up alongside it, parked, took off my helmet and told the grizzled gentleman inside that I was looking for a hotel. He can't have been police, because he didn't ask for papers, which it later turned out was just as well.

'Over there,' he said, pointing across the road.

I peered into the darkness and saw nothing. He kept pointing. 'Yes, yes, down there is the hotel.'

It was ridiculous, like a scene from the *Arabian Nights*. Why should there be a hotel there, when I had seen nothing for a hundred miles and there were no signs, and nothing visible? But now I could detect dimly an opening on to a dirt track a few yards further along on the left. Well, at least I might find a piece of ground to sleep on. I thanked him and rode on to the track, waiting for some magical manifestation. It came after about a hundred yards, in the form of a sign advertising the El Alamein Resort. It was probably the most redundant piece of advertising in the world, but it cheered me up.

Evidently the *chowkidar* in the road must have thought I already knew about the hotel but couldn't find it. What extraordinary good fortune! A little further along, the building itself appeared. It was big, luxurious even, with large landscaped grounds and an empty car park, dimly lit, framed by bushes. Ranged alongside the road were three big BMW motorcycles packed somewhat like mine, with German plates. Bingo, I thought, the hotel is functioning. Not only that, there's someone to talk to.

I found them inside, already sitting down to dinner with the manager who, it seemed, was also the chef, so I joined them. We were the only guests in this large, echoing establishment. The price turned out to be a bit stiff, but I was too relieved to find it at all to want to argue. Herbert, Klaus and Andreas told me they were on holiday to fulfil an ambition they had shared for years: to explore the oases in the Egyptian desert. They had flown their bikes into Cairo, so we compared customs horror stories. With only four weeks of vacation to realise their dream they had lost five days just getting their bikes through customs, and it had cost them $500 each. I began to feel a lot better about my ordeal at Salloum.

Next morning, in a flurry of picture-taking, they left for the desert, and I started on my way to Alexandria. I was very glad to be doing it by daylight because my first journey along this road in 1973 had been full of dramatic moments. The tension had been high, with troops and roadblocks everywhere because of the current war with Israel. I was fascinated by the fragments of armour and aeroplane parts still lying in the desert, remnants of that earlier, rather larger war that I had lived through as a child.

I remembered how the road had veered towards the coast after El Alamein, revealing to my left miles and miles of empty beach, of blinding white sand, and beyond it a strip of sea so intensely turquoise as to be quite vulgar. Then came that unforgettable scene to my right, an ocean of limestone, a tumult of pinnacles and troughs like a flash-frozen storm, with all the energy and wildness held in suspense and transmuted into gleaming white rock. Nothing like it had ever come my way before.

Now, twenty-eight years later, everything had changed. All traces of the Second World War had disappeared. The sea had vanished too, hidden behind an unbroken string of resort developments. And the extraordinary limestone ocean had also vanished, sawn up into blocks and carted across the road to build those same look-alike holiday condominiums. Miles of spectacular scenery reduced to packaged banality. Why should I have expected anything else?

Then the road closed in on me and I plunged into the fringes of Alexandria.

7

It seems at times that I have been struggling through this urban chaos for ever and that my attempt to reach the heart of Alexandria can never succeed; that this throbbing, convulsive city will eventually digest me and my motorcycle, and spill out my remains among the splintered crates, crushed cartons, decomposing refuse, crumbling bricks, rusting auto parts, donkey dung, splattered fruit, yawning potholes, heaving tar, protruding tram rails and oozing water mains, all passing endlessly under my tyres. Surely my faith is misguided, there is no centre here to reach, and I will go on hour after hour as the broken buildings and their unruly contents press further and further into the narrow streets until, exhausted and delirious, I am finally swallowed up and redistributed to become part of the detritus over which others will pass until it is their turn to join this ancient dustheap.

Then the grotesque fantasy lifts as I emerge from a crowded alley into a streaming thoroughfare of lopsided buses and battered taxis all moving purposefully as though there were a beginning and an end to their journeys. Here there are taller façades, an ornamental plaza, police blowing whistles, crowds hurrying along pavements. Surely I must be getting closer, but just as suddenly this show of pomp and progress dwindles again into a narrow, obstructed passage full of carts and bicycles, ravenous cats and indolent donkeys, and artisans hammering and sawing on the pavements.

All I can do is keep going east, trying to stay with the flow. Even if I had a map it would be useless to me. All street signs are in Arabic now. The Englishness of Egypt has quite drained away, as I discovered yesterday at the border. Already I am nostalgic for the Egypt I knew before.

Alexandria has swollen hideously. It was hard enough to break through in 1973, but since then entire suburbs have had time to grow and collapse around it. The road runs on, interminably, swelling and contracting, and despite everything I cannot help but think that it is still, after all this time, a damned good idea to be travelling on a motorcycle. Because of that slight element of risk, always present with a heavy machine on two wheels, I have a keen interest in knowing what passes beneath me, and what's happening in front and behind and on either side. Short of crawling on my hands and knees, how else could I become so intimate with the texture of this city?

Again the road opens out, but now I see a difference. The buildings are ranged in a more orderly European fashion, rising up high, with shops at street level. This is an avenue and undoubtedly it is leading somewhere, and before I know it, I turn the corner and there is the statue, and the old Hotel Cecil, and I have arrived in Zhagoul Square, for the third time.

I came there first a long time ago, as in a dream, on a hot summer's day in London in the fifties. It was an entirely mental trip, a journey I made in my imagination when I was winding my way through the volumes of Lawrence Durrell's ambitious and brilliant Alexandrian Quartet. Reaching his Alexandria (which he claimed 'could not be less unreal') involved no arduous physical trials. Durrell's words wafted me over sea and desert, marsh and lake, tumbling columns and prophets' tombs, into the living presence of his eclectic company of characters. I became immersed in that fictional city and my familiarity with it survived twenty years. So it was Durrell's Alexandria I was riding towards in 1973 when I first set out to discover the world for myself.

All of Islamic North Africa was bubbling with excitement and suspicion and, given all the promised obstacles, my progress across the border from Libya was little short of miraculous. After that, with occasional polite interference from the Egyptian army, I advanced on Alexandria by fits and starts. Finally, after riding through a smaller version of the same maze that nearly three decades later I have just penetrated, I reached the only landmarks familiar to me through Durrell's book: Zhagoul Square and the Hotel Cecil, where Nessim proposed a doomed marriage to Justine. And it was as I brought the Triumph to a halt outside the hotel that I first noticed portents of my own doom snaking from my exhaust pipe in a cloud of smoke.

The Alexandria I discovered then was nothing like Durrell's. I saw none of the great, mysterious wetlands he described, I went to no masked balls, and there were no foreign warships in the harbour as there had been in his day. The warships were Egyptian, and when I photographed them (having forgotten there was a war on) I was promptly arrested as an Israeli spy and carried off to be interrogated by an elderly, myopic general who regaled me with his memories of shopping expeditions to Harrods.

King Farouk's summer palace, the Montasah, was as close as I could come to the languid luxury of an earlier aristocratic Alex, but it had become a museum crammed with expensive objects in rather bad taste. The only item that fascinated me was a shower bath of convoluted nickel-plated pipes that must once have squirted water at all parts of His Obesity.

The centre of Alexandria was originally conceived in splendid Parisian style, with buildings like those radiating out from the Étoile: six-storey edifices presenting intricately moulded stone and stucco decoration, with wrought-iron lift cages rising and falling hydraulically at the core of sweeping circular staircases. But unlike Paris, which had become a white, fastidious and expensive courtesan, Alexandria was already a shabby old whore well past her bed-by date.

Zhagoul Square, however, was still an attractive place, and the Hotel Cecil, outwardly at least, seemed as grand as ever. In '73 it was far too grand for me and I found a billet on the fourth floor of another building behind the Cecil, in the Hotel Normandie, a small *pension* belonging to a Mme Mellasse. In those days the lift still worked. Given a coin to feed into the slot, it carried me and my luggage up the four floors to the Normandie, but slowly and with many a shudder, and I always arrived with a sense of triumphant relief. It was in Mme Mellasse's cramped French-speaking salon that I got my only authentic whiff of the past, from the widow of an exiled Russian aristocrat who languished there with an elderly expatriate professor from Paris.

Out in the streets I had been overwhelmed by more immediate experiences, brief but vivid, for I was arrested yet again on the same day and had a few hours of real anxiety. My brushes with authority and outraged citizenry brought me up abruptly against the current realities. Repairing the Triumph took me closer to the population. I found a garage near Ramilies railway station where some mechanics treated me with touching kindness and sincerity. I soon took the city away from Durrell and appropriated it to myself.

So it is at this real Alexandria that I am now arriving twenty-eight years later as, once again, I park outside the Hotel Cecil. The old lady is dressed in scaffolding. Maybe they're giving her a makeover. For the hell of it I walk inside for a taste of old-fashioned luxury. A black-suited manager, undeterred by my filthy appearance, comes over to offer me a room. I tell him I can't afford it, and he offers me a sixty per cent discount, but the truth is I don't want to stay there. I want to go back to the Normandie. I ride round the block, and there among a battery of brass plates outside the large open doorway is the sign.

I summon up my faith, and leave the bike parked outside the entrance to this once august but now utterly decrepit mansion where the Normandie still floats on the fourth floor. The grand old coin-operated lift, alas, has died. I climb up the four flights and pass the old lift cage, stuck on the second floor. It is half full of rubbish.

Of course I know that Mme Mellasse and her faithful servant George must have long since passed away, and yet it's a blow to find that the hotel is fully occupied by a busload of chemistry students on a field trip. However, there's another hotel, the El Gameel, on the same floor – that's how big these old mansion blocks were – and I settle for a room. The man who gives me the key is related to the owner in some way. He's about five feet tall, with a square brown face, worried, unshaven, with a moustache. His name is Hamid and he seems undernourished.

He comes down to help with the bike. He says I must bring it into the hallway, which is quite long, and has several steps up. So I take off my two big Ortlieb bags, and ride the bike in up the steps. All this takes a little while and makes noise. A door on the right of the hall opens and a robed woman looks out and starts yelling. I can see through the doorway that behind her is a single, smallish room, with dishes and clothes and children scattered around the floor. This is where the watchman and his wife and family live. She wants to be paid for the inconvenience. There's an altercation, and I settle it with a small payment to her to watch the bike.

The hotel guy seizes my bags, humps them on to his back, and heads for the stairs.

'No, no,' I cry. 'You can't carry all that?'

The bags look bigger than he is, but he insists. Short of using physical force (to which I am opposed), I can't get them away from him. I follow, carrying nothing more than my helmet and tank bag, feeling foolish. And there will be a reckoning, I know, and it comes quite soon.

The room's OK. What do you want for five dollars? It's a room with a bed. We're sitting at his desk, in a space just behind the front door, and with a curious mixture of hope and despair on his face he asks me to buy some whisky. It goes like this. There's a place I can go to, where only foreign visitors can buy alcohol. He will take me there. I can buy two bottles of whisky, and then he will give me the money because his sister, or his daughter or someone, is getting married tomorrow, and he wants to take the whisky to the wedding.

I don't really care what he does with the whisky. It occurs to me to go to the wedding, but I doubt that there is one, and anyway I am already feeling pressure to get to Cairo, and get the visa for Sudan, because I know there's a big Islamic holiday coming up and I'm supposed to be there, in Sudan, by 14 March to meet Manfred's crew. That's another reason why travelling and film-making really don't mix.

What I worry about most is getting caught up in some scam where I have to buy my way out with a heap of money because, as I said earlier, I am very inexperienced in the ways of bribery and corruption. On the other hand, I'm intrigued, and I like the man, and he did unquestionably carry a lot of my stuff up four flights of stairs. So I take him through the whole deal carefully, several times, and finally I agree to give it a try.

By now it's dark. The night is delicious. Soft, warm, full of promise, just like it says in the brochures. We walk through the streets, all nicely lit, still in an affluent part of the city, while I record my path mentally so that I can find my way back. And eventually we get to this place, like an emporium from the thirties, on two floors, with sumptuous carpets underfoot and rather grand attendants to direct my attention to the displays of costly liquor.

Hamid was very specific about the brand. It had to be Johnnie Walker Red, but that's no problem. The problem is that he's right there with me, and so it's obvious to anyone what we're up to, which makes me nervous. I shoo him off, quite sharply, but in the end I have to admit that nobody seems to care. I show my passport, pay, and leave. In a small café Hamid gives me my money back and takes the bottles. That's it.

In a B movie, of course, I would have got myself into all kinds of scrapes with sinister characters out of *The Maltese Falcon*. I still forget sometimes that I'm in an A movie now.

8

In the morning I wandered back across the landing to the Normandie, hoping to find something there to evoke the past, but the new Egyptian owners had rearranged the rooms and I had to make do with my memories. However, I did meet the professor in charge of the chemistry students who were staying there. Professional people in Egypt speak English as a matter of course, and we had a pleasant conversation. He was a small man, superficially grave, in a heavy black suit, and I prepared to drag out what shreds I could recall of my chemical engineering education, but he was more interested in hearing about my journeys.

Dreading the road out of Alexandria, thinking it would be a repeat of the journey in, I was delighted to discover that he was taking his party out towards Cairo that morning by bus. They were to visit a large chemical plant, he said. Their bus would be parked at the edge of Zhagoul Square and I could follow it out of the city.

When I arrived the students were already on board. They had all seen the bike in the hall and were leaning out of the windows waving, grinning and sticking their thumbs up. I followed the green bus and to my astonishment we were out of the city in hardly more than fifteen minutes. We were on what is called the Desert Road, and when we came to a junction where they were turning off, the bus stopped and the professor got out to make sure I knew where to go. Even in this fleeting relationship there was genuine warmth.

In Alexandria, for once my mobile phone had worked and I had made an arrangement to meet Stuart Larman at a roadside restaurant halfway to Cairo. Stuart was an American civil engineer and motorcyclist who had invited me to his home in Maahdi, one of the nicer parts of the city. He was one of the many who had emailed me, people I had never seen and knew virtually nothing about, but who wanted to be part of my adventure. I still think it remarkable that all of them, without exception, are people I would gladly meet again.

Stuart rode up on an older BMW. He turned out to be still quite young, though almost bald, and with a gentle disposition. He had the height and athleticism of a basketball player, and dwarfed his bike. We had a coffee and rode to Cairo together. Since I was there last Cairo had doubled in size, to twelve million people, an even bigger congested sprawl than Alexandria, but with Stuart to lead we arrived fairly soon at the Nile embankment and then rode upriver to Maahdi, a pleasant enclave of large houses and leafy squares.

In *Jupiter's Travels* I wrote nothing about Cairo, but not because my time there was uninteresting. Far from it. There was simply too much to tell. I had met someone, I forget whom or where, who told me about the Hotel Golden, on Talaat Harb, in the centre of the city, and I was there for eighteen days. Amin Simaika was the young Copt who managed it. It was his sword that I carried halfway round the world to Brazil – the umbrella on one side of the Triumph, the sword on the other. The proprietor of the Golden was Amin's uncle, Serafim, an elderly and distinguished-looking man whose family had founded El Minya, a prosperous city on the Nile. He had once been rich enough to regale his dinner guests off a forty-piece table setting of solid gold, but when Colonel Nasser came to power (what is it about colonels?) he was partially dispossessed. He accepted his situation philosophically, having had an extraordinary life. He had been at Oxford with Jawaharlal Nehru, Arnold Toynbee and other luminaries, and had stories to tell about that time.

There was another fellow there then, a tall, fair Englishman called Alan. (Amin and I decided between us that he was probably a spy.) We three had played chess and discussed politics interminably, while I tried to get permission, despite the war, to ride my bike up the Nile to Aswan, hoping to visit Serafim's city on the way. In the end I was unsuccessful and had to take a train. This time I expected no problems riding south to Aswan. My challenge now was quite different. In Cairo I finally had to confront my worst fear – that it might not be possible to get into Sudan – and without Sudan the journey through Africa would be wrecked.

Ever since Clinton's cruise missiles had struck a Sudanese aspirin factory, Americans were *personae non gratae* in Sudan, and because Britain was complicit with America a British passport was hardly any better. As if that wasn't bad enough, because of the approaching Islamic holiday of Eid and the generally indolent schedule of the embassy's passport department, I had at the most three days to crack their apparently impregnable position. After that, weeks or months might go by. The thought of not going through Sudan was anathema to me. My experiences in the Sudanese desert had been a crucial part of the first journey. I absolutely had to go back.

Stuart called around his expatriate friends. 'They all say it's pretty hopeless, but there's one Sudanese guy, Mustafa, who knows people at the embassy. He might be able to help.'

Mustafa – my third Mustafa so far – said he had fixed up an introduction to the official who managed the passport section at the embassy. His name, apparently, was Gorshy. He would be expecting me.

With high hopes I gathered up photos and dollars, and went in search of Sudan's embassy. It was hard to find, because I was looking for an embassy, and should have been looking for a demolition site. There was rubble all around. A muddy-looking sentry leaned against a sentry box that appeared also to be made of mud, like a termite mound. The building itself was difficult to discern behind scaffolding. Workmen seemed to be tearing it down, and throwing the bits across the entrance.

I dodged through this barrage and asked for Mr Gorshy. A very short male receptionist wearing a metallic-blue suit and a bitter expression gave me four identical forms to fill out, with no carbons.

Then he directed me forcefully to a waiting area in a state of such grime and disrepair that it was seriously depressing. The people sitting there, on folding metal chairs, wore the set, hopeless expressions of those who have been waiting for eternity. At the end of the room were two rectangular openings in the wall above counters, and behind them was a small empty space and a door. Like everyone else who came in, I walked up to these counters, ascertained that there was no one there, waited around a while to be first in the rush, and then gave up and joined the ranks of the defeated.

After an hour a man appeared behind the left-hand counter. There was a flurry of excitement but it quickly died. He was not there to accept applications, only to dispense documents to Sudanese nationals. Another hour passed. Then Mr Gorshy arrived. The crowd rushed to his window and it was hard to get near, but I managed to push my introduction across to him. It was obvious as he read it that he had never heard of me. 'You must get a letter from your embassy,' he said brusquely, and went back into Arabic mode.

The British embassy was not far away. I sped over there and, to my joy, found that the press attaché had actually read my books and was a self-confessed fan. I explained what I needed.

'Oh, yes,' he said. 'We do quite a lot of these. We've never had any trouble. This should do the job.' I suppose I should have known then and there that he was less than current. He wrote me out a handsome letter explaining who I was and that Her Majesty would be delighted to see Edward Simon and his motorcycle conducted safely into Sudan.

Back at the embassy Gorshy had left. The blue-metal man said, 'He will return', making it sound like a threat, and directed me back to purgatory.

Until then I had avoided contact with the denizens of the hall of despair, not wishing to be contaminated by their fate, but now I gave in and began conversation with a young South African lawyer called James travelling on a battered Enfield Bullet, and a New Zealand backpacker called Chris. Their stories were very dispiriting. Both had been hanging around for days, and getting nowhere. Mr Gorshy's appearances, they said, were unpredictable and very brief. We waited for five hours through the afternoon, and at five-thirty an official came to tell us the embassy was now closed. He smiled broadly. It was the first Sudanese smile I had seen there that day.

That was Wednesday. The embassy would open again on Saturday, and after that . . . holiday time in Islam. Meanwhile, Manfred and his crew had already bought their non-refundable tickets for Khartoum for 15 March, only two weeks away. Even worse, if my entry into Sudan was delayed by weeks, the rains might stop me from riding out of the country at all.

Next day I went to the offices of the United Nations in Cairo to begin fulfilling my ambassadorial obligations, but also in the desperate hope that there was something they could do to help. I had promised I would tell stories of volunteerism on my website, and they had some volunteers for me to visit and write about. Part of the curious jargon the UN adopted was to describe a person as a 'focal point'. Cairo's 'focal point' for the Year of the Volunteer was an Arab woman with strong but attractive features, an engaging smile, a rare self-assurance and a pair of sunglasses perched on her thick black hair. I also discovered later that she had some rather disconcerting opinions, but for now she had a cancer hospital for me to visit.

In the same office cubicle was a beautiful porcelain blonde Italian woman called Stefania, who worked for the UN development programme. Before leaving, I explained my problem to Stefania. Not only did she say she would see what could be done, she actually sounded as though she meant it.

For two days, while the Sudanese embassy was closed, I was immersed in the remarkable stories of people who devoted themselves to helping impoverished victims of cancer and others dispossessed by earthquake disaster. Meanwhile Stefania kept me informed. Messages were flying around the world on my behalf. Bonn was talking to Khartoum, and Khartoum, it seems, was talking to Sudan's ambassador in Egypt who happened to be visiting London. Something could come of this.

I took the metro back to Maahdi. It was crowded, but I noticed that the first carriages were fairly empty so I walked into one of them, just as the doors were closing. I knew immediately that something was wrong, but it took a minute to understand. Shawled women looked at me oddly. Then it struck me. I was the only man. Obviously I had transgressed, flouting an unwritten rule. Too old to blush, but embarrassed nonetheless, I slipped out at the next stop, but as I walked to the next carriage a man on the platform told me, severely, 'This carriage is for women only.' The remark was not only unnecessary and annoying, but it triggered a resentment in me I couldn't quite identify.

The first news at Stuart's apartment was not good. The British press attaché had called to say he couldn't raise anyone at the Sudanese embassy. But later Stefania brought me the best news of all. The UN had succeeded. The Sudanese ambassador had told his embassy to give me a visa. She would come there with me next day to help me get it. I rejoiced, but cautiously. My last experience at the embassy had left a bitter taste of frustration.

Stuart and I went out to celebrate, through the quiet middle-class streets, past roughly uniformed conscripts with ancient rifles, supposedly guarding against attacks by Muslim fundamentalists, and down to the market to eat. The market was a crowded cluster of shops and small restaurants behind the station. People were already excited over the coming feast days of Eid. Flocks of sheep stood tethered in the bustling streets, unaware of their impending fate.

We found a small, brightly lit shop where a man was busy with food behind a counter. There were chairs up on tables and we thought he was just closing, but in fact he was preparing to open. We bought *foul*, made from spiced fava beans, and *tarmeia* sandwiches, very satisfying and tasty, and sat down to a good, filling meal for about fifty pence each. Then we took a taxi to a café terrace on the banks of the Nile. The café had just been refurbished, and was crammed with middle-class Egyptian couples smoking, drinking coffee and soft drinks and listening to pop music.

Attendants splendidly gowned in blue carried magnificent sheesha pipes (what we used to call hubble-bubbles, or hookahs) to the tables, and many of the men were smoking the perfumed and flavoured tobacco. Stuart chose an apple flavour, and I tried it myself, but you can't draw enough air through these pipes without inhaling. Since I stopped smoking I find that uncomfortable, so I satisfied myself with the fragrance wafting through the warm night air.

Next day, Stuart brought his friend Mustafa to the embassy. Apparently Mustafa knew somebody upstairs. Stefania met us there, and when Gorshy arrived she thrust her card into his hand. I had the pleasure of watching him turn from hostile apparatchik into an apparently amiable person. However, there was still a problem. The ambassador's instructions referred to Ted Simon and his motor-cycle. My passport identified me as Edward Simon. How was he supposed to know, Gorshy said with an apologetic smile, that these were the same person? So my British embassy letter, describing me as Edward Simon with a motorcycle, did finally serve a purpose.

'Ah, the motorcycle,' said Gorshy. That was enough for him. Still we waited several hours, with Mustafa prodding his friend for progress reports from upstairs. We tried to get news of Chris Collie's desperate case too, but it was shrouded in mystery. As for James, it would seem only a miracle could change his fortunes.

My passport came down from the perfumed gardens above at about midday, bearing a suitably expensive-looking visa complete with hologram, and I was able to spend the afternoon in a daze of relief. I still have no idea how I would have proceeded without it.

There was only one more important thing left for me to do in Cairo, and Stuart and I set off to the pyramids on our bikes. On the front cover of one of my books is a picture of me sitting on a camel in my flying jacket and with my helmet on. I can never look at this picture without experiencing some of the sheer joy I felt when it was taken, so long ago. Having penetrated into Egypt in wartime I was enjoying one of the rewards.

At first, as the only foreigner in sight, I had been mobbed by a throng of guides, camel drivers and sellers of postcards, perfumes and sex, and through it all the pyramids themselves suffered a good deal in my estimation. Finally, though, I found two camel drivers with the good sense to realise that I was no target of opportunity for them. Instead, they joined in my pleasure, and we enjoyed ourselves together. They wondered at my bike and gave me tea in their tent as I described my journey. I delighted in the camels, with their rich trappings, because I had never been so close to these exotic animals before.

There were two drivers, both young men, and their names were Fares and Mandor. It was on Fares's camel (which had the unlikely name of Jack Hulbert) that I rode for an hour, and it is Fares who is standing beside his camel in that picture, holding my hand, as Egyptian men do.

We took photographs, lots of them, and Mandor took that one beautiful shot. If I ever needed reminding that the second journey, however wonderful it might be, can never compare with that first ecstatic rush out into the wide world, I had only to look at that picture. Now, after all these years, it didn't seem possible that either of these men would still be there. And even if they were, why would I matter to them? Why would they remember me, when so many thousands must have come and gone since then? I had come to find out.

We arrived to find tourists and their buses littering the streets all around. Barricades and police guarded both entrances to Gizeh, and through a misunderstanding we found ourselves at the wrong entrance, a long way from the pyramids, and unable to take our bikes through. As we started walking, a young camel driver spotted us and trotted his animal over to solicit business. Before he could begin his sales talk I called out that I was looking for Fares Hamse.

I could see that the name meant something. His English was shaky, but he said something like 'good man' and 'gone', and he looked sad, and I gathered at first that Fares was dead, or at best had gone away.

'Is he dead?' I asked bluntly.

'No, no, not dead. Come,' and he motioned to the saddle of his camel.

As the animal sank groaning to its knees and then settled on its haunches, I handed Stuart a few things I was carrying. I clambered up behind the driver with just my camera in my hand, and almost lost it as the camel's hind legs unfolded and jerked me forward at an alarming angle. I had forgotten how wild the bucking motion was. Then we rose up and padded off across the sands towards those huge tan triangles piercing the sky. Gradually, as we travelled, I learned the happy truth. Both Fares and Mandor were alive and well, and there was every likelihood that I would find them both there that day. I needed the prospect to offset my growing discomfort. It is one thing to sit alone on a camel, with legs folded over its neck, and quite another to sit behind with legs spread across the animal's girth. Unaccustomed to doing the splits, I was in agony well before we arrived, but mercifully I didn't have to ride the whole way. With a few hundred yards to go, my driver put me down.

There was evidently some kind of hierarchy among the drivers, and Fares was at the top of it. My driver belonged to a lesser order that had to scavenge for business on the more distant approaches, and was not allowed to carry passengers anywhere near the pyramids. So we walked on together to where a cluster of camels, buses and people were gathered. When we were within earshot, he called out and, hearing some shouts back, he pointed and said, 'They are there.' Then he turned his camel around, I gave him some money and thanked him, and he walked away.

It was extraordinary to see those two men I had met only once twenty-seven years earlier, and yet to recognise their faces. Mandor, in a dark robe, was heavier, his face fuller. Fares's face was lined with age, but I knew them both. Even more amazing, as I walked in, unexpected and unannounced, it was obvious that they knew me. Mandor looked pleased, but Fares was clearly overwhelmed, just as I was.

'You have come back,' he said, 'as you said you would.'

At last, a human connection with the past.

Both men had prospered in the meanwhile. They had cars, and families. Mandor had a profitable arrangement with a big hotel-restaurant and Fares gave me his business card. It read:

KAMEL * HORSE
Fares Hmza
Teacher and Trainer to ride horse and camel
Kfr El Gabl El Nadi st. tel. 3886836

Fares took me out into the desert with his camel, walking along-side it at first while I rode, and then climbing up himself. We spoke very little, but the depth of his feeling was unmistakable. We could have stayed out there all day if I had wanted, but I was anxious to fetch the bike and get it up to the pyramids somehow. I wanted him to see it, and also I wanted to repeat the picture that we had taken so long ago.

It took a long time to get back to the bike, leave messages for Stuart, and find a way to ride in. By the time I got back, Mandor had had to leave – a pity because I would have liked him to take the picture, as before. Repeating history is a fool's game, and of course the picture we took this time was a farcical caricature of that original one, but it serves its purpose. It marks the passage of time and the strong desire of two people, with nothing in common but one magic experience when we both felt young, to cling to what is best in us. When I had to leave he said, 'I am crying.'

His eyes glistened, and I expect mine did too.

9

We left Stuart's apartment at 8.30 a.m., and I filled up my enormous tank with rather expensive petrol. Then we rode out past the pyramids again, past the exit to the Agricultural Road and eventually on to the Desert Road south, a fine, smooth, empty highway which bypasses the crowded village roads running alongside the Nile but appears on no maps I have seen.

An infinite stony waste surrounded us for many miles before we passed an oasis of palms and irrigated land, then the Beni Suef oilfield, then more desert. There were police checkpoints, and at some the police were heavily armoured, but they didn't stop us. Stuart pointed out the Mai Doum pyramid, a step pyramid about ten miles off the road. We took the spur road and got close enough for pictures, when police rolled up in a small truck. A fellow with two pips on his shoulder jumped out and questioned us, politely. Who are you, where are you going, what are you doing?

'We're taking pictures,' said Stuart.

'No pictures,' he said.

Stuart laughed in exasperation. 'Oh, come on. What's the matter with you guys? If we come in and pay it's OK, and here it isn't?'

Smiling, the cop got on the phone and reported in Arabic, '*Wachad Americani, wachad Inglesi.* One American, one Englishman' and so on. Meanwhile we took the pictures.

The cop said, 'You come to pyramid?'

I said, 'Yes', though we had no such intention, and they drove off.

'You can see I've got no time for these Egyptians any more,' said Stuart, but in reality he was always very nice to them. Some months earlier a young boy had come to his door one day, needing 'money for school'. Stuart had been giving him something regularly ever since, though he complained about the frustrations of daily life. It was his wife Stephanie, a graceful Colorado girl almost as tall as Stuart, who really liked Egypt.

We went a little further together. Stuart took a set of pictures of me in various heroic poses. Then he shook my hand and went back to Cairo, while I rode on south.

I was stopped only once, by another two-pip cop talking on his phone who waved me on again. After that the desert changed, the sand loosened, flying in the wind and gathering in dunes that began to leak across the road. I stopped and examined a handful as it trickled through my fingers, a beautiful mixture of tiny multi-coloured crystals, like jewels.

These long periods of unworried riding are very precious. These are the times I think best about what has already happened, and what to make of it. It is one of the reasons I prefer to ride alone, and why I actually prefer to be wearing a helmet. It contains its own little universe.

The turn-off to El Minya, Serafim's city, came after about 150 miles, and led back to the Nile. I rode among cultivated fields of green wheat, diesel pumps spurting water into ditches, donkeys and water buffalo everywhere. The traffic, a sluggish medley of animals and machinery, oozed through a couple of dusty villages and crossed a bridge into Minya. I found myself alongside a wide canal. There was a choice between two more bridges and I took the bigger one. I had the name of a hotel, but a young man who spoke English said I had crossed the wrong bridge. He sent me over the other one, into a maze of streets where I got lost, until I met the same young man again. He grinned, pointed to a bus and told me to follow it, but at that moment a blue pick-up appeared, and the driver offered to take me to the hotel I was looking for.

'Yes,' said the young man, 'go with him.'

'Who is he?' I asked.

'The postman,' I thought he said. But in the back of the pick-up, under a canvas top, were packed ten or more men all peering out. Why is he making this detour for me? I wondered. Then behind me another blue pick-up appeared, obviously police. And together they escorted me to the Palace Hotel.

The drivers got out, smiling, and said, 'There it is.'

'So why does it take fourteen police to escort me to a hotel?' I asked, laughing.

'Oh, those aren't police,' said one, pointing to the men in the back, 'they are teef.' I was with Ali Baba and the fourteen thieves.

But the magnificent façade of the Palace was nothing but a shell. Inside was an abandoned and very filthy ruin. 'Try the Beach Hotel,' they urged, and that too was on my list, just a block away.

So began my extraordinary visit to El Minya, with a policeman at my side for every minute that I was not in my room. I knew they were there to protect me against real or imaginary danger from Islamic fanatics. My bodyguard spoke no English. He was an amiable man who wore a loose corduroy jacket with deep pockets, and buried in them on one side was a gun and on the other a walkie-talkie. As I wandered the streets with him I tried to imagine myself as someone important enough to need guarding, but my ego wasn't up to it, and I felt more like a prisoner.

The scene distracted me, though. I had come at a very important time in the Islamic calendar. It was a highly propitious day for weddings and an entire street was devoted to the ceremonies. Other streets were busy providing for them. Shops offered opulent dresses and decorations. I watched animals being slaughtered and butchered outside on the pavements. Minibuses and trucks crammed with families from the villages were rushing up and down, and cars processed through the streets honking loudly.

Everything felt very close and personal. A motherly woman with a hennaed face, crowded with others in the back of a pick-up, looked at me in a startlingly suggestive way and then warbled loudly at me, flicking her tongue. The women and the policeman all laughed. I didn't know whether to feel complimented or insulted, and of course it didn't matter either way, but that brief connection

was so direct, personal and aggressive that it stayed with me all
evening.

I ate quite well in a self-serve restaurant while my policeman
hovered outside. I got a large plate of rice and macaroni with some
kind of meat-flavoured sauce spread over it. On the tables were bottles of what looked like lemonade and I poured some in a glass and
tasted it, but it was unpleasantly strong and salty. After a bit one of
the servers came over and discreetly removed my glass and emptied
it. Then I noticed others were using it as a condiment. It was only
a minor gaffe. Everything was very cheap.

In the evening I was passed on to a strong, silent but handsome
man, fashionably unshaven, in a headcloth and a very full galabiya
with even deeper pockets, who stayed near me as I went back to the
Palace to photograph it and to walk around. The bike stood in the
gutter outside the hotel, and as night fell an elderly man in the
khaki uniform of the Tourist and Antiquities Police brought a chair
out of the hotel and sat there stroking his big white whiskers.
Apparently he was there on watch for the night.

I saw my same young man walking by with friends. It could
hardly be a coincidence, I thought, and suspected that he was
hoping to profit from our acquaintance, but I asked him in
anyway and we talked for a while. His name was Fakhry, and he
was a student. I learned that while the police were nice enough to
me, they treated the population with a rough hand, which
explained why he had left the scene earlier when they arrived. He
wanted nothing of me, not even an address, and I found that
truly refreshing.

I went to bed early, but sleep was hard to come by. At three in the
morning the town was still full of cars hooting for the weddings.
The horns beat out their tattoos into the night. Da-da, da-da-da, da-
da-da-da. There was shouting in the streets. A neighbour in the
hotel, the TV on full blast, was watching a show in which people
shouted at each other non-stop. Noise, I came to realise, is regarded
as an adornment rather than a pollutant in Egypt.

I slept fitfully, lying under rough blankets on a hard pillow, and
got up at seven. It promised to be a hard day's ride to Luxor, not so

much because of the distance, but because road conditions, traffic and police were bound to slow me down.

El Minya to Luxor is rather more than three hundred miles by the route I hoped to take, my problem being that the road I wanted wasn't on the map. At seven-thirty the strong, silent one accompanied me to a bakery. I bought a quarter-kilo of mixed fig and apricot rolls for about 20 pence, went to a café and sat down to breakfast. My consort had milk coffee and smoked sheesha. So we sat together for a while, bonding. There's no point in reporting our conversation, which consisted of various grunts and groans, unintelligible to either party.

By eight-thirty I was packed and ready to leave, and another detachment of police in a blue Toyota pick-up came to escort me and my bike out of town. I could hardly complain. It was a useful service, because I had certainly lost my way coming in. The Toyota, with two grinning khaki-clad men in the back pointing their assault rifles at me, took me out of the city. Then they waved me on.

For ten or more miles I was free of police, and my heart soared. All around me now was a broad, flat expanse of green wheat, beans and grasses, ornamented here and there by moving figures in white or brilliant colour. Water gushed from the pumps in thick columns, a symbol of abundant fertility. The scene was made to seem all the more lush by the bright-yellow sand dunes that hovered on the edge of it, temporarily beaten back, but always ready to rush in and reclaim it for the Western Desert.

Most of all I liked watching the donkeys. Egyptian donkeys are small and white. They trot along very briskly in a most un-donkey-like way, and I hate to think of what's done to them to make them so willing. Every village family seemed to have at least one, and of course they did all the donkey work. The trick of riding them seemed to involve swinging the legs out and in sideways. The silhouette of a tall Arab trotting on a small donkey would be my hieroglyph for Egypt.

The weather was glorious. Not since I'd left northern Italy had a drop of water fallen on me, and in Egypt there had always been cool breezes, blue skies and comfortable warmth. Then I left the green fields behind, and made my way to the Desert Road. A huge black armoured troop transport stood there waiting for me. My heart sank again, thinking I would have to follow this monster, but two smiling policemen sprang out and indicated that they would follow me.

I rode off and soon left them far behind. Then came another junction, where another of these thirty-foot monsters pointed its wedge-shaped snout at me. Would the police chastise me for fleeing my escort? Would they send me back to square one? With police, you never know. But they smiled, waved me on, and lumbered into the road behind me. Once more it happened and then, after another twenty miles, my 70 m.p.h. free ride came to an end. The Desert Road stopped at Asyut, and I was back on the Nile banks again, being shuttled from one police Toyota to another.

If a country that seems to have a policeman for every ten citizens is a police state, then this was one. Nowhere have I ever seen such a profusion of armed uniformed men as in Cairo and Alexandria, and they were only more visible there because they wore black, as opposed to the khaki uniforms of Upper Egypt.

But I must also say that from my perspective (though not from that of the local population) there was never such an unthreatening force of men. They laughed, smiled and waved, and not since I left Libya had I been asked for my papers. No doubt it was the assassination of Sadat that brought them out in the first place, but it was the massacre of tourists in Luxor that kept them there, and made them take such good care of me. After that tragedy the tourists simply stopped coming, and tourism is like wheat, sugar and oil to the Egyptian economy. So I was passed like a relay baton from post to post, and in retrospect I am glad I was forced back to the Nile.

The road is raised quite high and the life of the villages goes on below in the swales on either side. It is a world of brick – a Legoland of dusty, bare, red-brown brick, some baked, some mud – piled up in the most fantastic labyrinths, on several levels, but seeming to fall as they rise, everything unfinished, with ragged outlines, and gaps only for windows and doors.

People and animals swirled around. Sometimes a large area was shaded by a layer of interwoven twigs and brush raised a few feet above the ground on posts, and beneath this latticework lay herds of cows or buffalo. I was entranced by the intricate design of the dove-cots that often crowned the walls of the houses like battlements. The density and complexity of it all is hard to convey. I felt I was peering down on an utterly strange world, with dimensions I could never understand, and I cursed the Toyotas for dragging me through it too fast. Though I stopped twice to take out my cameras, for the most part it was an endless stream of missed opportunities. Finally, after hours of wonder and frustration, I was dumped at Dandera to join a convoy of tourists, and after a tedious wait we straggled into Luxor just after dark.

Still this day was far from over. Thinking of Luxor only as a destination, I had simply forgotten that it was the site of one of the most staggering of ancient buildings. I came suddenly upon the illuminated Temple of Luxor, and it caught me quite by surprise. The massive size of its columns took my breath away. Whatever tiredness or irritation I had been feeling simply vanished before this awe-inspiring sight. And it was right there, on the street, to be looked at any time, as long as I liked, without permit or ticket, or restrictions of any kind.

I found a hotel for thirteen dollars. The lift worked, there was hot water, and breakfast was included. I manoeuvred the BMW up two steps on to a little patch of marble forecourt, nervously, because it's always in these situations when I'm tired that I'm most likely to drop the bike, and least fit to deal with the consequences.

Then, showered and changed into somewhat less dirty clothes, I walked back to the Nile and found a restaurant on a terrace that overlooked the temple. There, with a cold beer in front of me, I thought this view of both the Nile and one of Egypt's most famous ancient monuments would be just about perfect, if it weren't for the fact that immediately below me they were tearing up the road with hydraulic drills.

And so this day in Egypt, rich and unusual in most respects, ended as it began, typically, with noise.

*

In Luxor I was exposed for the first time to the full Egyptian tourist treatment, and it is rather overwhelming. Every conceivable spin-off from the tombs and temples was thrust at me, but the most persistently promoted was the papyrus. These reed-based pieces of parchment with ancient Egyptian figures and hieroglyphics painted on them seem to be the bread-and-butter items of phoney pharaonics.

The forecourt of my hotel, the San Mark, was twenty square yards of eroding marble slab that just managed to raise the tone of the establishment about eighteen inches above the gutter. It gave access to the hotel entrance and, next to it, a souvenir shop. My bike was parked on it, beside a shaky sign advertising 'Snack Food' and 'Roof Garden'. There were also some chairs where the hotel proprietor sat in the evening with his cronies, a few feet from the nourishing noise of the traffic.

However, my attention was mostly fixed on Regeb, who was responsible for the shop. He was tall and thin, in nondescript clothes and athletic shoes, and with a maniacally friendly but patently insincere grin. He was a smirk on a stick. From his marble podium he launched himself at every foreigner that passed, with a swaggering energy that turned most of their faces to stone. At the same time as he was badgering them with 'Come. See papyrus. I make a very good price', he also shoved under their noses a piece of blue paper with an address written on it, and began an incomprehensible story about this address in Europe where they could write.

Sitting out there in the warm night with a beer, I watched him for an hour or more, as Swiss, Italian, German, British, French and other groups and couples of all ages and conditions drifted past his lair. He shot out and engaged them all, but without a single success. Most of them ignored him. Some gazed at his piece of blue paper in bewilderment, before shaking their heads and walking on. Yet he never showed the slightest sign of discouragement. On the contrary, he seemed buoyed up by it, as though this were exactly the effect he was seeking.

I couldn't stand it any longer, and asked him to explain about the paper.

'You see, this is a friend in Switzerland and they can write when they are home . . .'

He moved away as though the mystery was all cleared up, to pounce on a passing backpacker.

Later on I grabbed Regeb again. 'But why should they write?' I asked.

'Well, you see,' and his grin took on a sickly tinge, 'well, you see, actually, it is nothing. It is just a business trick.'

'Well, it doesn't seem to work,' I suggested.

'Oh yes, it works very well,' he said, rubbing his hands with glee.

'So you are doing all right?'

'Oh yes. I am doing good business.'

A little later he did sell some papyrus to two young women, but they never saw his piece of blue paper with the fake address. They came up to his shop from the side and entered unbidden, so that he almost missed them. On the basis of this evidence I calculated that the mark-up on papyrus must be somewhere in the region of ten thousand per cent.

All the time now I was saying to myself, I may never pass this way again; so it really became imperative to visit the tombs of the pharaohs, and having the bike made it relatively easy and cheap. The Valley of the Kings is approximately opposite Luxor on the other side of the Nile. About six miles south of Luxor was a bridge, so a thirteen-mile loop brought me to the ticket office, where I bought entrance to three tombs and Queen Hatshepsut's temple. I was astonished by the profusion of hieroglyphics in the tombs and took dozens of pictures.

On the basis of such a short visit, I thought it hardly worthwhile to write anything about them or about the extravagant constructions that housed them. Any reference work in any library would be a hundred times more informative and reliable. Rather, for my own sake, I recorded some thoughts I had when faced with the massive columns of the temple in Luxor, thoughts amplified by the day's visits. It occurred to me that throughout history there must have been men (and maybe women) with an insatiable desire to create something of superhuman proportions. This impulse to overwhelm nature, as it were, was always presented to me as glorious, enviable, enriching. Now I am not so sure. First the pyramids, then these extraordinary excavations in the Valley of the Kings and the massive stoneworks of Luxor and Karnak, were presumably accomplished by the labour of huge numbers of humans enslaved for the purpose, all too long ago for us to make moral judgements.

Then we have Alexander's empire and the Moguls, and Napoleon's lust for grandeur and dominion, and Hitler's demonic dreams driven by slave labour, and Werner von Braun's monstrous rockets. You can add your own list of candidates. And I wonder, when these men turned their giant fantasies into reality at the expense of so many little people, whether any of them really gave a damn what good might come of it.

I'm glad these Egyptian things exist, because they are fascinating in themselves and offer a benchmark of what people (however awful their circumstances) can accomplish. But we don't have to go on doing it. I have developed a deep suspicion and distaste for giantism.

We have engineers willing to risk grave consequences to build the biggest dam, and if they can't do it in their own backyard, they'll do it in India or China. There are scientists with grand ideas for changing the nature of life itself. I am not talking about the pursuit of knowledge, but the pursuit of effect. They must see their hubristic ideas carried into effect through any means available – which usually means bribing us (or our leaders) with the promise of equally exaggerated profits. As for the risks? Who cares! We'll fix it later.

10

I had my ferry ticket, obtained in a small back room up a rickety staircase in Aswan. With a touching stab at modernity, it was shaped like an airline ticket and the printed cover showed a picture of the new ferry in pale blue. Strangely enough the photograph seemed to reveal streaks of rust running along the ship's side. In any case the ferry in the picture, which supposedly had a drive-on ramp and could carry cars, was not the boat tied up in front of me now. Nobody could tell me what had happened to the 'new' ferry. Perhaps it had burned, like the one I crossed on in 1973.

This was a smaller boat, with a rough wooden gangway laid up to it at an angle. Sooner or later I would have to ride the bike up there. On the gravel of the quayside were mountains of crates, casks, cartons, jars, barrels, bales and boxes which small men in ragged clothes and varying states of bad health were carrying up the gangway in endless procession, like ants.

Nothing was as I remembered it. I had crossed the High Dam three times, at ten dollars a pop, trying to find a road that would show me how I had come off the train to the ferry in 1973. I recalled very well going from the station to the quay and having to ride down a short flight of stone steps, because I miscalculated at the bottom and finished up bouncing into the bushes. That old ferry had actually been two ramshackle boats tied together side to side. I had almost lost my bike in the Nile as a small mob tried to manhandle it from one boat to the other. Only the brake pedal, catching happily on a rail, had saved it from falling into Lake Nasser. The entire floating assembly was nudged across the water by one diesel donkey engine. And, come to think of it, we had to put in at Abu Simbel in the middle of the night, to offload a Turk who had smoked too much hash.

I remembered so clearly the magic of that time out of time; of nights spent sleeping on a tin roof under stars of unimaginable size and brilliance, of days singing and joking with Nubian camel drivers on their way home from the markets of Cairo. No doubt I was uncomfortable, but the discomfort was lost to memory. I recalled only my pleasure at being accepted by such exotic company, and my scarcely contained excitement over the mystery of what was to come.

Today there were no Nubian camel drivers, with their tackle and long gowns, hawking, spitting and chanting. Only merchants with tubs of fat and sacks of plastic sandals. It was a new age of commerce. And this ferry boasted that it would cross the lake, from Aswan to Wadi Halfa, in sixteen hours overnight, before the margarine had even melted.

I was quite lucky to be there at all. As I came through customs it turned out I was missing a vital document. After all the drudgery and expense of coming into Egypt they had not given me the one thing I needed, a plasticated card that entitled me to ride the bike.

'Impossible,' said the man, 'you must have lost it.'

'Never,' said I. 'I have never seen such a thing.'

'Impossible,' he repeated, 'you must have had it. What did you do when they asked you for it?'

'I was never asked for it, or anything else, and I never had it.'

And so we went on, as in a tennis match, hitting from the base line until I finally won the point, and wrote out a statement promising to dig up my grandmother if I'd lied. I won't say I wasn't nervous.

When enough stuff had been cleared out of the way, a fat man asked me to bring my bike on to the boat. Riding through the remaining merchandise and up the wooden ramp on to the deck was only mildly risky. After that the bike had to be lifted through a hatch and over an eighteen-inch steel coaming. It came down the other side with a satisfying crash and was stuffed into the dead end of a passage, about twenty feet long, that crossed the vessel amidships between the saloon and the canteen.

A young African from the Congo who had been kicked out of Egypt said he wanted to guard my luggage. He wore a striped woolly hat and a poignant smile, and he spoke good English and called me 'father'. I told him I was going to take the bags up on deck with me, but I could tell, with the foresight born of long experience, that before the journey was over I would give him money. How much or why, I didn't yet know, but it would happen.

The Egyptian traders on board spoke little English and showed even less inclination to try. The whole ship was jam-packed with their stuff. Clothing, biscuits, flour, dried milk and cheap electronics filled the passageways and obscured the hatches. Cooking oil oozed up between the steps of the gangways, and I'd already slid painfully while fetching my gear and searching the ship for company. I found two Westerners, a young Canadian fireman and a French teacher of *informatique*. They were both backpacking. We staked out a place on the deck to lay down our stuff for the night, and compared stories for a while. Then the Canadian offered me a book. He said he'd be glad to lighten his backpack.

So I sat on a shelf, leaning against the ironwork, reading *Crime and Punishment*, with my multicoloured golfing umbrella balanced to shield me from the sun. It was difficult to stay comfortable for more than a few minutes at a time. The umbrella kept slipping, the rivets dug into my thighs and the shelf was too wide, forcing me to lean back too far, but the story, which I hadn't read in decades, held me in its grip.

The incongruity fascinated me as well. I had always been lucky with these random readings. The most absurd juxtapositions – Thoreau's *On Walden Pond* in Benghazi, *Middlemarch* in Ceylon, *Bleak House* in Oaxaca – all produced some quite unexpected insight. Now I was waiting to see what Dostoevsky could come up with.

Around me the limpid waters of Lake Nasser reached to the horizon in all directions, bleached by an early afternoon sun that beat down relentlessly on the ship's metal. The port of Aswan was an hour or two behind us. Wadi Halfa was promised for seven the next morning. Meanwhile I was drawn back into the gloomy, poverty-stricken world of nineteenth-century St Petersburg, where Raskolnikov was sinking ever deeper into his melancholy fate. The contrast could hardly be starker. The book enveloped me in an atmosphere of paranoia, depression and feverish violence, but when I raised my head it was to savour only my great good fortune and my barely contained excitement at the prospect of being back in Sudan after twenty-seven years.

Then, abruptly, the spell was broken. Dostoevsky, as the narrator, loosed off a completely gratuitous anti-Semitic remark. It was a casual observation about Jews and their 'down-turned mouths', made with the same degree of easy authority that one might apply to the weather. A mild shock ran through me. I become attached to a writer, especially a writer as skilful as Dostoevsky, and after a while I am led to identify with him. It was almost as though I was telling the story myself, until he suddenly brought me up short with this incongruous, offensive assertion.

I retreated from the book and looked around me. Surely, I thought, it can't be true. Down-turned mouths? Rubbish! Arrant prejudice!

Tom, the Canadian, was lying on the deck, dozing on his sleeping-pad. Sylvain, the teacher, was leaning against the rail. Like me he had been travelling a while in Arab countries, and we had compared experiences, so it was not too suprising that his Jewishness had figured in our conversation. At that moment he turned towards me, his mouth set in a glum, inverted U, and a second shock rippled through me in the opposite direction. Punished by an alternating current of political incorrectness, I wondered, Could it be true? Could I have lived for seventy years without noticing that the default setting of the Jewish mouth was a moue?

And what of my own mouth? I took a quick revisionary glance at remembered images of my face in the mirror, and had to admit a tendency for the edges of the mouth to droop in a minimally miserable manner, as befits one who is only half-Jewish and generally unaware of it.

I was immediately reminded of a far more shocking moment in Cairo, at the UN offices when the Arab girl with those clear, attractive features and wide-set eyes that promised both intelligence and honesty, was talking about the Yom Kippur war of 1973. I was astonished to hear from her that Egypt had won the war, and Israel had suffered an unqualified defeat. I said this was certainly not what I had heard and read at the time. Although Egypt's surprise attack had been very successful, I believed that by the time the armistice was signed Israel, with some help from friends, had recovered, and Israeli tanks were only eighty miles from Cairo.

This didn't disturb her confidence at all. She explained that I must have got my false information from the Western media, which are all controlled by Jews. She then went on to say, as though she were stating an obvious truth, 'The Jews are the cause of all the trouble in the world.'

Perhaps my dismay at hearing this was visible, because she went on with the same light-hearted assurance, to add, 'This is what we believe.'

I saw Stefania, working at her desk a little way away, raise her head and roll her eyes. I accepted that there was nothing to be said or done, and the subject never came up again.

It was not so much those dogmatic beliefs that shocked me. It was the way they had been uttered, and even more that they should have been expressed under the roof of the United Nations. To be part, however temporarily, of an organisation dedicated to bringing the peoples of the world together in harmony, and at the same time to consign a whole race to hell – that seemed to me to be an extraordinarily violent act. And what does it mean to be 'the cause of all the trouble in the world' if it is not another way of saying 'doing the devil's work'?

Anyway, I gave Dostoevsky the benefit of the doubt, and read on.

The ferry arrived off the coast of Wadi Halfa at about ten in the morning, but the land was largely obscured by fog and we stayed out in the lake a long time, hooting dismally.

After midday they brought the boat in. There was a welcoming party of self-important officials standing there to meet us, and they took a long time going through protocol. I suppose it's unfair to be so critical. They had every right to treat us as though we were an ocean liner arriving from some distant continent rather than a rusty ferry that had drifted in across a lake. Meanwhile, the Congo Kid was hovering around me. He was desperate, he said, for money to make the train trip to Khartoum. He kept calling me 'father' and treating me with an absurd degree of reverence. In the end I promised him some help if he'd help me get my stuff off the boat. We were told to gather in the canteen. Two badly dressed immigration police with dull faces came on and examined everyone, at tedious length.

Sylvain was mocking me. 'How are things going with your employee?'

They weren't going anywhere at all, because one of the policemen was keeping him fully occupied. I sat in the canteen watching and waiting and the idiotic idea came to me to take a picture of what was going on. The digital camera is perfect for taking surreptitious shots and I thought I had it set for 'No Flash', but I made a mistake, and it flashed.

I saw the policeman interrogating the Congo Kid start. He came over quickly and demanded the film. He looked none too bright (though who was I to make such a judgement?), and I knew I was in trouble trying to explain why there *was* no film. I pulled out the batteries hoping to mollify him, but he wasn't *that* dumb, and in the end I had to show him the flash card.

He took the card, the camera and the batteries, and told me to report to the police station later. Why? That was never an issue. People who take pictures with policemen around should expect to go to jail. This is axiomatic. I didn't even think to question it, but my faith in the Sudanese had not entirely evaporated. However surly and resentful they seemed to have become, I was fairly sure they were still honest. In the end I might lose the pictures, but I felt sure I would get the card back. What scared me was the idea of missing the train, because I thought the train would be leaving for Atbara that afternoon, just as it had twenty-seven years ago.

Getting the bike off the boat was even less fun than getting it on, but I managed it by refusing to budge until they'd got the barrels and sacks out of the way and had the ramp pointing in the right direction. I rolled down under the scornful eyes of the assembled dignitaries, and followed the trail into the customs hall where I met Kamal Hassan Osman in his flowing white robe, turban and sandals.

Kamal is well known to travellers, and had been recommended to me. He is a genial old gent, short of teeth but long in the ways of bureaucrats. Given a little incentive, he lubricates the path for the prudent traveller. Kamal was pleased to see me through customs unscathed, 'but you must go to the police station for permission'. So I told him about the camera. He recommended the Nile Hotel, and said he would meet me later and help with the police.

As for the train, it hadn't even arrived from Khartoum, he said, and certainly wouldn't be leaving until the next day.

I should explain why I was taking the train. Why not ride? Well, there were two quite separate reasons. First, because that's what I did last time. Second, because I had promised to be in Atbara by 15 March, in two days' time, to meet Manfred and his film crew.

A glance at a map of Sudan reveals that between Wadi Halfa and Atbara there are two ways to go. One is a long lazy loop which actually follows the Nile. This I knew to be a very difficult route of six hundred miles, which might take any amount of time to accomplish. In 1973 it didn't even exist. The other is a 380-mile straight shot across open desert that follows the rail lines. There is no road there at all, the conditions are very uncertain, and it would certainly be dangerous to ride that way alone.

To be sure of making my date in Atbara, it seemed to me that I had to take the train. There would be plenty of other challenges to face further along on the journey. The wisdom of my decision was quickly underscored when I rode off towards town. Fully loaded, with eleven gallons in the tank and on dirt for the first time, I promptly toppled over in the sand. People rushed to my aid and there was no harm done, but it was not an auspicious start for my desert experience.

Wadi Halfa today is so low on the ground that it isn't visible from the port. The real Wadi Halfa is actually about fifty feet under water in Lake Nasser. Most of the inhabitants moved out thirty years before to New Halfa, much further south, where they are watered by the Kashm el Girbir dam, but about ten thousand of them refused to leave their memories behind and set up shop on higher ground.

To hear them talk about it, the old Wadi Halfa was a paradise of palm trees and beautiful buildings. In its place they have erected on this barren shore a shanty town of sticks and tin, with not a tree in sight. The government won't help them, and they live off the trade that the ferry brings. They are actually closer to Egypt than to the nearest city in Sudan, and all those groceries on the ferry were for them to buy.

What do they have to sell? Well, fish, for one thing, and that played an important part in my story, as you will see.

When I found Wadi Halfa, hiding behind some rocks, it came as an exhilarating shock. I had really forgotten how things were in this other world. The Nile Hotel, the best in town, consisted of sheets of corrugated iron erected as partitions in the sand to make cubicles about ten feet square, with a tin roof. Inside each cubicle were four string beds with straw mattresses, and a rough table in the middle. It only took a minute or two to realise that this was all I actually needed.

In the middle of this warren of cubicles was a large mud-brick basin, a water tap and buckets. I filled a bucket, took it to a small closet, and emptied it over myself. What could be more refreshing? And all this for three dollars a night.

My companions, thinking this was the price for a room, out-smarted themselves by packing in with two Japanese, hoping to split the cost four ways, but $3 was the price per bed. So I luxuriated in my empty sandbox for the same price. Even if their plan had succeeded, they would each have saved the royal sum of $2.25. These are the little games that make travelling such fun.

Money-changing is always an adventure too. I had only a rough idea what the dollar was worth. The Congo Kid, who was trying to redeem himself, said I should get 250 dinar, and went off to find a money-changer. But I had another friend now as well, a young Egyptian with very dark skin, a dazzling white smile, a superbly tailored white gown of superior material and a very sophisticated manner. He too said I should get 250, and if nobody else wanted to change dollars at that rate, he would be glad to, and any amount. He suggested I walk with him to the bazaar so he could show me around, and as we walked he told me stories about the old Wadi Halfa.

When we arrived at the bazaar, which was just a semicircular row of stalls, he zeroed in on one man and opened the small sack he had been carrying. It contained about a dozen pairs of cheap and gaudy shoes which the man had evidently commissioned him to bring. There was a little haggling about the price before my friend handed the shoes over. Then we left.

He seemed inordinately pleased with himself. 'It is so easy to make money,' he said, flashing his teeth in a broad grin.

Even if he had paid nothing for them, how much money could he possibly have made bringing a dozen pairs of cheap shoes all the way from Aswan? When I see how much satisfaction some people get from making a profit, however small, I realise why I have never made much money in my life, except by accident.

We met the bag man on our way back. He was carrying a bag full of money which may be why he seemed so nervous. My friend asked him what he would give me to the dollar and he said 245. We expressed polite interest and walked on. My friend chuckled. 'He'll be back later,' he said.

But I had other more important things to do. I had to register with the police, get a permit, and try to get my camera stuff back. I walked over to their offices, and had to part with more passport pictures and money. But the worst news was that they said I had to go to Khartoum before I could do anything else. This didn't suit me at all. I wanted to get off the train in Atbara, with my bike, and ride across the desert just as I had in 1973. Kamal was there too, pleading on my behalf, but nothing would shake them. And for the camera stuff I should come back tomorrow. Not a good afternoon's work.

I walked over to the station to see if I could find out anything more about the train, only to discover that there was a bank operating on the platform. It was offering, legally and without any commission, 267 dinars to the dollar, so for once I was saved from making a fool of myself. And the train, I heard, would probably arrive that night.

If there is night life in Wadi Halfa I didn't find it. I had a meal and slept. Next morning I met a superior policeman with pips who knew about digital cameras. To save face he instructed the dolt who had confiscated my flash card to search through every picture on it looking for bombs, military targets and other suspicious phenomena. If he had been serious he would, of course, have asked for my computer. Squinting at the tiny screen, and looking rather silly under his pork-pie hat, my persecutor searched through thirty-seven pictures of Egyptian hieroglyphics. He examined them all three times, trying to crack the code, before he gave up.

Small satisfaction. I still had to go to Khartoum.

'Mr Simon,' said Kamal in his gentle splashy voice, 'Mishter Shimon, don't worry. You can alight in Atbara and go. When you are already in Sudan nobody will mind.'

And he might have been right. On my own I would have risked it, but I had a film crew to think about. They would undoubtedly need a suitcaseful of permits. Manfred had already given me the phone number in Khartoum of his location manager, another Mohamad, and I decided to call him, though I had really no hope of success. The mobile phones, of course, didn't work – they were only good in big cities – but there was a telephone in town. The man who had it sat behind a table in a small shack. It was his business. I dialled the number and, miraculously, Mohamad answered through what sounded like a sandstorm. I told him I was getting on the train and he said he would meet me in Atbara. That sounded better.

Then I met a couple who were driving a van from New Zealand

to Belgium. They were on a mission of some kind – peace, love, joy, save the world. They were stuck, without enough money to get on the ferry. I listened to their stories and thought they were genuine so I lent them some dollars, which they eventually repaid. When I rode the bike to the station to book it on to the train they brought Kamal there in the van.

Every step of the process was fascinating. The old worn wooden ticket counter, the weary goodwill of the station master, an office that might have been teleported from pre-war Britain, the long, beaten-up train waiting at the platform and the weighing-in ceremony with the bike. In fact, when the men with the scales saw the bike they just decided to take my word for it.

Two hundred kilos, I said. I hardly cheated at all.

I bought my own ticket through to Khartoum (feeling paranoid as I did it), just in case the police checked up, but I only booked the bike to Atbara. The train would leave at 4 p.m., they said, so we went back to town for tea. We had three hours – and who ever heard of a train leaving early?

At 3 p.m. I noticed that Kamal was wriggling in his seat. 'Mishter Shimon, I am thinking. It is better to go now.'

I thought he was being fussy, but we'd been there long enough, so we paid and got in the van and I heard more rainbow stories as we drove to the station. Before we had even stopped it was obvious that something was up. There were men in galabiyas waving frantically and shouting. When I got down I heard them.

'Quick. Hurry. Train is leaving. Hurry. Quick.'

There wasn't much else to say, I suppose. I rushed on to the platform and saw three men huddled around the bike, with buckets and a hose. They were emptying all the petrol out of my tank. I was furious but powerless. They insisted that it was regulations. The train really was packed with people, and leaving. The locomotive was puffing away. They siphoned out the last drops. I had time to put the cap on the tank and with help push the bike up into an empty freight car. They wouldn't even give me time to secure it.

Kamal had my two bags and waddled with me to a passenger

car. The aisles were crowded. It would be impossible to get two bags through that mob, and I just took the bigger one. A little way along the carriage, where there was an open window, Kamal pushed the other bag through. The train was already moving. I waved – and that was that.

11

It could have been the same train I travelled on in 1973. If it was, I doubt that it had been cleaned since.

I found a seat, crammed into a compartment with six other people. There were seats for eight, but one man occupied two of them. Given the premium on space, this was a testament to his extraordinary personality because it was clear that nobody objected. He had a corner by the window with a large plastic keg of cooking oil filling the space where his legs should have been, so he sat across two seats with his legs folded beneath him. He was not an attractive person in appearance or in manner. His head was coconut-shaped and his skin was dark, oily and rutted. His fingers were short and stubby, and always busy rolling cigarettes, for he smoked constantly and spat out of the window at such regular intervals that I had a vision of tobacco plants growing in the desert alongside the track, as predictable as telegraph poles.

He wore a voluminous robe of a dark-grey material, and I could only guess at the bulky body beneath it. Yet he was one of those rare characters who by sheer energy and authority can command an audience wherever he is. For most of the twenty-seven hours we travelled together he was discoursing, and he held his audience not just captive but enthralled.

The conversation was in Arabic and incomprehensible to me, but his theatricality hypnotised me. He spoke slowly, musically, and with precision. I could almost see the words drop from his mouth. It was clear that he was telling stories, because the sounds were structured like stories. And they ended with general exclamations of agreement, or bursts of laughter. Only one man spoke a few words of English, a black man from the south, who had the other window seat to my left. Occasionally he tried to translate, but with little success.

The train made a great commotion as it travelled, but I doubt that it ever exceeded thirty miles an hour. We rattled through the barren desert, stopping a couple of times only at nameless stations so small and remote that they rated only numbers. As the sun set I watched the shadows stretch out further on the sand, including the shadow of someone hitch-hiking on the roof above us. It became dark. Then, after a few paroxysms, the train ground to a halt in the middle of nowhere. I could not imagine why, and the man on my left could not enlighten me. People started getting off, and eventually I also left the train to stretch my legs under the stars. I heard people singing and looked in vain for someone who could explain. I would have liked to go back to the luggage vans to check on the bike but the train was too long. I had no idea when we might start again, and dared not take the chance.

Finally the locomotive whistled several times and we all boarded again. It was then that I spotted my young Egyptian friend with the voluminous white robe and the brilliant smile. I asked him why we had stopped.

'Well, you see, the engine was not strong enough to pull the train, so they have left the luggage vans behind.' He smiled. He didn't seem at all surprised.

I couldn't believe it at first. It made complete nonsense of all my plans. How could they possibly do this?

'Can you make sure?' I asked, and soon he convinced me. It was true.

Well, there was nothing to be done. Utterly deflated, I sank back into my seat and let the little world of my compartment swallow me up. The carriage was filthy, and had a stale odour of yesterday's food. Much of the little leg room allowed us was taken up by boxes and bags. After a long night, dawn came and the sun began its slow climb up the eastern ramparts of the sky until it drilled down on us from above, and I wondered how the hitch-hiker on the roof was enduring it. Then it slid down to the west until the hitch-hiker's silhouette was once again visible, and we were still in the desert. Because we all had to survive in this offensive environment we developed a comradeship, the kind of affinity that allows people to suffer through much worse conditions even than these, and which in the end becomes attractive.

When the train at last arrived at Atbara in late afternoon I was so inured to the discomfort and the smells that it was a wrench to leave it. I even thought of going on to Khartoum, since I had the ticket, then recalled with a start that Mohamad, the location manager, was intending to meet me here in Atbara. Reanimated, I pulled myself and my stuff together. Perhaps I could find out something about the bike. Maybe I could even find the hotel where I had stayed in 1973. I retained a clear image from that time of the ragged, walled garden where I had taken tea and marijuana with a band of thieves, and of the red-brick buildings alongside the road from the station. So I emerged, stiff and grubby, on to the platform among the motley crowd.

I found an office and spoke to an official about the luggage vans. He was not very reassuring. 'Maybe in a few days from now we will be getting those cars here,' he said, 'but first we must find a locomotive.'

'A few days?' In a few days the film crew would be gone, and all the effort and money to get us here together would be wasted. I wandered on down the platform with the last remnants of the crowd to an open area where I could see cars and taxis coming and going.

The intense blue of the sky had changed to a pale eggshell, and the sun's light soaked into the dried mud walls making them glow like gold. I watched the bustle of departing people hoisting their robes as they clambered into vehicles, and waited in the warm air where the dusk gradually enveloped me.

The car park emptied. Nobody came.

I remembered the cellphone in my breast pocket. I had all but forgotten I had it because it had been useless since Cairo, and would probably be useless here, but I turned it on and to my surprise the satellite bars appeared on the screen. I dialled Mohamad's number and he came on the phone. Given where I was it seemed like a small miracle. He said he was in his car, heading out from Khartoum, and I should go to the hotel where he would find me.

'Which hotel?' I asked.

'The Nile,' he said.

Another Nile Hotel? A hotel chain, maybe? A string of hotels made of tin and sand?

Looking around from the taxi I saw nothing to revive a memory. The whole shape and structure of the place seemed different. I had no sense of where we were in town or how we got to the hotel, but it was very pleasant. No tin, very little sand, but plenty of open balcony, garden space and flowers. I got out my things, had a shower and a cold beer, and was prepared to spend the night when Mohamad arrived.

I could see straight away that he was someone to be reckoned with. Short, dark and inclined to plumpness, he had the busy, slightly condescending air of one who was accustomed to be obeyed. His English was fluent, though accented, and I learned quite soon that he had been an army officer, trained by the British at Sandhurst.

He told me I would have to drive back with him to Khartoum. I resisted, but he explained that he would have to get me an official permit to be in Atbara. The crew, he said, was already in bed after a horrific flight from Hamburg, but Manfred wanted to be with me in the morning. 'No problem,' he said, 'but we have to be there.'

'I should have stayed on the train,' I said.

Mohamad shook his head. 'Oh no. You see, you would not get there until midday tomorrow.'

I couldn't believe it. Sixteen hours for two hundred miles, even for that train, seemed outrageous, but I found out later he was right.

The next morning I came down from my hotel room in Khartoum to meet the crew at breakfast, and found them in good spirits and full of energy. In their own way they travel just as well as I do, maybe even better. Needing to save money, their schedules involve red-eye flights and long waits at uncomfortable airports, but they seem to survive these gruelling journeys remarkably well.

Bernd and Pascal hardly hit the ground before they start looking for interesting background shots and sound swatches to capture. Bernd carries a full-size movie camera, usually attached to a full-length tripod, but he treats it as lightly as I do my Nikon, poking its nose into all the business around him like some five-legged alien. The strange thing is that nobody seems to notice him while he's doing it. Perhaps all great cameramen are gifted with an invisibility cloak. And Pascal, for all that he's a huge, black and handsome Senegalese, seems to fade into the landscape just as easily. Flourishing his furry microphone on its long boom, he could be a modern witch-doctor with a dead cat on the end of a broomstick, but nobody seems to care.

If the news of the missing motorcycle bothered Manfred he didn't show it. His resilience is impressive. We made some sort of a plan. Obviously the first thing was to get back to Atbara. By lunchtime we had the permits and were back on the road. From the hotel bedroom at night Khartoum was a fairytale scene of lights on the banks of the Nile, but the daytime reality is not pretty, and the escape from the capital involves a tortuous trip. There is poverty, of course, at the edges of every city, but in addition it was clear that things were falling apart, on the roads just as they had been on the railway, and I caught a particularly gruesome glimpse of people squatting down in a storm drain.

In the car, a big four-wheel-drive SUV, we began to learn more about Mohamad. Sudan was in the news a lot, then as now. The American raid on the aspirin factory was still a major story, and now there was also publicity about slave-traders exploiting the civil war in the south. There were sensational accounts of Arabs seizing women and children and selling them into slavery in the north, and of right-wing Christians in America funding efforts to buy them back out of slavery.

Mohamad scoffed at the whole idea. 'Who is going to buy slaves these days?' he laughed. 'Where can they go to sell them?' The whole thing, he said, was a blatant propaganda campaign against Sudan.

Somewhere along the way we learned that he had been in military intelligence. For want of anything intelligent to say myself, I made some reference to the hoary old chestnut about military intelligence being an oxymoron. The remark was greeted with the silence it deserved, and I apologised for my bad joke.

'What kind of jokes do Sudanese tell?' I asked.

He thought for a minute and said, quite seriously, 'You know, we don't have jokes.'

The silence that followed this remark didn't disturb him. I already had the impression that he basked in a private pool of security and self-satisfaction, and whatever his motives in working for Manfred, they probably weren't financial.

We arrived in Atbara in mid-afternoon, and went back to the station. Naturally we wanted news, and thank heavens it was good. The motorcycle, they said, would arrive the next day. A locomotive was leaving any minute to fetch it. Of course, they weren't taking all that trouble just for me. Fortunately my bike was not the only thing they had abandoned in the scorching desert. The second baggage car contained four tons of fresh fish on ice and the owners of that fish were not at all keen on having it converted into fertiliser.

Manfred wanted to shoot at the station, and as he and Mohamad discussed the shots and the angles he would need, we could all see that there was trouble ahead. Mohamad was coming close to telling Manfred how to shoot the scene. Finally we left, satisfied that Manfred would get the pictures he needed, and they began looking for other things to do. I wanted very much to find the hotel I had stayed at before, and I had a photograph of the building, but eventually somebody told us it had been torn down so we filmed me having my hair cut instead.

In the morning Mohamad came to tell us that the bike had arrived at the station. When we got there it was already out on the platform, surrounded by railway officials. Some of them wore military uniform, and refused to allow Manfred to film, so Mohamad had to argue his way past them. While he was doing that, in Arabic of course, he was also telling them how the film would be shot, from what angles and so on, and translating for Manfred who was becoming increasingly irritated.

Finally he pulled Mohamad aside and told him, in no uncertain terms, that it was not his business to direct the film. He, Manfred, would decide how and where he was going to shoot. Mohamad's job was just to get permission, and not to interfere. I watched Mohamad swallowing this bitter pill. His army training must have helped – after all, the chain of command was clear – but it would have unfortunate repercussions for me later on.

Manfred wanted to film me receiving the bike, getting on it, riding down the platform and out of the station. I sat on the bike and looked into the tank. There was only a puddle of petrol left, and suddenly all my frustration at having lost ten gallons, on top of all the bureaucratic obstruction in Wadi Halfa, welled up in me. I lashed out at the assembled officials, lecturing them about their duties. They listened with grim faces while Bernd filmed the uncomfortable scene. Then, with my anger spent, I rode off the platform into the town.

We lunched on fish and chicken, and as I was tucking into the delicious Nile perch Manfred said, 'You know, we cannot use that scene. I must say, we were all really shocked.'

'Why?' I asked, naively. The others, I noticed, were all nodding.

'If we are using it we are losing the sympathy of the audience. It was just another ugly white guy telling the natives what to do.'

I argued, rather lamely, that stupidity was stupidity whatever the colour of the skin, and that if I could carry a tankful of petrol on the ship, why not on the train, and that I should be free to say so. But at heart I was a bit ashamed of losing my head. If there was one good thing, though, about having lost all that fuel it was this: I could at least ride into the sand with a much lighter tank, which should make the bike more manageable. Forty-three litres of petrol weighs something like sixty-five pounds, but I felt I would only need nine litres to do the relatively short trip we were planning.

Manfred wanted to film me getting petrol, so Mohamad set things up with a roadside pump nearby and the crew got into position to film my arrival. I rode up, took off my helmet and unscrewed the tank cap. Someone thrust the nozzle into the tank and started pumping. The crew and Mohamad were very close. I felt them all over me. I watched the old-fashioned gauge on the pump anxiously, repeating again and again, 'Nine litres please. Only nine litres.'

The needle seemed to be moving very slowly, but then suddenly I was awash in petrol as it flooded all over the tank. In Sudan, as it turned out, the pumps still registered gallons, not litres.

I was furious. I cursed in several languages as I wiped the fuel off the tank. 'Why the hell didn't anybody stop him?' I yelled, meaning Mohamad of course. He must have known what was happening.

'Manfred told me not to interfere,' was all he said to me. I suppose it was a Sudanese joke.

Not only did the incident make me feel foolish, but much worse than that I now had exactly what I didn't want: a huge dead weight over my front wheel.

Manfred thought I was blaming him (although that was not how I felt). 'You are always playing the blame game,' he said angrily.

'That's very unfair,' I retorted. 'I am just frustrated, that's all. I have never blamed you for anything.'

But he insisted that I had, and I insisted that he was imagining it, and he smiled a funny smile and said, 'Then you must find a way to stop me imagining it.'

'Look,' I said. 'It's just that I don't want to make a fool of myself, riding into the desert like this. I'm nervous anyway. I've never really been into desert with this bike, and I already fell over in Wadi Halfa. You must realise, I feel very vulnerable with the cameras and all that.'

'Forget about us,' he said, grandly, as though it would be the easiest thing in the world. 'We are just here to photograph what happens. I don't care what it is. If you have a bad diarrhoea and have to stay in bed all the days, we make a film of that. This is a documentary.'

To me that sounded like bullshit, but I felt I had gone far enough.

I reminded myself that I really loved this guy, and bit my tongue. All the same, I was not happy. I would have liked to dump the fuel, but it all seemed like a huge amount of trouble and I thought it would just inflame tempers further, so I said OK and we set off to find the desert.

Twenty-seven years is a long time, in my life and even in the life of a city. Atbara had seemed more like a large village in 1973 when I left the hotel to ride down a dirt road lined with workshops and the one-room 'hotels' where the prostitutes from Ethiopia did their business. There had been a garage where I filled my flask with distilled water, only to find later that it was full of battery acid. And a police station where I went twice, trying to find my way. Each time, following directions, I ran into an enormous mountain of garbage where scavenger storks with bloodshot eyes buried their scrofulous heads.

The idea was to repeat my journey into the desert, but Mohamad had never heard of Kinedra and Seedon, the two small places where I had found myself in 1973, and where I had had the extraordinary experiences that brought us all together here now. Given time, I could probably have found them myself. After all, I knew they were close to the Atbara River, but the entire geography of the place seemed to have changed. The huge rubbish dump I had circumnavigated to get to the desert had disappeared. The fact that such a vast volume of refuse had simply disappeared today said more to me about the changes than anything else.

On this day as we left there had been only open ground. The compacted sand which once showed only isolated tyre tracks was now churned up by an armada of heavy vehicles. Apparently the traffic across the desert had increased a thousandfold, but where it was all going to or from I could not say.

Following the car, I had no trouble staying upright on this stuff, but we were on a virtual highway to Kassala, which would skirt Kinedra by a large margin. Sooner or later I knew we would have to turn away towards the river, and then it would get more interesting, and difficult.

Occasionally on this featureless plain we came across a hut, or an encampment, and Mohamad stopped a couple of times to ask directions. Then he followed some tyre tracks off to the right, which led us around hillocks, over areas of stony ground that looked freshly laid, past bushes and a tree or two. All of it was utterly unfamiliar.

Not that I expected to remember any particular feature, but the entire nature of the landscape had changed, as though some cataclysmic event had occurred. Maybe a great flood had caused it. All the strange features seemed to extend from the direction of the river. Then we came suddenly on a dip where water had gouged out a long narrow valley and filled it with soft sand. It lay across our path, and Mohamad must have registered that I would have great difficulty crossing it. He turned left, on to firmer ground – hoping, I suppose, to get around it, and it did indeed taper off. The car stopped where the sand was only about forty feet wide, and Manfred came over to me.

'Do you think you can get across here?' he wanted to know.

It was not what I would have chosen to do, but obviously it would make for good pictures, whether I succeeded or failed.

'I'll try,' I said, though I was pretty sure I'd get buried.

They manoeuvred the car over to the other side. Bernd and Pascal set themselves up, and I made a run for it, trying to get the speed right, which was difficult because there were bushes growing out of the sand.

I made scarcely ten feet before the front wheel dug in. I fell over to the left, in a rather untidy fashion, and made a hole in my calf with one of the protruding Bing carburettors. The crew watched from the high ground as I unpacked the loose luggage and struggled miserably to get the bike upright. One of the disadvantages of the big Acerbis tank is that it makes it hard to get a good grip on the bike, and the soft sand let the bike slide away as I lifted. Somewhere during my efforts one of my mobile phones slid out of my breast pocket, and no doubt it lies buried in the desert even now.

Finally I was ready to make another attempt, but after fifteen feet I was down again. We didn't waste any more time. Manfred helped me raise the bike and I managed the rest of the distance without falling again. The film is quite dramatic and was worth the pain. Of course, had I been on my own, I would have done it all differently but that's showbusiness. It takes artifice to show truth, however pure the intention.

The film shows me going through the sand with my legs dangling, and I've had plenty of derisive comments about my 'riding style'. No doubt it is better to keep a good grip on the tank with your knees, but I never had time to train myself to ride over dirt. (It interested me to notice that the picture on the cover of Robert Fulton's excellent book, *One-Man Caravan*, also shows him dangling his legs. I think he set off on his journey in 1932 with much the same attitude as mine. His was certainly a motorcycle adventure that commands my highest respect, and it was a great joy to meet him, at ninety-something, on Martha's Vineyard some years ago shortly before his death. At the back of my mind lurks a notion that the people who know best how to ride don't necessarily go anywhere much.)

The going was better after that, but we clearly weren't going to get to Kinedra before dark. We came upon a nomadic encampment where there was also a small brick building, and Mohamad, after exchanging a few words, convinced us that it was safe for me to leave the bike in there overnight and go on by car. However much I hate to admit it, a four-wheel-drive SUV can do things I can't.

When Kinedra appeared I was shocked. My mind was still warmed by the memories I had preserved for so long, recharged through slide shows I had given in recent years. Around the village there had been children playing and men working with their animals, amazed at my sudden emergence out of the desert. I remembered Kinedra as a golden place lively with youngsters in spotless galabiyas, all frantic with curiosity, and young teachers eager to pamper me, interrogate me and incorporate me into their lives. This time we came upon the village unheralded, and what I saw now was a sparse collection of grey, dilapidated mud buildings spread out over vacant ground with scarcely anyone in sight.

I told Manfred I wanted to make the first contacts on my own, with my helmet in my hand, hoping that it might prompt some memory in someone. I did find a man to talk to and I asked him, with difficulty, where the school was. Then some other men gathered around showing diffident interest, and ushered me to the rickety gate of a small compound. Their English was minimal, and I waited while they went into the house to fetch the headmaster.

Of course this was not the same man who had received me so whole-heartedly in 1973, whose wife had prepared endless dishes specially for me, and who even after three days was reluctant to let me go. The man who came to the gate was exceptionally tall, thin and dark, elderly, and with a sombre and impassive countenance. I told him who I was and why I had come, and he remarked, 'Oh yes?' as though I was wasting his time.

I was feeling rather despondent, but by now news of my arrival had spread and the men with me spoke more excitedly in Arabic, and I gathered that something had sparked memories. So gradually the atmosphere grew livelier, the old man softened, and it seemed that there was one at least who remembered me from that other time. Soon he had joined us, a short fellow with crooked teeth and a large strawberry mark on his cheek. His name was Hassan, and he was clearly agitated by strong emotion. He had been a young employee at the school in 1973. He spoke no English, but the headmaster translated, and it became obvious that in some way Hassan and I shared the same romantic memories of a golden, almost legendary, event when a lone adventurer had come out of the desert on an iron horse, bearing weapons and messages from distant lands.

It is true that I was carrying a sword at the time, though I certainly had no intention of doing battle with it. But Hassan in his imagination had equipped me with a gun and a pistol as well, and nothing I could say then or later would shake his conviction. In his excited telling of the story to all around him the atmosphere gradually warmed up. Soon I heard there was another man, a doctor, who had known me too, and someone was running to fetch him. And also one other man, who was around somewhere.

So between us we built up the glow of mutual admiration and fellowship that, without realising it, I had been looking forward to so much. Hassan had only a very simple house with two rooms and a walled yard, but it became the scene of a big celebration. Soon we were all gathered inside, some ten or more men, with boys peeping in through the doors and windows. As usual in Sudan, all the women stayed out of sight but food was put out for us, and Manfred filmed Hassan talking about what it meant to him to have me return after so much time had passed. It became clear, just as it had in Cairo at the pyramids, that my appearance in the lives of these people had made a powerful impact.

Ever since my original journey I have been learning more about its significance. The idea that I might be making it for others, as well as myself, first occurred to me as I was crossing this same desert so long ago. But then, I was thinking more of the people at home. The fact that *Jupiter's Travels* is still read seems to show that I was right about that, but just as interesting and rewarding in a different way is the effect my arrival appears to have had on the people whose lives I entered so briefly. It seems that when you raise yourself up to achieve something beyond what is needed just to live day by day, the energy you generate has an effect on those around you.

I first became aware of this later on my first journey, at Kibwezi in Kenya, but something like it must have happened here too. The meeting in Hassan's room had a ceremonial feeling. Even those who had no recollection of the past event were warmed by it. The day ended very well, and we slept outside, on our string beds, under the stars, but for all the excitement of the day the stars did not seem as close as I remembered them in 1973.

We had some time next day to look around, and I could only confirm my first impression, that Kinedra had lost most of its vitality, however hard I wanted it to be the magical place I remembered. The school seemed pitifully diminished, and the headmaster, nice and sympathetic as he was, appeared rather depressed.

In the afternoon we drove back to where the bike was parked.

Manfred had to get to Atbara to do some technical stuff with his cassettes, but he suggested that I spend the night out and he'd come back next day. Pascal also wanted to stay. His ears were tuned to some wedding celebrations that were just beginning in the nomadic encampment close by, and he wanted to record the sounds.

The wedding was a tremendous event. The groom dashed about on a richly caparisoned camel waving his sword, and the tribe gathered around a big fire, with musicians playing and girls singing and ululating through the night, much to Pascal's delight.

The others returned in the morning as I was packing up my tent. Mohamad found a road back to Atbara that was a lot easier than the one we'd taken coming out, but even so, by the time we got to Khartoum it was dark and I was already weary. We stopped first at Mohamad's luxurious house, and I got a glimpse of what his life was really about. It turned out that he owned and ran an advertising agency. He made ads for TV, and often used his own house as a location. He invited us all to dinner, but first Manfred wanted pictures of me arriving exhausted at a suitably dingy hotel.

Mohamad had found one, the Shahrazad, near the bus terminals, and by the time we got there I was quite as overheated and worn out as he could have wished. We all crammed into this poky L-shaped room, and I flopped exhausted on the bed and took off my boots. I was dying to get into the shower, and took off my shirt and trousers, but that wasn't enough for Manfred. He wanted me to strip all the way, and just for the sake of getting into the water I grudgingly exposed my less than Greek proportions.

The humiliation was soon washed away. Refreshed but thirsty we made our way back, by car, to Mohamad's residence. He received us in long, gleaming white robes and a white hat. He seemed a different man. On a large well tended lawn behind the house we sat at a table, and he brought out a bottle of Johnnie Walker Black Label. There were servants everywhere, tending the grill and bringing food. In the course of dinner he confided that his family actually owned the whole street.

The whisky was the first alcohol I'd seen since I left Aswan. I may have abused it a little. Maybe more than a little. I know we got through more than one bottle, but the dishes were delicious and the evening was too lovely to be spoiled by thoughts of sobriety.

And so to bed.

Manfred and the crew flew out next day, and left me briefly with the same emptiness I'd experienced in Tunis. Filming engenders in me a feeling that is intense, but at the same time rather unreal. And, most significantly, it is quite different from the feeling of the travelling it is supposed to be documenting. There is no way to get around that. The observer affects the observed. I remember earlier travellers who allowed their exploits to be filmed, and I believe their experiences were much more upsetting than mine. Manfred's interruptions were relatively short and slight, and I can't deny that they were enjoyable. They were also profitable, because he picked up all the tabs; but they are still the exception to the rule that 'the interruptions are the journey'.

On the other hand, he ended up with a very good film.

Mohamad had promised to take care of my permit problems after the crew left. Now that he was no longer working for Manfred his attitude to me became much more patronising, but still he was helpful, and he also suggested somewhere to camp that would be cheaper than the hotel.

This was the Blue Nile Sailing Club, and he showed me the place that afternoon. It was pretty impressive and must have been handed down from the days of British rule. Now it belonged to an upper-class Sudan elite, who spoke English and prided themselves on a British way of doing things. There was an obvious awkwardness about this in a radically Islamic Sudan, and the point was made with full ironic force by the presence of an extraordinary item of naval history. Raised up from the river and beached about one hundred feet from the bank was Her Majesty Queen Victoria's ship, the 145-foot TSS *Melik*.

This had been the lead vessel in a fleet of ten iron gunboats that Kitchener brought up the Nile in 1899 to avenge the death of General Gordon. TSS means tunnel-screw ship. The tunnel screw

was an ingenious invention that allowed the screw to drive the ship
without becoming entangled by the weeds that flourish in the Nile.
The Maxim gun is still in place on the bow. It massacred thousands
of Dervish warriors in what Winston Churchill once described as
'the most signal triumph ever gained by the arms of science over
barbarians'.

Its presence must be a perpetual thorn in the side of an independent Sudan, but they can't let it go. On the one hand, Sudan is
an Islamic state, under Sharia law, and politically hostile to the
West; but on the other hand it is the familiarity with Britain and its
institutions that characterises at least a section of the ruling class.
The *Melik*, and Mohamad with his robes and his whisky, seemed to
symbolise that duality perfectly.

I spent one more night at the hotel, and next day I pitched my
tent at the club, which occupies a pleasant site alongside the river.
Because the temperature in Sudan varies between warm and
ferocious there was no need for indoor accommodation. All the
social events took place in a large canopied area of chairs and
tables. From an open kitchen a cook supplied simple food for
little money. On the other side of a scrub-grass lawn was a functioning toilet and a primitive shower, and outside it, a water tap
and a stone construction where it was possible to wash clothes.
There was also a small round kiosk where, as the heat mounted,
I found myself buying and drinking huge quantities of mango
juice.

On the roadside edge of the property was a small octagonal concrete shell, intended to be a mosque. It was begun seven years ago
and never finished. This was so characteristic of everything I had
seen since Tunis that I thought I had finally found a better description of those countries than 'Under-developed' or 'Third' World: I
was in the Unfinished World.

I didn't mean to be condescending. I knew very well that if the
people here could rely on a steady income and a stable economy
they could finish things just as well as we do. It was the legacy of our
empires that created the kind of corruption and uncertainty in
which nothing ever seemed to work out. Sudan was a mess,

exploited by zealots and opportunists. Decades of murderous and futile warfare had left most of the people weary and destitute. That was obvious in Kinedra. Mohamad and his crowd, of course, were OK because they had their pipelines out to the West, but even they couldn't manage to finish this little toy mosque.

12

Getting out of Khartoum was almost as difficult as getting in. One needs a permit to leave, and permits invariably involve waiting. So that's what I was doing.

The act of waiting is an important part of life in older societies. It is a discipline but also a humiliation, because an essential ingredient is futility. You can never know how long you must wait, or whether the waiting will bear fruit, and it is difficult or impossible to do anything useful while waiting. In the West we have reduced this kind of waiting to a minimum. It generally only afflicts us when we are sick, in hospitals or doctors' waiting rooms, and even then rarely for more than an hour. In a country like Sudan, an hour doesn't even count.

Most of the streets in Khartoum are like long, thin valleys with streams of asphalt running between broad banks of red earth. I sat on a pile of eight bricks on one of these banks in the shade of a tree outside the wall which surrounds the Aliens Registeration (*sic*) Office. Opposite me was the tea lady. She sat on a low stool behind a wooden box. On top of it was arranged a row of jars containing sugar, mint and various teas and spices. She was loosely enveloped in a gown patterned in shades of blue, brown and orange, and like most Sudanese women she had a fine head and attractive features.

Her hands were big and well proportioned, and it was a pleasure to watch them as she put sugar in a glass, packed a strainer with tea and mint, wetted it with something dark from a bottle, and poured boiling water through it into the glass. If I hadn't been waiting, with time on my hands, I probably wouldn't have noticed the sure elegance of her movements. Waiting concentrates attention on little things.

There were other little stacks of bricks around, most of them occupied. We were all waiters. I had been waiting since Mohamad took me into the registration office two hours earlier and gave me three long, identical forms to complete (without carbons) while he went out and somehow obtained faded photocopies of my passport and visa details. He hovered over me as I scribbled away, urging me to finish. Then he took the forms, four more of my passport pictures and, easing himself effortlessly ahead of the queue, got everything properly stamped, signed and stapled.

The Sudanese government now had fifteen of my passport pictures. For some reason this annoyed me more than the money they'd taken, about a hundred dollars in various fees, but there was no explaining any of it. Certainly Mohamad wasn't even going to try. Much of what happened around me in Sudan this time was shrouded in petty mysteries. None of them was in itself worth the effort of penetrating, but the cumulative effect was bewilderment and a sense of helplessness.

Mohamad ushered me out through the gate, and to another opening in the wall where there was a counter. There he passed my papers, my passport, and a bundle of 500-dinar notes to a young man with a moustache. Then he handed another bundle of banknotes to me. 'Wait. He will take care of you. Take some tea,' he said, and drove off.

That was two hours earlier. Even two hours is a short time to wait in North Africa: hardly more than dallying. Proper waiting, I should say, begins at about three hours. Most of it, of course, is done outside the offices of influential people who have the power to grant patronage or jobs or permissions of one kind or another. It is a measure of significance. Important persons should always have people waiting to see them, the more the better, and they should *never* be seen waiting themselves.

Then there is official waiting. I told Mohamad how, at the Sudanese embassy in Cairo, I had waited for a full day, from nine to five, merely for the opportunity to apply for a visa, while others had waited several days without seeing anyone. He replied, in a matter-of-fact way, 'Yes, you see, it is because it is the same for us when we want to come to London.'

Waiting, and making others wait, is also an instrument of foreign policy.

Eventually after three or four hours the young man came out smiling with some papers in his hand. In broken English he told me where I had to go next. It was a police station, but I had no notion of where it might be. Well, it seemed that Mohamad had supplied enough of the vital lubricant to provide a solution. The young man called to a taxi across the road, and we went off together.

It was a long way, on the other side of town, past the airport, at the top of an old office building that had no signs or indications of any kind. It is inconceivable that I could have found it on my own. Again it was obvious that Mohamad had greased enough palms, because I was well received, but unfortunately two signatures were necessary and they could only give me one of them. Not just the police, but also Military Intelligence had to sign me out, and they were as far away again in the opposite direction.

It could not be done that day, and because it was a Thursday it could not happen until Saturday. And since I also needed a visa from the Ethiopian consulate, which observed both Muslim and Christian holidays, I could not hope to get out before Tuesday, at best.

I resigned myself to four more days of waiting at the Blue Nile Sailing Club.

The next day I was sitting under the canopy nursing my Pepsi, which club members pronounced 'Bipps', when an athletic Arab with burning eyes perched next to me. Without much preamble, he said he was fed up with Sudan. He wanted me to help him go to America, and offered to tell me where Osama bin Laden had all his secret hide-outs in Sudan. The attempt to entrap me into espionage was so blatant I almost missed it. Luckily I showed no interest, and the next day Military Intelligence (Mohamad's old employer) signed off on my permit.

It pained me that I had to think of leaving Sudan as an escape, but there was no denying my discomfort there. A chance encounter with a UN official confirmed that I was almost certainly being watched all the time, and I found this very disagreeable.

My first encounter with tribespeople in the Sudanese desert, back in 1973, was a revelation. Their clarity, integrity and dignity filled me with awe. From Wadi Halfa through Atbara, Kassala and Gedaref I met with nothing but respect, hospitality and trust. The days I spent as a guest at the school in the desert village of Kinedra remained with me as one of the most luminous experiences of that four-year journey around the world.

It seemed to me during that idyllic voyage through the desert that I understood Islam much better than I had hitherto. Being without any religion myself, I tend to judge religions more by the behaviour of their adherents, and I was enormously impressed by the sense of wholeness in these people, and the guilt-free simplicity with which they led their lives. The contrast with Western materialism was stark, and if the two were incompatible, as it seemed to me, then I was ready to defend their choice.

Time had soured things. Even though the people might be as friendly and courteous as ever, the country was now under Islamic law, security was oppressive, and the atmosphere was infected with paranoia. I made the best of my time in Khartoum, but there was really very little there to inspire me. At one point my old friend Sylvain, the Frenchman, turned up and took me to the Museum of Anthropology. This was supposed to be a highlight of any visit to Khartoum and he wanted me to see it for myself. I certainly was astonished. The whole interior of the museum had been destroyed as if in a raging fury. One half-ruined exhibit leaned drunkenly against a stand, the rest was rubble. We were quite unable to account for the destruction – the old caretaker, who hadn't wanted to admit us, spoke only Arabic – but we feared the worst, and it only added to my eagerness to leave.

On the Tuesday I got my Ethiopian visa (my second one: the first had expired – another sixty dollars!) and hurried off to Gedaref. The road south was asphalt, but badly broken up and busy with heavy traffic. Buses were a menace. They moved very fast and came up behind me unexpectedly.

I stopped halfway for refreshment at a teahouse and a crowd of interested men stared at me, whereas twenty-seven years earlier they would have respected me and stared at the bike. There were other differences too. In 1973 they sat on rough wooden benches. Now they sat on the same moulded plastic furniture that Walmart sells in Europe or the States. And back then, as a foreign traveller, I was never able to pay for my tea – some anonymous donor would always have paid my bill – but this time there was no such automatic generosity. In these very mundane ways we are all becoming more alike.

Working my way through Gedaref I eventually found a large traditional hotel in the centre. It seemed to be the only one in town, so I parked the bike and climbed some steps to the entrance which led into a spacious hall and a restaurant area. The rooms were all on the floor above, accessed from galleries that ran round a big central open space. There were toilets and shower cubicles, but the water was taken in pails from huge pottery jars on the landing, jars of the kind Ali Baba might have recognised.

The owners were anxious to help. They found a shopkeeper at the back of the hotel who was willing to lock my bike in his premises overnight. Then they suggested, surprisingly, that there was a man who could be of interest to me. They urged me to meet him and of course I agreed.

He arrived quite quickly, a tall man – taller than me – and large in his robes and turban (everyone here wore robes or galabiyas). He had a bushy, glistening black beard, a genial manner and a gentle voice. He made polite conversation at first, and I mentioned my interest in the domestic structures I had seen from the road coming down, round huts with conical roofs. He said he himself had several in his compound, and explained that this was how most people lived, in an enclosure with separate huts for various functions – wives, kitchen, toiletry and so on. Would I like to see them?

So he drove me to another part of town and showed me into a very pleasant hut, about twenty feet in diameter, walls about six feet high, and with a beautifully constructed conical roof of poles and thatch.

A middle-aged friend of his joined us, and we talked a little, but soon it became clear that he had an agenda. There was a tape he wanted me to hear. It was a recording of a speech, delivered in London to a Muslim audience, by a man who had begun his adult life in Malaya as a Communist freedom-fighter (or a terrorist insurgent, depending on your views at the time). This was quite interesting to me. I had already been politically conscious when Britain was trying to hold on to Malaya back in the 1950s, in a bitter and deadly struggle. The fellow on the tape described how he had begun to lose faith in the people who were ordering him to lay down his life for the cause, so he went to Eastern Europe hoping to restore his beliefs, but that led from one disillusionment to another until finally, yes, you guessed it, he ended up in the arms of Allah.

It was an intelligent, even witty, account. Of course he was preaching to the choir. Every remark was greeted with knowing chuckles. At one point he recalled how it used to annoy him to be woken by the calls to prayer. The audience tittered at the thought of such an unenlightened attitude.

Under it all I detected something very familiar. It was the same insufferable air of self-congratulation that I knew so well in my youth when, for a while, my mother belonged to the Communist Party. There were always some people who thought their belief in Communism made them superior beings. Not Communists in general (many of them were fine people), just some of them. You can find such people everywhere, on the Christian right, among environmentalists, neo-Nazis, neo-Cons, Buddhists, Muslims, Hindus, Jains – any religion or party you care to name. It has nothing to do with their beliefs. I think of it as a personality disorder. For certain people it is absolutely essential to know The Truth and The Way, while the rest of us misguided creatures are doomed to wander in limbo.

My host wanted me to embrace Islam, but evangelists of all stripes find me a tough nut to crack. I still had problems being woken by the muezzins. Some were lyrical, most were just raucous. I'd rather have church bells, but it's not a religious choice.

13

I woke up before dawn, even before the call to prayers. It was easy. The bed wasn't that comfortable. I switched on a dim bulb and struggled into my clothes. There was no point in washing or shaving. Pretty soon, I imagined, I would be covered in grime and sweat, and nobody was going to judge me by my appearance. I faced the day with a curious mixture of emotions – resolve, fatalism and anxiety, in uncertain proportions. Of all the roads I had ridden in the seventies, the one I was going to take during the next few days was by far the hardest – harder than the desert, harder than the freezing wet dirt of the Altiplano. Back then it took me four days to cover 250 miles and it exhausted me at the age of forty-three. I had no idea what it would do to me this time.

I walked across the threadbare rug under a fly-specked ceiling fan and opened the flimsy door on to the gallery. The skylight above was black, but a few bulbs illuminated the big central well of the hotel. The tiled floor of the restaurant below was bare. The building was as still as a tomb. I made my way downstairs, and out to the back where the street was level with the ground floor. The only street life was a man washing down the pavement outside the shop where the motorcycle was locked away. It was important to get away early, and I was lucky that he was there to open up for me.

I rolled the bike out, and it started at the touch of a button, shattering the silence. As if by arrangement, the loudspeakers in the minarets began immediately to blare their chants across the rooftops.

The hotel was a big block of masonry built on a slope and I rode round it and down to the front where steep, broad stone steps climbed up to the open hallway. A man with a coat over his robes and a scarf to guard his face against the morning chill was arranging his tea-making things on the steps.

'*Salaam*,' I said. '*Wachad chai. Shukria.*'

I went back to my room and carried out my bags. The hotel still slept, and I left nine hundred dinars in notes wrapped round the room key on the rough wooden hotel counter. When I came down the darkness was beginning to drain from the sky, and the *chai* man had his charcoal fire going. By the time I'd packed, the *chai* was ready. I wrapped my hands gratefully around the mug of hot, sweet, milky tea, and drank. Then, feeling as ready as I'd ever be, I rode off down the road to Ethiopia.

There was virtually no traffic in the town, just a few bicycles and one Toyota LandCruiser ahead of me, far out in the middle of the road. Suddenly, without warning, it swerved to turn right. I was too close to stop. There was just time for me to curse myself before we hit and I went over. Next minute I was standing up and looking down on the mess, and my carefully cultivated morale slumped. The driver and two women came around me, agitated, calling out, 'Sorry, sorry. You are all right? You are not hurt?'

Of course it was their fault, technically, but I was a fool not to have anticipated their move. They helped me pick up the bike. What had at first looked like major destruction turned out to be minimal. The heavy fibreglass screen, which I never really liked, had been ripped off together with a chunk of the headlight housing, but otherwise everything seemed to work. I checked the forks and the front disc brake, and tried to calm myself. I couldn't get angry with the driver. I was too concerned to guard my emotional state for the trials ahead.

'It's OK. Don't worry,' I said. I strapped the shield over my bags. 'It's all right. I was too close.'

Much relieved, they drove off before I could change my mind. I got back on the bike. What a bastard, I thought, castigating myself. How stupid can you get!

I was unhurt, but definitely off balance. The bike trundled along like a wheelbarrow, barely under control as the asphalt turned to dirt. Gradually I got hold of it again, trying to recover some confidence.

The road was nothing like what it had been in 1973. Instead of a track through dried mud there was now an actual road bed of gravel. It was clearly intended one day to be tarred over, but meanwhile heavy traffic had murdered it. More and more trucks were travelling between Sudan and Ethiopia, and one day there might even be a decent road, but now the bike bounced and slithered over irregular corrugations and around potholes.

The struggle was all internal. I sensed, rather than knew, that my difficulties were of my own making. I had a bike that was more powerful and much better equipped than the old Triumph to handle this terrain, but I really didn't know how to use it, and like an old dog trying to learn new tricks I was awkward and uncomfortable with its size and weight. Many riders would have laughed at this road and flown over it with ease, but I was too scared to try. I told myself this was not the time to learn by trial and error, because one significant error could cost me the whole journey, so I continued to stagger over the ruts and loose rubbish in second gear, like ploughing a field with a Ferrari. This deep dissatisfaction with myself, this sense of my inadequacy, certainly sapped my strength, and it's fortunate that I was too busy watching the road to dwell on it too much.

It took me almost three hours to get through the first fifty miles to the police post at Doka, where on my first trip I had spent the night. My weariness must have shown because the police tried to encourage me. 'It will be better,' said one of them, smiling enthusiastically. 'A company is building it. You will see.'

It was the worst possible news. However bad a road may be, it can only get worse when the road-builders come. There might be a few short stretches of beautiful surface, though they are often barricaded off, but then they tear everything up to put in a culvert or a bridge, and send the traffic round through the countryside. In this part of the world the countryside is soft, black soil. Cotton grows in it, and bikes sink in it, especially when trucks have already churned it up, mixing it with the little water that trickles where the culverts and bridges would be.

For about twenty-five miles, at intervals of roughly a mile, I fought my way in and out of ditches and through slime, before the noble works of the road-builders came to an end. Through these last miles the road was slowly climbing, then abruptly it reverted to what it had been thirty years before, a superhighway for goats.

Probably as many as ten goats abreast could have advanced along this track that wound around rocky outcroppings and over crushed boulders, through a savannah of shrubs and thorn trees. Even so, I managed to negotiate it. In all this time I had not fallen once, and that at least was a considerable improvement over 1973. Then the track forked, and I had to guess which way to go. There seemed no point in waiting for someone to turn up. I'd seen only one lorry in five hours. I chose the right fork. And after about a mile of increasingly narrow and wild terrain I lost faith.

This can't possibly be a truck route, I thought, and stopped to think it out. There in my face, no longer hidden beneath the windscreen, was the GPS. Well, isn't that what a GPS is supposed to be for? Up to this point I'd only thought of it as a toy. It made a convenient clock and I could check my true speed. I'd thought it might help to keep a log of the journey, but it was always last on the list of things to do, and I really didn't want to spend all my time doing jobs. In truth I had only the haziest idea of what it could do.

Of course, this tiny border town I was aiming for – Galabat on the Sudanese side, Metema on the Ethiopian side – wasn't recorded in the GPS, and I had no coordinates, except for the spot I was on right then. But if I could get a coordinate off the map, maybe I could get a sense of the right direction. Using the millimetre rule on the side of my Leatherman I measured longitude and latitude, and fed the result into the little black box, and it told me to go back and take the other fork. So I turned around and scrambled back up the last steep, slithering descent, hit a boulder, bounced away, and fell against the sloping side of the track.

It was a gentle fall. The bike was nestled up against the hillside, at about thirty degrees to the horizontal, looking very peaceful. There was no sense of crisis, and it took me all of five minutes to discover that there was no way whatever to pick it up.

This is ridiculous, I said to myself, again and again.

I took everything off it I could get to, but the heaviest box was trapped below it. And because the ground continued to slope upwards above the bike it was impossible to get underneath it to lift it. The problem had me baffled. Probably, in a day or two I would have figured something out, but meanwhile a truck came bouncing merrily along where I was sure no truck could go. The passengers, riding above the load, must have been airborne most of the time, but they seemed quite cheerful, and between us we got the bike up.

'Galabat?' I asked, and they pointed in the direction I had been going in the first place. After that I never gave the GPS another chance.

Getting to Galabat was very hard work, just as it had been back then, but the experience this time was so very different. Then the Triumph seemed to be struggling just as hard as I was. I remembered how the engine had almost died of heat-stroke, how a box had been ripped off in a fall. Now I was doing all the suffering. The big BMW motor just ran on unperturbed, putting me to shame.

Galabat itself was changed too. Instead of the small garrison of soldiers who had been so surprised and delighted by my arrival in 1973, who fed me and cheered me on, there was now just an impersonal border post with an absentee official who was being entertained on the other side – where, of course, wine, women and song were legal. The Sudanese side of the frontier was dusty and lifeless, and he kept me waiting there for a couple of hours while I sat and contemplated my boots.

When he finally returned, in a freshly laundered white robe, he was neither drunk nor debauched, but very correct, rather imperious, and certainly indifferent to my presence.

'Do you see motorcycles here often?' I asked, trying for conversation as he dealt with my papers.

'They are passing here seldom,' he replied impassively, and pushed my passport across to me. 'Here, you can go now.'

On the other side I was received in a shady hut with an earthen floor. The immigration official was a small, eager man in a knitted jersey and brown trousers. He seemed pathetically anxious to please and before I left he gave me a questionnaire to fill out, rating his services on a scale of one to ten, as though he were running a hotel.

A few people travelling in the other direction in a Toyota were in there with me. They were impatient to get on but I was able to extract some information from them. They had come from Gondar that day, and at first I was reassured, until I reflected that a road that might be good for a LandCruiser could be pretty bad for a bike (and vice versa). Then one of them told me about an Australian biker who had broken off half his handlebar on the road, and had succeeded in riding it with only his right arm to hold the front wheel on course. Even though it sounded like a tall tale, for some reason the story depressed me.

Perhaps, given my age, I should have felt proud to have got as far as I had, but I wanted more than just to survive on this road. I wanted to relish the struggle, not to be drained by it. Already I was feeling quite battered physically, but the worst was that I couldn't find the spiritual energy to get on top of my tiredness. Was that the price of following in the footsteps of others rather than being buoyed up by the excitement of being the first? I was not helped by the irony that those others had been following in *my* footsteps.

Coming into Metema my mind easily conjured up memories of the past. I remembered it as a raw and squalid frontier town, but it had also been interesting. Prostitution had been an important element but it was institutionalised and almost respectable, catering for the appetites that the harsher laws in Sudan exported. Along the roadside there had been crude but colourful 'hotels' – nothing more than large bars really, with earthen floors and tin cubicles at the back. I had stayed the night at one that was owned by two single mothers who had saved enough from prostitution to buy this small measure of security for themselves and their illegitimate children.

Now the street was merely miserable. As I rode along it nothing caught my eye, no signs winked at me, no touts beckoned, the place seemed utterly desolate, and when I emerged from the town I could not bring myself to turn back and look again. Somewhere further along I knew there was another village where there was supposed to be a customs office, but there again I could see no sign of either officialdom or hospitality, and by this time I had decided to get as far along the road as I could and camp. If customs weren't interested in stopping me I had no desire to bother them, although I knew I might be storing up trouble for later.

I rode on for an hour or so in the gathering darkness, found some space under a tree, and set up my tent for only the second time on this journey. I made tea, cooked some rice, opened and ate a tin of beans, and then lay down. No cigarettes now to celebrate the end of the day. I stopped smoking in 1977 and had no desire at all to start again, but I recognised how useful those cigarettes had been as a way of punctuating time. My body was aching and my legs were bruised, but I slept undisturbed.

Ethiopia is a mountain kingdom. There is no other country remotely like it on the African continent. At its heart there are roughly 150,000 square miles of undulating highlands, nine or ten thousand feet above sea level. That's a third of its total area. It is the world's oldest Christian nation, and hidden among the valleys and peaks are relics, mysteries and wonders of this ancient religious practice. The Ark of the Covenant is said to be squirrelled away at Axum, while Lalibela is famous for its underground churches. Also cradled among these mountains is the huge Lake Tana, the source of the Blue Nile, and just north of that lake is Gondar (which Tolkien must surely have been thinking of when he wrote about Gondor in *The Lord of the Rings*).

From this mountainous core, Ethiopia spreads its skirts, east to Eritrea, the Red Sea and the lowlands of Somalia, south to Kenya and the Rift Valley, and west to Sudan. Metema is quite low. To reach Gondar, a city of ancient castles and churches, I would have to climb around nine thousand feet.

I started soon after dawn. The first stretch was fairly flat but it

wasn't long before the roadworks began again, slicing across the
road bed for culverts, and driving me on to long and difficult tracks
over loose soil where a four-wheel-drive Toyota would have a great
advantage. I had a hard time keeping my heavily laden GS upright.

Looking back on the two times I passed that way, it seems to me
that in the interim the countryside had been seriously damaged, if
not ruined. I remember from my earlier journey lightly forested
country with undisturbed ground, but now the land seemed hot
and bleak and bare, and this I am sure contributed to my growing
weariness. It would not be surprising to find that deforestation had
had something to do with it. I imagine that huge numbers of
refugees must have swarmed across this land since 1973, fleeing
from famine and almost continuous warfare, and they would all
need wood, to burn and to build shelters with. Aside from that the
population had increased greatly, and road-building is not kind to
the environment either.

There were streams to ford, too. The water itself was not a problem but the unstable sides of the gullies made me nervous. This
particular obstacle course came to an end after a few hours, to be
replaced by other trials. As the road began to ascend into the mountains the straight gravel bed on an earth floor became a narrower
winding path ripped out of pink and white rock. The heat was
becoming intense. This was where the Triumph had suffered the
most, but now the BMW met the challenge unfazed. I, on the other
hand, was tested to the limit as I tried to deal with my old nemesis.
On every sharp curve heaps of rubble were banked up at the outer
edge and my problem had always been to stay closer to the inside
while keeping up enough momentum to avoid stalling on the steep,
loose and powdery rock. Twice I found myself too far out in the
rubble and unable to stop the bike from falling.

The falls themselves were no danger, but the effort of unpacking
and raising the bike in the heat was distressing. There was very little
traffic. On the first occasion I had help, on the second not, and by
then I really did feel I was fighting for survival – oh, not for my life,
but for my mind. The heat, the strain, the fear of falling, or rather the
fear that I wouldn't have the strength and the will to pick myself up

again, were taking me to the edge. And here came another river, another chasm to dive into and another slope of rocks and mud to fight my way up on the other side. The bike whipped and wove from side to side as I barely made it to the top, but there was no sense of relief because there would just be more and more of the same.

Somewhere in my brain I had lodged the idea that I would get to Gondar that day. I should have reconsidered it, but I was too tired to think, and it drove me on. I knew that a well-meaning sympathiser had arranged a good hotel for me in Gondar, and I was hypnotised by the prospect. If there had been any kind of hospitable terrain, just a bit of flat ground and a tree maybe, I would have stopped and camped, but it just went on and on, and like an automaton, so did I. And then I came around a corner and there was a flat area ahead of me, with a few trees, and some huts. And beyond that I saw the ground drop steeply down to what must be a river. I knew that nothing would get me to go down into that river that day, and I stopped.

I stopped alongside a roofless, half-finished building of brick and cement. It was the only building in sight – all the rest were lightly constructed huts of stick and thatch. Four young men were working on or around it. Three of them wore the usual shorts and shawls, but one wore long trousers, a shirt and a baseball cap. Which meant that he probably spoke a few words of English.

Very carefully I put down the side-stand and dismounted, knowing that there was not an ounce of energy left in me to deal with a mistake. I took off my helmet and goggles and wiped the sweat from my eyes with my sleeve as they approached me.

'I want to stay here tonight,' I said, pointing to one of the huts and laying my head on my two hands. The boy in the cap had a long face and long teeth, a bit like a donkey, not too bright, but friendly. He seemed to be in charge, and he said, 'Okey-dokey.'

Where did he get that from? I wondered. Then, 'Come', and he beckoned me to the building. 'You can be here. Is good?'

Behind a wall, on the bare cement floor was a string bed, but what riveted my attention was a 55-gallon drum of water, with a tin can beside it.

I waved my hand at it. 'Can I?' He nodded.

Without a moment's thought, careless of who might see or what they might think, I stripped off my clothes and began emptying water over my head, standing stark naked in front of my fascinated audience. It could have been the Texas Girls' Choir standing out there, for all I cared. As the cool liquid coursed through my hair and over my skin it was like being brought back from the dead. Never in my life will I feel greater physical relief. But there was no corresponding flicker of animation in my mind. I felt brain-dead. I had to recognise that I had really gone beyond the limit of my endurance. This was a quite unfamiliar condition for me. Until that day, however bad things got I had always been able to count on some reserve of mental energy to get me out of trouble, but now, for the first time, the spring had dried up. I was moving like a zombie.

I went on pouring the precious stuff over myself for minutes on end until it occurred to me that they would have to carry the water up from the river, so I dried myself on my shirt, pulled a fresh one out of my bag, and dressed. Then I dragged the rest of my things in alongside the bed, fished out a twenty-birr note and gave it to them.

Twenty birr was only a bit more than two dollars, but in Ethiopia it was a handsome reward for a string bed and a few buckets of water, and I did it to avoid having to talk about it. Then I lay down on the bed. I was too exhausted to sleep. I was hoping that some synaptic event would occur and bring my brain to life again, but nothing happened. I just lay and stared at the sky while the kids went on with their desultory labours.

After a while I thought I'd better eat something. I wasn't hungry. I just thought I should eat. It was the only kind of thought I was capable of.

The head boy said, 'Okey-dokey.'

'Where did you get that from? Okey-dokey?'

'I learn from stranger. Come.'

I followed him down to the river. I could see more clearly now a profusion of scaffolding, handmade from rough wooden poles, where a bridge was taking shape, also handmade. It was quite an ambitious bridge over the broadest stream I had come to so far and a rough walkway for pedestrians was already made. On the other side was a considerable sprawl of huts, a sizeable village.

Suddenly it struck me that this must be where I had stopped twenty-eight years before, where I had got stuck in the middle of a river, where some road-builders had helped me out and invited me to join their little camp. A wave of nostalgia washed over me. That had been one of the best of nights, a few friendly men under a bright starry sky around a camp fire in unspoiled countryside. They were telling stories in Amharic and I listened to the tapestry of the language and the lyrical bursts of laughter as I dozed off in my sleeping-bag. There had been no village then, only trees. Now there was a village and very few trees. According to my map, it might be called Giunt, or perhaps Nagadebaher.

My guide took me to a hut with a table and left me there. A woman brought me the same meal I used to enjoy, *injera* and *wat*, a spongey millet pancake and a spiced goat stew, but I didn't like it any more and couldn't finish it. I swallowed a bottle of warm Italian beer. A small crowd in an adjacent shop, mostly women, turned to gaze and smiled at me, flashing brilliant white teeth. Even in my exhausted state I noticed how naturally beautiful the women were. I felt foolish and ungrateful, but I took their picture and then walked back to my bed.

You poor sod, I said to myself, you are really wasted.

That night all the muscles in my body – including many I had never met before – revolted against my harsh treatment of them, with painful spasms. I lay thinking of the bridge. Obviously the whole community existed to serve the bridge. I could see what a great story it would make, I could see the fascination of it, but I could not feel it. In the morning I tried to persuade myself to stay and find out more, but I couldn't do it. To all intents and purposes, my imagination had died, and without it I was a dry husk.

I gave the boys another twenty birr because I was grateful to them for tolerating this incompetent old fool instead of ripping him off. Then I got on the bike – it was all I could do – and headed for the river. There was no access to the walkway and the traffic still went through the water. I approached it and dived into it with fatalistic resignation. Somehow the BMW got me through and up the other side. I had little to do with it.

Not long after, on a hard climbing curve, I fell. This time my foot was trapped and crushed under one of the boxes. I managed to drag it out, but I felt absolutely finished. Left to myself I don't know what would have become of me, but a petrol tanker stopped and the driver and his young mate got the bike upright. Makonen Abay, the driver, could see I was wiped out. He stayed a while to talk to me, and got me an orange soda from his cab. I took a picture of him, and he accidentally knocked the bike over again. The laughter helped. I wasn't the only clumsy bloke around.

My foot hurt but I could ride with it, and when he was sure I was all right he left. I couldn't know then that petrol tankers and boxes would figure again in my story, and even more seriously.

That was my last fall before I got to Gondar, a few hours later. There was one more steep dive down into a river, and this time there were cows drinking at the bottom. I couldn't get round them so I rode straight at them, hoping they'd get out of the way in time – the shut-eye school of motorcycling. They were agile animals, and I scrambled up the other side to safety. Soon after that the road levelled off, the bridges and culverts had been finished, and there was no more risk, but I couldn't bring myself to believe it. The road was still gravel and I rode it as though traumatised, in perpetual fear of falling.

Closer to Azezo the land was agricultural and there were many people walking on the road. Most memorable were the men, in shorts, sandals and shawls, with a stick or a rifle slung horizontally behind the shoulders and both arms hooked over it, so that they gave the curious impression of walking marionettes hanging from an invisible string.

There were women in long dresses, half-naked boys, goats, donkeys, cattle and carts. They all seemed to regard me impassively, not smiling, not hostile, but beautiful to watch. I could observe their beauty, but I still could not feel it, so I reserved it for another time. I was still used up, mentally alienated from the world. It was a shame, and I knew it.

Finally, at Azezo, the road turned to tarmac and the last miles to Gondar were so smooth, it was like skating over ice, like a flying dream (and I remembered it was just like that the last time). The Hotel Goha is at the top of a steep hill with a stupendous view of the surrounding mountains. I parked the bike and limped up to the door, and then to the counter.

What I want, the only thing I want, is a cold beer.

'Yes, we were expecting you, and of course there is beer, but first there are these forms. . .'

Why can't I just have a beer, and then——?

'Please, the forms will only take a little time, and then . . .'

I was on the verge of behaving disgracefully, but I managed somehow to hold myself back and deal with the formalities. Then I was allowed to walk through to the terrace, beside the empty pool, and sit down with a beer.

I had arrived. In three days, from Gedaref. Less time than I took twenty-eight years ago. And I certainly fell down more often then. I was one month from my seventieth birthday and I suppose people would say it was a triumph. But the bitter truth is that in the only way that is important to me, I knew I had failed.

14

I am not much attracted to thoughts of failure, and I can usually let go of them quite quickly. The comforts of the Hotel Goha helped a lot. I owed this luxury to a certain Tony Hickey, whom I knew only as a name in an email and a distant voice over a mobile from Khartoum. I knew he was Irish, and had a travel business in Addis Ababa. He had fixed up two free nights at the Goha, and told me to contact his agent, Habte Selassie Asmare. I don't look gift horses in the mouth.

My foot hurt. I was worried that something had fractured. When Habte arrived at the hotel I asked him if I could get an X-ray. He turned out to be a very capable and self-assured young man who really knew his way around. He took me to a clinic the same day, and for eight dollars I got pictures to prove that nothing was broken.

The hotel gave me a discount on a few more days while my foot recovered. Relieved, I set out to enjoy myself. Even knowing in advance the dangers of trying to repeat unrepeatable experiences, I still fall into traps. It annoyed me that I hadn't liked the *injera* and *wat* they had given me back at that village, and I wondered whether it had just been badly prepared. Habte sent me to a restaurant where, he said, I would get the real thing. I was the only customer in a rather gloomy room, but the dishes were quite elaborate. There were several different kinds of stew and I tried them all, wrapped in pieces of *injera*. I didn't like any of them much, and was really disappointed in myself. I was even more disappointed that night when

I suffered the first stomach problems of my journey. I'd hate to lose my taste for exotic dishes, but losing my cast-iron digestive system would be even worse.

The thing to do in Gondar is to look at castles, and Habte showed me more castles in one afternoon than I had seen in the whole of my life. Most old cities are lucky if they have one castle, but the dynasty that ruled here four hundred years ago suffered from a congenital condition, castlemania. Every ruler had to build a new one and, if possible, one for his wife too.

Restoration by volunteers was in full swing, and there were buckets of lime and whitewash everywhere. I limped around in astonishment, and marvelled particularly at a gorgeous ceiling with eighty angelic faces painted on it, humbled to learn that it was world-famous though I'd never heard of it. With my appetite whetted I started reading *The Sign and the Seal*, a long and involved piece of historical detection in search of the Ark of the Covenant, and I heard about the churches of Lalibela. I discovered that for not much money I could fly there and back. Repeating the mantra, 'I may never pass this way again', I booked a flight, planning to stay in Lalibela overnight.

Gondar's airport is at Azezo, where the road south to Addis begins. I checked out of the Hotel Goha, with heartfelt thanks for their hospitality, and arranged to park the bike, fully packed, at the airport so that when I returned I could get straight on the road.

The flight over the mountains was dramatic, and the monolithic churches of Lalibela are nothing short of astounding. Instead of being built from the ground up they are simply carved out of the volcanic rock underfoot – down, I would guess, around thirty feet – with their doors, windows and decorative details all of a piece, and their roofs at ground level.

The atmosphere inside the churches is equally extraordinary, because although they are richly decorated with frescos, carvings, hangings and other treasured objects they still have the intimacy of caves rather than the grandeur of cathedrals. The priests, or monks (I didn't know which were which), wore white robes and turbans, and some of them brilliantly embroidered cloaks, and because it was Easter there were many of them, bustling around in the labyrinth. In the deep cuttings that surround the churches a whole monastic life subsists, apparently carried on in rooms carved into the rockface, and the smoke from the kitchens, mingling with the chanting of the monks, swirls through these man-made chasms.

The smoke also helps to keep down the flies, which are a plague above ground. Tourism is in its early days at Lalibela. The bus that should have taken me back to meet the plane never came, and I enjoyed a breakneck roller-coaster drive in a Toyota over the 'old road', which was almost no road at all. It was said to be faster, but whether to the airport or to perdition was not specified. As it happened, the plane was late, but the drive got me back into the right frame of mind for tackling the road to Addis.

There was no way of knowing what that road would be like to ride. Only another motorcyclist could tell you, and I hadn't seen a single one since Egypt. All I did know was that there were some 460 miles of it, with two obvious places to stop along the way. Bahir Dar, on Lake Tana, was a hundred miles off, and I assumed, starting at midday, that I would at least get there before dark. The other stop would be Debre Markos, about fifty miles north of the Blue Nile Gorge.

Well, the road was bad, but not as bad as the road to Gondar. There were stones in the middle and sand at the edges. I stayed in the middle, preferring to take the vibration rather than risk sliding out in the sand. On this first leg there were no road-builders, so I was able to keep up a reasonable pace, and twenty miles along a mystery was resolved. Locked into my memories of the first journey was a tall, slender finger of rock pointing at the sky. It's a quite startling phenomenon. I thought somehow I had missed it on the road to Gondar, but I had simply misplaced it in my memory because here it was, still surprising and still apparently unremarked.

A little further along I came across Fabio. He was a good-looking young Italian kid, with a white bandanna round his head and a helmet tied to his baggage, and baggage was the right word for it. His Yamaha Teneré was parked by the roadside with a huge pile of stuff on the back wrapped up in a torn tarp which badly needed attention. He couldn't afford proper luggage, he explained in halting English, so he made up this bundle, and it was coming apart, but he'd already come a long way with it and he knew what to do.

We were going the same way, so obviously we went on together. I knew nothing about him, and he knew nothing about me, but just being two people on bikes on that road already gave us a lot in common. I found out that he was a nurse in Milan. He had very little money but he wanted to make a big journey through Africa, so he found this old Yamaha for $500, fixed it up, and here he was.

He was not only a lot younger than me, but braver too. He rode closer to the edge, literally, looking for a softer ride on the sandy verge and taking his chances. But then he had knobbly tyres. Well, that was my excuse for staying in the middle and taking the knocks.

Although we were actually circling around the enormous Lake Tana it was out of sight. The country was barren and empty, and after four hard hours we got to Bahir Dar, a resort on the southern shore of the lake. I found a pretty nice hotel and told Fabio I wanted to stay there for a day, write a bit, maybe go out on the lake. The hotel had pleasant verandas overlooking it where I could sit and write, and unlike Lalibela it was fairly free of flies. Fabio said he'd wait too so that we could ride on together, but at six dollars a night my place was too pricey for him so he went off to find something cheaper.

Two days later Fabio turned up in mid-morning thinking we'd have plenty of time to do the 175 miles to Debre Markos, but conditions had changed. Up until then we had met scarcely any traffic, but now the numbers of diesel trucks with their filthy exhaust grew, and the surface became worse. Some parts of the road were laid with black cobblestones, which were both puzzling and painful. I had no recollection of them from 1973, and they were certainly older than that, I thought. Who could have laid them? Was it the Italians in the thirties when they invaded what was then Abyssinia, or the British when they drove Mussolini out? Whoever put them there earned my hatred.

On the other hand there were wonderful things to see. The great undulating uplands rolled away into the far distance. We were in a much more productive part of the country and the agriculture was fascinating to observe. It was all animal-powered. Everything seemed to be at the highest level of organisation for a pre-industrial age. It is where we all come from, and to see it displayed at its best was inspiring. The elegant way the compounds were laid out, the clever use made of materials to build them, the intriguing implements that have evolved and the way animals fit into the scheme of things, were wonderful to observe.

Because the roads, for the most part, were still terrible, most tourists would fly between the more easily advertised sites and so miss the best of this rural experience, meeting it only at its worst in the form of flies and beggars. I couldn't for a moment begrudge the pounding I took on those stony roads through Bahir Dar and Debre Markos. Our own roads across the moors, fells and downs must once have looked very similar, with donkeys packing sacks of grain, men driving their flocks and herds to pasture or market, oxen trampling heaps of straw, women bowed down under loads of firewood or towering stacks of cow dung.

Although the roads were much the same, the people had changed through the decades of war and liberation. Riding through a crowded village was always much like running the gauntlet, but I felt no hostility this time, just a great hunger to be observed and recognised, with hundreds of people waving, stretching out their hands, seeming to say, 'Hey, I'm here. Look at me. Let me into your life.' How crazy, I thought, that soon these people will be replaced by machinery and driven to live in city slums, while the machines pollute the landscape and food has to be carried to those slums by those same dirty diesel trucks I was fighting on the road. Why couldn't we, instead, bring the benefits of modernity out to these people here, so that they could continue to sustain the land, and themselves? And the answer, as usual: there's no money in it.

Then, as we got closer to Debre Markos, the road-builders reappeared and I came within an ace of destruction. It was very hard to get past the trucks on the narrow road, but it was dusk and we needed to arrive. To be out there in the dark would be really dangerous. The best place to overtake the trucks was when they had to slow down for the diversions, and here came a big one, diving down to a riverbed. Determined to get around a group of the monsters I went down much faster than usual, only to have the surface change and become unstable. It was impossible to brake, but the trucks had speeded up. How I managed to get round the lead truck in time I'll never know, but the adrenalin rush and the exhilaration are with me still.

When I looked in the mirror at the hotel, a masked bandit, smothered in diesel soot and dust, stared back at me. We ate and slept well in the almost modern hotel, and left early next day with two hundred miles to go and not much faith in road reports. For a while the roads seemed to be getting better. Then we got to the Blue Nile Gorge.

This is such an extraordinary geological feature that the state of the roads is almost irrelevant. The gorge is approximately five thousand feet deep – as deep as the Grand Canyon – and the descent to the river is many, many miles long. Although attempts have been made to surface the road, the work only survives in patches, and the gorge is, of course, a huge obstacle between north and south Ethiopia. It is also one of the great features of the journey, the river having cut its way through millions of years of geological history. The views are quite spectacular, but I was luckier on my first journey, travelling in winter, when the air was clearer. Now a moist haze obscured the far side of the gorge, so many miles distant.

The climb up the other side was slow and tortuous, and that was followed by another section of poor highway – through gorgeous countryside – before it gradually improved. Then, dramatically, everything changed. Suddenly we were on a broad, smooth asphalt highway as good as any in the world.

It's hard to describe the sense of freedom. To be able to fly along without a care, to look around without fear of potholes and weird obstacles, felt like a reward from the gods. We sailed through those last sixty miles close to heaven, and came down into the great bowl of seething humanity that is Addis Ababa.

15

I had an arrangement to meet with Tony Hickey and, after some confusion, we found each other in the centre of town. Fabio came with me, but then went off to meet some friends he knew. He promised to reach me through Hickey's phone, so that we could go on together later, but I never heard from him again.

Tony Hickey is very tall, thin and fair, and quite contradicted the image I had somehow created in my mind. In Addis he outdid himself for me. He had persuaded the Sheraton hotel to do the same for me as the Goha had in Gondar, but this is no ordinary Sheraton. The Addis Sheraton is beyond stars, and possibly the most luxurious hotel on the African continent. I was received by a delegation with flowers, a gilt-edged celebrity guestbook where I sandwiched my signature between those of prime ministers and other potentates, and I was waylaid at the entrance by photographers anxious to snap this latest Indiana Jones. As usual I felt rather foolish, but I endured, and my ultimately elegant quarters were my reward. The room was hotel heaven.

Determined to take every advantage, I stored away all the expensive soaps and shampoos I could nab. I puzzled the staff by asking for as many household rags as they could give me, and then brought all the filthy contents of my boxes up to my room, cleaned them, wrapped all the spare parts in rag and packed them away nicely, trying not to soil the bedspread. As I went up and down in the lift in my deplorable clothes with my unsuitable accessories, patrician diplomats from Nairobi in their Savile Row suits turned politely away. It was all very enjoyable and ended all too soon, after forty-eight hours, when I returned to reality at the Wutma Hotel in the Piassa district.

Tony found the Wutma for me and helped me to enjoy Addis enormously. Through him I met Thomas Mattanovic, an older man originally from Croatia and a one-time famous 'white hunter' who now worked to preserve and promote wildlife, and who was a link to an Africa that was fast disappearing even when I first travelled through it.

Tony's business, Village Ethiopia, had developed an eco-village among tribespeople in the Afari region, east of Addis, and a few days after my arrival he took me there with a couple of travel journalists. Not since I was with the Turkana in north Kenya in 1974 had I been so close to tribal life, but there were obvious differences. Instead of spears, Kalashnikovs; instead of goatskins, cotton cloth; instead of cows, camels; and for all the black skin, European features. I felt easily at home with them, admired Tony's project and was sorry to leave. We returned to Addis next day to a scene of unimaginable violence.

As the car came to the edge of the city we heard bursts of gunfire. Along a street nearby we could see crowds milling about. Then across the roofs of the city where the land rises up, we saw pillars of smoke. Before long Tony had established that a student uprising was in progress, that some fifty people had already been shot dead, cars and buildings were being burned, and areas of the city, including mine, Piassa, were too dangerous to enter.

He dropped me off at a luxury hotel in the city centre where it was safe and I could wait for the danger to subside. I watched CNN – 'Be the first to know' – where there was no mention of the riots going on around me. In fact I never saw them reported anywhere, then or after.

Across the lobby I noticed a young woman sobbing uncontrollably in the arms of an older woman. She had bruises on her face and blood on her blouse. When she had calmed down a little I went over to talk to her. She was an English girl called Heidi. She told me that she had been coming into Addis by bus when it ran into a riot. The driver and all the passengers simply ran away, but she didn't know where to run. Then a group of men seized her, kicking and half-strangling her, trying to get hold of her backpack. It seems they were just criminals taking advantage of the chaos. Finally the pack fell to the ground and as they dived for the loot she escaped.

It was quite late that night before I found a taxi willing to take me back to Piassa. I liked Addis a lot, even though the popular European view of it was as a nest of thieves, beggars and cripples infesting a slum on a rubbish heap over a vast latrine. The violence I'd seen was very uncharacteristic.

The Wutma was cheap and adequate. The restaurant served a few decent dishes, the beer was good, and backpackers came through from all over. I lingered on for several days – too long, as it transpired. If I had left even one day earlier my fortunes would have been very different, but one can never know.

Finally I fixed a day. Thomas and his wife Samwrit gave me a farewell dinner at the Armenian Club. The food was rich and delicious. That night I was sicker than I could remember being in my life. I writhed in abdominal misery for hours until finally I was able to lose it all in the tiny bathroom, accompanying my efforts with all the usual barbaric animal sounds. Even after that relief I couldn't sleep. I got up at six-thirty feeling and moving like the old man I really am, thinking, I wish I didn't have to do this. Why do I have to do this?

Packing the bike was painfully slow. When I tottered out on to the road, which is on a very steep slope, I felt like falling over. Fortunately I had already learned from Tony the best way out of town. There was still a lot of tension in the air, with soldiers and police everywhere, but nobody interfered with me, and making a smooth exit from this complicated city improved my state of mind.

I expected to get to the frontier with Kenya in two days, stopping first at Lake Awasa. The road was extremely good asphalt, utterly transformed from what I remembered, and I got to Awasa early feeling better if still a little queasy. I'd already been tipped off to look for the quaintly named Unique Park Hotel which had a lovely garden stocked with a remarkable range of plant life. I tried to eat some scrambled eggs, but had to leave most of it, and went out to walk by the lake for a while. The lake is famous for bird life. I had once seen two spectacular red-beaked cranes cavorting there, but this time it was a party of British birdwatchers I watched, with amusement, arguing about the difference between 'the spotted' and 'the banded' something or other.

Back at the hotel I met Anthony, one of those entrepreneurs you only find in the Unfinished World. He said he was a tour guide and a circus impresario, as though it was an entirely natural combination of careers. He wanted to warn me that I would be in serious trouble the next day because I would be passing a big school at Chuko, where they were rioting. He wanted to come with me next morning and protect me and, not having my wits about me, I agreed.

In the morning I realised that he was expecting to ride on the back of the bike. I pointed out that there was nowhere on my bike to sit, and said I would take my chances. So then he asked me for some money. Feeling manipulated, I refused, but none of it felt good. That's how it goes sometimes.

In fact I almost met my fate long before Chuko, at a village called Dila where the road is raised above the shops and walkways on either side. As I came through I saw a white minibus parked on the other side of the road facing away from me. Then to my horror it did a complete reverse U-turn right across the pavement in front of me, driving me off the road on to the steeply inclined dirt. Luckily there was nobody in the way, the tyres held, and I was able to scramble back up to the road.

But when I went through Chuko, which was supposed to be rioting, everybody yelled 'Welcome to Ethiopia' and cheered me on. What goes around comes around.

The road climbed to over six thousand feet and the ride was very pleasant. At the villages people put things out for sale by the roadside. Each village specialised. One sold nothing but carved stone decorations and gravestones. Another sold baskets and woven goods. At another, a flock of women in purple dashed out into the road with bottles of golden *tej*, a popular honey wine, or mead. The only product that was sold everywhere, that lined the roads of Ethiopia (and indeed all of Africa, as I was to discover later), was charcoal, big white plastic bags of it, in huge quantities, and that was where I began to wonder about the future of Africa's forests.

Most of the road was completely new. In 1973 I had seen them building it, and it followed a different path from the one I had followed then. I got to Moyale, the frontier town, at two-thirty in the afternoon. In fact, compared with '73, I thought, this was hardly more than a commute.

16

Moyale is at the southernmost border of Ethiopia, and the northern entrance to Kenya. The country is dry savannah, a landscape of thin grasses, termite mounds and acacia trees, inhabited by giraffe, ostrich, wart hogs, various gazelle-type animals, lions of course, and the Borana tribe.

The Borani live on both sides of the frontier and are semi-nomadic. Their sketchy dwellings made from brushwood and thatch can be put up and taken down pretty quickly. The women look fine in their brilliantly coloured clothes, but are usually bent double under a load of stones, or forage or cowpats, because they do all the hard work.

The men are a lazy lot who keep goats, cows and camels, and stand around all day with sticks prodding their animals out of the way of trucks. This doesn't prevent them from believing that they are the victims of government abuse and discrimination (which is probably true – almost every tribe in Kenya is). So occasionally some of them go on a rampage and kill policemen, soldiers and anyone else they associate with authority, before disappearing into Ethiopia.

Hence the convoys. There is virtually no danger to pale-faced tourists, in my opinion, but I'm told we have to join the police convoys which are organised largely to protect themselves and non-Borani Kenyans. My recollection from 1974 is that from Moyale to Marsabit is about 150 miles, and that there is nothing in between. I've been reading email accounts from others who have ridden this road recently, and they all talked about stones. The road south from Moyale, they said, is a horrible, bone-shaking, tyre-ripping bed of stones. Well, I've done stones already in Ethiopia, six hundred miles of them, and I don't mind them any more. I know the bike can handle them, and I probably won't fall off.

The road should be dry. There has been no rain in two weeks. If there is going to be a problem it could be the dust. That really could be difficult if I am made to ride in convoy.

That, more or less, is the state of my knowledge this Saturday afternoon on the Ethiopian side of Moyale. It is really too much to expect me to remember, after twenty-seven years, that the first part of the road is not stones, but plain red dirt.

I've got a room at the Tourist Hotel because I haven't seen anything better, and it is situated very conveniently right there by the metal pole that bars the road between the two countries. The room is only moderately awful – a bed and a cold-water shower stall. I ask them to replace the missing hook in the ceiling so that I can hang my mosquito net. I haven't investigated the toilets yet, which turn out later to be unusably horrible. And all this for only $2.30 a night.

My friends at the Tourist (in Ethiopia one always has 'friends') are a tall, slim ex-soldier dressed in blue, and a short fellow rather stylishly outfitted in loose jacket, trousers, shirt and trilby, all white. He carries a cane and has an interestingly remote expression. I know they will both profit from me in ways I don't even suspect, but they are undeniably helpful. The blue fellow is the one who invited me into the hotel and showed me the room. I thought he worked there, but he's just a gentle hustler trying to make a few pennies in the tourist industry. He's alert and pleasant, and useful to the hotel because he speaks good English.

I ask him if it would be possible to telephone to London.

'Maybe from the other side,' he says.

He is not talking about spirit guides (handy though they would be with Africa's phone systems), but Kenya. With his patronage, I can duck under the metal pole and into Kenya. I see that the sky is now uniformly grey, but not dark. Nobody thinks it will rain. In a small office run by Asians I try, persistently, to call the *Independent* in London and tell them what I know about the riots in Addis Ababa. It's no good. After much fruitless dialling I give up.

We return to Ethiopia to meet with the man in white. Between them they roust out the immigration officer and the customs man from their homes and bring them to their offices, so that I can be ready to leave first thing in the morning. Undeniably helpful.

There's a minimum of formality at this border, just as there was at Metema, coming in. With all the right stamps in my passport, Mr Blue tells me that if I want to take advantage of cheaper Ethiopian petrol I need to fill up now because the pumps won't be working in the morning; so I do that, and then manoeuvre the bike through the ruts and the rubbish into the back gate of the hotel.

After all this activity there is suddenly nothing left to do. The bike is safely parked, and the three of us are sitting outside the metal door of my room, surveying the squalid hotel yard. Across from us are the stinking toilets, and a tiny hutch where the night guard sleeps. I would do anything not to live in this environment, but for my 'friends' this is their life. Tentatively I broach the subject of Kenyan shillings. I am at a serious disadvantage here because, having forgotten to ask on the other side, I have absolutely no idea what they are worth.

'Ah,' says Mr Blue, indicating Mr White, 'he is the money-changer. You have birr?'

'What are they worth?' I ask.

'Seven shillings to the birr,' says Mr White firmly. The birr is Ethiopian money, worth about eight-fifty to the dollar, but I've used most of my birr to buy petrol.

'Actually, I wanted to change some dollars.'

Mr White is looking down nonchalantly at a stone that he's pushing around with his stick. I observe him with more attention. Mr Blue is nicer, but Mr White is more intriguing. He has created some kind of an aura around himself, and lives inside it in a self-contained way.

'How many dollars?' he asks.

'Maybe ten.'

Mr White gets out his calculator. He is not looking enthusiastic. He can't even bring himself to name the figure, but hands me the calculator. It shows 360. Plainly ridiculous. Even I know that seven eights are fifty-six, so I should be getting at least 560.

'That's not much,' I say.

Mr Blue looks sympathetically sad. 'Well, you see, they are not much liking small notes. Fives and tens. That sort of thing.'

It's got to be a ten or a hundred. I have nothing in between.

'For a hundred,' says Mr White, busy with his calculator, 'I can give you sixty-six fifty.'

That's a spectacular leap upward. I can't help feeling that it must be somewhere near the true value. And I do want some shillings. The bank is shut and it's important to have some usable money.

'It's a good rate,' says Mr White. 'He will tell you.'

I glance at Mr Blue, but he says nothing. Even so, I eventually agree to the deal.

Mr White doesn't actually have the money. Aside from the partitioned shacks where I will sleep there is a café, and inside is a desk where a pretty woman with a hard face listens stonily to his proposition. They speak in Amharic. I imagine they are splitting the profit. Then, grudgingly, she hands over the money, and I order a beer. They don't have Bedele, my favourite, but Harar is not bad. I buy one for Mr Blue as well. After all, he is my friend.

We take our beers outside on to a cement walkway with a few metal chairs. Below it is another level, because the ground slopes away, and down there, covered by an awning, are several men pulling small green leaves out of large plastic bags and chewing them. They don't speak, and have a distant look in their eyes. The leaves are called *chat* and exude a mild narcotic. I sit there with my beer and toy with the comic possibilities of the Tourist Hotel having a 'chat room'. Then Mr Blue suggests I might want dinner. He knows of a better place. Not surprisingly it happens to be run by his younger brother, but that's all right too. We stroll up the hill a little way, and into his brother's yard. The kitchen is in a hut and the stove is a bed of glowing charcoal. I like it. It's clean, and I get a plate of goat's meat fried with onions and peppers, with bread and a soft drink, all for seven birr.

While I'm eating, Mr Blue takes his leave. He will be back in the morning, he says, and entreats me, with a smile, to remember to reward him for his services. But Mr White has meanwhile appeared to take his place, sitting silently by my side and tracing patterns in the dust with his stick. I'm sure he wants money too, but he won't open the conversation. He follows me back to my room, then he gets it out.

'You should give me something for helping you,' he says. I grumble a bit, and argue that I'm already paying Mr Blue, but my heart's not in it. The amounts are so small. So I fob him off with a hundred shillings. He declares himself a happy man. I reckon he must have made enough already on the money-changing.

It's time for bed. What else is there to do? I climb under the mosquito net and try to sleep. Gradually I become aware of a dreadful smell seeping into the room. I suspect it is coming in from the shower drain, like a poisonous gas, and that it originates in those ghastly toilets. The stench becomes unbearable. I cannot recall ever being kept awake by a smell before. I can't think what to do. Tomorrow will be a difficult day, but sleep is impossible with this stink in my nostrils. Then I remember the soap, that expensive scented soap that I liberated from the Sheraton in Addis. With the soap up against my nose on the pillow I finally fall asleep.

When I wake it is still dark, and I hear rain falling on the tin roof. As I listen the sound mounts to a deafening downpour, and I have my first presentiment of disaster.

I try to cheer myself up. It will probably be just enough to lay the dust, I tell myself.

I'm out of bed at first light to pack. The sky is dark. The cloud is almost at ground level, and releases sporadic showers. I'm not interested in breakfast, or even coffee. I just want to get out. Mr Blue appears and I give him 300 shillings, which is plenty, and then I'm under the barrier and into Kenya. Even on a Sunday they are open for business. My visa costs fifty dollars – a new and unwelcome change in the rules – but I can't get excited over it. Since I was here last, all of Africa has joined the visa racket. I am in favour of giving money to poor African countries. I just don't think this is the way to

do it. Customs for the bike is swift and careless, and the customs officer tells me that with a bike they will let me ride ahead of the convoy.

I ride up the hill for a few hundred yards to where the convoy is
gathering. Everything is grey and wet. I can't see anything that
resembles Moyale as I remember it. There are many trucks and I
think I must get ahead of them, so I take the road south that leads
out through a narrow, rutted detour. It's dirt, but the ground seems
firm. It brings me out to the main road where police shout at me
from their post, but I shout back and keep going. Then there's a
police barrier across the road and they hold me up for a while, but
they are sensible people. They understand, and after a bit they let
me through.

'There's a LandCruiser ahead of you,' they say. ' Try to catch up
with it.'

I nod, thinking, Not a chance. No way am I going to catch a
LandCruiser.

The road bed is flat earth, and about twenty feet wide. It runs
across a broad plain of low scrub and gaunt thorn trees, where I
once long ago saw ostriches and giraffe, but there is no sign of any
wildlife now.

So far there seems to have been no heavy traffic on this road.
Although it is wet and glistening the surface looks undisturbed, the
red murram soil feels firm and the tyres hold. Encouraged, I put on
speed and manage thirty, even forty miles an hour, only rarely feeling the wheel slip a little. But it is all earth, and no stone, and then
I come to a part where trucks obviously have preceded me, and the
surface is churned up. In places the mud is too deep to risk rushing
over it, and I have to almost walk the bike through.

Then, quite unexpectedly, comes the first fall. I can't explain it. It
just happens. The front wheel twists and the back slides over. The
bike leans on the pannier in the mud, and I can't move it. I take fifteen minutes unpacking stuff until, with all my strength, I can lift it.
Finally, after forty minutes, I've got it together again, but in the
meantime two big open trucks have gone past. Clustered in the top
of each truck, presumably standing on the load, are thirty or more
Africans. The trucks drive very fast, and they all wave and shout as

they pass, but I am not happy to see them. There will be trouble ahead and there's no doubt about it.

I have arrived one day too late.

Another ten miles, and a truck passes me. I see it stop, and a soldier gets off. There's some heavy road equipment at the side, and the soldier joins a man in overalls. I wave as I pass, but immediately confront a long morass of red mud. Gingerly I make my way along a deep tyre rut, but at last I can't hold it, and the machine overturns on to its side. As I scramble to shut the petrol-tank taps I see the two men running towards me.

They help me stand the bike up. There is thick mud everywhere, on me and the bike. The soldier asks for money to buy a soda. The road worker tells me he's about to grade and cover this stretch. He says it continues bad for another twenty miles, and then, after a bridge-building detour, it gets better. Slowly and painfully I literally paddle the bike through this quagmire and out the other end.

My thoughts are sombre. The weather is not lifting, the bike is too heavy, and these tyres, which have been so good so far, are not good for this mud. And it doesn't help to have sixty-five pounds of petrol sitting over the front wheel. Nevertheless, the next stretch is not too bad. Then there's a detour, but it's come much too soon to presage relief. Down in the gully Africans are labouring and a grey-bearded Indian oversees them. They look miserable, but he is smiling, a pattern I have seen repeated several times. We exchange banter.

'Are you enjoying yourself?' I ask.

'Not as much as you,' he says.

'You think this is fun? Well, we'll both be happy when it's done.' I expect never to see him again.

Another few miles and I get to a junction. It surprises me. I can't remember there being anything like it on this road. There are khaki-clad police here, and a shack with a painted sign – Sisters Café – so I stop for a cup of tea. I can see that the turn-off is a really bad road. A sign points to Sololo. I have no idea what or where Sololo is, and I'm too stupid or tired or mentally paralysed to ask.

It is already midday, and I have gone less than a third of the way to Marsabit. If the road doesn't get better soon, I realise I may have to sleep out. I've already resigned myself to it. I'll take my time – the penalty for falling is too great. As I'm drinking I hear a motorcycle engine. A Swiss rider pulls in on a Japanese dirt bike with the knobbly tyres I wish I had, but unfortunately he's coming from Marsabit. I would have liked company. He promises me another twenty miles of mud before it gets better, and I offer him more of the same.

When I set off again, I can already see a long stretch of thick mud ahead. Painstakingly I work my way through it, recognising how tiring it is, particularly on my legs, only to encounter another stretch soon after.

I am already out of sight of the junction and halfway through the second patch of mud when I lose it, but this time my right foot is stuck in the glutinous clay, and the forward motion of the bike drags it under the alloy pannier before I fall. It's very bad. For the first time in my life I hear the loud snap of a bone breaking. Then I'm on my side in the soft mud with the full weight of the bike pressing down on my boot.

I feel the panic rising, and have a moment of pure horror: Oh Christ! Oh God. You've done it now. Oh shit.

But there's no time for histrionics. I can't get the foot out. The lip of the box has caught the heel of the boot. I keep pulling on the boot and then wriggle around to get at the toe, trying to lever it and worm it out. At last it comes. I have no idea what's broken. I can't feel anything. Why is there no pain? Is it shock?

The break must be low down, because above the boot my leg still seems to be in one piece. I can think only of getting out of the road to the side, and I stand up on my left leg and hop around the prostrate bike to the verge, but at one point I lose my balance and can't help putting my right foot down, twice, only to see it flop over uselessly – a sickening sight – before I fling myself to the ground.

Now what? Sooner or later – probably later – someone will come. Meanwhile, what can I do? Still no pain? I can't feel a thing, but maybe the shock is protecting me. Surely the pain must hit me soon. I drag myself to the back of the bike and open the top box.

Stuff falls out, including the first-aid bag. All I've got for pain is Tylenol. Seems pretty inadequate, but I take two capsules anyway.

Then I put the bag under my head, and lie down in the mud to wait.

I am very aware of being in the middle of a vast plain populated only by a tribe with a bad reputation, but I can't worry about that. I have faith in people. And the junction is not far. Someone will find me. Still no pain.

It's only five minutes before the children come, a crowd of them, all ages from four to fourteen. They filter through the bushes on to the road about a hundred yards away and approach cautiously, fascinated, the older boys in front. One of them dares to come within ten yards. Then he holds his hand out and says, 'Money?' They all giggle. They see me in the mud, and the bike on its side, and it doesn't add up to them. I'm a white man, an *m'zungo*. Maybe this is something *m'zungos* do.

I shout out 'Police!' and 'Army!' and 'Sisters Café!' and 'Go, go, go!' and 'Accident!' and 'Ambulance!', but the words mean nothing. The girls back off, frightened by my noisy behaviour but still, despite the urgency in my voice, they seem to have no idea that there's anything wrong. Then I stumble on the magic word, 'Doctor'. It didn't occur to me before. How could there be a doctor out here? But the boy nearest me, in tan shorts and shirt, repeats, 'Doctor.'

'Yes, yes,' I shout. 'Get the doctor.'

Hesitantly he moves back up the road.

'Go, go!' I shout, waving, and now I think he's got it. He starts to run, slowly, and I sink back into the mud, too tired even to think what 'doctor' could mean to him. Maybe he'll bring a witch-doctor. I don't care.

17

With the smaller children still watching me with fascination from a safe distance, I lay in the soft wet mud and considered my prospects. It stopped raining quite soon, but I kept my multi-coloured golfing umbrella up for shade, enjoying the theatricality of the spectacle.

I was sixty miles of bad road away from Moyale, and 120 miles of equally bad road from Marsabit. Moyale, I thought, would hardly have anything more to offer than a clinic. Marsabit was just a staging-post and a turn-off for the national park. From Marsabit to Nairobi was three hundred miles, most of it really bad going, but I was sure Nairobi was where I would have to end up. I still felt no pain, but surely that couldn't last? By road could be excruciating. By air, if it were even possible, would be financially horrific. I stopped speculating, and thought about the children. And I remembered the Afari kids I had visited with Tony Hickey.

Those children had all worn simple cotton shifts and lived far from the modern world, yet they were not in the least intimidated by me. While the kids around me now were dressed in Western clothes and lived close to a highway where white travellers, even on motorcycles, were no longer a rare sight. So why were they so scared to approach me?

I remembered an experiment that Konrad Lorenz, the behavioural scientist, had carried out with ducks. He cut out the silhouette of a hawk, strung a line across a pond, and flew the cut-out across it. And all the ducks . . . well, ducked. Then he flew it across backwards and the ducks paid no attention. Probably the same thing here. It's not just what you are that counts, it's also what you're doing. They were used to seeing types like me upstanding. An *m'zungo* flat on the ground must be a different species, and could be dangerous.

So I whiled away some time, and then the first vehicle arrived. It was one of those tall trucks that had contributed to my downfall by churning up the mud ahead of me. The usual crowd of men were bunched together on top. It slowed as it approached the supine motorcycle, went through the slippery patch and then stopped, and some of the men came over.

I was struck by how different they seemed when they were on the ground. On top of the truck, outlined against the sky and waving their arms, they looked like a featureless and vaguely fearsome mob. Now they were just pleasant, considerate, well dressed individuals concerned about my condition. Obviously the duck analogy applied to me too. They had been told at the junction to let me know help was coming. Then they lifted the bike up and set the side-stand down. A lot of petrol had poured out by then, but I asked them to close the taps. There was nothing more they could do for me, but they couldn't just drive off and leave me lying there.

'Shall we take you in the lorry?' one of them asked.

'What have you got in there?' I replied.

'Beans.'

'How would you get me in there?' I asked.

He smiled, and shrugged, and we left it at that, but they stayed, looking down at me until a car drove up. There were two men in the car, not in uniform, but they said they were police, and they were both very pleasant, practical men. They said they had come to fetch me.

I had looked at my watch just after the accident happened, and now I looked again. It was one-thirty. I had been lying there for an hour, and I thought it little short of miraculous to be rescued so quickly, but what they told me next was quite astounding.

'There is a big hospital at Sololo. It is eight kilometres away. We can take you there.'

What astonishing good fortune. Truly Africa was doing its stuff again. It was on this same road, twenty-seven years before, that my luggage rack had suddenly cracked apart under the vibration. It was impossible to go on, but within minutes, although I had seen no one on the road all day, a Danish aid volunteer drove up, told me that a few miles down the road was a man with a welding set, took my luggage in the car, and an hour later I was fixed up. These are serendipities you don't forget. In Africa, somehow, things always seemed to work out.

I had given some thought to how I would stop my foot from flopping about when I was moved, and had managed to get the boot off. One of the cops squatted beside me to ask what I wanted to do, and I suggested making some kind of splint with a stick. He reached out to one of the boys, who had all come closer now, and took his stick from him, snapped it and folded it in two. Then with bandages from my kit, we strapped it to the side of my leg and foot. Still no pain.

The other cop was busy unloading the bike, and putting my things in the car. A third man came up, wearing a fez-shaped hat with a coloured geometric design on it, and he was introduced as the village chief. I liked the look of him too.

'You know, he can ride,' said the cop. 'So he can take the bike to the hospital.'

'Sure.' I shrugged. With all the luggage off and half the petrol on the ground, maybe even I could manage it, so why not him? I wasn't feeling too proud of my riding skills.

They laid a sheet of plastic over the front passenger seat, since I was covered in mud, and lifted me into it. I was concerned about the boy's stick. It was a very nice, straight stick. I thought he should get something for it.

'No, no,' they said, 'it is nothing. He was glad to give it to you,' but I had seen no pleasure on his face at the time. It still bothers me that I never thanked him for his stick.

And then the caravan took off. The hospital was at the end of that long and atrocious dirt track I had seen earlier and ignored, to my cost. As we crept along it, working our way through and around the ditches and wash-outs, the cops, who had been drafted from the south, were chatting in Swahili.

'This is a hell of a road for a hospital,' I interrupted, and they laughed and said, 'This is just what we are saying.'

But the approach was misleading. When we arrived I saw quite an extensive establishment of single-storey buildings, well laid out. Sololo Mission Hospital is Catholic, run by two Italians, Roberto Faccin, who is both doctor and surgeon, and Ms Peira Sala, who is the hospital administrator. I'm sure they have help, but it was a Sunday and they were the only two I saw.

The police helped me to hop along a veranda to a room with a bed, and Faccin came in soon after. He was a tall, exceptionally lean and lanky man, probably in his late fifties, with short iron-grey hair and grey eyes, and dressed in green hospital trousers and a white shirt. His face, I noticed over time, was normally composed in a perfectly neutral expression, but capable of breaking into an infectious grin full of teeth. He invited me to lie on the bed and tell him what had happened.

Peira Sala came in too, and brought some pineapple cordial. I discovered that I was incredibly thirsty, and drained off glass after glass. She was younger than Faccin, by maybe ten or fifteen years, with dark hair. She too had a likeable face that expressed quiet contentment, with a warm and cheerful smile in which teeth also played a prominent part.

I had the thought, quite unbidden, that in the whole of this episode I had seen nobody I didn't like, and drew unreasoning comfort from it, seeing it as a good omen. Of course the broken leg, in itself, was unfortunate, and I hoped it wouldn't have lasting consequences, but my main concern was that it shouldn't cause too much of an interruption to my progress. Interruptions are all well and good – and so far this one had been quite absorbing – but you can have too much of a good thing. I was hoping that Faccin would soon be able to tell me just what had happened, and what it would entail.

I was to be disappointed. He carefully removed the sock and touched the area all over, looking for sensation. There was still, remarkably, no pain at all, but also no numbness. Then he told me the bad news.

'I am sorry, but without X-ray it is impossible to know what is broken.' His English was laboured and poor. 'We have the X-ray machine, but there is no bulb. Not the bulb for the X-ray. It is the one to develop the film. It is nothing, but we don't have it.' And he showed his chagrin.

For want of a dollar item, I would have to go to Nairobi.

The precarious state of these hospitals was suddenly dramatised for me. The Catholic Mission hospitals have a great reputation (I have heard nothing about the others) and undoubtedly they receive much charitable support. I heard later from Peira that Faccin himself has a personal fan club in Cortina, where he originated and is much admired, and they try to provide for his needs. But a hospital as isolated as this one is terribly vulnerable to sudden shortages of the most trivial items. Although I was there for a mere twenty-four hours, I learned enough to conceive a tremendous admiration for these two Italians and the work they do, and promised myself I would find a way to help them later.

Faccin said the best he could do was immobilise the leg in plaster until I could get to Nairobi.

'Can you tell anything from feeling it?' I asked.

'Without X-ray' – he shrugged – 'very difficult. But I think maybe both bones.'

There are two bones? Oh yes, those well known twins, Tibia and Fibula. Which was which? Tibia was the big fellow down the middle, and Fibula was the smaller one. Well, there was no point pushing him. Obviously he didn't want to make any more guesses.

Peira had put water on to boil, and set a large bowl on a table next to the bed as though I were about to give birth. Faccin was unwrapping packages of cotton wool and gauze, and another pack of long white cylinders. Then he took hold of my heel, pushed the sole of my foot up to make a right-angle, and tugged gently. Still I felt no pain. He got Peira to hold it in that position, wrapped gauze and cotton wool round the leg, and started dunking the white cylinders in the hot water, grimacing from the heat.

The cylinders unravelled into sheets of cloth and wet plaster, and he wound them around the cotton wool, bending my leg at the knee as he did so until only my toes and upper thigh were visible. And that was it. The plaster set in minutes, and with the help of a pair of crutches ('Made in Cortina,' said Faccin – of course, all those skiers) I made my way to the doctor's house nearby. They sat me in a chair by the phone, gave me a stool to raise my leg on, and left me to try to make contact with the outside world.

Peira held out little hope of success. Sololo phones ran on a manual exchange, she said, and often there was nobody there. I couldn't get a line.

While Peira and I were trying, the two policemen came back. They sat down with me, and were tremendously solicitous and gentle, but finally said they wanted to take the motorcycle into police custody, for safe keeping. I said I was sure that was unnecessary, that it would be safe here at the hospital. Gradually it emerged that they were concerned they might be held responsible, in some way, for what had befallen me. So in the end I wrote out a statement exonerating them from any liability, and saying that it was all my fault.

They helped by bringing in stuff from the bike that I might need, and Peira asked them, when they went back into Sololo, to get somebody to take care of the exchange. By mid-afternoon, I was making phone calls. Both Peira and Faccin were amazed. They had never seen so many calls go through in one afternoon.

I talked to Nairobi, to Germany and to England, and got calls back. It was unheard of. By the end of the day, everybody knew what had happened to me. Lorraine, a friend who was expecting me in Nairobi, had identified a plane that could fly me from Moyale on Tuesday for $120. Faccin said the hospital car would take me there.

Meanwhile I was a guest in their house. Peira was cooking dinner and I was drinking more pineapple cordial, for want of anything stronger, when an elderly man appeared on the veranda outside, and came in.

'I was hearing what happened to you,' he said, exuding benevolence. 'I am sorry. Are you all right? You know, I am here to tell you that we have a man who is sick and has to go to Nairobi. The plane is coming for him, tomorrow, here to Sololo. The plane is covered by insurance, so maybe you can go on it too as a passenger. You may have to pay something, I don't know.'

It was hard to believe my luck. Of course I agreed. Knowing that, one way or another, I would be taken care of in good time, I settled down to an evening with those two wonderful Italians that fate had brought into my life. And in his broken English, Roberto Faccin began to reveal to me the extraordinary challenges that a mission hospital doctor has to face.

There was, for example, the time when the tribe in that area had decided that one of his patients would have to be killed. She was a sick woman, but she belonged to a different tribe. Luckily Faccin was tipped off by someone that the tribe had convened and sentenced her to death. When they came, in seeming innocence, saying they wanted to take her to her home, he refused to hand her over. They besieged the hospital. He refused to let them in. For two days they surrounded the place, trying to get in. He confronted them and said it would have to be over his dead body. But eventually one of them succeeded in entering by a subterfuge, having convinced a young volunteer that he wanted to help protect them from the mob.

Once inside, he made his way to the sick woman's ward and shot her five times. Hearing the shots, Faccin rushed in, and the sixth bullet whistled past his ear as the man escaped through a window. The shots had all gone through her arms and legs, but missed any vital organs, and he was able in the end to save her, and get her back to her family.

Faccin enjoyed telling these stories. Even though he was a spare, rather austere man from the mountains, he had enough of Italian theatricality to make the most of them. It had even occurred to him that they would make a good television series – so much more interesting than those hospital dramas about predictable events in mundane surroundings, and I had to agree with him.

So we had a good evening, with delicious food, and even though the Chianti was absent, I went to bed both satisfied and astonished by the day's events.

There was nothing to do next day but pack a bag, pay my bill and wait to see if the plane materialised. At lunchtime the old man returned, this time with a young man who stayed outside, walking up and down, and it turned out that this was his son, and it was for him that the plane was coming. I was surprised to hear it, and Faccin, who was by my side looking out, said to me quietly with a grin, 'That is not a very sick man.'

But that was none of my business. The main thing was, the plane was coming, at two o'clock. An hour later they came to fetch me, in the back of a pick-up. I surrendered my crutches to Roberto, because they were the only ones the hospital possessed, and we drove to the grass airstrip. The plane, a Flying Doctors' Caravan, was already there. When I got into it I was taken aback to see two stretchers, and find that one of them was for me, since I was expecting to be given a seat. There were four seats but they were all taken, by the pilot, a doctor, a paramedic and a young woman who turned out to be the wife of the patient. I assumed it was just easier for them to put me on the stretcher, and let it go.

They were fussing over the young man as though he were in a serious condition, and wanted to do the same with me, but I resisted and the medic had the sense to leave me alone. So then we took off. I had the pleasure of looking down over the huge expanse of savannah with its powdery green cover of acacias and a silver thread of river winding among them, but it was pleasure tinged with sadness. However rough the road, I would rather have been down there.

We landed just after dark and Lorraine, the friend who had worked so hard to help me, was there to meet the plane. Then I was whisked off to Nairobi Hospital, with Lorraine just behind, and the rest followed with remarkable speed. The X-ray showed, mercifully, that only the fibula was fractured. It was a relatively clean break, and – better still – the broken parts were perfectly placed but not touching, which explained why I had experienced no pain. I was extremely lucky. The break could be easily repaired with a metal plate and screws, and I could be back on my feet in a month.

I was lucky with the surgeon too. Professor Mbindyi was obviously respected by the junior doctors, and had a very pleasant, jovial personality. They had me into a ward, then on to a trolley, and into the theatre within a couple of hours. I went under the anaesthetic feeling secure and happy, and stayed that way until I woke up next morning.

I woke to sunshine in a pleasant bedroom, separated from the only other inhabitant of the ward by a curtain on my left. My mind was sharp and clear, and I felt no pain or discomfort. All there was to suggest that anything unusual might have happened to me was the IV tube linked to my wrist, and another long thin plastic tube emerging from under the covers leading to a semi-transparent plastic object, round and flattened like a toy flying saucer. There was some suspiciously dark fluid in it. After thinking about it for a while I guessed that it must be there to drain the wound.

No hotel I have ever stayed in was more pleasant than Nairobi Hospital that morning. I was waited on hand and, particularly, foot. Kindly nurses gifted with foresight popped in to fulfil desires before I had even properly conceived them. I got tea and newspapers, and a breakfast menu with appetising choices. The IV tube was disconnected. I was able to wash and shave in bed with very little effort.

I ate a very nice lunch, and then was wheeled down to the X-ray department where they photographed my leg, which was now tastefully encased in a shorter cast that came up just below the knee. As before, I was shown the film, and was fascinated to see something that looked more like carpentry than surgery – with six quite large screws fastening a metal plate to the bone. It looked comfortingly strong.

Then came another trip to the physiotherapy department, where they fitted me out with crutches and showed me how best to use them. Back in the ward, my benefactor, Professor Mbindyi, came to visit me. Everything had gone very well, he said. Ever on the lookout for the silver lining, I asked what condition he had found my bones to be in, and he said they were good and strong, adding that I should be able to walk again in three or four weeks. Certainly I could leave the hospital that day.

A payphone was wheeled in so that I could call Lorraine, and we fixed up for her husband, John, to come and fetch me on the way home from his teaching job. Then a nurse came in to pull the drain tube out from between my toes. I had almost finished dressing in the early afternoon and was sitting on my bed, when a woman came in, asked for me by name, and handed me a posy of flowers and a card.

I must have looked rather puzzled, so she said, 'We always like to follow up', and I took it for granted that she must be from AMREF, the African Medical Research Foundation, whose plane I had flown down in. Then she pointed to a figure, scribbled in pencil on the back of the card.

'We would like you to write a cheque for this amount,' she said.

The amount was more than eleven hundred dollars. For a moment I was stupefied.

'I can't possibly do this,' I stuttered. 'I mean, if I had known I would never have agreed. I would have taken the plane from Moyale for $120. You must understand . . . this is just not possible.'

I looked at her, helpless to think of anything more to say, and she was obviously taken aback too. She mumbled something and left the ward. In some confusion, but sure that there had been a mistake, I finished dressing. Then she returned, but with her was the brother of the patient in the plane. His pale face had an ugly expression, and he didn't even bother to be nice. In a sharp, aggressive voice, he said, 'Why don't you pay?'

I said I had never expected to pay anything like this amount.

'It was confirmed,' he said. 'You confirmed it with the radio operator.'

'Absolutely not,' I said. 'Your father said I would travel as a passenger and that I might have to pay something. Nothing else was said to me. I was never told about anything like this. I would have taken the plane from Moyale, as I said earlier.'

'What plane? Who was flying this plane?'

I tried to remember what Lorraine had said about the plane. She mentioned a company called Maff. 'I think it was Maff,' I said.

'Maff doesn't fly to Moyale,' he said bitterly, and started shouting. 'I know all about people like you. We do you a bloody favour. We send up a bigger plane because there's someone with a broken leg. And now you won't bloody well pay. We know about people like you.'

'You know absolutely nothing about me—' I shouted back, but I was wasting my breath. He was already out of the door.

Perhaps I shouldn't have felt so shocked. It's a weakness of mine to feel hurt by baseless charges like that. I should have been able to shrug it off, but to have someone come into a hospital ward and call me a liar and a cheat was defiling. Curiously enough, I recalled that the last time I had been in a hospital was 1976 in Penang, at about the same time of year, where I lay with my eyes bandaged over while a thief stole all my possessions from my bedside locker. Maybe astrologers would have something to say about it. I should stay away from hospitals.

I left the flowers and the card behind me and tried to shake off the nasty residue but it stayed with me a long time. I knew the incident could have worrisome consequences. The man's father might cause trouble in Sololo. The bike, and most of my belongings, were still up there, four hundred miles away, and I had to trust Dr Faccin to take care of them. How, and when, I would get them I had no idea. For the moment, rain was making the road impassable. I read that even those big trucks were stuck.

Meanwhile, I was as comfortable as could be imagined, on the terrace of Lorraine's home, overlooking an incredible gorge stocked with rhinoceros, giraffe, impala, baboons and who knew what else, lurking in the bush.

On 27 April, in three more days, Manfred and his film crew would be flying in to Nairobi. I supposed it would make an interesting change of pace for them to film me on crutches instead of on a motorcycle. On the phone he had seemed unworried. 'It'll be good for the film,' he said. Then, three days after that, the world would be celebrating May Day and, without knowing it, my seventieth birthday. That'll be something! I thought.

18

Journeys like this, as I keep saying, are made in the imagination, and nothing seems to shrink my imagination more than a crippling injury. The first days were exciting enough – the fall, the rescue, the air dash to Nairobi and so forth. But then the weeks dragged on, waiting for the day the cast could come off. After a while I moved into town and stayed with Christoph Handschuh, who managed the service department for BMW in Nairobi. He was an adventurous motorcyclist himself and very hospitable, but as I limped around the cosy confines of Nairobi's pseudo-English suburbs where he lived, the idea of what I was supposed to be doing seemed more and more remote.

As did the bike I was supposed to be doing it on. It sat four hundred miles away on Kenya's wild north-west frontier, and between us lay savage country and horrific roads, with no scheduled flights or regular transport of any sort. In my feeble state of mind, the problem of getting the bike back without riding it seemed insuperable, and riding it so soon, they said, was out of the question.

Through a growing circle of Nairobi friends I chased every possible solution. The kind of vehicle that could make such a journey and carry a big bike was prohibitively expensive to hire. A keen pilot offered to fly the bike out for me. He reckoned he could squeeze it into his Cessna for the knock-down price of £1000. I knew that was cheap, but it was still far beyond my means.

Then Alex Hooper, a photographer with a liking for bikes, had an idea. We would take his 4 × 4 Suzuki up there together. He would ride back on the stripped-off bike and I would drive with all the luggage in the Suzuki. This sounded feasible, and he was keen to do it. He found five days free, we filled the car with supplies the night before, and the next morning, a Saturday, he set off to collect me. He had hardly got down the road before his four-wheel-drive unit seized up – and that was the end of that plan.

But it led to another. Researching the state of the roads, Alex heard that the 150 miles from Isiolo to Marsabit were in a terrible condition and it would be better to take the long way round through Naivasha, Nyahururu, Maralal, Baragoi, South Horr, and then west through Kargi to Marsabit. And this information came from an Israeli called Yoav – it was the route he took to his camp.

Gradually it came together. Yoav was married to Emma, the daughter of an English family in Nairobi, and together they owned a resort, or 'camp', as these things are known in Kenya, a long way north of Nairobi among the mountains and tribal desert lands west of Lake Turkana. They were going back up there with two LandCruisers and I could ride with them. Then Yoav, for a price which I thought steep at the time, would take me and his pick-up to Sololo, and bring the bike back. So on Sunday 10 June, with my leg out of its cast but still swollen and hurting, I drove off with them, sitting first with Emma and then Yoav.

The first nine hours of the drive were fairly easy. Emma, an attractive dark-haired woman with two children in boarding school, told me their story. Against all odds they had decided to carve a luxury resort out of the most remote and unforgiving terrain in northern Kenya. In ten years of unremitting labour, with the help of only two local men, they had dug it out of the rock by hand – and not just the site itself, but also over a mile of road. They called it Desert Rose, and I became very curious to see just what they had accomplished.

After a while I switched cars and sat with Yoav, a short, tough, agile man who appeared to confront his life rather than living in it. I was sympathising with him because Emma had told me that bookings were very slow this year, but Yoav seemed to have no use for sympathy, either received or given. 'You have to be positive,' he said. 'We decided this was how we want to live our lives.' He accompanied this statement with a slight smile, but there was no humour in it. It was the smile of a fighter getting ready to hit back.

After Baragoi we ran into mud, pools of water, loose rock and sand, and I began to have second thoughts about coming back that way. As night fell, a steering linkage on Emma's car broke away from the axle. It would have stopped most people, but Yoav took it in his stride. Working by torchlight, he replaced sheered and broken studs with filed-down bolts to get the car going again. Finally, after twelve hours, with the vehicles climbing like animals at walking pace, we made our way up that handmade road and arrived. I had to admit that the road alone was an awe-inspiring achievement.

The effect of coming out of such demanding country into the ultra-sophistication of Desert Rose was quite dramatic, and I was full of admiration for what they had created. The small apartments were carved out of the mountainside, and paved and roofed with natural local materials. They had brought cedar down from the forests above, and in their own workshop turned it into elegant and idiosyncratic furniture using the natural shapes of the wood. If it had been merely competent rustic work I would still have been impressed, but the standard of design and the degree of finish were far above that, and the accommodation was truly luxurious. Emma assured me that the food and wine were of an equal standard, and as for the views, they were simply stunning. Together, with impeccable taste, clever use of natural materials and the employment of local Samburu tribespeople they had designed and made something extraordinarily attractive.

Desert Rose was designed for affluent tourists on safari who would fly to a nearby landing strip and drive in for a few days of incongruous luxury. She said they charged $295 a day.

'Isn't that rather a lot?' I said.

'Well, what can you get for that in New York these days?' said Emma with some acerbity, and I had to agree that coming there would be an utterly unique experience.

Yoav explained that he had a day's work to do before we could go to Sololo. There were no guests there at the time and when they put me into one of their gorgeous apartments, I assumed it was for their convenience, or perhaps for the pleasure of showing me just how fine their hospitality could be. I would have been happy to sleep anywhere since my main purpose was simply to recover my bike, but after the long drive I had come to assume a degree of mutual respect and friendship.

Emma and Yoav were well matched. She had her own unmistakable toughness, which I soon got a taste of when she proposed that I should pay hotel prices for my food and accommodation. It came as a shock to realise that I had completely misjudged our relationship and that I was, after all, no more than a cash customer. There was an echo, too, of that unpleasant affair in the hospital ward and the angry accusation flung at me about 'people like you'.

Who were those 'people like you'? Was I one of them? Was Nairobi afflicted by troops of dodgy characters from the mother country preying on the gullibility of the locals and hardening their hearts? Perhaps, I thought, this was an aspect of African life I had somehow missed. I examined my own conscience and found it moderately clean. I was already committed to paying Yoav quite a lot to get the bike for me. Surely there was no way Emma could have imagined that I was a tourist looking for a luxury holiday. I tried to hide how offended I felt, and said that I'd be glad to contribute something later but I didn't know how much, since it had never been part of our deal, and she let it go.

The incident never affected my respect for their extraordinary accomplishment, which had more the feeling of an obsession than a business. I would recommend anyone with the money to go there. I even came to sympathise with Emma's efforts to make a little extra in what was obviously a very difficult time, but I kept things cool from then on.

Next day Yoav and I were on our way again, this time across the Chabi Desert to Marsabit, 125 miles of sandy track with the pickup steering more like a boat than a car. In Marsabit, at the police post on the way out, we collected two armed guards. We had to. Either we waited overnight for a convoy, or I paid for an escort, so we took them with us to Sololo, at 900 shillings a head, with a promise to feed them and give them beds.

They sat behind us now in the pick-up bed, two camouflaged Kikuyu policemen armed with G3 automatics, as well as Yoav's own man, a Samburu tribesman. Everything went peacefully as it usually, but not always, did. A week earlier, the police told us, one of their corporals had been shot dead on the road by bandits.

There were highwaymen on the road to Nairobi and they occasionally ambushed vehicles. Or sometimes it was just tribal kids doing target practice, showing off. Not long ago, in another part of the country, a white man had been shot. The killer explained afterwards that he had never seen a white man die, and wanted to know how they did it. These were still only occasional events, but when I first came in the seventies they were unheard of. Guns and corruption have changed Africa. Old values have collapsed, new values will have to be erected or old ones restored. Meanwhile the times continue bloody.

We made good time over the last 120 miles and arrived in Sololo well before dark. Dr Faccin was at the hospital to receive us and assured me that all my stuff was just as I had left it. In gratitude I brought him wine and sausage, showed him my X-rays and donated my crutches to the hospital.

There was a tragic mystery to this man's life that I hoped one day to uncover. When I asked him when he next expected to revisit Italy he said vehemently, 'Never! For me Italy does not exist. It is a hole in the map.'

We took our policemen to a 'hotel' across the road for dinner. We had stewed goat, chapatis, maize meal and tea. The tribes here were mostly Muslim, and there was not much booze around, although I managed to score a bottle of beer later in the evening. Yoav and I thought the goat tasted very good. The police, I heard later, were not very happy with it, but they hid their disappointment well. The hospital found us all beds for the night, and we got up early to coffee and biscuits. Then we loaded up the bike, still liberally coated with red mud and, after sentimental farewells, drove off. It was going to be another long day.

The road we were on, the road I should have been riding, the road on which I had broken my leg in April, was dry now and quite manageable. I watched it roll past with mixed feelings. Away from the city, with its comforts and its phobias, I felt the courage seeping back into my veins and I was very tempted to get back on the bike. Yoav put me off in Marsabit. It was my idea. Better this road, I thought, than the one we had come on. And after what we'd been through together I thought he had undercharged me, so I added to it, waved him goodbye, and settled down to wait for a lift to Nairobi.

I was there for three fascinating days. Marsabit is a random collection of buildings, shacks and huts spread out over a square mile or so of red dirt, at the foot of a small mountain in the middle of a desert. The more important buildings, of course, face the big road, and Jey Jey's was the main hotel. Jey Jey was the MP for this district for quite a while, and he still retained some of the parliamentary gloss of his days as chief whip. His hotel boasted singles, doubles, a restaurant and something proudly described as the Conference Wing, all built around a contained courtyard rather like a stockade, which was very securely locked and guarded at night by watchmen gathered around a glowing charcoal brazier.

Do not be misled by the 'Conference Wing'. A single room here cost two pounds, and so did the best meal you could buy, but the rooms were clean and so were the toilets, and there was hot water in the showers too.

Behind this front line were rows of single-storey shops of plastered cement block bearing painted slogans like 'Millennium 2000 Fashions', and behind them was the market area of rusty tin shacks and stalls made of sticks and sacking. In some ways Marsabit made me think of the old Western cow towns of a hundred years ago. It was the mixture of people that did it. There were black Kikuyu truckers passing through, and white aid workers scurrying about, all in western dress. And mingling with them, without a trace of self-consciousness on either side, Samburu tribesmen wrapped in brilliant red shawls and skirts, hair reddened and ornamented with little beaded flowers and figures, faces framed by beaded strands, foreheads decorated with pendant silver, ears sprouting more beadwork; leaning languidly on impossibly thin spears, with other sticks of significance protruding at various angles.

The Rendille, another tribe in this area, came to town in similarly distinctive tribal dress. Women of both tribes, also gorgeously decorated, sat in the market behind sacks of beans, maize and other goods they brought in from the surrounding desert. How these people came in I'm not sure, but they left in the afternoon, sitting on the sacks of grain in the food relief lorries that went out to the villages. And it is something to see Samburu warriors riding out of town in the rosy evening light on top of those trucks.

At first I thought I would be leaving town on a heavy-machinery trailer. It was due to bring an excavator back from Moyale, and over a couple of cold Tuskers at the Blue Mountain, Sonny, the driver, offered to pick me up on his way back in three days' time. By now I had begun to wonder why I had made such a big deal out of this in Nairobi. Clearly, all I had needed to do was get on the road somehow. All the rest would follow.

On Friday afternoon a German aid worker took me to visit the game park, and at the lodge, by chance, I met Bonaya Adhi Godana, Kenya's new Minister of Agriculture. He had been Minister of Foreign Affairs a week earlier, before President Moi reshuffled his cabinet in another of his many intricate ploys to hold on to power and to keep sucking the economy dry. Godana, a pleasant man, owned some or all of the lodge, and made himself very accessible. I photographed him in front of the lake, a quite beautiful setting, and he pointed out some elephants I had missed.

He seemed genuinely enthusiastic about his new post, and spoke eloquently of his plans to revolutionise agriculture in Kenya. However, when he left and I wished him well in his new job he asked, 'What job?', making me wonder just how he viewed his responsibilities.

I had only just got back down to Marsabit when a self-appointed 'friend' of mine rushed up with the news that there was a LandCruiser waiting to take me to Nairobi. In fact not one, but four.

The Toyota is Africa's favourite overland vehicle and these four white pick-ups belonged to Oxfam, which was moving them from

Ethiopia to the Congo. The drivers were Robert Wanjiku and his three colleagues, John, Francis and (a name to savour) Philharmonius. All four were Kenyans who belonged to the Kikuyu tribe. Robert seemed to be the boss. He was a solid, stocky extrovert, in his late thirties I guessed, with a round head, big limbs and an obvious appetite for life. Philharmonius was taller, lankier, older, and seemed contentedly preoccupied with his own thoughts. John was young and happy-go-lucky, and Francis was the practical, easy-going fellow.

I did my deal with Robert. Lacking a ramp we backed the pick-up to an earth bank and managed to stuff the bike in from there. Then we all met again at seven in the morning when the convoy was set to leave Marsabit, though I saw no sign of other vehicles. I rode with Robert and he made mincemeat of the 'terrible' road, charging over the corrugations at 65 m.p.h. All the time I was thinking, What would it have been like to ride over this? Of course it would have been uncomfortable, and there was a short stretch where black lava rock made progress more painful even in the pick-up, but on the whole it was no worse than Ethiopia. I felt sad and a little ashamed at having avoided it.

The cab was very noisy and conversation was difficult. I wanted to know more about the four of them, but couldn't find a starting-point. After an hour or so, Robert's mobile phone rang (they all carried them) and we had to stop. One of the vehicles was choking up, and needed a new fuel filter. We got going again. There were 150 miles of this bad road, and then about the same again on better roads to Nairobi. I was expecting about six hours. But Robert was on the phone again, calling out this time, and a little later he turned to me: 'We are going to stop here soon. I have been talking and we are going to get some goats.'

'Goats? How many goats?' I asked.

'I think three.'

'What for?'

'We are going to take them to my place, my *shamba*, and we will have a feast. Will you come? We will sleep there tonight, and tomorrow we will have the feast. You will be welcome.'

'Of course,' I said. 'Where do you live?'

'My place is in Thika,' he told me. 'It is on the way.'

We were still in open desert but the road was gradually rising towards the high ground around Mt Kenya, which is what makes the climate of that whole area so agreeable. Somewhere before Archer's Post we met a man by the roadside with a small herd of tethered goats. Robert and Philharmonius chose three and, amidst much bleating, loaded them into one of the pick-ups.

We forged on. Gradually the country became more hospitable, and soon we were riding over tarmac among lush cultivated gardens and coffee plantations at around seven thousand feet. But now there was more trouble. John's brakes had developed a serious problem. They decided to stop at an inn that was famous from colonial times, the Blue Posts. While John examined his vehicle in the car park, we sat comfortably at tea on a terrace surrounded by flowers and over-looking a lawn that swept down to a burbling stream – a place where forty years ago no black man could ever have been served. It gave me enormous pleasure to see how well these four men dealt with modern technology and appropriated the best of what colonialism had left behind.

Eventually John came to tell us there was nothing he could do here. We would have to drive slowly and get the repair done later. We turned off the main highway to Thika just before dark. So far the road surface had been excellent, but almost immediately it turned to dirt and became abysmal. We all drew up outside a bar, and before going in Robert hailed a man from across the road and arranged for mechanics to work on John's Toyota. Then we entered a world as different from the Blue Posts as night is from day.

Instead of the carefully designed and elegantly decorated interior of a nineteenth-century English hostelry we were in a place that had obviously grown organically from a single shack of rough wood and tin, all decked out in bright paint. One room led to another and another in an endless succession of kitchen, pool room, eating place, lounge, bathroom area, and so on and on. There were no windows – only dim electric light – which gave the whole warren an atmosphere of cavernous mystery. I loved it.

We ate fried chicken and other spicy snacks and drank enormous quantities of beer, while Robert explained about the road. 'This is all Kikuyu country,' he said, 'and the government is punishing us.'

It was the Kikuyus who spearheaded the fight for independence back in the fifties with their ferocious Mau-Mau rebellion. It was the Kikuyus, under Jomo Kenyatta, who ruled the country when I came there first, and it is the Kikuyus who are generally considered the most industrious of the tribes, the go-getters, the economic engine of Kenya. But according to Robert, when Daniel Arap Moi, who came from a different tribe, was elected president, he combined with other tribes to keep the Kikuyus out of power. To cripple them, he refused to spend anything on their infrastructure.

'Everything is broken. You will see afterwards how bad. The phones, the water. The road to my home you will not believe.'

And it was true. When we finally left, with John's pick-up repaired, we could hardly exceed five miles an hour over the hills and gulleys of red dirt that passed for a road, and given our condition perhaps this was no bad thing.

Robert's house had a tiled floor and I slept on a bed of sofa cushions. The next day started very slowly, and drifted gradually to the main event. Robert had a largish piece of ground which was littered with useful objects like chairs, benches, tables, small sheds of one kind or another. Appearance was clearly not a consideration.

There was nothing for me to do but watch and wait. Through the bushes and trees I could see an undulating landscape of similar homesteads, of green leaves and red earth and small buildings. A few women came and went, doing useful things, but this was a strongly patriarchal group. Women played no part in the men's communal enjoyment.

At mid-morning an elderly man with grizzled grey hair and a green cap came to oversee the slaughter and butchering of one of the goats. He had special knowledge, said Robert, and it couldn't be done without him. There were very strict rules about how the animal was to be divided up, how the various parts were prepared and, equally important, who was to eat them. Some parts were for young men, some for pregnant women, some for the elderly, some to promote healing. I was to get the broth of the marrow to help with my leg.

More men ambled in, and two large crates of beer appeared. Women arrived to leave basins of *posho*, or what we call polenta. A fire was lit. Two large aluminium pots of water were set on it to heat up – some of the meat was to be parboiled before it was roasted. The goat's head and hooves lay on the stones beside the pots, and the old man squatted down, cutting up the carcass. My friends sat at a table watching the fire, or helping to chop wood. Philharmonius gazed on dreamily. Robert sucked on a toothpick. John made jokes, and Francis laughed. The atmosphere began to warm up and we started on the beer. It could have been any backyard barbecue any- where, except for the absence of women and music, and the strong undercurrent of ritual.

In the end there were fourteen men assembled there to drink and eat, and I was struck by the gentleness of the gathering. Plenty of laughter, but nothing too loud. Nobody postured or became aggressive, or noticeably drunk. They all seemed to like each other. I sipped my soup and chewed happily on some delicious but uniden- tifiable pieces of roast meat and felt at peace with the world.

In mid-afternoon Robert was ready to take me back to Lavington, in Nairobi, where I was staying. I said goodbye to the other three. They all felt like very good friends. Christoph was at home, and using his ramp we easily unloaded the bike. I was hoping that Christoph would find Robert interesting, but there was a curi- ous coldness between them which I never understood. I took Robert's mobile number, shook his hand, and watched him drive away.

A week earlier I had not been able to imagine how I would ever manage to get the bike back. I wanted a reliable plan, something predictable. How wrong I was. All you have to do is get out there, and things just fall into place. What an incredible week it had been.

19

What keeps me going? I know there are people who expected me to give up after the accident, and if I were just doing this for fun, perhaps I would have. Although my leg is healing well I am nervous and I can't honestly say, right now, that I enjoy riding the bike. Well, let me qualify that. In Nairobi, stripped of all the bags and boxes, I was happy enough nipping down to Ya-Ya's Mall with it. But now, fully loaded and on my way to Mombasa, I feel stressed. Perhaps sometime it *will* be fun again, but meanwhile I have to be clear about why I'm doing this.

On my first trip I had an overwhelming need to finish the job, to complete the circle, but I don't feel that imperative any more. It's true that I have an obligation to everyone who has supported me, but that's not what's urging me on. I could have used a broken leg to get me off that hook, if I had wanted.

So it's not for fun. And it's not for money (what money?) And it's not out of a sense of duty. It's for significance. I am cursed by the need for significance. It may be arrogant, but I can't help it. I want to tell people something important, something valuable about the world, before I leave it. Some things I know already. I know there are too many of us. Of course, that's only an opinion. Maybe there are people who want to live on a crowded planet, but surely not without water, fuel or security. All those things are threatened.

The cultural stew of Marsabit was exciting, but that also is obviously in transition. What will follow it? Further south, the Nairobi slums are bursting, and the city earns its nickname 'Nairobbery'. When the villages can no longer support their growing populations, where are the teenagers to go? Not all of them fall for a life of crime, but it doesn't take that many to launch a crime wave. And crime creates employment too, in private security forces. They talk of Kenya as a place where one-third of the population works to protect another third from the other third.

Another big difference I've already noticed – there seems to be no wildlife left. At least, not outside the parks. I am riding now past a big park called Tsavo, on my way to Mombasa and the coast. We went filming in the park, Manfred with his crew, me with my crutches, and of course there were plenty of animals, but were they really wild? Last time I came this way there were elephants at the roadside. Not now.

Well, we'll see.

At least the bike is in perfect nick. Christoph did a lot of work servicing it, and repairing the damage I did in Gedaref. Avon sent new tyres, and Stephen Burgess sent me some tall riding-boots to protect my shins from being Binged by those big BMW carburettors. And there was a bottle of fine French wine in each boot to boost my morale.

I can see Kilimanjaro way off to the right, and I've just passed Kibwezi Junction where I had such memorable encounters in 1974. This time I didn't stop. We have already been filming there, so I know that the Curry Pot Inn has vanished without trace, and so have Pius, and Paul, and Sampson and the bar girl. Did they just move? Or did AIDS carry them off? I'll never know.

The road is all asphalt, which suits me down to the ground. I'm not ready for dirt. I'm scared of it, even though I know that's absurd. They say it will be nothing but tarmac all the way to Cape Town. I wish I could believe them. And right here, coming into Mombasa, this good road suddenly disintegrates into a mess of wet sand, puddles and potholes. I'm riding on tiptoe, afraid of falling. How ridiculous. The mud at Sololo has traumatised me. I hate to think of going round the world in a permanent state of funk. Surely I will get over it? The bike just feels too big, too heavy, too ungainly. It doesn't feel like part of me, the way the Triumph did.

Into the city and the surface gets better again. I have fond memories of Mombasa, and particularly of the Sunshine Club on Kilindini Street. What a wonderful, wicked barnful of blaring noise and sex and sensation that was, with those girls in their extravagant costumes and those shady customers doing dodgy deals in dark corners. Just too good and too bad to have survived – and I'm right, it's gone. Even Kilindini Street has been hi-jacked by Kenya's despicable president, who has turned it into Moi Avenue.

And the Castle Hotel, that great white four-storey building that was once the epitome of classy colonialism, now stands in ruin, broken windows gaping, weeds sprouting from balconies, and the word is that it was the victim of another of Moi's political vendettas. Damn. I had a great lunch there in 1974.

It's time to move on, but not before I sit on my glasses. Yes, I've finally done it. I put them down on the bed and sat on them. Squashed them flat, and I can't read without them. I remember so clearly the moment when I first knew I was mortal. I was in a telephone booth in Colombia, in 1975, with the bike parked outside. The light was fading and I was looking up a phone number and I couldn't tell the ones from the zeroes. In a way it's been downhill ever since.

These are difficult moments. How can I make this journey if I'm constantly being reminded of my age? Now I have no idea whether the glasses can be repaired, or how long it might take to get new ones. The hotel owner sends me two hundred yards up the street to an optician, and I hang around until his assistant opens up the shop. He's a young Kenyan and I show him the sorry mess I've made, feeling like an idiot.

'Give them to me, please,' he says, and takes them into a little back room. Five minutes later he hands them back to me, in perfect repair. I'm amazed and bubbling over with gratitude.

'How much?' I already have a fistful of shillings ready.

'No. It's nothing.' He flashes me a big smile, and this simple act of kindness comes as a huge release. I feel whole again, and ready to roll.

The euphoria doesn't last long. Outside the hotel is a busload of teachers also going to Tanzania, and they tell me that across the border the road turns to dirt. 'Don't fall into the holes,' they laugh. 'There are some big ones.'

Tarmac all the way to Cape Town? How naive can you get?

First there's a ferry to cross, and a fine road along the coast, past cashew plantations and palms, with lovely glimpses of the Indian Ocean. I'm trying to control my anxiety. Black rainclouds are massing, and my heart is sinking, and I say to myself, To hell with this, and stop at a small village and buy two oranges. And while I'm sitting there eating them and talking to the stallholder, the clouds seem to lighten and pass over. By the time I get to the border, the sky is blue again, and when all the idiotic formalities are finished and I'm through into Tanzania I see the dirt road, and with great relief I see that it's dry. Even so there are a lot of deep potholes and it's slow, hard work avoiding them. I am not happy with myself, although it improves as I go along, and after thirty miles heavenly asphalt takes me all the way to Tanga.

Tanga is a quiet seaside town and I've found a pleasant hotel. It must be Muslim. The calls to prayer at dawn are louder and longer than any I heard in Sudan, but when they're done the town subsides into a gentle torpor relieved by a refreshing breeze off the ocean. I wouldn't mind staying here longer if I hadn't lost so much time in Nairobi.

I was planning to go to the capital, Dar es Salaam, but an Indian at the Internet shop convinces me it's not worth the detour. 'Just another big city full of noise and cars and fumes,' he says. Something I can do without, so now my route takes me inland, the length of Tanzania, almost seven hundred miles, towards Zambia. Most of it is the old TanZam highway. It used to be a hell run for oil tankers and trucks beating the blockade when Zimbabwe was Southern Rhodesia. They were still building it when I was here last, and that really was a hell of a ride. The road was strewn with wrecks. It rained the whole way, and the country was poor and miserable.

Today the riding is a joy. I'm on good roads with light traffic, under a blue sky fluffed up with white cumulus, cruising through a broad green landscape of maize, sisal and pineapple plantations, ruptured dramatically here and there by heaps of forested rock thrust up through the earth's crust by some ancient igneous event. The air is just pleasantly warm and the whole country comes to life for me.

Here comes Mwebwe, a small town that played a crucial part in the mental life of my first journey. I stop here briefly for a snack, sitting at a plank table by the roadside next to a comfortably plump local lady who instructs me in the Swahili names of things, and I refresh myself with a few small savoury doughnuts called *badiyas* and a couple of bananas. The bike is parked behind me, and people are buzzing around it. Here they still get excited about it, but not in the awestruck way they did back then. Today there are small bikes everywhere, and it is merely the size of mine that provokes giggles and amazement.

'Is this one a pikky-pikky or a *car*? No, me, I couldn't. It is too big.'

Later, from Morogoro, I take the wrong road and have to spend the night at a roadhouse where everything is behind steel bars, including the TV in the lounge which hangs from the ceiling locked in a steel cage. Bathed in sickly green fluorescent light, solitary males sit staring at the TV from behind bottles of beer, but they can't be following the action because the soundtrack is drowned by loud Latin music. This seems common in Africa. The meaning of what appears on the screen in public places is irrelevant. What is wanted, it seems, are figures going wordlessly through their routines, as a focal point for glazing eyes to fix on.

But when I think about it, we do that a lot too.

None of this spoils my pleasure in Tanzania. The ride continues to be beautiful. Now that I'm back on the right road, I pass through the Mikumi Game Park, where I had encounters with elephants and zebra in 1974. Nothing this time, but the landscape becomes ever more exciting as the road climbs to more than six thousand feet. A bus sweeps past me, very fast, catching me by surprise. I see it moves slightly crabwise. That can't be good.

This must be one of the few areas of productive farmland. There are onions, peanuts, potatoes and tomatoes for sale at the roadside, as well as the ever-present charcoal. Bicycles are the main form of transport, and carry enormous loads, often being just pushed along. Kids here have a particular kind of old-fashioned heavy yellow scooter and tie bundles of sugar cane to it. But why no donkeys? I wonder.

Lots of mission buildings, though, of every denomination, strung out alongside the highway just as they were in Kenya, all desperate, it seems, to bag the largest share of souls. People look happy, and I'm tempted to believe that Tanzania is a better place than it was twenty-seven years ago, but it could just be the weather. Last time I saw it all in the rain. This is still one of the poorest countries on earth.

Up here is where the tea estates begin, because they need the altitude as well as the rainfall. I'm at Mbeya now, close to the Zambian border, and I've made a momentous decision to change my route. I intended to go through Lusaka and then over the Livingstone Bridge at the Victoria Falls, but I hear that they have turned the Falls into a kind of Disneyland, and I have such good memories of them that I don't want them corrupted. Anyway, I have already discovered that trying to track anyone down in this part of Africa after so long away is pointless. With all the fighting that went on around here when black Rhodesians, under Mugabe and Nkomo, were struggling for independence, people have moved away. The only family I knew in Zambia were missionaries, and I know they've long since gone.

So I'm going to go through Malawi instead. That will take me past an enormous lake, supposedly with beautiful beaches, and then through Mozambique into Zimbabwe where I will rejoin the original route to Cape Town. So at Mbeya I turn south, and here I discover one of the world's most beautiful rides, about eighty miles long and a good surface, that lets me take my eyes off the road. It soars to 7,500 feet alongside the tea gardens, where the rolling hillsides are clothed in a glorious emerald green. Then it winds down gradually through banana plantations and tropical forest until it comes finally to the shore of Lake Malawi and the border.

The border crossing offers the usual mixture of boredom, irritation and mirth, but doesn't take me too long. Others are less lucky. A party of backpacking holidaymakers in what we used to call a 'hippy bus' are stuck there in some kind of bureaucratic glue. They envy me my freedom on the bike, of course. They're going to Nkhata Bay, a resort on the lake. I decide to check that scene out for myself. Then I discover that, unwittingly, I've put myself to the test. The map showed tarmac, but the road is being rebuilt and I'm shunted on to a temporary dirt road for a hundred miles. And quite suddenly I get so sick of my own pathetic fears and anxieties that I just decide to let go.

Amazing. That's all it took. It's not a bad surface, really. Most of it is graded, honey-coloured gravel, with some loose patches. Ethiopia was much worse. I charge at it, and the bike just swallows it up, and I feel a huge sense of relief. I can do this. It's going to be all right.

Lake Malawi is about 360 miles long, north to south. The main road runs above and parallel to it but has so many twists and turns that it is almost twice as long. To get down to the shore at Nkhata, where the hippy bus was heading, I have to turn left at Mzuzu, but already the light is failing. Better to stop. In an old-fashioned hotel run by Indians I enjoy the luxury of a hot bath, but sleep comes hard because of a shattering volume of noise pouring in through the window. Is it a rock concert, or a national celebration? It continues all night. I am flabbergasted to be told in the morning that it all issued from one small bar. Was it a measure, perhaps, of the sorrows that needed drowning?

It would be easy to travel through Malawi oblivious to the desperate condition of the people. Economically this has always been a basket case, and now in addition Malawi is among the countries most heavily infected by AIDS/HIV – out of a population of twelve million, at least 900,000 have the virus – but it is not in the nature of Africans to walk around in the sunshine looking miserable, even when wives, children and husbands lie dying in their huts.

The road down to Nkhata is a long sequence of potholed hair-pins, but the attraction of the lake is immediate. It is too wide to see across to Mozambique on the other side, so it is really an inland sea, and the beaches are beautiful. A cockney ice-cream salesman called Bryn brought his money here and put up an extremely rustic but idyllic resort called Big Blue, where it costs almost nothing to eat, drink, sleep, swim and, if you're luckier than me, make love. I feel lucky even without the love, and after two days I have to tear myself away and ride on.

I'm warned off the lake shore road – there's a bridge out, they say – so to go south I have to climb back up to Mzuzu. At the petrol station a German couple on impeccably equipped dirt bikes put me to shame. They could have stepped out of the pages of *Motorrad* – young, slim, handsome in perfectly fitting matching outfits. Next to them in my baggy jacket and generic jeans I feel like a tramp. His face is narrow with ice-blue eyes. She has my favourite features, wide eyes and a Mia Farrow mouth, open and smiling.

'It's cold in the Kalahari,' he says, just so I know where they've been.

The road rises through farms of red-barked conifers, an easy ride until suddenly I hit three big potholes in a row. Each one is so severe that I have no chance of avoiding the next. It feels as though something's broken. The fibreglass screen has broken off its bracket, but that's not serious. I search for other problems and find nothing, but the bike feels a bit weird at first. When I take my hands off the bar it goes into a wobble rather easily.

At Kasungu, halfway along the road to Lilongwe, I turn off to look for food and strike lucky. There's a market, a throng of people, and here they're frying up potatoes and meat. The appliances are simple and ingenious, just square sheets of tin with hollows stamped into the middle, suspended over wood fires. The crowd is in great, boisterous humour.

'Come here. This one is very good. You must try it. You are hungry, isn't it! Take the plate.'

They swept me up, happily swarming around the bike. It was like old times, only better, because then between black and white there was always underlying strain. So looking around, as I munch contentedly on these delicious cubes of fried beef, I can't imagine how things can be so bad here in Malawi.

Back on the road I start consciously looking for signs of trouble, but everything looks so normal until here, in the middle of a village, there is a sign, literally. Some energetic entrepreneur has put up a bold notice by the roadside with the breezy slogan: 'ENERGY COFFINS' – and they can be yours, he announces, in twenty-four hours. I find it hard to get my mind around the concept, but there's no doubt about the product, which is obviously in demand.

Lilongwe, the capital, is a small colonial town gone native, but it has a core of nice buildings, and in an arcade I find a remarkably good restaurant which calls itself Don Brioni's Bistro, where the diplomats go. In the gents' washroom, pinned to the wall, there's a large floral menu from London's famous Trocadero Restaurant where, I learn later, the proprietor began his culinary career. It dates back to the heady days when you could buy a good bottle of Nuits St Georges for under a pound, and in a fit of nostalgia I can almost taste the wine. In the far-flung corners of the Unfinished World you find these windows into the past, like the railway booking-office in Wadi Halfa, or the old British clubs in Buenos Aires.

Five hundred light years away, physicists tell us, the very dilute images of Shakespeare and Queen Elizabeth are fleeing through space. I think of this menu as a modest terrestrial version of the same phenomenon.

All this time I have been following a timetable. Manfred's cameraman, Bernd, is flying into Zimbabwe, on his own, in three days' time. We are to meet in Mutare and do some filming. So today, Saturday, I plan to enter Mozambique at Dezda, not too far from here, and ride to the Zambezi River. Then tomorrow I'll come out the other side into Zimbabwe. There's a spur road from the highway to the frontier, and when I get there my heart slumps into my boots. Instead of the tar I took for granted I find a dirt road, but worse than that, it's covered with about four inches of soft white sand.

It seems as though every time I overcome one level of fear, the bar is raised to a new level. I should have the courage to blow right through it, but I am too scared of falling again.

Slowly and painfully I struggle along in the sand for half a mile, and think seriously of giving up and turning round, but I see two men coming towards me. 'How many kilometres is it to the border?' I ask nervously.

They laugh and point to a building two hundred yards away. 'See there? The flag? That's it.'

With huge relief I make my exit from Malawi, surrounded by money-changers who are so impressed by the size of my bike that one of them gives me a pocket calculator. Money-changers do not usually give away anything. To them I am a hero. In my heart I feel like a coward, but the adulation helps.

I ride up to the Mozambique barrier, see the tar road stretching ahead, and think my troubles are over. They are not. Somehow I had it fixed in my mind that Mozambique, like all the countries around it, gives visas at the border. Mozambique does not. This could be a moment of truth.

Essentially we all live two different lives simultaneously. One of them is made up of all the plans, hopes, ambitions and expectations that we have woven around ourselves. The other consists in just being alive. Sometimes it is extremely hard to switch from one to the other, from expectations to reality.

I am stuck in the first mode, and stand in front of the immigration counter in a state of shock. Being alive isn't good enough. I am supposed to go to Mutare. Instead I will have to go back into Malawi (and pay another fifty dollars for the privilege). I will have to ride through that sand again. Then I will have to ride 150 miles to Blantyre and spend two nights there until on Monday, maybe, I can apply for a visa. Bernd, who has taken these specific days off from an expensive production, will fly in for nothing, but at huge expense to Manfred, who is already losing money. With luck I might just get to see Bernd before he leaves for home.

The thought of it all is appalling. So I just stand there, staring at the immigration officer, thinking, It can't be true.

It's not a busy border. There is only one other traveller going through, a tubby Tanzanian businessman in a beautifully laundered striped shirt who is doing some kind of deal with the immigration official. He is a ball of energy, and speaks English, Portuguese and of course his own languages, probably at least two of them. I had not realised, until this trip, what great linguists Africans are. Almost everyone speaks at least three languages.

Anyway, he sees me in my pit of despair and says, 'My dear fellow. This is Africa. In Africa everything is possible. I think, for some money, you will be able to get your visa.'

He talks to the officer (which I can't do, having forgotten my Portuguese) and the officer goes away to fetch his chief.

'Maybe twenty dollars will be enough,' says the ball of fire. I put a twenty dollar bill on the counter, and cross my fingers.

Back comes the official with his boss, a woman with a very contented expression, like a cat eyeing a saucer of cream. They all talk together for a while.

'It will cost fifty dollars,' says my friend.

Of course, I think. That is the logical price.

They give me change for a hundred dollar note, and the smiling woman stamps my passport. No visa. Just a stamp.

And with a huge sigh of relief I ride into Mozambique, tragedy averted, but already I'm wondering what they will say at the other end. The roads are rough, some tarmac, some dirt, and gradually I recover my confidence; but I have to keep my eyes on the road, and so I am a little slow to spot the most extraordinary sight on the journey so far. Striding up the hill towards me, followed by a crowd of people, are two quite bewildering creatures. Their appearance is so strange that at first I don't recognise them as human, even though they must be. From the shoulders up they are just a huge head of feathers. There's something quite powerful, even aggressive, in their movements.

Bird men? I've heard some mention of them, but I'm too shy to ride back and goggle at them.

Only two years ago there were massive and lethal floods in the Zambezi basin, but I think that was further east towards the coast. As the land descends to the river it gets hotter and more humid. The huts all around are nothing but thatch roofs supported on sticks so the air can blow through them.

The ball of fire has told me which hotel to go to when I get to Tete, but it's full. Instead I have to stay at a modern hotel driven into senility by a collapsed economy. Everything's broken. Nothing works. The power has been cut off. And yet, strangely, on the top floor, lit by candles, is another marvellous restaurant, this one run by two young Portuguese, cooking over charcoal.

In the morning, before I leave, I notice something I missed the day before. A spoke on the rear wheel has broken, and is sticking into the tyre wall. With much effort I'm able to bend it away and prevent it from puncturing the tyre. I wonder what other damage has been done that I haven't seen.

When I do get to the other side of Mozambique the next day, the border is being run in a rather more professional manner.

A man in a well cut suit riffles through my passport. 'Where is the visa?' he asks. He speaks good English.

I explain that I paid fifty dollars and got my entry stamp.

He looks worried. More than that, he seems resentful. 'Do you have a receipt for this fifty dollars?' He calls it 'a resseety' which sounds comical because his pronunciation is otherwise perfect.

I say that I regrettably failed to obtain one.

He hums and haws and frowns a lot. 'It is not correct', he says.

I agree.

'You should have asked for a resseety.'

'Yes,' I say, with a hangdog expression.

He knows damned well in whose pocket the fifty dollars have gone. He pushes my passport at me and jerks his head towards the exit. He's too disgusted even to look at me.

On the other side, the Zimbabwe office is run by black women in neat blue uniforms. They seem happy to see me. I fill in a form. The young woman reading it exclaims to the room at large, 'What is a writer?'

'Give it to me,' says the severe matriarch at the back of the room.

They give me two days to explain myself to the immigration office in Mutare. President Mugabe doesn't like writers. They write bad things about him. So when I go to the immigration office, I decide to go into retirement. As a retired person I am more welcome, and they give me a month. So I get to play at making movies with Bernd Meiners after all.

One important observation: in Zimbabwe, I notice, the fuel is paraffin, which drives home my observation that ever since Egypt – that's about six thousand miles – I have become used to seeing sacks of charcoal along the roadside. I'm racking my brains, but I simply can't remember seeing this in 1974. Of course, there are many reasons for clearing forest, but a large portion of now-vanished European forest was consumed as charcoal, I believe, and the same may be happening here in Africa. And with it, of course, goes the wildlife such as it is.

Why not in Zimbabwe, which is now close to disaster? I think because twenty years ago this was an economically advanced society with access to Western products, and probably all the old oil-burning heating and cooking devices still survive, but I would speculate that people will soon revert to charcoal unless there is drastic change for the better.

Just like elsewhere in Africa, it is difficult for a casual observer in Zimbabwe to perceive the country's problems. Bernd and I, and John, the black location manager from Harare, are staying at a comfortable motel owned and run by whites, and there's no hint of crisis. I ride my bike around in picturesque settings for the camera, then join a group of black Africans lunching off a barbecue behind a petrol station. We are all in good spirits, spooning delicious stewed beans out of a huge pot, to add to our curried beef. Nobody's starving, or sick. My only problem is that the South African beer is frozen in the bottle.

Riding along a country road in the dusk one evening I pass a group of men gathered outside the gates of a farm, and one of them steps out and raises his fist, shouting something. He might have been threatening me, or he might have been drunk. It could have happened anywhere.

There are another three thousand miles between me and Cape Town, a huge distance, like crossing America coast to coast, and yet I feel as though I am almost there. It is still the year 2001, and although Zimbabwe has begun its slide into dissolution, the infrastructure is still intact and the roads are good. The South African border is only a few hundred miles away, and from now on it will be more like tourism than travel.

Of course I could seek out difficulty and danger. There are plenty of opportunities, but I have the rest of the world ahead of me. I need to get on. Bernd leaves me, satisfied with what he has in the can, and I head south to the border at Beit Bridge.

South Africa seems like Zimbabwe, only more so. On the surface everything is orderly, and bland. When I was here before there was apartheid. I got my first tragicomic slice of it at the frontier, when a plump white official tried to confiscate my Egyptian friend's sword, in case 'the natives' got their hands on it. Then I was served an even larger portion of apartheid at a hotel restaurant in a town called Louis Trichardt, where the black kitchen staff operated like slaves in a glass cage under the eyes of the white customers. I stop in Louis Trichardt to find out how they work it now, but that hotel too has gone, demolished. So much of the past is associated with buildings that have simply been wiped off the map.

I hated apartheid, and it was something to get passionate about. I met Afrikaaners who spoke their mind, and I met many white people who hated the system even more than I did. Now, thank goodness, official discrimination is a thing of the past, and no doubt many have benefited from their freedom, but most whites still live in good houses, and most blacks still live in slums. I don't know how it could have been otherwise. The disparity in wealth is so huge that even the most benevolent, philanthropic whites know that what they have to give would only be a drop in a black ocean of need. Still, I can't help wishing they had the courage to narrow the gap.

In the bad old days, when the issues were black and white, you could be excited about the prospect of change. You could hope that when apartheid finally went, it would usher in a brave new world. Now that only the people are black and white, the prospects are murky. I hope there doesn't have to be a Mugabe in South Africa, willing to bring the whole house down in the name of egality. All my friends in South Africa are white, and prosperous. It's inevitable. When I was here last it was difficult to meet blacks. I remember asking a mechanic in Port Elizabeth to come out for a drink, and seeing the expression on his face. It was illegal. My friends did the best they could then, and they do now. In Johannesburg I find a dear old lady, Trish Ord, who remembers me well.

'You're the one who laid out all his oily motorcycle parts on one of my bedspreads,' she says, but I am forgiven, of course, and she has me in for tea. She lives in a fortress, like all my other friends. Crime in Johannesburg is like crime in Nairobi, except that it is more usually fatal.

Within the walls of her domain Trish runs an egalitarian society, as does Elmarie, another friend I met in Nairobi, who offers me shelter in one of the suburbs, where her extended family occupies a large area surrounded by electric fencing. The hospitality is warm and generous, and my friends are generally optimistic. They recognise the problems, of course, but are accustomed to them. I'm sure they think I exaggerate.

I have decided to change my route again. I need to go back to Mozambique, to Maputo. Maputo used to be Lourenço Marques, and it was where I went in 1974 to take a ship to Brazil. It was a momentous time for me, and also for Mozambique. I was there when the first of the revolutions against foreign rule from Portugal took place. It was a white revolution, by the white population of the country, and mostly a non-violent affair, but anyone could see that the black revolution was coming. Black insurgents had been fighting in the country for years.

Eventually, of course, they won their independence, and for decades Mozambique has been a predominantly black socialist state. It's important for me to see how it is today, but to follow the 1974 route would take too long. So instead of crossing the veldt as I did then, I'm riding east from Jo'burg towards the Indian Ocean, armed this time with a visa. The road is first-class highway, and has some very beautiful stretches, especially around Nelspruit where the high land breaks down to the coastal plain.

For all the problems of South Africa there are enough whites there to keep their own standard of living high. Crossing into Mozambique reminds me of the border between America and Mexico. Enough of South African prosperity spills over to relieve the shock of transition, but the change is dramatic nonetheless. Maputo is a big city, and inevitably there are opulent patches to be seen, but much of it is badly neglected.

I follow the coast out to a hotel that I've heard of. It's the Costa do Sol, and it's a really fine place. It has lovely, airy rooms in the old colonial style, high ceilings and beautiful solid woodwork. But there's a touch of old Eastern Bloc mentality on the management's part. On the door is an inventory of the room's contents, down to the tiniest detail, with a stern warning. Woe betide me if I should walk off with an ashtray. As against that, downstairs there's an incredibly good restaurant where I finally get the lobster I couldn't find in Mombasa.

As well as wanting to see the place, I'm on a bit of a wild goose chase too. There's a man I want to find. While I was waiting, for the *Zoë. G* to sail, I got to know a young Indian shipping clerk, who was taking care of my departure. I knew him only by his first name. Ahmad was already married, with children, and the prospects of life in Mozambique were dismal. He had fought for four years in the army against the Mozambican liberation movement, the Frelimo, and he knew what to expect.

Leaving him there on the dockside as I sailed away was one of the most poignant moments of that journey. I have no real hope of finding him again after all this time, but a shipping agent in Johannesburg told me that the company still exists, and it's in the hotel phone book. To my amazement not only do I track Ahmad down, I discover that he now owns the company he once worked for. This company, which used to be South African, is admittedly in bad shape. With all the more wasteful aspects of socialism to contend with, the owners were willing to sell it off for pennies. Ahmad will be lucky to keep it afloat but, for the moment, he's the boss. Surprised that I found him, and not a little intrigued as well, he agrees to meet me.

In the morning, on the veranda overlooking a peaceful beach and a green ocean, I wait for Ahmad. Across the road, under the palms, families are setting up stalls to sell souvenirs and furniture. A car comes rapidly along the road from my right. The driver suddenly decides to stop. Tyres screaming, he loses control and the car hurtles into the row of stalls. A man is injured. I watch the drama of remorse, anger, fear and resignation before the ambulance arrives. How quickly life can change.

Ahmad arrives with his wife, Galima. They sit opposite me, calm and composed, and I can sense the love between them as he describes the troubled waters he and his wife have navigated since I saw him last: 'You cannot imagine the difficulties. We had to stay here, for the family, but everything collapsed around us. We just had to keep on somehow, both of us working. No power. No light. Hardly any food.'

It was a remarkable story, through crisis after crisis, with the country's economy going from bad to worse. And yet somehow, with ingenuity and perseverance, they kept themselves afloat: 'Things got a bit better a few years ago, but it is almost impossible to run a business. The government restrictions are so severe.'

But they are alive. They look well, and content. People survive.

Ahmad agrees that things in Maputo itself don't look too bad, but he tells me that it doesn't represent the state of the country, and I know that already, of course. Tourism keeps Maputo in slightly better shape. Ahmad has no idea that his story appeared in my book. He has a son in the USA, and I promise to send a copy to him. I keep the conversation going as long as I can, but then he has to leave. So strange, these meetings. After twenty-eight years we meet for half an hour. There is real feeling between us, and then we part, probably never to meet again.

My route back to South Africa and Cape Town takes me through the tiny kingdom of Swaziland, which seems to survive on sugar and wood – at least that's what I mostly see. At the lower altitudes the hills are covered with sugar plantations. Up higher, all the native forest seems to have been replaced by tree plantations. I ride through huge areas, devastated by clear-cutting, where there's nothing but tree stumps and slashed branches, and pass monster mills throwing out great plumes of smoke. There is no temptation to linger.

The border post to South Africa is very modest, and perhaps because it's Sunday, it seems to be deserted. There's an open gate with no one around, so I ride through. I don't realise I'm already in South Africa. Then I hear a loud whistle behind me, and see a man beckoning me back into his office. He's tall and thin, in tight-fitting blue uniform trousers and jersey. His round black face has a blotchy appearance, and his eyelids droop. He sways as he walks, more like a plant than a person. His mouth makes a round O shape when he opens it, which he does now.

'You are under arrest,' he says, staring at me belligerently across the immigration office.

'What for?' I ask politely.

'For trespassing,' he says.

I think there's little chance of my going to jail in Swaziland, of all places, and if I have trespassed at all it wasn't on his little kingdom but on the much bigger neighbouring republic of South Africa. All the same, it pays to be careful. I caught a whiff of liquor as he passed by me. A drunken immigration officer can cause all kinds of trouble. Fortunately the other man in the room, a customs officer with four impressive gold rings on his sleeve, is smiling.

'You white people,' the first man goes on, 'you think you can . . .' The rest is lost in a mumble.

'I am not white,' I protest. 'I'm light brown.'

'Huh!' He spits it out. 'You think you can play with the law? It's no different for you.'

Well, I suppose I have taken something of a liberty just riding through like that.

'It was a mistake,' says the customs man, chuckling.

My inebriated interlocutor mumbles on in his indignation for a minute or two, then the air goes out of him. He decides it's all too much trouble and he stamps me out: SWAZILAND 2001 07-29 EXIT SANDLANE.

20

I hardly ever ride in company because I have very few close friends who ride, and if it's not for the pleasure of being with a friend I can't see the point. Why should I expose my dreadful riding habits to strangers who are probably only there to make themselves feel good? Off the bike I'm a pretty gregarious person, but when I'm on it I'm too interested in my own thoughts to listen to yacking through the intercom.

Besides, all my instincts for self-preservation were acquired as a lone rider, so I'm inclined to think of riders in bunches as a major safety hazard. And then, on top of that there's my firm belief that two or more people are going to have a much harder time insinuating themselves into the family life of, say, a Bedouin herdsman or an Indian sitar maestro. I could be wrong, but I doubt it.

However, this bit of the journey having become more of a tourist excursion, when a friend of mine suggested riding the last fifteen hundred miles to Cape Town with me I was happy. Emerson Milenski may be the brightest American I know. His intelligence alone gives me pleasure. He is so bright that he could probably get the Bedouin and the sitar player to form a touring company. Anyway, Emerson, or 'Bubbles' as I know him for reasons I have forgotten, left his oil rigs in Angola, flew to Jo'burg to rent an 1100 GS, and rode to meet me at Piet Retief, which is just down the road from Swaziland.

I wish I could say I chose Piet Retief for its remarkable historical interest, or its cathedral or its cave paintings. I wish. All I can say for

Piet Retief is that it was comfortable and convenient, and had a restaurant named Mama Mia where you could get spaghetti. That was the cultural highpoint.

Actually there was plenty of history in the vicinity. We were on the edge of Zululand, where the British, the Boers and the Zulus slaughtered each other in colourful and exciting ways at places like Rorke's Drift, but the countryside itself is so attractive that I thought I'd let the history go by for another time. Emerson and I just made our way slowly along back roads through lovely hill country to Durban, where an old friend had offered to shelter us.

Pip Lorentz was one of a group of young people I met long ago in Cape Town. No longer so young, but very vigorous, he runs a car and motorcycle dealership in a wealthy suburb of Durban, and lives in fine style. He looked after us both very well, but best of all he introduced me to Rob Brogiolo, who runs a great machine shop. I happened to mention that there were 'a couple of things – you know how it is', and Rob ended up working on my bike for the best part of a day, with Emerson and me hanging around trying to help. My luggage rack was fractured in several places and one of the alloy boxes had split along the corner. Rob did a masterful job of welding the rack and he also found a way to move the boxes back. The fact that they were too far forward had certainly contributed to my accident in Kenya. I offered to pay him but he said I couldn't afford it, and took a sandwich off me instead. So I left Pip in much better shape than he had found me.

Kokstad was another place I had a sentimental attachment to. It was where I once saw a black hotel servant dancing to the rhythm of my engine. We arrived there the following evening, but once again the hotel had disappeared and the whole place was unrecognisable. What's more, the town was full. We did find two beds, but in different establishments. My host was a thickset Afrikaaner, a retired South African rugby player, and one of those men who cannot bear a moment's silence. I stood at the bar among several strangers and he stood behind it bubbling and seething like an old Dickensian kettle. It didn't matter how inane his remarks were, as long as he was saying something.

'Hey, Ted, are you all right there? Have you got what you want? Now, would you believe it, Ted here has come all the way from Johannesburg on his bike. Oh, from London, is it? Yes, all the way from London.'

Well, what's twelve thousand miles between friends?

'Now John here, he travels a lot too, eh! I'm sure he'd like to hear some of your stories. What do you do, John? Oh, prisons, is it? That's wonderful. I am sure Ted here will be very interested to hear . . .'

Well, to tell the truth I was. It seems they were going up at an astonishing rate. Full of blacks, too. Needless to say there were no blacks to be seen here, or anywhere we'd been, except as servants. So much for the passing of apartheid.

Later, as we rode on to East London and Port Elizabeth, we glimpsed big housing developments out in the hills, but too far off to know what they were like, and there was no apparent access. The road along the south coast to Cape Town is known as the Garden Route, and most of it is quite pretty. We stayed at good places and, on one occasion, some well-wishers even fixed me up with satin sheets. As I said, it didn't really count as travelling any more, but when you thought of it as the reward for coming a very long way, it had its place in the scheme of things.

'Bubbles' had a gorgeous blonde girlfriend, Sophie, with an apartment overlooking the ocean at Camps Bay, just east of Cape Town, and even though he had to leave the following day, they let me stay on, which speaks volumes for our friendship, or my ineligibility. Manfred and his crew arrived soon after for the final shoot, and we spent four hectic days filming on the roads and in various locales.

I made one more attempt to follow up with the UN volunteers, and they made contact for me with a shelter for homeless children on the streets of Cape Town. It was a riveting experience. I learned how extraordinarily accomplished these kids became at survival, with all their little tricks and techniques. They are so proud of their skills that despite the brutality of their day-to-day lives, they usually preferred it to any kind of home that was offered them. So, in a way,

I finally found out where Africa's wildlife had got to. It's to be found in the streets of the cities. It's a species called Street Kids.

The crew flew away on 11 August. I had a ticket on British Airways for the 13th. In that forty-eight-hour window I had to organise the shipping of my bike to Brazil. Transport by sea was impossible, but I thought I had arranged for South African Airways to fly the bike to Rio de Janeiro strapped to a pallet. It almost didn't happen. All the information I had gathered turned out to be wrong, and if it hadn't been for Mark Chandler, body-builder, motorcyclist and one-time contender for the title of Mr South Africa, I would have had to cancel my flight. Mark's packing business, Cape Crating, boxed the bike and solved all my problems with no notice at all.

Mark was a tall white man in his thirties with a shaven head. Fifteen years earlier he had crashed a big Kawasaki, broken count-less bones, lost half his bodyweight in recovery and got diabetes to boot; but now he had all his strength and vigour back, and if he was a bit cocky with it I could hardly blame him. All the men who worked for him were black or 'coloured'. They seemed to have a great working relationship, and yet Mark was no more politically correct than I am. He didn't think much had changed for the better since apartheid. He said he heard blacks say it was better in the old days.

It's not the first time I found myself liking someone I disagreed with so strongly, but it's happened more often in South Africa than anywhere else. I didn't say much. He lived there, I didn't.

21

It was a bit difficult to come back to Rio in 2001 as an old man. Not that I felt old. After all, I had just ridden my bike from London to Cape Town and managed to survive, and I was told often enough that I looked young for my years. But in a way that made it worse, to be an old man pretending to be young. A man of seventy is never going to be looked at in the same light as a man of forty-three. I was all too aware of my fading powers. The pheromones were flowing in the opposite direction, and the aphrodisiac thrill was decidedly lacking. I couldn't even ride in, heroically, from the mountains because my bike was sitting at the airport in a box.

In this new century there was no ship of dreams to carry me across the Atlantic. That was just one of the reasons why my journey of the seventies could not be made today. Shipping is containerised. Ports are inhospitable to people. To insist on remaining close to the surface when crossing oceans has become unreasonable, expensive and sometimes impossible. To want to do it in the company of a motorcycle is eccentric, to say the least. My BMW arrived in Rio in a crate, and I flew in myself a while later.

Does it matter? Of course it does: everything matters. How does it matter? Who can say what those precious days afloat between continents might be worth? I only know that my days on the *Zoë. G* were priceless. I believe that to be flipped through the air from one continent to another diminishes them both, in a way that is contemptuous of space. But contempt for space and time characterises the age we live in, and it would be foolish to deny it.

Since the purpose of this journey (the public purpose at least) is to give an account of how things have changed in getting on for three decades, I am not going to pretend they haven't. There was a time, not so very long ago, when people who crossed oceans to live on another continent knew that they could not expect to see their homelands ever again. Then, for a while, when air travel was still in its infancy, small merchant ships were accessible to passengers. That seems to me to have been a golden age of travel, and I caught the last rusty particle of it on the *Zoë. G*, but now it is past.

The people who go to sea as passengers these days are as containerised in their vast floating hotels as the cargo that chugs past them in the night. And if a hundred flying-fish were to burst out of the water below them I don't suppose that from the tenth floor they would even be visible.

Rio was enjoying a beautiful warm spring day when I came off the plane on Saturday morning, 1 September. I had lost four hours on the way, but I was in excellent shape thanks to my friend Jacques, he with the miraculous Air Pass. In the absence of tramp steamers, 'Shuttle Jacques' had offered to become the official carrier for Jupiter Two – a marvellously generous gift.

He flew me from Cape Town to San Francisco in ultimate luxury and, two weeks later, again travelling first-class, we came off the plane together in Rio. We went through the nothing-to-declare channel, sharing my carry-on luggage because Jacques typically carries almost nothing. Among other things I had a new helmet (a Schuberth 4 to replace the Nolan which, sadly, had come to the end of its useful life) and a pair of slick BMW boots that fitted me well. What pleased me even more was that I had managed to reduce my total load by fifty pounds.

Jacques sat with the luggage while I figured out what to do next. That was the deal. He took care of the air. I looked after the ground. At airports, every taxi driver becomes your instant bosom buddy, and with the help of a self-appointed 'friend' I bought a few reales at a lousy rate of exchange, so that I could buy a phone card, so that I could phone my dear friend Lulu.

Yes, Lulu. Lovely Lulu was still there. She was rather tired from a late night out, but she knew where to send me, and I passed the phone over to my new 'friends' (there were now two of them). They tried to tell her that what I really wanted was a hotel in the thick of Copacabana's sex industry, but she was firmly unflattering about my immediate needs, and insisted on a hotel opposite a museum. As a result the 'friends' (who by now had become three) got away only with doubling the taxi fare.

Twelve dollars seemed a not unreasonable surcharge to apply to two Anglo-Saxon non-Portuguese-speaking, apparently witless tourists arriving in Rio. We got a good view of the Sugar Loaf and the Corcovada, and I was happy to let the imposition go. The hotel was close to the studio where Lulu was putting some young girls through their routines, and we went to watch for a while. Then we all had dinner together before Jacques took a taxi back to the airport and was wafted away into the friendly skies.

If it hadn't been for Lulu, I think I might have been quite desolate. My crown of laurels had long since withered and shed its leaves. The millionaire Baby Bocayuva had gone, having died much earlier from some kind of cancer. So had Marcia Kubitschek, from a disease that had been dogging her for years. (How I mourned that beautiful face.) Esmeralda was polite. I met Dalal, Bocayuva's widow, later at a performance of *Swan Lake*, a strange 'concept' production in which men with hairy legs also danced in tutus. Dalal smiled sweetly, but she was too busy now to spend time on me.

The hotel Lulu had found for me was the Imperial, in a street called Catete, and I came to like it very well. The price, equivalent to twenty-seven dollars a night, was acceptable, especially given that a breakfast there could last you through the day. My room was rather like an old-fashioned steamer cabin, with a lot of polished wood, built-in furniture and a partially obscured window, and it suited the rather nostalgic mood I had fallen into.

The hotel had cable television and I spent quite a bit of time wandering through the channels. I could get CNN, of course, which was almost entirely preoccupied with stock prices, Israelistine and the weather. The BBC seemed to be aping CNN, and was more exciting for its theme music and graphics than for the news it presented. I remembered how good the soaps used to be in Brazil and went searching for them. One night I wandered too far beyond the pale and came across a pornography channel which showed virtually non-stop close-ups of a penis hard at work in various human orifices. There was nothing erotic about it at all, and it did not hold my attention for long, but I found it shocking, and it invaded my mind. From that time on, whatever else I might be watching, I was always vaguely aware that somewhere in the vicinity there was a penis relentlessly plunging away.

Of course the hotel, and all its amenities, were only a backdrop to Rio and everything I had to accomplish, and the first thing was to get my bike out of its box and back on the road. This was more than just a practical necessity. All the flying about I had done, and my brief return home to deal with mundane domestic matters, had weakened my attachment to the journey. I wanted badly to be identified again as a traveller, an adventurer, something apart. I needed the bike to validate my mission.

But first I had Sunday to become reacquainted with Lulu. Being a ballet dancer, the years had hardly changed her, either in manner or in appearance, even though in the interim she had been married and widowed. Incredible what that physical discipline can do for a body. Then on Monday Lulu drove me out to the old airport, called Galeão, where the cargo terminal is now. I have countless reasons to be grateful to Lulu, and this was only one more of them, but it was a very big favour indeed.

I have learned only two ways to approach bureaucracies. One is to think of them as a horrible and obstructive waste of time, energy and money, and a dreadful debasement of the human spirit. This naturally leads to bad feelings all round. It usually makes the process even longer and more tedious than it needs to be, and I come out dripping venom and feeling sorry for myself. The other way is to regard it as a useful opportunity to observe a class of humanity I usually avoid, offering rich prospects of comedy and satire, at a price almost worth paying.

At the airline office Lulu put everyone immediately in a good mood. As a result Roberto, the clerk, explained to her in detail everything we would have to do, and also gave us *cafesinhos*, little cups of strong, sweet coffee. This was a very good sign. He then gave us a bundle of papers, charged me a twenty dollars tax, and sent us into the bonded area. We had to show our IDs at a gate, and get passes. Then we went to see Marcello.

Marcello was a new bureaucrat. He had pastel-coloured steel filing cabinets, metal furniture and a modern computer, and he wore blue and white clothes. He was a chubby young man, seemingly pleasant, with obvious intelligence which allowed me to overlook his self-important manner. Lulu worked her charms on him, and he became our point man, as it were, pointing us to all the various offices we had to visit.

First we went around the corner and up the stairs to find Fernando. He was a thin, tobacco-stained individual who belonged to the old bureaucracy. All his furniture was brown and wooden, people were crammed into small spaces, under deluges of paper, and he wore brown clothes. All the same, he was very nice. I have to stress that everybody was extremely nice and laughed a lot. This is the effect that Lulu has on people, but it is only fair to add that *brasileiros* like to laugh.

Wooden crates, they say, can harbour parasites, so we went to visit the Ministry of Agriculture, in the shape of a pleasant woman who gave us a form in triplicate. It had a lot of information on it, but the carbons were no good, so none of it came through. This didn't matter. The only important thing on it was the number on top. We brought this trophy back to Marcello and he set about inventing a new document, probably the most serious work a bureaucrat can do. It was printed out five times, and I signed four of the copies.

We now had the beginnings of a dossier, which included:

1. two original waybills, one blue, one pink, and two photocopies of it
2. photocopies of my passport details and entry stamp

3. a printout showing what Varig had done with the crate, and
   where it now was
4. the agriculture release
5. Marcello's four-page document in triplicate
6. a photocopy of my *carnet de passage*
7. a photocopy of the orginal title to the bike.

Then we were out of time, so we gathered up our dossier, and brought it back next morning.

Marcello was still in good humour. He sent us up to another office on the first floor where I paid the price for all this entertainment. It came in the form of storage fees, because the bike had been there almost two weeks. I swallowed bravely, paid two hundred dollars, and brought the receipt back to Marcello who added it to our bundle. And now, dear reader, we were finally ready to approach the customs officer.

She was a charming black lady with glasses, whose name was Cely. Lulu got on very well with her. Cely browsed through our stack of paper, and then ordered the crate to be brought outside her office. Lunchtime intervened but Cely returned even before the appointed hour, and I was impressed.

The crate now stood outside, on the floor of the customs facility, and when I went out there I was quite overwhelmed. I saw an enormous space, of cathedral proportions, obviously just constructed and full of immense, newly painted steel racks and imposing, supermodern machinery. Lulu asked about it on my behalf, and she said it was able to stack and move something like ninety thousand items. For the first time I could really believe that Brazil had made some kind of quantum leap since I was here last, but at the same time I was glad that the massive space was still largely empty.

Cely gave the word, and men with hammers and crowbars took off the top and one of the sides of the crate. Crouched there, with its front wheel tucked alongside it, the bike looked rather like a beast at bay, hemmed in by straps and tapes. The huge white Acerbis tank looked even more enormous than usual, like the barrel chest of a one-eyed bull, and the bars, set askew to fit in the box, might have been the horns of the animal, swerving to hook an unwary matador.

Cely looked at it from every angle. She read the registration plate and the chassis number. The engine number is almost impossible to see, and she took my word for it. Everybody posed for pictures, and then Cely had them nail the boards back in place. It was only going to be moved about a hundred yards, but nothing must leave the facility unpacked. It's a rule, or maybe it's a mystery.

I had already asked permission to put the bike together again outside, and it was happily granted. Lulu drove herself home and for an hour I had an enthusiastic audience as I slowly recreated the motorcycle on the loading dock. We had even remembered to bring petrol, and at 4 p.m. I rode into Rio. We had got the bike out in a record time of two days. In 1974 it took me two weeks just to get a front wheel through customs.

I gave myself four days to enjoy Rio, to repack the bike and to make sure everything was working properly, and on Sunday morning I started out on the long ride north.

22

To be in Brazil and not to revisit the place where I was locked up and afraid for my life would be unthinkable. For all the trauma that I suffered there at the time, the port of Fortaleza also fascinated me. It was a direct link to scenes of intrigue, corruption and decay in the tropics that I used to read about in Conrad and Greene and Maugham. I wanted to know how it would feel to be back where I had once experienced so much fear.

Close to two thousand miles of road lay between me and Fortaleza, two-thirds of an enormous country, and afterwards I would have to come back south again to continue towards Argentina. I contrived a loop that would take me up the coast and then bring me back a little way inland on the route I had taken in 1974. One could spend a rewarding year travelling all those miles through such a wildly entertaining country, but I gave myself only two weeks. Why? Because much later on in this journey, when I had circled the south of the continent and was coming north again through the high Andes, I wanted to avoid the rains of January that had almost cut me off the first time around.

Short of becoming an aimless wanderer, there seemed no way to escape these calculations, and yet I know better than most how much is lost by them. I was going to ride about four hundred miles a day in uncertain conditions, so there would be little hope of chance meetings and spontaneous hospitality. I was resigned to staying at hotels, and chose Linhares as a useful first stop,

although it had nothing to offer, apparently, but furniture factories.

The coastal road north from Rio, the BR 101, leads across the
Niteroi Bridge, a long viaduct with a hump in the middle that spans
the neck of the bay, and I found it easily enough after making only
one mistake, which is about par for the course. The road surface was
decent, the weather good, and the bike lighter than it had been in
Africa.

Sunday, as it happened, was Brazil's Independence Day. I saw
parades with prancing horses, and uniformed riders flourishing
flags. Just looking around me, I thought that people in Brazil were
better off than they had been. Clothes, vehicles, houses, roadside
services, all appeared to have improved. The people of Brazil are
naturally cheerful, but it seemed that they had good reason to be
optimistic, which made a pleasant change after Africa. I passed a
factory, dormant because of the public holiday, but obviously very
productive. Thousands of brand-new cars, in protective coatings,
were marshalled around it.

The traffic was all on the other side, going south, and that's where
I saw my first accident. The Polícia Militar (which is not really military) was coming up fast behind me, lights flashing, and at first I
thought it was coming for me, but it stopped a little way ahead
where a crowd had gathered across the road. Cars were passing
slowly, with drivers gawping at an adolescent boy stretched out
motionless on his back, surrounded by a litter of palm fronds or
thatching materials. I thought he could easily have been dead. He
wasn't poor: I could see he was wearing a good-quality grey woollen
jumper. Then I was past, and it was behind me. I started thinking,
How would it be to lose my son Will now, just as he was turning into
such a fine young man? For a while, every lithe young male seen
from behind looked like Will.

At one point along the road I was suddenly in serious trouble. I
was experimenting for the first time with earplugs, and the instant
dramatic silence was so overwhelming that I lost the sense of my
own speed. I came into a junction too fast, and couldn't avoid a
small forest of cats' eyes. I was in among them before I realised that

they were raised about six inches above the surface on apparently
rigid supports. I had never seen anything on the road like it before.
To fall among them would have been disastrous, and for a moment
I was in real danger, but got through it without being thrown. I was
sharply reminded that roads in Brazil are not designed with motorcycles in mind.

Aside from that, the only recurring menace was a particular kind
of driver I encountered from time to time. He would be about fifty,
with carefully groomed greying hair and a fabulous tan, and he
would be driving a fairly expensive car containing beautiful young
people. Obviously it would be supremely important for him to prove
that he was a match for Montoya, or any other Grand Prix driver,
and it was essential to overtake me regardless of the consequences.
I did my best to help him prove his virility by staying out of his way.

The scenery was enticing. The Sugar Loaf peaks of Rio flattened into those well remembered jelly-mould hills, clothed in green
and decorated with cows, pretty wooden fences and interesting
older buildings. Police road blocks and inspection points appeared
frequently, which meant slowing down almost to walking pace, but
I was never stopped, and in spite of them I made good time to
Linhares, where I worked my way into the centre of town just as the
sun was going down.

An important football match was in progress. It was warm out.
Crowds of men were gathered around cafés and shop windows,
watching television. Two uniformed cops in a car were parked outside one café, staring at the screen. Mentally brushing up my
Portuguese, I asked the way to the Linhares hotel.

'Turn right up there,' said one, pointing, 'then left after the
church.'

I found the hotel. A room was thirty reals, cash, or thirty-eight
reals on a credit card. Which would *you* choose?

Dinner was in a restaurant across the road, under fluorescent
white light guaranteed to kill any atmosphere there might have
been, but otherwise comfortable. I had two fillets of fish smothered
with tiny rubbery shrimps in a sauce. The little squiggles under the
sauce looked like a dead language waiting to be deciphered. I love

shrimp, which is why I have eaten more tasteless shrimp than any other food. I keep hoping, and trying. There *is* good shrimp, so why not here? It's only a few miles to the ocean.

Afterwards I walked around the corner to the church, which was extremely ugly. Of all the ugly churches I have seen in the world, the majority were in Brazil and they were invariably made of concrete. Maybe some penitent industrialist bequeathed a cement plant to the church. The style would be 'modern', licensed I suppose by the revolutionary architecture of Brasilia, but the inspiration was lost somewhere along the way, and they all had the look of something you might buy from a catalogue. This one was made of two tall concrete wedges, placed in parallel, pointy edge up, with a barn in between. The wedge facing the road had a sixty-foot cement cross on the front of it; and the suggestion of a sixty-foot body, bleeding, I found very oppressive.

The entrance was beneath the cross, and the interior was large, white and featureless. At the far right stood a group of five musicians, all with their own microphones, playing and singing hymns to a soft rock beat. It was strictly background music, and the congregation paid no attention. At the far end a priest went about the business of saying mass, also curiously detached from everything around him.

A lot of young women sporting their navels over low-cut jeans were clustered around the entrance, practising their cool, as though they were waiting for something or for someone to spot them. The pews were full, so I supposed the church was a success, but I couldn't really see what brought them in. There was no sense of occasion or ceremony, let alone spirituality. Perhaps, after the football game, it was the only show in town. Facing the church from a strip of grass in the middle of the road was a figure of Pope John in stone, set there in 1966. He at least seemed satisfied with what he saw. I found it fascinating. Thank goodness one doesn't have to like something to find it interesting.

The second day's ride to Itabuna was hard work, but still largely without incident, and my only problem was with an increasingly painful saddle rash on my thighs. This surprised me, because I had been quite comfortable all the way through Africa. I put on some sticky yellow ointment, intended originally for dogs' ears, that a medical friend had passed on to me, and eventually it gave me some relief.

On the third day I aimed for Aracaju, another coastal city I knew nothing about. The country north of Itabuna seemed specially nice. The greens were brighter, the reds of the tiles more vivid, and the road crossed some very attractive rivers. It was another very long ride and I was tired, my muscles were aching, and it was already dark when I got to the edge of Aracaju. The city seemed enormous. I had picked out a hotel to aim for but, as usual with guides, the map showed only a small section of the town with no hint of how to get there. Often, in fact, the guides (and I include them all) give a completely false impression of the scale of cities. You think you are headed for some modest community of ancient churches, monuments, plazas and museums, and find yourself in a megalopolis of slums and oil refineries.

I rode for a long time, trying to maintain a sense of direction, looking for a sign with a recognisable name and finally, with some luck, I found the place I was looking for, but it was full. They gave me a map of the city, and suggested there were more hotels along the *costa*. When I got there I assumed I was on the edge of the ocean, but in fact I was on the south shore of a river, the Sergipe, Aracaju being built on an estuary.

It might as well have been the ocean. There were coconut palms, sandy beaches and water in the darkness on one side of the esplanade, and on the other, big houses and a few hotels. I wound up in a much bigger hotel than I would normally have chosen, but I didn't feel the incentive to go on looking because, in terms of dollars, everything was so cheap. It was the low season. All the hotels were cutting their prices, and I found myself in luxury, across from the beach, for thirty dollars.

The hotel was so good that I was able to pick up my email, and I got a message from a friend in America who was training to be an airline pilot. I had asked him how it was going, and his message said that in spite of the horrific news he was still going ahead with his plan.

I didn't know what he was talking about.

I had a shower, opened a can of Brahma beer from the *frigobar*, and switched on the TV.

The first thing I saw as the screen lit up was a plane flying into a tall building. The voice-over was in rapid Portuguese. Like millions of others, I assumed I was watching a Hollywood disaster movie, and switched over to CNN. The disaster was no movie. It was 11 September 2001.

The terrible events of that day were, of course, a turning-point, and led to far-reaching effects on the world at large and on my personal fortunes. At the time it was impossible to comprehend the meaning of it. Some Arabs had pulled off an extraordinarily destructive stunt, but who they were or what their ultimate purpose might be was obscure.

Lying on the bed of my hotel room in Aracaju, I watched the Twin Towers collapse for the tenth time, and I still could not connect with the disaster emotionally. I had no family or close friends in New York. There was no one in the room with me, so I was spared from having to make hypocritical proclamations of grief. Thousands had died, but then thousands had died many times in my long life. I could feel more grief for the thousands who were massacred at Srebrenica, staring into the eyes of their murderous countrymen, or for the hundreds of thousands slashed to a pulp by their neighbours in Rwanda. To see it coming, to see the guns being raised, to see the pangas flashing in the sunlight, that would be pure horror.

But this thing in New York, from where I watched it, was overwhelmingly a spectacle. And so remote. Not just distant in miles, but culturally in another world. It was unreal.

Almost immediately my mind flashed back to my time as a newspaper editor in London. Looking for items to pad out the news pages of the early editions, before the day had really begun, we went to the news services, Reuters, Associated Press, who wired what were called overnight fillers. Often they would be short, laconic reports of distant calamities. To grab our attention the calamity would have to be proportional to the distance. An avalanche that killed ten in Austria would have to kill a hundred in Chile to be worth its space. To match a house that collapsed in Rome, an entire skyscraper would have to disintegrate in Brazil. A thousand would have to drown in the Yangtse to equal a small boy falling into the Thames.

Here in Aracaju it was happening in reverse. The fantastic events in New York had that same disembodied quality, strained of feeling.

By now twelve hours had passed since the planes hit the towers and it was known who had planned and carried out the attack. Like most people I knew nothing about Al Qaeda or bin Laden, but I was certainly aware that in poorer parts of the world there was much resentment of American power and influence, and not just from those Muslims who regarded America as their anti-Christ – the enemy of Allah.

By an unhappy coincidence, 11 September was also the date when a junta of Chilean generals, aided and abetted by the USA, had bombed and killed their own president, Salvador Allende, in 1973 and ushered in a decade of dreadful torture and repression. The military dictatorship that had locked me up in Brazil also found favour in Washington. So did the generals who later conducted the 'dirty war' in Argentina, not to mention the death squads of El Salvador and Guatemala, and many other instances of manipulation by American interests. With these thoughts, and many others, in the back of my mind, it came as no surprise that someone would want to punch Uncle Sam on the nose. I just could not, at that time, bring myself to dwell on the awful fate of those thousands of innocent victims. In fact it was their very innocence that seemed to me to be part of the problem. Far too many Americans, I felt, were innocent of the impact their country was making on the world at large.

I went out into the soft tropical night to find something to eat, and walked a long way over sand, among palms and clusters of kiosks closed for the night, my thoughts darting all over the place as I still tried to grasp what had happened. There was a strange silence in the darkness around me, as though the world were receding.

Eventually I came to an outdoor restaurant where everything seemed comfortingly normal and peaceful. Confident that the food would be good, I ordered fish and a *caipirinha*, a favourite drink made from cane liquor and limes.

The gaily painted tables were spread out on a wooden platform over the sand. A boy was shining the shoes of a man at the next table, and flicked me a questioning glance to see if I wanted to be his next customer. I shook my head. The man must have heard me ordering and, assuming I was a gringo, leaned over and said in Portuguese, 'What a tragedy. So many dead.'

I agreed, solemnly, and he went back to his meal.

I reflected that all day people had known about this, but nowhere along the way had I seen or heard a hint of anything unusual. Whatever it was that had happened, out here it was on the margins of life. It would take a while to realise that this was not going to go away, and that it would change things, for the world, and for me.

23

From Aracaju to Recife should not have taken so long, but apparently something had happened to a bridge somewhere and I was sent on a huge diversion. Not that I was resentful, for it led me into a much more rural part of the country, but unfortunately I arrived in Recife too late to find my way to the beautiful old Portuguese centre. Like all the other cities, it had grown too big to penetrate easily.

I spent the night on the edge of it, and rode on to Canoa Quebrada. Now I was in the state of Ceará, and close to Fortaleza, but I wanted to visit Paul Moody first. He had sent me an email, and there was something about his way of expressing himself that intrigued me. I guessed that he was dyslexic, intelligent and imaginative. He had been a motorcycle courier in London, a desperately heroic way to make good money, both filthy and dangerous, and now he had become a hotel manager on a paradisiacal beach in Brazil. These remarkable self-transformations fascinate me – Bryn on Lake Malawi was another – because, having seen the myriad varieties of life it is possible to live on this earth, I am amazed that so many people condemn themselves to an unfulfilling existence in dreary circumstances. If I had to choose one reason above all others for taking pride in *Jupiter's Travels*, it lies in the numbers of people who say the book inspired them to change their lives. ('Thanks for giving me the strength to give up this sod-awful job,' wrote one of them.)

Paul had made the change without my help. He had used his earnings to take exotic holidays, until he found what he was looking for – a fabulous beach, a young Brazilian girl who wanted to marry him, and a friend with some money to invest in a hotel. They built it together and called it Pousada California.

Canoa grew fast. I'm sure when I was first in Brazil it was only a fishing village. Now every house on the main street had its hand out for tourists, but it was still small, intimate and enjoyable. Paul welcomed me in his laconic, noncommittal London way, and I stayed there a few days because I needed to stop and absorb the meaning of what had happened in the world before I moved on to Fortaleza.

My experiences in Fortaleza in '74 were so intense that the feel and smell and shape of it, as it was then, are as deeply ingrained in me as any formative locale in my life's story. I had never heard of the place before I arrived there, and so of course I took it as I found it, which was old, and poor and sodden with rain. May is a rainy season on the north coast, but that year was exceptionally wet. I still see the soaked and decrepit façades of the old buildings alongside the docks where I landed. All over the city broken pavements reared up through sand and floodwater. The grim black brick cathedral loomed over a cobbled square where thinly clad peasants, driven out of the flood-stricken countryside, lay huddled on the paving, sleeping like the dead. Epic amounts of rain fell from the thick grey blanket of cloud, so that even three degrees south of the equator I shivered at night, locked up with only a thin nylon shirt on. I had to cover myself with a filthy straw mattress to ward off the cold, damp air.

It was not an entirely miserable time. The Irish missionary priests who sheltered me before and after my incarceration inspired me by their selfless aid to the wretched and downtrodden. With Father Marcello – also known as Patrick Lavery – I had taken a bus trip to a flooded town in the interior called Iguatu, where I saw just how bad things were, and it was this visit, when I photographed a bridge, that triggered my imprisonment. I was held for two weeks. Afterwards the priests helped me to recover from the moral and physical sickness of the ordeal, and I never forgot them.

Of course the dictatorship, by now, was long gone, and the entire coast was bathed in September sunshine, but even so I was quite unprepared for the shock I felt on entering Fortaleza. The other cities I had passed through since Rio I had hardly known, if at all. I could tell only that they had grown enormously. By contrast, the Fortaleza I *had* known, had simply disappeared. In its place what I saw was a modern, prosperous city, with shopping malls, luxury shops and hotels, pedestrian precincts and well maintained streets. The docks appeared to have been completely rebuilt, and the coast gloried in a fashionable esplanade, the Praia do Iracema, lined with modern twenty-storey apartment blocks. The population had increased from one million to three. Money from the textile and shoe industries had showered down on the city and its beaches, and Fortaleza had become one of the most popular tourist resorts in Brazil.

At first it was impossible for me to find my bearings. The key was the cathedral, once only a short walk from the headquarters of the Polícia Federal, and I had to rub my eyes in amazement before I could finally accept that I had found it. That gaunt black structure had been entirely covered over in pale-grey cement, which left it even uglier, but also strangely diminished. The cobbles had gone, replaced by tarmac. The cathedral was fenced in. Whole roads had been built over. There was no place here for displaced *flagelados* to sleep, and the prostitutes who used to swing their bags around the cathedral had been moved off.

I found the place where I was once locked up. Now it was just an innocent-looking villa. Once it had sprouted seriously imposing radio antennae, and a fleet of menacing black cars had roared in and out of a basement garage. From this building General Ernesto Geisel, the military dictator, extended his iron rule over the whole state of Ceará. Now it had been converted, of all things, into a cultural centre. I stood in front of it trying to relive the fear I had experienced there, and couldn't do it. Too many years had passed. It was history. I would have to read my own book to know how I had felt. Even so, my curiosity was intense. What would it be like inside? I remembered well the place where I was interrogated, the tiled room where I shivered for hours on end, the dark stairs that led to what I fancifully thought of as dungeons.

But once inside I could see that it had all been rebuilt. The room where they held me was now the office of a grey-bearded poet who listened to my story with a half-smile. 'How long were you in here?' he asked.

'Fourteen days,' I replied.

'Ah,' he said. 'I was here for a hundred and twenty.'

He was gracious enough to shake my hand. I asked to see the basement, still hoping for a thrill, remembering the coughs and groans I had heard down there. The director, an older man, took me down but it was not the same. The cells had all been remodelled, except for one. With its iron-barred door still intact it was used for storing office supplies.

I asked the director if there was some sense of triumph at having turned this hateful place into a cultural centre. He looked at me intently, struggling to express his bitter thoughts. 'There was no triumph. This was not Cuba. There was no revolution. People just let it slip by. If we take down this last cell door, everything will be forgotten.'

I could see what he meant. When you mentioned the *ditadura* to people they were likely to say 'That was bad', then move on quickly to other topics. Unlike the Chileans and Argentines, they just didn't want to think about it.

I wasn't entirely fooled by all the glitter. Just because peasants couldn't sleep in the streets any more didn't mean there was no poverty, and I knew that if I could find the priests I had known there I would also find the poor. Again it was hard to orientate myself. Whole neighbourhoods seemed to have changed, but eventually I did locate the diocese of São Raimundo, and the hostel where, in my convalescence, I had once watched fruit-bats swooping about in the garden at dusk. To my delight Father Marcello was still there, sixty-seven years old now, thin and stooped but bright as ever, with an impish eccentricity about him. He enjoyed my arrival very much, I felt, and showed me around all the critical scenes of my past drama, but again it was all ancient history.

Then he told me where to find Ned Going. Ned and Brendan

Walsh (who later left the priesthood) were the two I remembered as the firebrands of the group, the ones most anxious to deal practically with the injustices inflicted on the people. So it came as no surprise that Ned was living in one of the slums, known in Brazil as *favelas*. We got him on the phone and I heard his big, bold voice inviting me to come and see for myself.

These priests belonged to the Redemptionist order. Their vows are chastity, poverty and obedience. For myself, of course, I regard chastity as optional, and the obedience is between them and their superiors in the order, but their willingness to live in poverty is a great gift to the world. Although the poor may be helped in other ways, I am sure that only by sharing their conditions can one really understand what is useful to them, and Ned was shining proof of that.

It was hot when I arrived, and he came out of his hovel to greet me with a wide smile, wearing nothing but jeans, sandals and his spectacles, but he later covered his greying chest hair with a shirt for the camera. He lived and worked in two tiny rooms built of unfinished hollow-core bricks, but he was very well connected, with a computer and a mobile phone. He seemed strong and healthy, and needed to be. He and his colleague had been given the job of 'looking after' twenty *favelas* altogether, and they got around on small motorbikes. The *favela* he lived in was not too bad. Most of the buildings were of brick, but he explained that it had taken a while to get that far.

'When they first moved in here, they were kicked out and their homes were destroyed,' Ned told me. 'That happened seven times. Then they were left alone because they became very clever.

'You see, this whole area has been laid out for development. There are spaces for private houses, and spaces for public streets. They managed to get hold of the plans, and they've only put up their houses where the streets would be. Because they're on public property it will be much harder for the municipality to kick them off without rehousing them.'

Especially since it would have to take place under the nose of the powerful state governor. High above us, overlooking the *favela* and the ocean, the governor had his mansion, and next to it was the equally imposing home of one of Brazil's star footballers, Jardel.

Ned delighted in these stratagems, although he would deny indignantly (with a wink) having had any part in them himself.

'Have you heard of the MST?' he asked. 'No? Oh you must get into that. 'The Movimento dos Sem Terra [the landless movement] is very strong now, all over the country. They had a big demonstration here recently. The governor wouldn't speak to them, so they got a crowd out on the big avenue along the beach and blocked it completely.'

The police couldn't move them, and in the end they decided to surround them and starve them out. But people came up behind the police cordon and threw food over their heads. Ned, of course, was in the thick of it.

'When that first loaf of bread came flying over,' he said, beaming through his glasses, his Irish brogue getting broader all the time, 'well, I can't tell you how good it felt.'

Finally one night the governor sent a fleet of buses and ordered the police to ship them out by any means, but someone got wind of the plan. Journalists rushed down there.

'I hurried down myself. We all had cellphones and we were calling all over the world, human rights organisations and so on.'

The governor was suddenly flooded with calls of protest, and couldn't go through with it. Eventually he agreed to meet with them. 'Actually most of their demands were met. They went away quite peacefully.'

Even Ned agreed that for the poor in Brazil things are better than they were, but he reminded me that while I had been away the population had increased from 100 million to 170 million. The improvement lay in the fact that there had in the past been 30 million living below the subsistence level, and that figure had not changed.

24

At times the inland route south from Fortaleza was very difficult. Most of it was still two-lane and this was where most of the heavy truck traffic went. North of Salvador, there were many miles so broken up that they were more pothole than road surface. Truck drivers would do anything to save their suspensions, and swung wildly from one side of the road to the other looking for any smooth tarmac they could find. When two strings of traffic met, the effect was awesome. Huge twenty-six-wheel vehicles cavorted around each other as in a drunk-driving nightmare. This tipsy tarantella of titanic trucks and tankers was a wonder to behold, but a dangerous distraction for a motorcyclist.

Iguatu, where I once went to see only floods, disaster and poverty, was now a thriving town. I still had a very clear recollection of how the town had looked then, and I thought it would be a good measure of how things had really changed. The improvements were dramatic.

If you have a copy of *Jupiter's Travels* you will be able to find in it a picture I took in Iguatu at that time. It shows a church and another religious building and some almost naked children standing in front of the camera. I took the picture because of the misery those buildings and their surroundings reflected. They stood grey, grimy and oppressive on a patch of muddy ground. Those same buildings were still there today, but clean, resurfaced, handsomely decorated, and in paved and landscaped grounds. If it were only the churches that had dressed themselves up like this I would of course have felt deceived, but the whole town was bright, pleasant and prosperous.

One of the more striking things I noticed, coming back to Brazil after so long, was that people no longer had any true recollection of how it was then, even if they were old enough to have known it at that time. There have been so many small changes over a long period, that their views were formed largely by what had happened in recent years. Sometimes they would tell me that things were worse, when to me the opposite was abundantly obvious. It was very pleasant to be able to say how much better things were in Brazil, but I could see that I was not taken very seriously.

The petrol stations in the north of the country are like sprawling villages, full of life and with a culture all their own. There would be a central row of buildings, with an office, a shop, a service station and a restaurant, called a *lanchonete* or *churrascaria*. There might be facilities for washing cars and trucks, maybe a separate shop for *eletro-mecânica*, and other freelance operations. As well as the pump attendants there were always others, men and boys, floating around looking for a chance to make a few centavos. They would generally hang out under the canopy near the pumps, or around the trucks where the *borracheiros* work.

Borracha in Portuguese means rubber, and the *borracheiro* was obviously the tyre repair man. His place of work, the *borracheria*, was usually separated from the pumps across a vast open space, to allow for trucks to be parked out of the way. Until this day I had had nothing to do with *borracheiros*, my Avon tyres having brought me all the way from England without a single puncture, but I noticed their existence everywhere, not only at the petrol stations but operating independently by the roadside. It may well have been the *borracheiro*, more than any other, that kept Brazil moving.

I was filling up on *gasolina comum* when two boys came up to look at the bike. It still attracted attention, even though motorcycles were very common now in Brazil, and having relearned a certain amount of Portuguese I could begin to take some pleasure in answering their questions. The boys were quite small, in tattered T-shirts, shorts and cheap sandals, and they carried their homemade shoe-shine boxes. I would have guessed they were about ten years old. One of them was brown-skinned, with a triangular face and exceptionally alert eyes. I found out later that he was thirteen. The other, a white boy with fairer hair, was eleven.

I am ashamed to say that it was the first of these two who pointed out to me that my rear tyre was flat. I had got so used to the Avons being impregnable that I rarely even looked at them. It was my time to meet the *borracheiros*. The tyre was not completely flat or it would certainly have let me know, and I was able to ride over to the rubber people.

In our own past history, and in parts of Asia today, you could tell certain groups of people apart because of the way their trade and way of life affected their appearance. I don't suppose I could have picked out a *borracheiro* in a crowd, but in his artisanal habitat he seemed to be remarkably consistent. For one thing, he was filthy. For another, he wore shorts, and a singlet (tank-top, if you like) the colour of washed grease. His place of work, compared with the rest of the buildings, was a brick hovel, but almost always whitewashed on the outside as if to proclaim that a man should not be judged by the colour of his material. And finally, he wore a sour expression until you talked to him, when, surprisingly, he smiled and became extraordinarily helpful.

About the smile I learned later. At the time I only knew that I felt totally insignificant among all the huge vehicles surrounding me, and doubted that my little machine would be taken seriously, so I was surprised when one of the men gathered around a dislocated truck detached himself, came over to me and, when I explained my problem, showed immediate enthusiasm.

I explained, as best I could, that I needed first to remove the boxes from the bike, and then the wheel, and his instant comprehension of my stunted Portuguese was even more impressive. So I began to undo the nuts that held the left box on to the carrier frame. By this time the boys had arrived. There were four lock-nuts to undo, and almost instantly the older boy grasped what had to be done. My routine was to loosen all the nuts first with a socket wrench and then to remove them and their washers by hand, but I had hardly loosened them before he began to unscrew them. I was annoyed. I didn't want him meddling with them – possibly losing them. He backed off but couldn't help, in the end, coming back to get at least one of them free.

I began to see that he really knew what he was doing, but what I liked most was his intent fascination with the process. I had got so used to people pretending interest in order to extract money. So we began to get on with each other.

Removing the wheel was relatively easy. Just four wheel-nuts to take out. All along he didn't make a false move. How can I explain this? In almost no time at all we generated a mutual respect that to me, at least, was immensely pleasing, and I have no doubt that at the back of my mind was the thought, If only I could share this same easy complicity with my own son.

The *borracheiro* took my wheel, pumped it up, and plunged it into his bath-tub. But however hard we looked there was no sign of a bubble. There was no puncture. What could I do but put the inflated wheel back again? The boys stayed with me, the older one helping without ever getting in the way. I developed a great respect for him, but still I was waiting for the pitch, the outstretched palm, and I could never have blamed them for asking – what a huge difference there was in our circumstances!

But it never came, and when finally I had put everything together, and pulled on my jacket, I gave them each a one-real note and felt very good about it. They walked off with much dignity. It was only then that I realised how soiled my hands were. I guessed the bathrooms were over by the main building, and as I made my way across I showed the younger boy the dirt on my hands. He whistled to his friend, who came over and instantly, with an extraordinary flourish, pulled out of his box a plastic bottle of mechanic's soap.

I wish I could convey all that was in that gesture. Pride, competence, alertness, individuality, self-respect. This kid, I thought, could become anything. This was what gave me faith in the human race.

*

The tyre, which was tubeless, continued to fall flat. In the end I got another *borracheiro* to put a tube inside it. I thought the tyre must have been damaged by those three potholes in Malawi. Avon sent me a new tyre in Rio, and that one stayed inflated.

25

It took almost three weeks to complete that four-thousand-mile loop and return to Rio, to the hotel on Catete, and to more good times with Lulu. How I love that city! It amazes me that people can be so easily intimidated by tales of violence into missing some of the best experiences the world has to offer. The pavements of Catete outside the Imperial Hotel are pure theatre at night. It was hard to leave.

I took the road south along the Emerald Coast and spent a couple of nights in Campinas with Amin Simaika, my friend from Cairo, hoping to set eyes one more time on the sword I had once carried halfway around the globe on my Triumph, but it was an heirloom that he shared with his brother, who had it for the time being. Amin and I had been in touch beforehand, so my arrival was no great surprise, but it was wonderful to see him again, with a little less hair perhaps and a bit more waist, but happily married and working as a translator. He still wore the same gruff, unsentimental, almost cynical manner which only barely hid a huge heart.

I was in the prosperous south of Brazil now, not too far from Argentina, and I knew the road would take me through Curitiba. I decided I would have to make an effort to find Marcio Grise. When I first set eyes on Marcio, in the stylish centre of Curitiba in 1974, he was hanging out with his biker friends in the main square. I had just come over the high road from São Paulo, a long, dirty and somewhat hazardous ride through freezing rain, fog and diesel fumes. Spattered with mud in my improvised rain gear, I must have looked like a homeless biker, which of course is what I was.

What I noticed first about them was the fat. All his friends, standing around with their clean new motorcycles, had comfortably plump bellies which they would stroke or pat from time to time in a self-conscious way. I was aware of it because in northern Brazil, where I had been for four months, everyone was lean if not positively emaciated. Marcio, however, was more than plump. He was a very fat man, and jolly too. I guessed him to be in his late twenties. Under a black helmet and long black hair his broad face sported a lavish black moustache, and he beamed amiably at me from his polished and spotless Suzuki.

'Come to my house,' he had said in Portuguese. 'You can sleep there tonight. You must be hungry, and cold.'

I had heard the words many times in various languages but they had never been more welcome. His pregnant wife Albaneira welcomed me into their bare apartment. He was a travelling rep for a drug company and still struggling to furnish the place, so we all had mattresses on the floor. I was there for two nights, bathing in their warmth and generosity. When I eventually left for Argentina Marcio insisted that we swap helmets so that he would have something to remember me by. I took a picture of this nice, friendly man and later put it into my book, but once I had left we were never in touch again.

Until twenty-eight years later, when I discovered his number in my notes and found, by sheer chance, that by putting a 2 in front of it I could still reach him on the phone. I called him from Amin's house. It was a bad line and I could get no sense of his mood, but I told him that I would be in Curitiba the next day.

'I was planning to go to Matto Grosso,' he said through static, 'but I will postpone the trip. Call me when you are in town.'

I was on the other side of São Paulo, Brazil's biggest city, and the ride through was an endless traffic jam alongside a stinking river, but once I got to the road over the mountains it was a pleasant, easy journey in sunshine on a much improved surface. I arrived in

Curitiba, a prosperous and tidy city, in the early afternoon and found a public phone. Marcio asked me to meet him in a car park on a big, well known square.

I waited there a while until he came walking towards me. I knew it had to be Marcio but I could not believe my eyes. In a crowd I would never have known him. This was a tall, slim man, almost hairless, in dress trousers and a formal pink shirt. His height surprised me. Remembering him fat I had assumed him to be short, but he was several inches taller than me.

He grasped my hand in a quite unexpected effusion of emotion.

'*Não posso* . . . I can't imagine it,' he cried, and there were tears in his eyes. 'This is like a dream. How incredible that you are here. You cannot know how wonderful—'

Almost speechless, he shook my hand again and again. As embarrassed as I was delighted, I listened to his outpouring of joy, which seemed at first so incongruous in a man of such formal appearance. He pulled himself together at last and pointed to his BMW saloon, asking me to follow him. After a short while we drove into the underground car park of some luxurious high-rise apartments on the Alameda Dom Pedro. He owned the two top floors, he said, and I realised that something remarkable must have happened to Marcio in those twenty-eight years.

We came through some heavy oak doors into his living area and there stood Albaneira, almost unchanged and smiling broadly. Then he asked her to fetch something, and she returned a moment later bearing, as though it were a bejewelled crown on a velvet cushion, my white polycarbonate helmet of 1974, polished, restored and curated like a museum piece.

For a moment I was overwhelmed and speechless. Then I could only laugh.

That was the beginning of two whirlwind days of hospitality and nostalgia. Marcio had become a supplier of medical equipment and had made a fortune. He had acquired a cattle ranch, a paint shop and various other businesses. He was a pilot and an instructor, and had his own plane. The unborn child of 1974 was his daughter Marcia, who now held a degree in agricultural science. She arrived soon after, and in good English explained that her father had never stopped talking about his meeting with me.

Something in that chance encounter had fired his imagination and he had drawn strength from it, strength he had needed, because some years later, having become grossly obese, he suffered a massive heart attack.

'I was dead,' he told me, 'but I came back. I don't know how, but it was to be born again, you know? I had to completely change my life, or I would die again for sure. I found this,' and he waved a white book at me, written by a doctor whose name I failed to record. 'He saved my life. You could say he is my religion, my guru. I eat only what he says,' and he reeled off the details of a draconian diet that had stripped away literally hundreds of pounds.

We had a wonderful couple of days and they did everything they could for me. Marcio took me all over Curitiba to visit the provinces of his personal empire, the white helmet dangling from one hand and my book in the other, ready to flip it open at his photograph and astonish his friends with this picture of the person he had once been.

I marvelled that merely by doing what I had wanted to do, by travelling around the world with no altruistic motive whatsoever, my appearance in their lives could have had such an invigorating effect on the people I had met along the way. Of course the virtue was theirs. They had to be willing to let me in, in the first place.

26

An enormous river, the Paraná, with its source in the very heart of Brazil, runs south to where the frontiers of Brazil, Paraguay and Argentina meet. There it gathers up the waters of the River Iguaçu, and rushes on down the continent to spill out finally into the ocean at Buenos Aires. That point where the three countries meet was a day's run of about four hundred miles from Curitiba.

One of my fondest memories from 1974 was of that ride, when I had stopped halfway in a cornfield to sling my hammock under a primitive thatched canopy that field workers had put up to shelter a threshing-floor. In the night an owl woke me, diving into the corn husks for a mouse.

The countryside was open, fertile and beautiful. It was one of the places where I had thought, I could come back and live on this land. I was glad to see now that it was still beautiful, but much more heavily populated, and there was no longer an obvious place to camp out. So I rode all the way to Foz, a little town on the border, and found lodging with a vivacious middle-aged Bulgarian blonde called Laura who was so turned on by the bike that I'm sure she would have come away on it if I'd asked.

Before the Iguaçu loses itself in the Paraná it creates one of the world's most spectacular sights, the Iguaçu Falls. Thank goodness I'd seen them when I had. Then, I just rode my bike out to the edge of the gorge and stared, trying to comprehend this astounding display of water crashing over the top of a mile and a half of precipice. Today, because of the pressure of sightseers, the viewing is strictly organised, with obligatory bus tours. I decided to leave my memories intact, and crossed over into Argentina. There is a new bridge over the Iguaçu which makes it easy, but the old ferry was so much better. You can't beat floating in.

I rode south through Misiones, where the crumbling remains of the old Jesuit missions still stand, and into the province of Entre Ríos. I remembered very well how much it had rained here in 1974, even if I didn't have my notes to remind me. In this part of the country, when it rains the dirt roads are impassable by anything on wheels. Geologically it's an area named after Mesopotamia, meaning it was formed by the silt laid down in a delta, so that the topsoil is very deep, extremely fertile, and without stone of any kind. When wet it's like soap.

Back then I came to visit the parents of a friend who had a ranch several miles from the small town of Villaguay. I was lucky and managed to sneak in between rain storms – back then, these were all dirt roads. Once there I was trapped (very comfortably, I should say) for weeks, but between storms I managed to get a Villaguay leather-worker started on some ambitious bags for the tank of my Triumph.

Now my elderly acquaintances at Campo Stella are long gone, but I stopped at Villaguay on my way to Buenos Aires, and to my delight I found Delio Quiroz, the saddler, shrivelled but alive at the age of ninety-three and still functioning. His shop was unchanged, although everything around it had grown and modernised so that now it seemed minuscule and Dickensian. It was a warm and wonderful meeting for me because I had once spent two days working with him, and it was with him that I learned what it is like to be apprenticed to a master. I told him that his bags were now in a British museum, and his eyes grew even larger and more luminous. He insisted on giving me a belt, and I insisted on him signing it. I wore it from then on, tucking my camel-leather belt from Cairo away in my bags.

This area is home to some of the most famous Argentine beef ranches. There actually is a town called Fray Bentos and another called Bovril, but the commercial centre is the provincial city of

Concordia, and I was able to get there despite more heavy rain along the way. I found a hotel, Las Palmas, near the Plaza de Mayo, which is one of those big squares that are such a happy feature of all Latin American towns. The rain stopped, and I spent the evening on the square, eating cheap and delicious beef and wandering around in the warm night air.

Concordia had obviously seen richer and better days, but now the whole of Argentina was once again plunged into one of its recurring crises. For the moment the peso was still clinging to the dollar, which made everything very expensive, but the economy was collapsing. How does one explain how a population of thirty million generally industrious and educated people, living in such a large, rich and fertile land, can be perpetually broke?

All the government offices were on the square, and I looked in through an open window of the police station. It was the records office. I couldn't believe what I saw there. On three walls, stacked to the high ceiling, were paper files, dark brown with age and frayed at the edges. Everything that was ever known about anybody in the entire province must have been recorded there – quite uselessly, I imagined – waiting to be excavated by some future historian. In the middle of the room stood one small wooden table holding an Underwood typewriter and a pile of carbon papers.

All of it, in the dim yellow lamplight, had a soft sepia glow. It was like an archaeological find, and this single image of a bureaucracy stranded in another age seemed to answer at least some of my questions about Argentina. It stayed with me a long time. What also stayed with me was a string of irritating bites I found on my skin when I got up in the morning. So the Palmas, while otherwise excellent, would not be my choice of hotel again.

I had friends on the edge of Buenos Aires, and one of them took me to a theatrical rehearsal in the city. Afterwards, at midnight, four of us went trundling back to the station in an old car. The other three were Argentine actors. They had been rehearsing *Titus Andronicus*, Shakespeare's political bloodbath, in Spanish, and all three had been murdered several times that day.

'What do they think of us in England?' asked the Emperor Saturnin, who was driving. 'Are we barbarians who eat grass?'

I told him the unpalatable truth. 'People who don't have connections with Argentina just don't think about you at all. It doesn't come up.'

Nobody seemed surprised, except me. It is astonishing how remote this part of the world seemed, both when I was at home and when I was there. Africa came up all the time. How could the two hundred million people in Brazil and Argentina, most of them of European descent, seem so irrelevant to our world?

Of course I was particularly aware of that now, when most of my world was threatened by a common enemy. It felt almost frivolous to be riding around South America on a motorcycle. Since the planes hit the towers I had been living in two worlds. One was the world of CNN/BBC/cable TV, a non-stop frenzy of recycled film clips and speculation. The other was life on the streets, where the 'war on terror' seemed about as menacing as an outbreak of sunspot activity.

Pretty much everyone in Argentina believed that the US incited and funded all the murderous military crack-downs in South America. You couldn't be surprised if their grief over the events in New York was tinged with a sniff of come-uppance. Especially in Argentina, where people took politics much more seriously than in Brazil.

'We wuz robbed,' was how they explained their own crisis. And who by? Foreign business, mainly from the US (you couldn't call it 'America' down here), in league with their own politicians. Presidents came and went, sometimes to prison like the previous president, Menem, who was caught up in an intricate web of conspiracy, fraud and murder. What Argentines would like to do to their politicians probably explained my friends' otherwise bizarre choice of *Titus Andronicus*.

From Buenos Aires I rode first to Bahía Blanca, and I think it was there that I first became aware of the plethora of gambling joints I had seen on this journey. There were many in southern Africa, and now I was seeing mini-casinos all over Brazil and

Argentina. This was certainly something new, and I found it depressing.

Up to this time of my life – and that's a long time – I have been a lucky person. Not that everything has turned out the way I wanted it. Almost the opposite, in fact, but every disappointment has led to new and better prospects, so that looking back on my failures I can't bring myself to regret any of them. If the magazine I once owned hadn't failed I would never have had that seminal experience in France. If my love affairs had been more stable I would probably never have travelled as I did. If I had been more sensible when I returned, I would not have my wonderful son to admire. And I am willing to believe that my erratic progress through life has somehow contributed to my unexpectedly good health, because I was born a wimp.

I would even go so far in tempting fate as to say that I was blessed, somehow, with the ability to make my own luck. How could one be more fortunate than that? Being as lucky as I am, if I have money to spare it seems absurd to gamble with it. Far better to invest it in myself, or simply give it away.

This leads me to think that people who do gamble can't really be very lucky. All that frenzy of 'fun' and throwing caution to the winds, to my eyes, is a thin disguise for a kind of despair, for lives out of control, for people desperate to change their luck. As I see casinos springing up everywhere, and more governments encouraging new lotteries, it worries me to think that people see no better way to improve their lives. I do hope I am wrong.

It rained furiously in the night. All I'd had for dinner was fish and wine, but I had strange druggy dreams, and woke late. On my way out of Bahía Blanca I stopped on the dirt verge to check my map, and the bike just flipped over in the mud. Nobody stopped. I had to take two of the boxes off to get the bike up again. Then I sailed off across the great sea of grass called the Pampa, and headed towards the Andes on the other side of the continent six hundred miles away.

This is a world inhabited by cows and gauchos and a string of little towns named after military men, like Colonel Pringles. There were pools of floodwater everywhere, and curiously I saw men fishing in them. Past Neuquén I had a fascinating interlude examining the remains of the Gigantosaurus, a carnivore even bigger than T-Rex, and ended the day under a blazing red-ochre sunset at a little place called Picún Leufú. The following day I arrived in Bariloche, and something extraordinary happened to me on that leg of the journey. I was overcome by an overwhelming sense of joy.

Not that I am normally miserable. Far from it. But my mind is usually occupied by a variety of concerns, and not all of them are happy. That day, quite abruptly, they all disappeared. I felt as I would hope to feel in paradise. I had the River Limay on my left, fantastically shaped rocks above me, a perfect winding road through gorgeous vegetation, a bright blue sky with a few artistically arranged clouds, fresh cool air – all these things contributed – but the sheer joy came from somewhere else. I wish I knew where. I'd get some more.

In Bariloche I found another old friend I knew from the first time around. Knowing him came as the result of one of those lucky encounters that happen on the road. I was changing my clothes in a bus shelter in Bahía Blanca in September 1974 (it was raining then too), when a passing Welshman saw my number plate and said, 'Are you going to Bariloche? Then you must look up Teddy Wesley, on the Ruta de Llao-Llao.'

I said OK, and that's pretty much all that happened, but when I got to Bariloche I took his advice, and was very glad I did. Teddy, his wife Leo, and his many children made me at home in what must be among the most beautiful spots on the planet. He took me around, introduced me to some extraordinary characters, and impressed me deeply.

Now, at eighty-four, he was in a wheelchair and near the end of his life. His wife had died, but his children lived around him. He didn't talk much, and I was never sure that he really knew who I was, but he seemed comfortable, and we were able to laugh quite a bit together. He had fought in the Second World War as a commando, and won the Military Cross (a very potent medal) in Burma for some act of valour he couldn't bring himself to describe. I know he was in a canoe – they used to raid enemy positions at night in canoes – and he got shot doing something brave.

But he was able to tell me that he was visited in hospital by Lady Mountbatten, wife of the British Viceroy of India, and she said to him, 'Have you boys been getting into trouble again?'

27

Crossing the Andes for the first time I had felt like a conquistador. Not that I faced quite the same problems, but I understand how the joy of discovery can blow obstacles away. In my case there had been a very difficult road coming down into Chile from Argentina. First I recalled the intimidating border post, the jack-booted guards, the menacing displays of weapons, to remind me that I was entering another, even worse, military dictatorship. Then came the road, a bad version of what they call *ripio*, with about three inches of loose gravel strewn across the surface, but it didn't affect my triumphant mood.

Perhaps it's just as well that the road was now good asphalt, but along with the *ripio* much else had gone. The vegetation, which fascinated me then because it seemed subtropical, had become ordinary and dull. How could that be? And there were no more milk churns waiting by the roadside.

Further down, the road was developed for tourism, with *cabañas* and fishponds everywhere. To get to town I crossed over a four-lane toll road, which is what the PanAmerican Highway has become, and then into Osorno. What a revelation that was. It used to be a small, dull provincial town. The most exciting distraction I could remember was examining ancient corsets in a shop window. Now it was big, vibrant and prosperous-looking, with the exception of one burnt-out building on a corner. Above the ruined doorway was a business sign which had survived the fire. It proclaimed that they sold fire alarms.

I had a great lunch in a very nice place, before setting off for the coast to attempt to recover another long-lost dream. When I left Teddy Wesley the first time to cross over into Chile he told me of a charming and cheap hotel perched on a rock by the ocean, and I had gone there to reap my reward for having reached the Pacific.

The long dirt road to the coast was another of the beautiful ones I remembered from back then. The countryside had been Elysian, totally unspoiled, and behind me, above it all, was that perfect snow-capped mountain we all know thanks to Paramount Pictures, only real and in stone. The hotel was there too, as inviting as Teddy Wesley had said it would be, but they refused to let me in because I only had dollars. A new law prohibited them from accepting foreign exchange, and they were petrified of contravening it. The penalties under that military regime were dire.

I'd had to sleep hungry on the beach, and ride back to Osorno next day to find a bank. Only later did I learn that I could have been shot on sight for sleeping out after dark.

Well, this time was going to be different. And it was.

The road was asphalt. The hedgerows were broken, and there were wires and concrete posts everywhere. I passed a eucalyptus farm, and various wood projects. Road-builders were desecrating the coastline with a new highway. Shacks and shanties surrounded the hotel, which looked so dingy that I didn't even bother to go in. I had got there in a quarter of the time but, as Gertrude Stein said, there was no there there. I'm happy to confirm, though, that the mountain still exists.

I rode north on the new PanAmerican Highway, built on the lines of an American interstate, but with an important exception: there is access to it along most of its length. People can walk across it with babies and bicycles, and so can animals. The speed limit is strict, but it is over 60 m.p.h.

On 1 November, the Day of the Dead, I arrived in Santiago, but only just. Traffic was getting thicker, all travelling at the limit. Suddenly, from between the legs of some people standing on an island on my left, a medium-sized brown dog ran full tilt across my path, so close to my front wheel that for a moment, as it passed, I couldn't even see it. It felt great to be alive.

Few people have had as much practice at leaving as I have, and though practice doesn't make perfect, as I was taught to believe at school, it does help. I hardly ever feel, when I am leaving people who are dear to me, that I won't see them again. I simply conduct my relationships over a longer time span. Without this discipline, I would have found it extremely difficult to leave Santiago de Chile again. This city has been very important in my life. It is one of the places where I could easily choose to live, and indeed it might come to that.

First the Dittborns.

When I came to Santiago in 1974 I was sponsored by Lucas, the company that manufactured the electrical parts for my Triumph. They had branches everywhere in the world, and Tito Dittborn ran the Santiago branch. He passed me on to his young son Adolfo, who was in his early twenties, and during the weeks I was there I came to know the family very well.

Adolfo had several brothers and sisters, and together they had acquired a piece of land high up outside the city that once belonged to Trappist monks, and they had just put up the first of their own small homes. Adolfo had an older brother, Alberto, who was a designer, and the five of us, Adolfo and his girlfriend Chicky, Alberto and his wife Paula, and I, became firm friends. Now, Tito had died and Adolfo ran the business. Alberto had lived in Spain, France, England. He had designed several important museums, and still taught intermittently at a prestigious Paris school of design, as well as at the university in Santiago.

The ground they bought had been engulfed by the city, which sprawled out ever further into the country around. There were now seven family houses and a guest-house on their parcel, all quite luxurious with the idiosyncratic exception of Alberto's. Adolfo and Chicky were married, with a big family. Alberto had a smaller one.

When I emailed Adolfo to say that I was going around again, and could Avon send the tyres to his place as before, he replied, 'You are crazy, but you can count on us. And you can stay at our place, if you want.'

How could I not want? To be greeted with such warmth after so many years is to reassert the power of humanity over all the negative influences that come between us. I stayed in the guest-house. We had many fine meals together, and I got a lot of work done.

So leaving the Dittborns was not easy.

And then there was Malú Sierra.

There are some women fortunate enough to remain physically beautiful regardless of time and age, and Malú has that happy gift. I have known her through only three of her many incarnations, and each time, despite great superficial changes, the perfect oval of her face and the symmetry of her features conquer all.

I was on my way around the world, and she was a successful professional woman in her thirties when we first met. She had jet-black hair and the rosy lips of a Titian cupid, the eyes of an adventuress, a will of steel and a mind to match. We were politically and culturally in sympathy and I fell utterly in love with her. She returned my affection abundantly, and but for the sanctity of my 'mission' I might never have left Chile.

We met briefly eight years later. By then she was a formal and composed mother of four in her forties, her hair already frosted, with wrinkles at her eyes and clearly far removed from the person I had known, but still stunningly lovely. She had become an important political journalist, against her own inclination but to protect herself and her family from military persecution, and it was clear that she lived under great pressure.

And now another twenty years had passed. With the country safely democratic she no longer had to pander to politicians and generals, most of whom she frankly despised, and instead had become a powerful voice in defence of the environment, and in particular the forests of Chile.

I confess I was a bit nervous when I rode up to her new home in the hills on the edge of Santiago. I had nothing in mind but to hope for a friendship, since whatever else might have changed, our beliefs and interests had not. I try not to be too concerned about my appearance, but I probably don't try hard enough. And of course I could not help wondering how Malú had weathered those twenty years.

She came down a flight of garden steps to meet me in cargo pants and a sweater, as lissome and energetic as ever. She wore a great mane of silver-grey hair, and the wrinkles had spread, but her eyes sparkled and that heavenly oval face was as gorgeous as ever. The rapport was instant, and we talked as freely as we always had. She explained that she regarded her age as a liberation from all the *Sturm und Drang* of love and sex and was perfectly happy now to live alone with her children, who were all but grown up.

For my part, I did my best to express my own feelings about life and love in general. I said that I had not given up the hope that I would still be able to share my life with a woman, and that if I did I would want to make love to her, but that I felt no sense of urgency. I would let it happen if it was meant to.

We met several times, and enjoyed each other's company tremendously. To find her so strong and enthusiastic and clear in her maturity was a great joy. The two youngest of her four children, Celeste and Pablo, lived with her in this sprawling house that had grown organically over the hillside, and we had much good food and wine and conversation. She told me that she had to go to Oregon the following April to a conference on wood products, and would take the opportunity to come to California, and visit Isabel Allende, the writer, who was a very old and close friend. It seemed likely that I might by then also be in California and that was how we left each other, as friends who hoped to meet.

If there was anything else in our minds, it was unexamined, and certainly unspoken.

28

Leaving Chile for Mendoza, in Argentina, is exciting. It involves climbing over the Andes to ten thousand feet. Back in '74 it included riding through a dripping railway tunnel on slippery boards, one of the nastiest experiences on a bike I've ever had, but now the railway is a thing of the past. The remains of the old one are visible as I climb. At times the track dives into a mountain of scree, at others it hangs helplessly over a washed-out gulch. The snow-sheds are crumbling away. It's a sad sight. I hate to see railways die.

The climb is thrilling and a little intimidating. The steepest ascent begins at six thousand feet and rises rapidly through twenty-nine hairpin bends. You see the hairpins stacked above you as you ride, and the wind gets stronger and colder. In reality there is no problem. The road is very broad to accommodate heavy trucks, and the surface is good. It's just the idea of it that excites.

At the top the Chilean officials let me through very easily with just a six-hundred-peso road tax, but I'm in line behind a truck driver who has a document comprising eighteen copies, each of which has to be stamped three times. I have nothing better to do than count.

It's on the Argentine side that I am anticipating all kinds of delay, because I remember the trouble I had coming into Argentina a month ago from Brazil. As I ride across, a series of menacing posters warn me that *all* food, of whatever origin, is absolutely forbidden. Maybe crossing frontiers is not as thrilling as it used to be, but still it has its moments, even if they are self-invented. When I came into Chile two weeks ago (is it really only two weeks?), I had a salami sausage in my top box. It was inside a voluminous white plastic bag.

In the immigration office I was given a piece of printed paper saying that I had to declare whether I was carrying any foodstuffs of any description, and that to make a false declaration could expose me to fines and imprisonment. I didn't want to take it seriously. Why should I lose my salami to some stupid bureaucracy? So I put a cross in the box marked 'None' thinking, They'll never look.

When I went out to the bike, an agent came up, took the paper and said, 'Open the box!' So I opened it and, with the adrenalin surging, I grabbed the white plastic as though it was merely an empty obstruction to his search, and thank goodness he fell for it.

And now here I am again with a salami (yes, I really like the stuff). Not the same salami I smuggled into Chile, but an even bigger one. I don't want to run that risk again, so as the customs building comes into sight I stop and eat as much of it as I can, to the amusement of a policeman who comes out of his hut to watch me. Then I stuff the remains in my pocket with the knife, planning to bring it out with a flourish when I'm challenged.

But the agents process me in minutes. I don't even have to get off the bike. No questions, no carnet. Just a *papelito* to guard with my life. And I am burping salami for the rest of the day.

Once through the new tunnel, everything is rosy. It might have been planned as an advertisement for Beautiful Argentina. No vertiginous hairpins, just a long and lovely ride down the Mendoza Valley between towering copper-coloured rocks streaked with verdigris.

I'm now sitting at a café table – one of my favourite occupations – on the Paseo Sarmiento in Mendoza reflecting that this is really a world-class setting, as good as Aix-en-Provence, or Cologne or the Via Veneto. It's a beautifully designed avenue, with fountains, pretty lighting and expensive shops, and no traffic allowed. People are strolling about as stylishly dressed as in any European capital, and it's hard to take seriously all the complaints about hard times, but there is an undercurrent of poverty.

The waiters are out in the street hustling for custom. Rather well dressed urchins are constantly whispering in my ear with their hands full of Chiclets. Women with babes-in-arms are begging, so is an old lady with arthritic legs, and a guitarist is singing (very well) a peasant song.

Two small boys, I would guess seven and five, with white paint and lipstick on their faces, come up with a little dog, a hoop and a metal stand. The older boy makes a statement I can't follow, then the dog sits up and begs. The smaller boy stretches the stand out in front of him and the dog jumps over it three times. Then it jumps through the hoop.

The older boy is carrying a bag, and out of it he hauls a dove and a white rat. He looks at the rat closely for a minute as though he sees something wrong with it, then puts it on his shoulder. Then he pulls out another dove, but meanwhile the rat has got under his shirt, and there's another short pause while he disentangles it. Then the two doves sit on the stand – and that's it. The rat is not part of the act.

The whole thing is so wonderfully artless I want to laugh and cry at the same time. Who sends them out here, I wonder? I would follow them to find out, but they are doing the same little show in front of every café, and they will be there all night.

Mendoza is a city for lovers. I see them clinging together everywhere, but here it seems to be the girls who seize the men and envelop them, while the men smile nicely and endure it.

I'm on my way to Bolivia – that's a thousand miles from Mendoza. This part of the journey was difficult but full of fascination when I did it the first time. The road skirts the edge of the Andes, curling over dry ribs of rock that separate the towns from each other. There is a long string of them, each nestling into a valley where water comes down from the mountains, but overall the road is hot and dry.

On the first day I ride through San Juan, and then on to San Jose de Jachal, a small, rather primitive town but with the usual big square, or *plaza*, in the middle. There are many ice-cream parlours but although beer is advertised everywhere, there is nowhere to sit and drink it.

In Mendoza I paid twenty dollars for a hotel room, with breakfast and parking included, which was OK, but here they are asking eighteen dollars which seems like a lot for not very much. I compensate by making do with salami, olives and wine for dinner, and walk out into the darkness. It's a beautiful, warm night, and a new moon is hanging belly up over the square, but the town is fast asleep. Back at the hotel the TV is on with a football match between Argentina and Uruguay, and I watch it over a quart of beer.

I am upset with myself. I can't seem to stop eating and drinking and going to hotels, even though I'm carrying everything I need to camp. I have become one of those travellers I used to despise. Is my age my excuse? I had better make my mind up soon.

Jachal and the next town, La Rioja, are only 125 miles apart as the crow flies, but the road distance is 350 miles, so you can see something fairly dramatic is going on here. The road shoots north, and turns to gravel and dirt, looking for a pass over a range of rocks; then it turns right and up over the top where it's quite bad, and then down to Valle Unión which is nothing but a junction. All of this is a big dusty desert, where a long time ago I saw foxes and armadillos, but not now. A man on a bicycle pulling a small cart comes labouring towards me. He's flying a blue flag and I assume he's an Argentine. I wonder at the effort it must take to do this on a hot day, and I'm afraid of disturbing his rhythm. The road climbs up again, and over another lower range, and then dives south to Patquia.

I remember Patquia because the last time I came I was desperate for water and fuel, and I was disappointed. There was nothing there then, but now it is much improved. I can get a decent meal here, and there is petrol. The attendant is an older man who tells me the cyclist was a Scotsman, so that blue flag must have been the cross of St Andrew. Then he asks, 'Have you been around Argentina?'

I say I have.

'*Qué tal?*' he asks. 'How did you find it?'

'Good,' I say.

He flutters his hands, meaning 'Maybe yes, maybe no.'

'Yes, I know,' I say. 'Things are supposed to be bad, but on the whole people seem to be all right.'

'*Sí,*' he comments. 'They complain, but they have forgotten what it used to be like. Here we had nothing. There was no flour, no sugar, no oil . . .' He rattles off a list of staple foods.

'I know. I was here in nineteen seventy-four, and there really was nothing.' In fact in my notes I called it a dump, not worth stopping for.

Now the road does a huge hairpin round the tail end of another rib of the Andes, and goes north again to La Rioja. And here's another cyclist, going my way. Two in one day, and I've never met any before. This one's got a more streamlined trailer. I slow down and ride alongside him. He's a Frenchman, Bertrand from Perpignan, and he has already been all down the west coast of Africa. He has legs like small tree trunks.

'How on earth did you go over those rocks back there?' I ask.

He smiles. 'Slowly.'

He says he enjoys it all, and I marvel at it.

Out here it's not easy to know what's going on in the world. In La Rioja, I got a newspaper. It had thirty-two pages. Fourteen of them were about who had been robbed, murdered or accidentally dismembered in the immediate locality, three were about goings-on in Buenos Aires, twelve of them were sport, one was entertainment, two were editorials. At the bottom of page 12 was the only news from outside Argentina. There were 150 words about Afghanistan. Apparently they're still bombing it.

La Rioja to Catamarca is a hundred miles of long, straight road past huge ranches. Every few miles I'm enveloped by the stench of a dead cow rotting in the ditch. The land is flat and covered with brush, where hawks rise up and hover and then just as abruptly plunge. There's a long, high range of mountains to my left, and another stretching across my path, both of them topped with cloud. At first I can't see how this road can escape, but then I see that where they intersect there is a pass.

It suddenly struck me today how much I am enjoying this. Even though I get pretty tired at the end of the day (and succumb to the hotels), most of the time I'm comfortable and happy on the bike. Sometimes, when the wind is right, I can just sit back with my hands in my lap and let the bike ride itself. It's very relaxing. I notice that I seem to be settling down to the same 50 m.p.h. that I rode at in '74. The bike can, of course, cruise much faster than that, but 50 seems best.

Today I finally forced myself to admit that my head is the wrong shape for my new German helmet. As a helmet it is superb with a built-in retractable sun visor and lots of different ways to adjust airflow. But on my head the helmet slumps too far forward. When I hold it up, even just a centimetre, vision improves dramatically, and the wind noise decreases. My head just doesn't go back far enough. Maybe Germanic heads have more bone at the back.

This may account for some things that have happened to me in my life. Maybe this is why my first girlfriend dumped me when I was seventeen, and why I had trouble with calculus. I could go to a phrenologist, I suppose, but I am afraid to learn the truth. I can just imagine his diagnosis.

'Vell, Mister Simon' – he would have to be German, I think – 've haff made ze measurements, und zere is, sorry zu sagen, a certain leck of depth, a shallowness, a distinct absence of profundity. You vill heff to live wiz it. Ve can do nussing, but you must be avare zat wiz ziz hendicep you vill never amount to much. Zat vill be ten guineas.'

Meanwhile, I may have to stuff some foam in where my head should be.

Once through the gap between the ranges, everything is suddenly different. I'm in a huge agricultural plain watered by tributaries of the Río Dulce. It's large-scale agribusiness, but business is obviously bad. Fleets of trucks standing idle, many buildings and factories unfinished, or derelict, surrounded by messy rural slums. There are colonies of new cottages, very small, with funny-looking chimney-pots on them that look like large silencers – until I realise they are not chimneys at all, but solar heated water tanks. Obviously there has been some attempt to house rural workers better, but all these social programmes, I gather, are doomed by the IMF.

Salta is a big and important city with a major military base, but I went straight for the centre and got into a very nice old-style hotel (again!) for not much money. It's called the Colonial Hotel and it's right on the plaza. The Plaza 9 de Julio is rather fine. It has a convent at one end, and at the other there's a cathedral. I heard a very serious-sounding sermon in there today from an intensely intellectual priest, who may even have been an archbishop.

The cathedral is an impressive pile of masonry, and so it's a bit of a let-down when, instead of bells ringing out the time, it gives forth a silly electronic tune, like a mobile phone. In fact, when I first heard it at night that's what I thought it was. Maybe it is. Maybe it's the world's biggest cellphone, and that's God calling every fifteen minutes.

The other day in Jachal, when I opened my eyes in the morning I saw the word GANCIA. It was on an old aluminium ashtray beside the bed. Decades ago, when I started travelling in Europe, I used to see this word, usually alongside MARTINI and CINZANO, on café umbrellas, so I know it's a drink, but I have never even seen a bottle of Gancia. Until today in Salta. There it was at the back of the hotel bar. These are important moments in life, and let me tell you, it's some drink. It's a pale-yellow aperitif, and the barman beat it up with some lemon juice – about eight to one is what it looked like. Throw in ice, and drink it through a straw. Try it. One won't be enough.

Salta is still only about 3,700 feet above sea level. I could quite easily get to Bolivia in one day, because La Quiaca is only 230 miles away, but it's at 12,000 feet. I'm a little concerned that I might not deal with altitude quite so well at my advanced age so I think I'll go about halfway up, and stop for a bit. That means going through Jujuy, which is not very far, and on to the next place.

So I'm on my way out, through heavy traffic, and as I squeeze past a little white car I feel a jolt on the bike. Not much of a jolt, but still . . . I go ahead but the lights are red and the traffic is stalled. In my mirror I see a woman get out of the car and walk around to the back, grim-faced, to look. Then the lights change, and I roar off.

Well, I don't want to get caught up in some silly little argument, but I feel rotten about it. It gnaws at me. What if I did some real damage? What if she gets a cop? Outside every city in Argentina there are police controlling who comes in and out. Now I know why. It's to catch delinquents like me. Well, if I can get out before she has time. . . Damn, I can't. My tank's empty. It takes an age to find a petrol station.

Now I'm back on the road and, sure enough, there they are, five cops, and a row of red plastic cones down the middle of the road. So what do I do to make sure they see me coming? I knock over a cone. Something I have never ever done before. You can't beat guilt. A cop comes trotting over, smiles broadly, waves me on and picks up the cone. All's well. But maybe they'll get me at Jujuy . . . Oh, come on Ted, knock it off.

This is a really lovely little road from Salta to Jujuy. All green and leafy on a spring morning, winding up and down through pretty country. It comes out at the end on the big highway, number 9, and then, just before Jujuy, the road's on fire.

It's a protest by people who work in the tobacco fields here.

'What's up?' I ask the nearest one.

'We haven't been paid for three months,' he shouts angrily.

They've dragged trees and tyres across the road and set fire to them. Fortunately for me, the fires are nearly out. They've made their point, and ten minutes later it's over, but it's brought home the nasty end of this economic crisis. While the sophisticates in the big cities complain that they can't keep up their payments, I realise that there are a lot of poor people out in the countryside who might be starving.

I was aiming for Humahuaca, about halfway to the Bolivian border, thinking it would be about halfway up as well. Not so. I was at 10,000 feet before I knew it. The altitude doesn't affect me at all on the bike, but when I get off and start doing things I find myself gasping every few minutes. There are several campsites at Humahuaca, and I am determined to justify carrying all this camping gear, so I set up my tent across the river and then take a walk around town.

Everything is stone, and very lovely stone too, suffused with pink which glows in the late afternoon sun. The amount of effort that it took to put this town together amazes me. It is really beautifully built, architecturally coherent, and it's clean. Suddenly it strikes me just how dirty all the towns I have been passing through were. Another nice thing about it is that practically all the inhabitants appear to be Indians (or native South Americans, if you prefer.)

I like it so much here that I am glad to stay another day just to see what happens to it as the light changes. Camping was fun, but the night was very cold, and as a small hotel costs only three dollars more than the campsite, I move into town for the second night, my last night in Argentina.

From Humahuaca to the frontier is easy, except for ten miles where the road-builders are at it again. At the border things are much more simple and civilised than they used to be. Officials go out of their way to be helpful. Posters at the Bolivian customs office announce mission statements, promising prompt and honest service. Twenty-six years ago this would have been a laughable pretension, but today they actually fulfil their promise. I am through and into Bolivia by midday.

29

The first view of Bolivia is rather daunting. There's nothing to be seen in any direction but a sea of stone, darkened here and there by patches of wizened vegetation, like lichen on a rock. Across this sterile plateau run two bands of rubble, as though a giant tiller had run over it, chopping up the surface and levelling it.

These are the two roads to Potosí. The shorter one on the left, passing through Tupiza, is said to be most used and in better condition, but these are car drivers talking. Cars are more forgiving of corrugation than motorcycles, and on the short stretch before the road divides it is obvious that corrugation will be a problem.

Actually I had already chosen the other road, because it was the one I travelled last time. I wanted to see how much of it I could remember, and although it was rough – sometimes very rough – it was not corrugated. In fact there could hardly be a more beautiful road than the one that crosses the Bolivian Altiplano from La Quiaca to Potosí. The fact that it is also a very difficult road makes it better. You have to stay on it a lot longer.

A good deal of the road is at 13,000 or 14,000 feet, and most of what you see is bare rock, but this is fairy-tale rock, designer rock, rock-a-bye-baby rock. Brilliant strata of red, green, blue, brown, black, purple and ochre minerals sling silicon rainbows across the horizon, and behind them is a sky so intensely blue that it should only happen on picture postcards. Twice the road plunges down (although the descent itself is slow and tortuous) to a riverbed three thousand feet below, and at the lower levels there is life. But up above it is stark, and for the first half of the journey there is barely even a llama to be seen.

The earliest of those deep descents took an hour or more to negotiate, and then I was up again to a huge and windy plain under another flawless blue sky, with banks of cloud guarding its far distant outer edge. The road across that plain was very rough (it has to do with the size of the stones). Eventually it rose back up to 14,000 feet and then came down into a more fertile area.

At about five I arrived at a small crossroads village called Ismayachi, and knowing I couldn't get much further that day, covered in white dust and looking like a ghost rider I stopped and walked around it. The buildings were primitive, but I found a bed in a dosshouse called the Bermejo, and a good meal in a place that catered for buses.

Next day, having gained an hour coming in to Bolivia, I was up very early from a hard bed with an even harder pillow. I found coffee (but no milk) and bread (but no butter) at Heberto's grand *cabaña* Il Momentito, but I don't wish to be disparaging. For where it is it's pretty good, and the cheese is great. Who needs butter? Heberto is a fireball. He's very proud of his place. He has a big bronze plaque on the wall dedicated to the friends who helped him erect it in 1993.

I got my stuff together and asked some truck drivers how long it took them to do the two hundred miles to Potosí. They smiled.

'*Todo el día*,' they said. 'All day.'

'Anything particularly difficult?' I asked.

'Well, there's water to go through at Puente, though it shouldn't be much.'

I said I thought *puente* meant bridge.

'Yes, but it's the name of the river. *Río Puente. Pero no hay puente.* There's no bridge.'

To me it sounded like a bad joke. I filled my tank from a drum and got going.

The riding was much like the day before, but I kept worrying about the water. When I got to Puente, I found there *was* a bridge there after all. It just wasn't big enough for trucks. I heaved a sigh of relief at not having to go through water, and almost around the next corner, laughing at me . . . was water.

The ford was about two feet deep and I splashed through it more by luck than judgement. Otherwise, apart from a tricky bit of sand that almost got me, the road was just an unending bed of stones. Not since Ethiopia had the bike been shaken up so badly, and it was this shattering vibration that later settled my fate.

But the views were simply sensational, overwhelming, glorious. And I realised that I must have missed a lot of this experience back in '75, because then it was cloudy and even rained a little.

As happens so often on a difficult ride, 'they', whoever they are, had saved up the worst bits for the end. If there is one word in Spanish I hate above all others, it's *desvío*, and it means diversion. They were building a new road out of Potosí, and for ten miles or more I was pushed out into the countryside. It was tantalising and frustrating to ride alongside a beautiful, smooth highway and not to be on it, but they had made sure I couldn't ride it by piling road blocks on it at frequent intervals.

And then, just before the city, truck drivers had jammed the road in a labour dispute, but I saw a narrow gap at the edge between a truck and a large boulder. I just managed to squeeze through it under the angry eyes of a protester, but he did nothing to stop me. Ten hours of riding, almost non-stop, and I circled down into the city feeling quite pleased with myself.

Potosí and Sucre are two fine cities, a hundred miles apart, on this particular roof of the world, and they are separated by a smooth tarmac highway. Potosí is the world's highest major city, and is built next to a famous mountain of the same name that was the source of almost half the silver ever mined anywhere during past centuries. The stories and relics of those times are fascinating and gruesome, and are told very well through a museum called the Moneda, which is in the building where first the Spanish, and later the Bolivians, made their silver coinage.

Many millions of native Bolivians died an unpleasant death to unlock these riches, and even today the mining goes on in dangerous and difficult conditions, having been turned over from the state to private cooperatives. The town has some lovely colonial buildings and the handsome plaza is set at an appropriately giddy angle. The city had not changed much in twenty-seven years, though there were cash machines everywhere, more traffic and less coca leaf for sale. I spent a day there before going on to Sucre, another city of beautiful buildings and elegant squares, and the legal capital of Bolivia, although in practice everything is decided in La Paz.

On my first journey through Bolivia I was in the company, loosely speaking, of Bruno and Antoine, two Frenchmen I had met in La Quiaca who were driving a little Renault van. We got as far as Potosí together, but then they wanted to go the long way round through Sucre and Cochabamba. Because it was raining, I wanted to go directly to Oruro, so we separated for a while, though we did find each other again in La Paz.

Now, in Sucre, and with fine weather, I wondered whether the road they had taken might be better, but the advice I got was unanimous. I should go back to Potosí, and then through Oruro. I didn't mind going back to Potosí. That ride had been fast and very pleasant. As for the road to Oruro, after all those years perhaps there was a chance that it had improved.

I remember that road quite well, even though I have never written about it before – there was always too much, even for two books. It was about two hundred miles long, and like all the roads in those days it was surfaced with rubble, very coarse, with some big stones thrown in. You had to look where you were going. It had been quite cold and raining intermittently on the first day. As I was climbing a winding road to cross over a pass at about 15,000 feet I saw a truck tucked into the verge. The cab was facing me and I could see there was someone inside it so I stopped. He was the driver, a young man, and he seemed quite cheerful. I could see a pile of blankets behind him on the seat.

'*Está roto*,' he explained. '*Hay un fallo mecánico.*'

The truck had broken down and he was waiting for help. I was astonished to learn that he had been there six days. It was necessary to stay with the truck, he said, to protect it. He gave no hint that he regarded this as an exceptional hardship, and suddenly I had a glimpse of a quite different view of life, and time, and expectations. Six miserable days, six freezing nights, in a bare metal box (for the truck was old and very basic) and on a mere subsistence diet. What for me would have been a triumph of survival for him was a run-of-the-mill event.

There was nothing I could do for him, and nothing he wanted, so I rode on. When I came down from the pass I encountered a river to ford, and it seemed that I had two choices. A stone weir had been built across it, and the water running over the weir was only inches deep. The stones were about eighteen inches wide and made a perfect flat path for me to ride across, whereas below the weir, where all the four-wheeled traffic obviously went, the water tumbled over boulders a foot or two in depth.

So I had chosen to ride across the weir, which was very foolish of me because the stone had attracted a coating of slimy algae and the bike immediately slipped off the weir and fell over into the deeper water. I was able to get it upright again, but not before I and one of the boxes had been thoroughly soused.

The engine, of course, had stalled and I couldn't kick-start it in water. I didn't have the strength to push the bike out but, by one of those lucky flukes, on this quite deserted road a Land-Rover appeared with a group of tourists, and using a rope they pulled me out. I was pretty wet and glad to stop at the only hotel on the road, which was mercifully nearby. I brought the bike in through the front door, and took the waterlogged box into the bedroom. The worst damage was to the workshop manual for the Triumph, so I took it apart, page by page, and plastered the pages all over the bedroom and the hot-water radiator. So yes, I remember the road to Oruro.

I asked a number of people in Sucre how the road was now and got a startling variety of answers, all given with certainty. Some said it was all tar, some all stone, and some a bit of both. I wasn't worried about riding over rubble any more, and my anxieties about dirt had been finally laid to rest, although I did sometimes wonder how much vibration the bike could absorb. It was more a question of gauging the time it would take. It seemed better to assume stones all the way, which meant I might be riding for anything up to ten hours.

I set out early, enjoying again the smooth ride to Potosí, where I filled the tank. There they told me it was definitely *tierra* all the way. So it seemed that the road was just as it had always been, but the weather was dry and the sun was up, and even at 12,000 feet it was pleasantly warm. After an hour or so I came to a junction and a smattering of buildings where, in the past, I would have been asked to show my papers. The crude barrier was still there, but it was raised and I rode through without stopping, paying only enough attention to notice a few *indios* slumped against the side of a green adobe police post. Of course, I had no idea how intimately I would get to know this place before long.

The road soon left the last mud-brick shack behind and began to wind and climb in stages to a higher plateau, where it ran straight for many miles towards another range of hills. The land around me was bare, the colour of toast, and decorated with a tracery of stone walls defining, I supposed, fields and paddocks, though there were neither people nor animals in sight.

I was about twenty miles beyond the crossroads when a loud, urgent clattering erupted just behind me, breaking into my reveries. I didn't know what caused it, but I knew immediately what kind of noise this was. It spoke to me and said, 'Whatever it was you were planning, or looking forward to, forget it.'

I changed down to neutral and came to a halt at the roadside as quickly as I dared, afraid of doing more damage to whatever the hell it was. Parking was difficult. The camber was steep and even with the stand down the bike was almost vertical. There was a ditch on my right, but I had left enough room to stand in front of it, and I slid off the bike to the right, letting the suspension rise and push it over the stand.

I could see fairly quickly where the problem was. A long bolt had unscrewed itself and was still hanging there, balanced in a hole in the frame. At that moment I hadn't quite grasped its significance, but I took hold of it and prepared to move the bike to a better place. I should have known enough to hang on to that bolt at all costs because with it I could probably have repaired the damage myself, but I stepped around the bike, preparing to shift it, and at that moment a strong gust of wind blew across the road and, improbable as it may sound, knocked the bike upside down into the ditch.

Petrol started gushing out of the carburettors and the breather pipe like blood from a blast victim, and in my rush to stop the bleeding I dropped the bolt in the ditch. Strangely enough, as though scripted, the only vehicle I had seen on the road that day, a very small minibus, drew up alongside and two men jumped out and helped me raise the bike. Then they drove off.

As soon as I'd got the bike somewhere stable on the other side of the road I could begin to appreciate what had happened. The bolt was a pivot that held the drive shaft in place. Without it, the shaft had disengaged from the gearbox. The racket I'd heard was the last despairing effort of the gears to mesh. If I could find it, I might be able to put Humpty-Dumpty together again, but after we had all trampled around in the ditch, any chance of finding the bolt was gone. I searched and searched in vain.

There are many places in the world where the chances of finding a part for a sophisticated German motorcycle are close to nil, and Bolivia is one of them. I was stuck, but not too unhappy. I was sure that sooner or later a truck would come by. After all, on previous days I had had to overtake several through the great clouds of dust that surrounded them. I assumed I could get the truck to take me somewhere where I could make a plan. Anyway, I thought this could be the beginning of something interesting.

I had four or five hours of sun still, and although I was now at around 14,000 feet it wouldn't get really cold until the sun went down. So I occupied myself at first with unpacking the bike and unscrewing the boxes so they would be easier to load. But nothing came. I sat on one of the boxes and waited. I took pictures of the austere but beautiful landscape. A few clouds blew over. Then suddenly a fierce hailstorm came and went, and I was grateful for my umbrella. Still not a single vehicle. Then, after three hours, a bus came by and stopped, but what could a bus do for me? I asked the driver to look out for a truck and waved him on.

What if I had to spend the night here? Just how cold does it get at 14,000 feet? I thought of building a shelter or a windbreak with the bigger stones lying around, but when I started moving them I discovered I couldn't get enough oxygen into my lungs. Finding myself so short of breath induced a sense of panic. How interesting, I thought. Panic itself provokes shortness of breath, so it works both ways.

I gave up on the stones and sat for a while, and then an enormous oil tanker came over the hill from Oruro. I waved and it ground to a halt beside me, hissing and groaning. The driver who jumped out was a nice fellow in a T-shirt and jeans, with a white baseball cap on backwards.

'Have you seen any trucks coming this way?' I asked, after explaining my situation.

'No,' he said. 'But perhaps I could give you a tow to Las Cruces.'

A tow? The idea was insane. To be towed over these rocks behind a behemoth seemed like certain disaster. He wouldn't be able to see me. I wouldn't be able to see what was coming at me. Anyway, towed with what? I said I didn't think so.

Then a car came from the other direction. A middle-aged man, driving his family, stopped to join the discussion. Then in a surprisingly authoritative tone he said, 'You can't stay out here at night. You must let him help you.'

All we had between us was a ten-foot length of cord, which could not be disconnected if I fell. I thought I'd be very likely to fall and be dragged along the ground. The thought was frightening, but my Spanish wasn't good enough to argue my way out of it so I agreed to try.

The paterfamilias drove off satisfied, and José Luís – for that was the driver's name – and I started to plan this thing. Instead of tying it, we would wrap the rope around the handlebar a few times so that if I fell, with luck the rope would eventually come away. I would try to ride out to the side like a water skier so that he might catch me in a wing mirror. He would not drive at more than twenty kilometres an hour, and on downhill stretches he would let me free-wheel on my own.

José took all the bags and boxes into his cab, and in great trepidation I got on the bike. It was just as scary as I had imagined. I did
fall once, but it was when we started again after I had been rolling
downhill alone. A quick jerk and a big stone combined to throw me,
but somehow José caught it in his mirror and stopped instantly.
The whole exercise took an hour and a half, and was more har-
rowing even than that wet railway tunnel in '74. I bounced around,
willy-nilly, at the mercy of any obstacles that appeared under the
rear of the tanker, and guiding the bike over them was made even
harder by having to keep a grip on the end of the rope. José was
remarkably conscientious, stopping several times just to make sure
I was all right, and finally he brought me back to the crossroads
alive. I was extremely grateful to him, and demonstrated it in a
practical fashion although he had expected nothing. The ordeal
created a strong bond for me, and I was sad to see him drive off.

So here I was back where I had been five hours earlier. The place
was called Cruce Culta, and now I saw that it boasted a single-
storey hotel grandly entitled Hotel Copacabana. It was a
dismal-looking place, inside and out. The once white walls were
spattered with mud. The dining-room was bare board, grubby walls,
chipped furniture; the staff consisted of two young boys in filthy
clothes who had a large Alsatian with them on a leash. A passage led
through the building past the dining-room door into a cobbled
courtyard with a well in the middle, quantities of junk in the corners, and two small cubicles serving as bedrooms. There was a
primitive toilet at the back, and the best that could be said for it was
that it didn't stink, perhaps because of the prevailing coolness.

My first response to all this was utter dismay, but there was no
alternative. I rolled the bike into the yard, parked it in the corner
nearest to my cell, and went back to the dining-room to explore possibilities. The owner was a rather taciturn individual who lurked in
shadow behind a counter just inside the door, where he sold everything I didn't want, and nothing that I did.

Of course, what I hoped he would tell me was that trucks came
through this way all the time, so that's what he told me. However,
there had been no truck that day, to my own knowledge, and so I

had my doubts. The other thing I thought I needed was a telephone. I soon established that there wasn't one. Well, not in the hotel. There was one somewhere in the village and he would have one of the boys show me, but not tonight. Anyway, I wasn't ready for it yet. I hadn't figured out what to do.

It was getting dark outside, and there was no electricity in Cruce Culta, but soon the oil lamps began hissing and as the grime faded into the shadows things looked a little more appetising.

Did I want dinner? Without much enthusiasm I agreed that I did. Soon a large plate brimming with soup appeared through a hatch from the kitchen, and the older boy brought it over with great panache without spilling a drop and served it with a big display of brilliant white teeth. I was struck by how alert and willing he seemed. There was none of that fake cool, that studied indifference that you see in kids in the West.

The soup was excellent. It was made with quinoa and some kind of rich meat broth and vegetables. It would be hard to overstate the virtues of good soup. It feeds every human need. My stomach welcomed it, my whole body was warmed by it, my senses were stimulated by it and my spirits were raised and relaxed by it. From being a grubby way station the Hotel Copacabana was transformed into a cosy refuge, and the owner became a genial, avuncular figure. But beyond all that, there is something about the concentrated goodness of a great soup that affirms the generosity of nature and of the world we are made to survive in – more so even than the plate piled with good things that followed it, perhaps because being suspended in water it matches more exactly our own composition and the primeval soup from which we all sprang.

There was little custom that night. A couple came in from a car, and a young man in a green jacket sat and ate alone for a while. I went to bed early with two candles to light my way. The bed was clean and comfortable enough, although it was hard to get used to the weight of the closely woven blankets, four or five of them stacked on top of me to keep in the warmth. I woke in the morning knowing that I had had good dreams, without being able to remember them.

The men in Bolivia no longer wore the traditional homespun garments I remembered, but the women still clung to their old customs. When I walked out into the street in the morning, the ladies were already assembled outside the hotel. In their bowler hats, big embroidered blouses and shawls, full pleated skirts, stockings and shoes they looked at first very much alike. They sat in a row behind their wheelbarrows, each barrow covered with a cloth.

It was not immediately clear to me what they were doing there. They saw me looking at them, and the nearest one dug into her barrow and produced two eggs which she held out to me, thrusting them at me repeatedly. I felt strangely intimidated, and it interfered with my thinking. Why would I want eggs? I asked myself. Where would I cook them? I refused. She looked angry, and I walked off.

I was on my way with the younger boy to find the telephone. I planned to phone Dave, in Dorchester, to see what he could do about replacing the lost part. I wasn't being entirely naive. I knew that phoning England from Cruce Culta would be a challenge, but I thought I had to try.

There was a woman who had been appointed custodian of the telephone, and first we had to find her. She had the key to unlock the small cell where the phone slept, and she was not at home. So that disposed of half the morning. Then, when we found her and unlocked the magic instrument there were many more rituals to perform before the number could actually be dialled, but by then it appeared that all connections with foreign parts had dried up, and I would have to try again next day. Meanwhile a few buses had come and gone, and I discovered what should have been obvious: the wheelbarrows were loaded with snacks to be sold to the passengers, so naturally the eggs would have been cooked.

Eventually my friend José also reappeared with his tanker on his way back to Oruro and we passed the time of day, but there were no trucks.

That night the young man came into the hotel again and this time we began to talk. His name was Nestor, and I learned that he too was waiting to be rescued. At first I couldn't understand what he was saying. Something about a house full of ore.

'*Tengo mi cazzo acá fuera, pero el cambio está roto.*'

Cazzo? What was that? Finally I twigged. Here in Bolivia 'r's became 'z's. And a truck, or *camión*, was called a *carro* and pronounced *cazzo*.

So he had come down from a mine at 17,000 feet with a truck-load of ore to take to Oruro, but his truck was on the point of dying. His transmission had all but collapsed, and he only had two gears left. Now he was sleeping in the cab of his truck and waiting for a man with a bigger vehicle to come and help him to Oruro. I saw light at the end of the tunnel, and Nestor agreed that if no other solution presented itself, I could get a lift with them. But there was a price to pay. It was not a monetary price, although for sure I would have to give them something. It was my eternal soul. I became the target of Nestor's evangelical zeal. He was absolutely determined to set me on the straight and narrow path to salvation.

Even when there is nothing at stake, I am generally reluctant to tell people that I don't believe in God. My experience tells me that believers are not open to argument on the subject, and that I can only end up by offending them, although it never seems to occur to them that the opposite might also be true. In this situation I had all the more reason not to offend Nestor, who thought of me simply as one of those wishy-washy Christians who can't be bothered to pray. Given my modest grasp of Spanish, keeping Nestor at bay was a demanding exercise. Still, I managed to get him off the subject occasionally, and discovered that the bigger truck belonged to a man called Tomás, who lived closer to Oruro. There was no knowing when he might come.

The next morning at the telephone I tried a different tactic. I thought it might be easier to connect with my friend Adolfo in Chile, so I kept trying both numbers, and in fact I did get Adolfo in his office, told him what had happened and gave him Dave's number and also the number in Cruce Culta. My idea was that if I couldn't reach Dave, maybe Dave could reach me. Miraculously, an hour later, the phone emitted its rather pathetic version of a ring. But it wasn't Dave, it was Stephen, the owner of my bike.

It was great to hear him, because he has an excellent sense of humour, and I told him what had happened and we joked about it. Of course, he promised to get the part to La Paz when I needed it. I said that I thought maybe it would be a good idea to change the shaft as well, because there was a rumour that the universal joints sometimes died after 30,000 miles. 'We can do that,' he said.

I think he enjoyed the involvement, if not necessarily the expense, and for the moment I was buoyed up by it; but I realised even as we were talking that the exercise was a bit pointless, and the more I thought about it the more disappointed I became with myself. Here I was, cast by chance into a quite unique situation, with people whose way of life, whose values and beliefs and expectations were wildly different from my own, and all I could think about was getting away as quickly as possible. These phone calls really had no practical purpose. They would achieve nothing that I couldn't do as well from La Paz when I got there. I was simply grasping at communication for its own sake, keeping busy, longing for a familiar voice almost as though I were under threat.

It came as a shock to realise how much I had changed. I had become a creature of communication, constantly sending and receiving emails, posting messages to my website, incapable of sinking peacefully into my surroundings. Where was that man, that 'Jupiter', who once sat contentedly under a tree by the roadside in India, confident that somehow, someone would bring help and usher in some new adventure?

I couldn't blame myself entirely. It is hard to resist the culture, which had become so much more intense in the last decades. We were all trapped in an ever more tightly woven net of communication. Even older people, like myself, could only resist mobile phones for so long. Now everyone was in permanent connection. People walked around talking into the air, scarcely aware of what was around them. Thanks to the Cold War we were all caught up in a technology that not only allowed us to be everywhere at once, but also monitored everything we said, and did, and spent.

Now I found myself by chance in one of the rare places still outside the Net, and I couldn't wait to rush back in. I was disgusted with myself. I went back to the hotel, got out my camera, and walked around taking pictures. I pointed the lens at the barrow-girls and got a couple of pictures, but they didn't like it, and the egg lady actually tossed a stone in my direction. I couldn't blame her.

On one side of the road the ground rose steeply among rocks, and I photographed a woman climbing up to a small stone hut which might have been her home. Nestor's truck was parked around the corner, in a side street where rivulets of water separated islands of garbage, and I took a few pictures there. I knew that I should really be talking to people, but feeling the way I did I couldn't even try. I went back into the hotel, got out my notebook, and interrogated myself.

It rained heavily in the night, but the morning was bright and clear with just a few white clouds. At 7 a.m. Tomás arrived with his *cazzo* and employed a gang of about six men to shovel the ore *zapido* from Nestor's truck into his. I learned that my bike was to be bedded on a mixture of zinc, tin, lead and silver.

Tomás was older than the fresh-faced Nestor – in his late thirties, I guessed – and very firm in everything he did, though always in good humour. He had already decided how much to charge me, and there was no question of bargaining. It was a fair enough price, if on the high side, and I had no say in the matter.

The shovelling was a long, slow business, and when it was done Nestor pushed me on the bike to an earthen ramp (*zampa*), refusing my help because I was still panting from lack of breath. Then with much laughing disagreement on how to do it, we all pushed the bike up the ramp and plonked it in the ore.

Tomás drove off, and we followed, but after three miles Nestor's truck died completely on a steep turn. It was time to tow, and I saw with surprise that they had not even considered how they would do it. Tomás's truck had a towbar, but there was no point of attachment to Nestor's vehicle. After two and a half hours of roadside mechanics they took the bumper off and found a way to secure the bar by flattening one end of it with a sledge-hammer. I held the bar down while Nestor hammered it an inch from my feet until the hammer flew apart between my legs.

Finally, with the two trucks joined together I thought we were ready to leave, but instead they spent an hour underneath Tomás's engine – for fear, they said, that the gearbox might be falling out. Waiting in Nestor's cab I heard their muffled conversation and laughter, and fantasised that they were having a party under there.

At 5.30 p.m., with a jemmy holding one end of the towbar and a bolt with a couple of nuts at the other end, we got going again. For two more hours we rumbled over the stones at the pace of a gypsy wagon, passing herds of llama, mud villages and high horizons.

At Tomás's village we stopped to put down a passenger and pick up two others. His house was the only one with stucco over the mud bricks, and I imagined he was an important man in the village. He would be a natural leader. He clearly had great practical intelligence, and commanded respect. Both of them exhibited great competence – if he hadn't been such a self-righteous Christian, Nestor would have been a perfect travelling companion. The cheerful and imperturbable way in which they accepted whatever fate threw their way was very impressive. They were evidently willing to take any pains to get the job done. As Nestor said, '*Es mi trabajo.* It's my work.'

Several times Nestor stopped us all to make sure the jemmy was still in place, and once, just before we reached the asphalt, it jumped out of its sockets. By then of course it was dark, but on the asphalt we moved much faster. At Challapata we stopped to eat. They ordered the fixed meal, a big plate of chicken, rice and beans, and Tomás was about to dig in when, seeing Nestor put his hands together, he jerked back from the food and whipped off his cap as Nestor sank into prayer.

It was 11 p.m. and I expected we would sleep there, but Challapata, they said, had a bad reputation for thievery. Hard as it was to imagine, it seemed there was a lot of it on those long, deserted roads in Bolivia. So we got back on the road. Both drivers were very sleepy. I could see Tomás's truck weaving erratically, and Nestor stopped us and got out. They met in the road and talked a while before continuing. We arrived in Oruro at one in the morning where we found our way into an enormous walled compound, or stockade, jammed with trucks and trailers. It was so full that Tomás had to bargain to get us in, promising to leave before 8 a.m. so as to unblock the others.

There were three free beds, under the usual compress of blankets, and I slept soundly.

At the workshop next day where Nestor was having his truck repaired, the mechanics became interested in my bike. They said they thought they could put it all together again and I could see no harm in letting them try. I wouldn't pay them if they failed, and getting the bike lifted to La Paz would be expensive, so I left it with them, and we three *campesinos* went to lunch, and to visit the contractor who would buy Nestor's ore.

Oruro owes its existence to a scarified mountain range that has been mined to exhaustion and that now loomed above us. A watery light shone down on puddles and glistening mud as we walked seven blocks on the Avenida del Ejército to a restaurant. Lunch was tongue, rice and *chuño*, literally defrosted potatoes. They are frozen naturally in the sub-zero temperatures of winter nights, and brought out when needed, starchy and devoid of flavour.

Now to the assayer's. Behind steel shutters was a yard surrounded by offices and, in the centre of the yard, a heap of black ore. Six men in company overalls walked around the pile, shovelling it into a ring of ore, like a mechanical ballet. Then, when they'd finished, and every last scrap in the middle had been swept up, they did the whole thing again in reverse, circling with measured steps until the pile in the middle had been restored. It had a feeling of madness about it, but I was assured it was necessary to evenly mix the ore, which was tin and very heavy.

The lads were in the office meanwhile, and now emerged. We walked back up the avenue and, to my amazement, sat down again for another huge meal. They mocked me for not eating, and I stared at the soup wishing I had an appetite.

The truck mechanics said they were having the missing part of the BMW fabricated for them. They promised the bike would be ready to ride the following afternoon. I found a hotel in the centre of town, and that night I gave Nestor and Tomás a slide show on my computer. It was interesting to see how, in the comparative luxury of the hotel and in the presence of this hi-tech equipment, their confidence seemed diminished. Or perhaps it was just that my own confidence was restored, and I was no longer this hapless elderly man with a broken bike who depended on their goodwill and expertise.

We met again next day but things didn't feel the same. The bike was ready and running well. I took it round the block several times, paid the mechanics well, and shook hands with everyone. Nestor wrote his name and address into a small evangelical tract, commanding me one last time to repent the error of my ways.

I thought hard about that long road back to Cruce Culta, and then I set off on the asphalt highway to La Paz.

30

I was in La Paz longer than I intended. Not that there's anything terrible about having to spend time in La Paz. Puffing up and down those steep cobbled streets, counting the number of different ways a woman can wrap a bundle on her back, rummaging through shops full of brilliant fabrics and exploring markets vibrating with life can take up a lot of time. Because of the beautiful dresses of the women La Paz is like theatre. It can easily blind one to reality. When you see two women in their colourful native costume sorting through a pile of rubbish and restaurant waste at midnight, looking for food, you realise they are just wearing clothes.

The part that the mechanics of Oruro had made was obviously doing fine, and I would have let well alone, but an oil leak had started from the drive shaft and, all in all, it seemed better to take advantage of Stephen's offer to replace the shaft and to clear up the leak at the same time.

There is one excellent motorcycle shop just outside the city owned by Walter Nosiglias, who is Bolivia's dirt-bike champion. Although his is a Honda shop he was willing to learn about BMWs, and I had the manual. The parts were excruciatingly slow to arrive from Britain, and the taxes were big, but little Fredy, the mechanic, and his even tinier *ayudante*, both with their hats on backwards, did a fantastic job, and Walter made up for everything else by giving it all to me for nothing.

I was about to leave La Paz when I got an email that changed my plan.

A man once wrote to me from Chicago to tell me that his wife was leaving on a long motorcycle journey. I'm not sure whether at that time he talked of her going around the world, but I know there was a lot of excitement and enthusiasm in the letter. He wanted me to send her a copy of my book with some kind of dedication in it. I know how it feels to commit oneself to an undertaking like that: the soaring energy, the complete change of perspective, the feeling that for better or worse you have gambled everything on your own destiny. Of course, I was glad to play a small part in her story. Then I got involved in planning my own journey, and forgot about her.

From time to time I saw emails from Mariola Cichon describing her travels from Alaska to Latin America.They were full of joy, wonder and excitement, but I read only one or two of them. I have other friends and acquaintances who are riding around the globe, and I don't read much of their stuff either. Not that I'm uninterested. It's just that you either travel and write yourself, or you read about what others are doing. There isn't time to do both.

Then, when I was hung up in La Paz, she emailed to say she was in Arequipa, in Peru, with her husband who had flown out to spend Christmas with her. Could we meet?

Essentially there are two ways to go north from La Paz. One is the route I took in 1975, with Bruno and Antoine. That one goes along the top of the Andes, from Lake Titicaca through Puno, Sicuani, Cuzco, Ayacucho, Huancayo, and then down to Lima. Back then the native populations in these central highlands were almost completely cut off from the big urban centres on the coast. It was a wonderland to travel through, a land of terrible roads, incredible views, beautiful costumes and miserable poverty. The other way north is along the coast on the PanAmerican Highway through Arequipa, Nazca and Ica, to Lima. Until recently I had felt like sticking, as far as possible, to my original route, but now I was beginning to recognise the patterns. I didn't need to follow so slavishly in my own footsteps.

In broad terms I already knew what I would find. Where once

there were distinct, largely isolated indigenous groups, there is now miscegenation with urban populations. City habits and morals were spreading throughout the rural populations. Anyone looking for the world I saw in the seventies would already be too late. Admittedly Peru was a special case. It had gone through fire since I was there last. I remembered the contempt and indifference that the mainly Hispanic population of Lima felt for the *indios* – those indigenous people eking out an existence far above them in the mountains – and their smug neglect brought retribution. Two separate revolutionary movements, called Sendera Luminosa and Tupac Amaru, went to war with the government. Those conflicts cost around thirty thousand lives, and lasted for two decades.

By 2001 they were more or less over, and the government was paying a lot more attention to the people of the Central Highlands. Among the improvements I had heard about were two new highways linking the crest of the Andes with the coast, both said to be staggeringly good. So I formed a new plan. I wrote to Mariola saying I would meet her in Puno, which is alongside Lake Titicaca, just over a hundred miles inside Peru. Then I'd take one of those new roads down to the coast at Moquegua, follow the coast to Pisco, and then up the other new road to Ayacucho.

With the bike running beautifully, I said goodbye to my hotel on the Calle Illampu and set off for Desaguadero, at the border. In 1975 this took most of a day's work. I was interested to see, reading my old notes, how I took all that for granted. I accepted the effort and the time it took with the equanimity of a Mr Pickwick posting all day from St Albans to London; but asphalt had completely transformed those journeys. Now I was there in two hours.

Everything along the way looked different. Where before there had been only solitary figures crouching under their ponchos in freezing drizzle on the bare pampa, there were now quite vigorous agricultural projects under way. Only where the two countries meet had they preserved about four hundred yards of the old road, a mixture of stones and mud. *Nostalgie de la boue*, perhaps. Two long lines of trucks stood on the wet dirt, nose to tail, barely leaving room for me to squeeze between them. Then I was back on tar, and two hours later I was in Puno. Had I wanted to I could have ridden on to Cuzco and got there before dark, a journey that once took me three days.

I found Mariola in a cheap and cosy hotel behind the cathedral, and I'm happy to say that I liked her, very much. It's true that I do like most people – travelling would be painful, otherwise – but people who do unusual things can't always be counted on to be nice as well. And then there's the hype effect. When you're looking for support and money to realise an ambition, it can be hard to avoid leaving a trail of bullshit. I should know.

I thought Mariola did pretty well in that respect. She called her journey a 'ride of the heart', and her heart seemed to be in the right place for it. Tall, red-headed and strikingly attractive, she looked quite dramatic astride her Kawasaki. Her husband Kris was a big, effervescent and very accomplished Polish guy (they're both Polish Americans). We ate roast guinea pig, drank wine, and he gave me some good tips on how to stay upright on dirt, so it was definitely worth the two-hundred-mile diversion.

The following four days that got me to Ayacucho were quite remarkable. The first road down to the coast was a thrilling series of hairpins through rocks and desert, followed by an enchanted ride through multicoloured dunes, a view of the extraordinary Nazca lines and a glimpse of what a tsunami can do to a coastal town. But nothing prepared me for the road that brought me up to Ayacucho. I thought I might have stumbled on the most beautiful road in the world, at least in the world I had seen.

What made it so wonderful? As always, the whole was so much greater than the sum of its parts, but I'll try. First, the fact that it was a brand-new highway, in perfect condition, was not to be sniffed at when it meant that I could take my eyes off the road in confidence and dwell on the beauty around me. This road went through three distinctly different kinds of world. At the lower level, the country was very reminiscent of Provence, though at an earlier, less evolved period, with fields of fruit, stone walls and buildings, trees planted as windbreaks, bridges and rivers. It rose slowly at first, then as the angle of the hills became steeper the mountains gradually enveloped me and soon I was among them, staring at incredible rock formations and marvellous vistas up and down and all around.

And so it went on, with something new at every turn, soaring up to 15,000 feet and then over the top and into a quite different kind of alpine fertility, of sheep, llama, alpaca and native shepherds, all under a glorious blue sky with white cumulus cloud. And all of this in one afternoon.

Ayacucho, which had been the heart of the rebellion, seemed now to be a peaceful- and prosperous-looking county town – nothing like the wet and dreary hole I remembered from my first visit. I found a small hotel in a side street, opposite a covered market which displayed the usual colourful extravaganza of trop-ical produce. The street was obstructed by carts, and littered with smashed mangoes. It was one of those hotels full of second-hand furniture and adolescent men who all seemed to work there, but it was friendly and comfortable. I enjoyed it, but I was nervous too. This was the end of the asphalt. From here to Huancayo I was back in the dirt, and the clouds above were thickening.

This journey was teaching me things about my first journey that I don't think I had appreciated before. Or maybe I had just forgot-ten. One of those things was the profound importance of the commitment I had made. To me, then, just making the journey and doing it right was all that mattered. It was my life, and long before I got to the Andes I had made my peace with the fact that it might cost me my life.

Because of that my approach to the difficulties as they arose was quite fatalistic. I took them as they came, and hardly worried. I chose the route I wanted to take, and pursued it regardless, and I don't think there was ever a time when I deviated to a safer course after hearing about dangers or difficulties that might lie ahead.

I realise now how much easier that made it. By denying myself the choice, I removed much of the anxiety. The die was cast. I had only to follow my fortune, and to back me up I had a powerful resolve and the confidence that came from almost two years of success, of 'getting away with it'.

Today's experience was very different. Of course it was. Age played a part, but there were other much more significant factors. I love this world I'm in, but it was like revisiting an old friend, and I was not quite so ready to lay down my life for the privilege. I have a son, and I want to know what would happen to him. There were other important people I wanted to go back to, and other things I still wanted to accomplish. So when I heard about a bad road ahead, it was a threat. Then there was the undeniable fact that there were far fewer bad roads. I was on asphalt so often that when I got back on dirt it was like starting all over again. And finally, there was the lingering memory of a broken leg to remind me that though I may have been immortal once, I am certainly mortal now.

It was the road that I was going to take to Huancayo next day that brought all these thoughts to mind, a road that would certainly be dirt and might be very difficult. This was only part of a long stretch of wonderful adventure that occupied an entire month in 1975. The distance from La Quiaca, where I entered Bolivia, to Huancayo where I was headed now was 1300 miles, and of that only 150 at most had been on asphalt back then. By the time I arrived at Ayacucho I had forgotten what tar was. This time, I had been on tar ever since Oruro.

It rained heavily in the night, the street outside was streaming and low fog hung around the town, but the boss of the hotel claimed to know that it would clear up. He told me there were two roads to Huancayo, an old one and a new, improved one. 'Be sure to take the new road, the *mejorada*, not the one that goes through Moccoche.' And the good news was that the first fifty kilometres to Huanta were paved.

So off I went, and he was right about the tar to Huanta. There I came to a roundabout, and met a man driving a truck for the municipality who ought to know about the roads. A sign pointed to Huancayo.

'Is this the *mejorada*?' I asked.

'*Sí,*' he insisted, '*es mejorada.*'

But I didn't just rely on him. Two other men were sitting on a wall, and they too said this was the way to Huancayo.

'Four hours on the bus,' they said.

Reassured, I rode on, but the road got narrower and narrower until it was nothing more than a twisting footpath sliding down a steep hill. How can this be the new road? I wondered.

Turning with difficulty, I went back and found yet another man. Yes indeed, he said, this is the way the taxis go. 'Don't worry. *No te preocupes!* Down below it will meet the main road.'

The sandy, rutted track wound and dropped for miles until I thought I was the victim of a practical joke, when to my huge relief it did meet with a wider dirt road, and I found myself riding alongside a river. The sky had cleared. The road, cut into the side of a steep river gorge, was quite decent. Things were looking better. Occasionally the road climbed quite high, and when it dropped again it would be to cross a stream, but the water was shallow. After an hour it bridged the river, and a few miles on it crossed back again to a small town. The name of the town was Moccoche. So I was on the wrong road after all, and too far on to go back.

There were some women waiting at a bus stop. 'How far to Huancayo?' I asked.

'Seven or eight hours,' replied one of them, emphatically.

'But the men in Huanta said it was only four.'

'They lied.'

In eight hours it would be dark. I cursed under my breath. Confused and discouraged, I went on. The mountain climbed steeply to my right, with sheer drops over the side at my left. There were many tight bends.

I was reminded of a story I heard about two Midwesterners, Frank and Bob, going through Peru on dirt bikes. Someone had sold them the idea that from Ayacucho to Cuzco was a short ride (which it certainly isn't), and by dusk they were less than halfway, on a similar road to this. In the dark, Frank lost his focus, drove into the mountainside and knocked himself out. At that point a truck approached. Bob drew his bike over to the other side of the road, but the ground gave way and he and his bike disappeared over the edge.

When Frank came to, Bob was nowhere to be seen. He shouted his name, and a faint voice came up from below: 'I'm OK – the bike got caught on a tree.' Below them, in the dark, Frank saw the lights of a village, and the villagers, having heard the shouts, came up the road with a rope. After much effort they successfully hauled the bike up to the road, and with joy and mutual congratulation they set off back to the village, before they recalled that they had forgotten about Bob.

They got him up, eventually. By then Frank had discovered that he'd broken his collar bone, but they went on next day, regardless.

At the time I heard the story, I thought it was hilarious. It didn't seem quite so funny now, and I was careful to pull over to the right on the rare occasions when a truck approached. The road ran all the way along the valley of the Mantaro River. There were wonderful views, and in one place a spectacular flood of what I took to be alabaster surged over the crest of a gorge, frozen in place.

Occasional little wooden plank bridges over streams presented a problem, The planks were nailed together with strips of wood just far enough apart to jam my front tyre, and I did get caught by one of them but escaped being thrown. I was averaging twenty miles an hour, and after three hours came to a town called Cáceres Mariscal with a hydro-electric installation.

Inside the gate were two men leaning on motorcycles, and we talked. I told them I seemed to have been misled, and intended to be on the *mejorada*.

'This *is* the *mejorada*,' they said. 'This is the quick, improved route. How fast do you ride? Sixty, seventy kilometres an hour?'

I thought they were just boasting. No way could you ride at that speed on the road I'd just been on. But as soon as I left them the road improved dramatically, and I was doing forty or more miles an hour. Perhaps they had never gone the other way? But the final confusion came a little further on, when I passed through another town. Its name was Mejorada.

Soon after that, 110 miles from Huanta, a brilliant new tarmac road swept me into Huancayo. The whole journey from Ayacucho had taken five and a half hours.

The descent from Huancayo to Lima began with a climb on a badly broken asphalt road leading out of the huge and fertile Mantaro Valley to La Oroya, which is a centre of Peru's mining industry. I remembered this part of the trip well from 1975, because it was here that I saw what I described in *Jupiter's Travels* as 'the highest ecological disaster area in the world . . . Pitiful rows of slum cottages, squalid railway yards, factories belching acrid smoke, vast slag heaps oozing lurid and poisonous wastes into stagnant yellow pools where ragged children splashed barefoot, and all among unmelted drifts of soiled snow and bitter cold.'

Things looked a lot better after a quarter of a century, and not just because the weather was good. I don't think a mining town can ever be called pretty, but La Oroya itself didn't seem too bad. The scene I'd described was above La Oroya, though, at Morococha, and the road no longer passes through it. By the time I realised this, I was well above it, but I could see enough to know that the houses at least were much improved, and there was no smoke, acrid or otherwise.

The road climbed well above 15,000 feet, past a brilliant turquoise lake, and then began the long drop to the coast among increasingly dense traffic, through roadworks, past more and more mining operations, through ever bigger towns, until finally I found myself on a straight avenue choked with buses, trucks and cars that ran for twenty miles into the heart of Lima. The driving would have been insane if the drivers' reflexes hadn't been so good. I was hardly ever more than a foot away from some vehicle or other. The pace was furious, and the climax came when a pick-up laden with construction debris crashed into the back of a minibus immediately to my right. Bits of wood and plaster flew everywhere. A lump of two-by-four hit my front wheel, but I was past it before it could do any damage.

In the relative calm of the city itself, I saw two big white police Harleys parked outside a public lavatory, so I stuck my BMW behind them, took out my mobile phone (which actually worked in Lima) and called a friend of Adolfo's who said he'd come and find me.

As I waited, two gorgeous women in tight-fitting police uniforms emerged from the toilets and rode off on their Harleys. I was very impressed. Apparently they belonged to the Fénix Squad of traffic police which was made up entirely of women. They were said to be incorruptible, unlike the men they replaced. I saw a lot more of them later, and they were all very good-looking. They may all be women, but I bet they were recruited by men.

31

There's no doubt that after leaving Brazil, my thoughts were drawn to Colombia as if by a magnet. My memories of it were so warm that ever since leaving England I had been impatient to see it again. At the same time I knew it would be a serious challenge to my state of mind. Colombia has always posed problems, but now there was an altogether different kind of threat.

Sometimes I think information is the enemy. There were many times on this journey when I longed for the blissful ignorance of my first venture into the world. Only once in those four years did it get me into real trouble, in Brazil, and even then I doubt that I could have or should have avoided it. Risk management on a trip like mine still seems to me to be a largely futile endeavour. The anticipated dangers hardly ever materialise, and obviously there's no way to prepare for the others. In any case, I learned many years ago that the odds in our favour are vastly higher than we imagine.

A modicum of fear is a useful preservative, but I try not to let it affect my behaviour. Sometimes I fail. Even in the seventies Colombia's reputation for violence and theft reached out to me long before I got there, and induced me to take precautions. I remember sharpening my kitchen knife (though what I had in mind to do with it escapes me). I also put padlocks on my boxes, but they were of little use as I soon lost the keys and had to have the locks sawn off.

No aggression came my way and I experienced only wonder at

the beauty of the country, and admiration for its people. But things had changed. Now a distinctly different set of horror stories emanated from Colombia.

Two major guerrilla groups had de facto control over sizeable areas of the country. The FARC, more to the east, were financed mainly by drug money, and carried out widespread bombings, raids and assassinations. The ELN, still thought to be the more ideological bunch, specialised in kidnapping and extortion, with a special presence on the very roads I meant to travel. And paramilitary death squads added to the mayhem in the name of peremptory right-wing justice. The only positive note was that Pablo Escobar's reign of terror in Medellín had ended in his death.

One could hardly approach this kind of situation without qualms, but I was determined to shrug off the dangers. I knew that with a reasonable amount of caution the odds against running into trouble were acceptable. And then I had the misfortune to meet Glen Heggstad. Not that I was unhappy about meeting Glen himself, although we are certainly very different kinds of people. It was what he said he had just been through that dented my composure.

I was visiting Ricardo Rocco, a passionate rider who lives in Quito and lavishes hospitality on every biker who comes that way, when I met Heggstad. Ricardo told me that Glen had just been rescued from the ELN. They had kidnapped him five weeks earlier when he was riding along the road from Bogotá to Medellín. At Ricardo's home I met this tall, pale, gaunt man who appeared to be deeply depressed and withdrawn. How or why the ELN let him go was obscure, and Glen didn't want to talk about that, or anything else to do with his ordeal except that they had delivered him into the hands of the Red Cross. The bike he was riding at the time, an olive-green Kawasaki, had disappeared, but supporters in his native Minnesota had delivered another one.

'It was worse than anything I could have imagined,' was all he'd say about his experiences, and then he showed me a larva, about the size of a fingernail, that he'd dug out from under his skin and saved in a plastic bag. He did his best to dissuade me from going into Colombia at all, but when that failed he said, 'If I had to do it again, I'd carry a red cross. The Red Cross is about the only thing they respect.'

I thought about it and didn't care for the idea at first. The ethics seemed shaky, and anyway I couldn't imagine a guerrilla saying to himself, Oh, he must be one of those Red Cross bikers I've never heard of.

Ricardo, on the other hand, was very taken with the plan. He had some poster materials, including a sheet of red contact paper, and made me a big red cross. I rolled it up and took it away, planning to lose it somewhere later, but there's no question that the whole episode shook my confidence. What was a biker to do?

I did the only sensible thing and asked around for as much advice as I could get. The response was pretty straightforward. On the route I planned to take, the danger was mainly on the more deserted stretches of the highway, either between Pasto and Popayán or north of Medellín. In these areas where the ELN is active, ride early in the day and never at night, because guerrillas like to get away under cover of darkness. Watch for oncoming traffic, because its absence could signal a road block. And keep asking the locals what's happening.

Somehow I couldn't quite bring myself to toss out that red cross, and on my way to the border I began what became a long series of imaginary conversations with guerrilla *comandantes*.

'Yes indeed,' I would say, trying to ignore the muzzle of the AK47 nudging my ribs, 'I really am a Red Cross volunteer. We carry urgent medical supplies and blood.'

'So where is this blood, this medicine, Señor?'

'Well, I don't have any with me at this moment, actually, but they're waiting for me anxiously in Medellín.'

After a bit of rehearsing I had almost convinced myself it could work. Anyway, it was better than nothing.

I swept my ethical doubts aside, and as soon as I'd crossed into Colombia I stopped at the roadside and got the red cross out of my tank bag. An old man saw me from his garden, and came out through the gate to talk.

'*Qué tal?* How's life?' I asked.

He sighed, mournfully. 'It is very difficult, very dangerous.'

Then, as the big, bold cross unfolded on to my windshield like the banner of St George, he exclaimed, '*Ah, la Cruz Roja!* Nobody will molest you now.'

I took his words as a blessing and set off for Pasto.

Even after the glories of the Peruvian and Ecuadorian Andes, Colombia is astonishing. It was a bitter-sweet experience, riding with the thought that there could be a road block around the next corner, but the mountains exerted their monumental presence and after a while I just couldn't think about anything else.

The road climbed to 10,000 feet, and swooped around the high passes. Where the southern Andes were rock, bare and sharp-peaked, here they were more rounded and clothed in green velvet, which somehow managed to make them seem even more enormous. Before long the landscape had captured me, and by the time I came down again to the valley and Pasto it had completely distracted me from my paranoid dialogues with imaginary terrorists.

Pasto was within easy reach of the border and the road surfaces were great, so I arrived at midday with plenty of time to look around at the apparent ease and affluence of a prosperous city centre. I saw crowds of well dressed men and women, late-model cars, girls in mini-skirts and heavy makeup, all thronging the cafés, bars, restaurants, ice-cream parlours and shops along the arcaded sidewalks of the plaza. Because the news from Colombia is all about jungle warfare and urban terror, bombings, shootings, massacres and extortion, it comes as a shock to find such sophistication in the cities.

The poverty and the misery are in the countryside, and I got a very close look at it next day, on the way to Popayán. The road climbed up again, but there was nothing majestic about this part of the country. It was arid, dusty, blighted land. I saw mean hovels, barren earth and, worst of all, there were people begging at the roadside – wrinkled old men, shapeless old women, some offering a handful of dry fruits, others just holding out calloused hands. It was as though a curse had descended on this particular part of the world, because I never before or after saw anything so bad, and a shiver went through me as I left.

It was just this section of the road that I had been warned about, of course. Between them, the guerrillas and the paramilitary appeared to have condemned it to death. I watched the traffic carefully and anxiously, and was glad to see that the army had a frequent presence on the road.

Popayán, again, was an easy objective for me, and I was there in good time. This is an old colonial town, and the plaza is ringed by buildings of white adobe and Roman tiles. It seemed to be bursting with activity. I was looking for a hotel where Bruno and I had splashed out in 1975. There had been a devastating earthquake since then, and I feared that it might have been destroyed, but my guidebook promised me that the Hotel Monasterio was still there. My memories of that time were very happy, and I was sure that when I saw the hotel I would have a powerful sense of recognition. In fact when I found it I was perplexed. It was completely unfamiliar. It was obviously the same building that had stood there for centuries, first as a monastery, then as a hotel: a grand two-storey structure built around a decorative garden with fountains. The cells had been converted into bedrooms, opening on to a broad, stone-flagged balcony, but apart from the addition of fixtures, little had been changed. The essential nature of the old monastery remained.

I couldn't imagine how I had ever thought of it as luxurious, cosseting, vibrant. What I saw now was an emotionally chilly, bare and echoing – in short, monastic – space. It took some effort to explain to myself why I found it so unrecognisable, but in the end I thought it was simply because the place was empty. My recollection was of a hotel busy with lively people, of tables laid with colourful cloths, of buffets laden with brilliant displays of food, of waiters rushing here and there.

Now, with tourism at a standstill, all the life had left it. I was never so aware of what a difference that can make. I stayed there anyway, partly for old times' sake and also because some chauffeurs of fancy limousines, parked next to my bike, told me that negotiations were going on in the hotel between the government and the ELN. If there were, they were whispering in a broom cupboard. I couldn't find a trace of them.

The route I had chosen led me up the centre of Colombia to the Cauca Valley. It was too dangerous to go off on side trips, but the main road north was considered all right so I was headed directly to Medellín, where an email contact, Tiberio Jaramillo, was expecting me.

The city was still more than five hundred miles away. Although these roads were safer, I decided to stick to my routine, and stop for the night somewhere on the way. Now that I was down in the valley the heat was building up. I thought of going into Cali, Colombia's second biggest city, but lost my way on the edge of it and decided to skirt it. The truck traffic was becoming difficult, slowing me up, blackening me with diesel fumes and making me even hotter. I worked my way north past sugar cane plantations, round Palmira and Cerrito, and by the time I got to Buga I felt too hot to go on.

I stopped at a crossroads, undecided, and an elderly, pot-bellied gentleman astride a small Honda rode up to me.

'*Hola! Qué tal?* Can I help you?'

'I was thinking of stopping here,' I said.

He asked me about my travels, and told me he was retired from the army. If I was going to Medellín, he said, I should go around through Armenia, Pereira and Manizales. 'It will be safer that way. Are you going to stay here tonight?'

'Do you know a cheap hotel?'

'Come,' he said. 'I will take you,' and he puttered off into town, leading me past an enormous red-brick cathedral to an area where the streets were laid out in a numbered grid. The hotel he showed me was decent, cheap, and could house the bike. The small court-yard was entirely taken up by a pool, with a walkway that crossed over it like a bridge. I said a hurried thank you to my guide, took a room, and within five minutes I was in the pool. I swear I heard the water hiss as it touched my skin.

Later that evening I walked into town for a meal and to look around. I passed a cinema, fried chicken outlets, a mini-casino, ice-cream parlours, juice bars, shoe shops and wound up on a pleasant plaza where I had a good dinner. It was about eleven when I realised that I had forgotten the name of the hotel and had no idea

what number street it was on. It took me an hour of increasing desperation wandering through the dark and deserted city before I
stumbled on it, so I can vouch for the safety of Buga by night.

With about three hundred miles to go the next day, and nothing
much to worry about, this last leg to Medellín should have been a
free ride. I have looked back on it many times wondering just what
it was that unseated my judgement on this particular day.

It was hot, no question about that, but I was quite accustomed to
heat. There was always the temptation to take off my jacket, but
even after all these years I can't forget how miserable it made me to
lose my flying-jacket in Mexico because the heat had made me too
careless to tie it on properly. Besides, this jacket was so well venti-
lated, under the arms and across the back, that it wouldn't have
made much difference. A few hours later I was deeply grateful to it.

Probably it was the traffic more than anything. I didn't expect so
much heavy traffic. I was riding now on one of the busiest roads in
Colombia, between manufacturing towns. The trucks were not
huge – twenty to forty tons – but they were dirty, and riding behind
them I became filthy too. They were covered by canvas rather than
hard tops, and I was behind them long enough to notice that most
of the tarpaulins were made in Medellín. As for the road itself,
while the surface was good, it was usually just a narrrow two lanes,
and overtaking was always a problem. By mid-afternoon I had come
through the bigger towns along the way, and was approaching
Medellín from La Pintada.

The road was winding uphill and the trucks were slower and
more numerous than ever when a little silver Civic nipped past me,
coming dangerously close.

I can still see that car in front of me now. The driver was
obscured by a headrest, but the passenger was a woman with a long
pony-tail which swung from side to side as the Honda darted about,
making failed attempts to pass the trucks in front of us. It annoyed
me that even when I could have got past them on the bike, the car
blocked me every time.

I should have just fallen back and let it be, but the stupid driver
got me mad. I couldn't know, when I saw a chance to get round

him, that I had chosen the most notorious curve on that whole sixty-mile stretch. I was already through, at maybe 40 m.p.h., when the road curved dramatically to the left.

However many times you read about it, or try to imagine it, nothing can prepare you for that moment when you find yourself staring into the face of fate, knowing that it's too late, knowing that whether you live or die is out of your hands, and having perhaps just one last flash of insight into your own unbelievable stupidity. That was the moment when I looked up and saw the rocks and the concrete storm-drain coming at me like the wall of death.

Then I was on my back between the bike and the concrete gutter, in utter stillness, wondering whether I was still alive. I don't know how long I lay there. It was probably less than a minute, but it seemed like an age. I didn't want to move. I didn't want to know what had happened to me.

By the time I knew that I was still breathing, two pick-ups and a motorcycle had stopped. The response was instant and generous. There were people all around and one couple was kneeling beside me. Carefully I moved my limbs, one by one, and they seemed OK. I got my helmet off, and nothing terrible happened. The visor was so badly scratched that it was opaque. That would have been my face, I thought. The jacket too had done its job: some of the fabric was melted by the abrasion and the padding must have saved me from much worse injury. One glove was ripped open, but the hand was only lightly skinned. My jeans had done their best, although beneath the fabric I later found a huge bloody mess above one knee.

I staggered to my feet, amazed that nothing inside me seemed to have broken. The lids had blown off the boxes, and my things were all over the road – my tools, the Pelican case with my computer still in it, spare parts, clothes and so on. While others gathered up my stuff, the couple, whom I got to know later as Nelson and Lucelly Montoya, helped me to hobble over to one of the pick-ups, belonging to another member of their family, Sergio Santistebán.

Then they all got together to load the badly abused Beemer into the Montoyas' pick-up with all my bits and pieces, and we drove back in convoy down the hill to La Pintada where there was a clinic. There they unloaded me and the bike, and after many effusive wishes for my health and safety they left me there. None of them seemed to realise that I had done something supremely stupid to cause all this trouble, so I kept my shame to myself. They treated me as though I were one of the family, and when I finally got round to checking, days later, not a single one of my things had been lost.

As we drove down I had become aware of something jiggling just below my neck and realised that I hadn't quite got away with it. So that's the clavicula, I thought. Another broken bone, and still no pain. How can I be so lucky? But the pain came later.

At the clinic I met a handsome young doctor, Miguel, who seemed to be on top of things in a sensible and practical way. I was not his usual kind of patient, so we talked a bit, and I learned that he had been trained at a faculty funded from Moscow. He confirmed that I had broken my collar bone and was very offhand about it. 'Don't move it around too much, and it will repair itself,' he said. 'It is a good break. The ends are still together. In ten days you will be fine.'

The clinic couldn't supply a sling, so he made one up out of loops of bandage. The mess on my leg was another matter. Quite a bit of me seemed to have been gouged out. There was a lot of cleaning and dressing to be done by pretty nurses, but the treatment was all very practical and matter-of-fact. This was a clinic mainly for rural workers who could not afford to take time off.

It was around this time, as I was being patched up, that I became painfully aware of a couple of cracked ribs, and it was these that caused me the most trouble in the end. I told Miguel about them, expecting that he would strap them up or something, but he said that was an ancient practice and not done any more. 'They must be free to move. It's better to go with the pain,' and he grinned in a friendly way.

So he gave me the bill, for twenty-five dollars, and they called a taxi. There was a hotel in town, Miguel said, and that's where they had booked me in. I went outside to wait for the taxi, and saw the bike standing there. At the time of the accident I was too much in shock to pay attention to it, and when I first saw it I couldn't see the damage, until I realised that the headlight was sitting on the front tyre. Then I also saw that the steering head was fractured and the instruments were a complete mess. But the forks and the wheel looked all right. Miguel said I could leave it there until I was able to have it repaired, and I asked him to take a picture for me. Then the taxi took me away to Los Reyes de Pintada.

Perhaps Los Reyes was not the best choice of hotel for an elderly invalid trying to come to terms with his own folly. In fact it might have been devised as a hell for incompetent, superannuated heroes. It was a resort hotel for yuppies escaping the relative cold of Medellín. An enormous pool at its centre was full of sleek athletic bodies, muscular limbs flying through the air and thrashing about in the water. Gorgeous young couples added twenty years to my age as I limped pathetically among them like the invisible man.

And then came the night. I had had no idea what a torture cracked ribs could be. My first mistake was to lie down on the bed. The pain was excruciating, exceeded only by the pain of trying to get up again. After managing finally to roll myself off on to my knees, I could see I would have to sleep in a chair, and in fact for the following six nights that was all I could do, but I spent only one of them in Los Reyes.

The next day I got Tiberio Jaramillo on the phone, and within three hours of my talking to him he and a friend had arrived with a pick-up to carry me and the bike off to Medellín. Tiberio was a tower of strength and encouragement. This stocky forty-year-old with an engaging grin had a BMW repair shop in the middle of town. My good fortune seemed to be ineffable.

Tiberio found a small hotel in the Candelaria area of Medellín, right in the centre. The nights were a pain for a while, although they found me a comfortable chair to sleep in, but I was all right during the day provided I didn't laugh or cough. I took a taxi over to Tiberio's shop in the mornings and worked on my computer – there was always so much to do with the website and the email.

In the evenings, I tottered out on to the big avenue called La Playa (The Beach) and, curiously enough, although it was many hours from either the Pacific or the Caribbean, there was a feeling about it as though the sea might actually be behind the next row of buildings. Particularly after dark. It could have been the warm air, the palm trees and the profusion of ice-cream parlours, or perhaps it was the people – even when they were busy they seemed relaxed, and in the evening very few were busy. There were cafés, restaurants, quick-chicken places, roadside grills, and heaps of fruit on the pavements.

CD shops fired snatches of music into the air. People at all levels of prosperity, in glad rags and sad rags, stood and sat around, eating, drinking, talking. Medellín is a big textile centre, and very fashion-conscious. The girls in their low-cut jeans were thinner and more beautiful than I remembered them from twenty-seven years back. Breasts and slim waists were obviously a very big deal in Medellín. Because the weather is generally warm, the girls wore short, tight-fitting tops, so breasts were prominent, and I was told the silicone business was brisk. I would not have liked to be a girl competing for attention in Medellín, but as a man who couldn't tell the difference between real and false I enjoyed them all and felt fairly blameless, since I knew they weren't being aimed at me.

Medellín has interesting art, good music, and there was a fine library nearby. It was a great city to be recovering in, and it was hard to believe that ten years earlier, under Escobar, bombings and assassinations had been everyday events.

Tiberio's girlfriend, Paulina, was a victim of Escobar. She was the young widow of an assassinated CEO, and had inherited a beautiful weekend house up in the hills at Valparaíso. One long weekend she took us there, and I snoozed on the terrace, drank in the view of the hazy hills and valleys stretching out for ever, and wandered about the village admiring the care given to the adobe houses and the streets. An enormous ceiba tree shaded the square, the Saturday market was going through an early-afternoon slump while the stall owners dozed. A brilliantly painted old wooden bus stood empty like an exhibit. A brief burst of noise ruptured the calm as a horseman in a cowboy hat clattered up a cobbled street. Back on the terrace we ate fruit and tried to name all the varieties that grew in Colombia, but at sixty gave up counting. It was a perfect weekend.

Tiberio had to wait for more parts to come from England, and then the reconstruction process began. There was no hurry. I determined to pay some respect to my age and, regardless of Dr Miguel, gave myself a full month before resuming the journey.

When the bike was ready, we went out for the day, Tiberio, Paulina and I. The bike felt great, but the handling had changed dramatically. Tiberio told me that the old head bearings had been shot. Steering must have been getting stiffer without my realising it. Suddenly everything swung so easily that coming slowly out of a garage on an awkward slope I almost lost control.

By this time I had found that I could fly the bike directly from Medellín to Panama at a very reasonable price, and I decided to sacrifice the ride to Cartagena for the sake of gaining some time. I was becoming more and more anxious to be in California when Malú arrived. We were corresponding by email and old feelings were stirring again.

32

Mauricio Tirado was a close friend of Tiberio's and became a good friend of mine. He was a tall, handsome man and in very good shape. He rode a big 1100 GS and his ambition was to run motorcycle tours for Colombians in Spain. He came from a family with important business interests and he felt a deep responsibility to them, but his passion was for motorcycles, which the family disdained, and his normally mild features sometimes seemed to express his frustration. He was married to a delightful sculptress, and they lived in moderate luxury outside Medellín in Río Negro, on the way to the airport. Both he and Macky were happy to have me stay with them during my last days in Colombia, and he helped me get the bike on to the plane to Panama.

The facilities at the airport were less than ideal. The loading deck was three feet above the tarmac, but there was no ramp, and not enough of us to lift the bike. After fruitless attempts to find planks it seemed the only way to get the bike up there was to ride it up and along a steeply sloping embankment of grass-covered dirt that abutted the dock. I was annoyed that I should have to take the risk of dropping the bike just to compensate for the airport's shortcomings, and frankly I was unsure that I could accomplish it safely, so I refused.

After a moment, Mauricio said, quietly, 'I think I can do it.'

Mauricio was a man of convincing modesty. I knew this was no brash boast, and I also knew that if he failed he could certainly afford to make good the damage, so I said OK. He took the bike, very slowly, slantwise up the treacherous slope in a beautiful demonstration of trials riding, and the bike was safely delivered into the cargo area and strapped to a pallet.

On one of my last nights they took me out to a small town of fifty thousand people called Retiro where pine furniture was manufactured. It seemed that every first Saturday of the month Retiro organises a party in the main square. They showed films on a makeshift screen and the municipal band played traditional Colombian music from different parts of the country. It's thrilling music, with lots of trumpet, flute and clarinet, and the band played very well. They were followed by a guitar trio, doing sentimental ballads.

The square was packed with people. We sat at café tables drinking rum and Coke, and eating *chicharrones* and delicious small *empanadas*. Others sat on benches, or on the stone borders of the flower beds, or on the plinths of the monuments, gazing at the band under its brightly lit awning. From where I sat I could see the tiled roofs and finely proportioned balconies of the colonial buildings surrounding the square. Three big laurel trees, sculpted to look like fat green plum puddings, seemed to float above me in the lambent sky. The weather was perfect, as it almost always is there. The atmosphere was pure pleasure, with not a hint of violence or unsociable behaviour. I danced and felt happy.

I guard these memories carefully. Two years later, on his GS with Macky on the back, Mauricio met a truck coming round a blind corner on the wrong side of the road and was killed instantly. His wife was seriously injured, and we mourn his loss. The truck driver is still driving. For some mysterious reason the case never seems to come to court.

On a more cheerful note, in the five years since my accident large parts of Colombia have become safe and Tiberio, among others, is running motorcycle tours up and down this beautiful country.

The trouble with Central America is that there are too many countries packed together, all small, and all different. To give them their due, I would have needed the month I'd lost in Colombia.

Regretfully I found myself doing what I did the first time round, and whistled through them.

Panama continued not to impress me. It's unfair, I know, to judge a country by what you see from the highway, but the landscape looks messy. Cattle country mostly, cleared and fenced, but untidy . . . and hot. Then I rode up into the hills to Boquete, and that was better. They were nice people on the whole. I thought it would be the sort of place you'd go to when Costa Rica became too expensive. This was confirmed for me by the elderly American gent who owned Bookmark, a green-painted villa full of used paperbacks. He was snoozing in his chair, but came to life when I asked him how long he'd been there.

'Ah came down eight years ago from Coasta Reeky. Gettin' too expensive, and anyways it's fulla thieves. Fella Ah knows tells me Caracas is more expensive now than Paris, and thet used to be the third most expensive city in the world. I guess the world is changing.'

I said Paris was still very expensive. I said I wished I could afford to live there.

'So do I,' he said vehemently. 'So do I.'

I tried to picture him in Paris, wearing a beret and selling his paperbacks on the banks of the Seine, but I couldn't.

With the exception of Costa Rica, which has always been a sort of American protectorate, all the countries of Central America had been through hell and back since I was there in the seventies. Panama had Noriega, and an American invasion. Nicaragua had a revolution to get rid of the detestable Somoza, only to have to fight a disastrous war against America's proxies, the Contras, a war which also implicated its neighbour, Honduras. Guatemala was the scene of continuous and murderous military repression, and the brutality of the regimes in El Salvador, which I have never visited, is well known.

Riding through as I did, I saw none of this. I had a particularly good week in Costa Rica, chasing the *piña colada* all along the coast and having my clothes stolen off a hotel washing-line. I had a great evening in the beautiful colonnaded square of ancient Granada, in Nicaragua, the latest swinging tourist phenomenon of the region. I revisited the Mayan temple site at Copán, and saw how many marvels had been unearthed in the interim, and had the enormous good fortune to be in Antigua Guatemala for the Easter parade of the angels.

From Guatemala I followed my original route into Mexico, first to San Cristóbal de las Casas and then, picking up a quart of mescal on the way, to Oaxaca. Both of these places used to be wonderful and were now congested with tourism, overpriced and crime ridden. In fact I learned that the murder rate per capita in Oaxaca had outstripped even Medellín. Which is not to say that there aren't marvellous things to see there, or that you will necessarily be murdered while seeing them, but time is not on your side.

So I escaped over the mountains to the coast, and the more reasonable pleasures of the beaches of Puerto Ángel.

Acapulco is a place I had never been, although I'd heard about it all my life. John Wayne used to hang out there. So did Johnny 'Tarzan' Weissmuller and countless other stars of stage, screen and radio. It used to be on newsreels when I was a kid. I bet Carmen Miranda was there a lot. Everybody, I thought, should have their day in Acapulco, so I dragged myself off the beach at Puerto Ángel and headed in that direction.

But a funny thing happened on my way to Acapulco.

With less than a hundred miles to go I was riding quite happily along a perfectly good straight road at about 55 m.p.h. The air was coursing through my hyperventilated jacket, and I was thinking about good times ahead, when suddenly I was sitting seven or eight inches lower than I had been an instant before. Quick to realise that something was wrong, I stopped. The shoulder was an uncertain mixture of brush and loose earth so I had to stop on the tarmac.

Then I met my first predicament.

The side-stand was useless, because the engine was almost on the ground. Likewise, it was impossible to lift the bike on to the centre-stand. Evidently I was condemned to stand there holding it up for ever, or letting it drop. I still couldn't see what was wrong, though I had a pretty good idea.

Still balancing the bike, I began to unstrap the soft luggage. Then I found I could put my main black bag under one of the panniers and lean the bike on it comfortably, allowing me to let go and view the damage.

My BMW had one shock absorber, a handsome and rather expensive thing called an Ohlins, with a big, beautiful yellow spring. It was still there, but at a jaunty angle, not at all where it was supposed to be. I took off the pannier that was obstructing my view, and applying my enviable intellect to the problem I discovered what had happened: a bolt that was supposed to hold the shock in place had sheared off, and the bottom end of the shock had jumped off its seat. This, I thought, was not supposed to happen to BMWs, but that was not a new thought. I'd had it before, in Bolivia.

Another thought was that the *topes* had finally got me. Ever since Africa speed bumps had been infuriating me, but they'd never been as bad as they were there in Mexico, where they are called *topes*. You run into them all the time, sometimes three or four in a row, even on major highways. Sometimes there's a sign to tell you they're coming, sometimes not. They can be ruinous to cars, which have to crawl over them. Usually I would slow down for them too, but the bike could actually take them in its stride, and anyway I had another problem right now which inclined me to keep going and absorb the bumps: my tyres were wearing out fast, especially the front one.

It was my own fault. Avon would have given me all the tyres I asked for. I just didn't want to bother them. Now the set I had would have to get me to the US, with another 1700 miles to go, but they were looking awfully thin and nothing wears out tyres so much as banging on the brakes.

So I was trying to ride through Mexico without using my front brake. If somebody were to suggest that you do something impossible like jump out of a plane with nothing but an umbrella, you could say, 'Why, that would be like riding in Mexico with no brakes!' Nevertheless, it was what I was trying to do. And braking for every *tope* would skin the rubber off my front wheel before you could say Mazatlán. Sometimes I changed down fast enough to avoid the jolt, but mostly I just rode over them. The bike could do it. My Ohlins could take it. But maybe that bolt couldn't. Or maybe it fractured ages ago in Africa, and now was when it decided to pop.

Whatever. There I was on the edge of a not too wide road, with maniacs whizzing back and forth at the end of their Easter holiday. I stayed calm. It is a well known fact that help will come. I busied myself taking everything I could off the bike to make it lighter. I knew it would have to be lifted into something.

A truckload of police wearing guns and dark-blue cloth drove past waving and smiling.

'Well, Gee, thanks guys! What do you think I'm doing here?'

Then a *pesero*, which is a pick-up with seats in the back for passengers, came along and I stopped him.

'*Hola hombre. Qué pasó?*' He said there was a mechanic just down the road. He would come back soon with three men to lift the bike into his pick-up. He drove off.

A white delivery van stopped behind me to let a bus pass in the opposite direction. A taxi driver travelling very fast behind the van was thinking of other things, and woke up almost too late, stopping inches from the van in a cloud of burnt rubber. This made the van driver angry with me, and we had a futile conversation during which he told me to do all the things I couldn't do, like taking the bike off the road. I switched on the left indicator to please him, and he drove off.

Then I switched it off again. Anyone who couldn't see the bike, wouldn't see the indicator. Then the police came past again, still waving and smiling.

I spread out my arms as if to say 'What the . . . !'

Having registered that I wasn't just stopping for a sandwich, they turned around and came back. There were six of them, and immediately two started directing traffic around me, with red flags. Actually it was a good idea, but it didn't look like an idea at all. I think they would have done it in the middle of a field.

But the others came to talk to me. They were sympathetic, and nice, and wanted to help. They thought they would put the bike in their truck. I told them about the *pesero* but their boss, who was in plain clothes, said the *pesero* would not come back. He turned out to be right, but I don't know how he knew. He didn't seem to know anything else. They tried to let down the tailgate of their truck, but it wouldn't open. Two of them struggled away at it for a long time. Then finally it popped down.

When it did I saw that there was a wooden structure right down the middle of the truck bed for the cops to sit on. There was no room in there for a bike. As delicately as I could I pointed this out, and while they were absorbing this information, a highway patrol car stopped, and the officer stepped out. He was in a different class, spick and span and spunky, with a polished badge and visible gleams of intelligence in his eyes. I was able to explain to him that if we could just lift the back of the bike high enough to get it on to the centre-stand I might be able to perform some magic and get it running again.

So that's what we did, and I popped the end of the Ohlins back over its stub, good enough to get me to the next village, but obviously not much further. Meanwhile two things happened.

First of all Officer Nambo (that was his name) told me he also rode motorcycles, and he knew a shop in Acapulco where they could fix me up. Then another pick-up stopped, this time with a car mechanic in it, a dark bristly man with a cheerful smile whose name was Ángel, and he wanted to be my angel too.

We now had the elements of a plan. We had enough muscle to load the bike into Ángel's pick-up, and he was willing to take me and the bike to Acapulco, for gas money and a little on top. Officer Nambo said he would phone the fellow he knew there, and tell him to wait for us. To do that, though, we had first to drive fifteen miles to Nambo's station house. There seemed to be communications equipment in his car, but for some reason he couldn't use it. So I rode with him that far, and learned what it's like to be a highway patrol officer in Mexico.

He had a forty-five-mile stretch to patrol. He worked twelve hours every day, and had three days off a month, all year long. There were no holidays. He had to deal with all and every kind of crime, whether highway-related or not, and just a few weeks ago one of his colleagues was shot dead when some robbers assaulted a bus. I said I thought that the police in Mexico were better than they used to be. He agreed. I said of course there was also corruption, and he said it was mainly at the borders.

'If they paid us better, there would be less.'

It wouldn't be long before I learned the truth of that.

At the station house, Nambo gave Ángel a piece of paper with the name and phone number of the fellow in Acapulco he knew, and also put some kind of rubber stamp on it. I moved in with Ángel and his young assistant, and we set off on the seventy-five-mile drive to Acapulco.

Ángel had been in Salt Lake City for about seven years (illegally, I'm sure), sending money back to his family, until he had saved enough to buy a 1986 Nissan pick-up, the one we were in, and drive it back to Mexico. He was very interested in my journey. As it gradually sank in how far I'd come he whistled in amazement. 'I thought I'd come a long way from Utah.'

We stopped to buy petrol, but not at a petrol station. It was a place where they were bagging limes. We ate some delicious mangoes, and I threw the peels to the pig that was wandering around the back of the truck. A man brought out a big plastic jerry-can of petrol and poured it into Ángel's tank through a cloth. I gave Ángel 200 pesos for petrol and a bit extra, meaning to give him more later.

'Why are you buying petrol at a fruit stand?' I asked him, but I suppose the answer was obvious.

'It's cheaper here. Six pesos for a litre. The price went up today, but here they will still sell at the old price.'

We chased the pig out from under the pick-up and set off again. I said how impressed I was with the police, how pleasant and cooperative they'd been.

'Didn't they ask you for anything back there?'

On the contrary, I replied. Nambo had even gone out of his way to get me some bottled water.

Ángel said, Yes, things were better with the police these days, which it turned out later was a rather premature judgement.

I told him how I hated the *topes*. Crazy drivers went so fast through his village, he said, that many people had been killed by them, so they had to have *topes*. We had lots of time for conversation. The drive took for ever, and it was getting dark when we reached Acapulco. The traffic was terrible, and we almost came to a halt squeezing through a long tunnel. When we came out the other side a police car stopped us, shouting instructions through a loudspeaker. I could see that Ángel was not amused.

We stopped. A perky little cop came over. He looked suspicious from the start. He had lots of metal in his teeth and wore a redesigned baseball cap, a white shirt and pale pants with a stripe. He had a gun, a tin whistle and a clipboard. He thrust his chest out as he talked and tried to look pretty damned important.

There was a lot of to and fro between them, too fast for me to follow, but you could tell from the cop's body language that he was inventing the whole incident. Angel showed the cop the piece of paper we had with Nambo's stamp on it, but it didn't shake the man's confidence one bit. According to Ángel, he was insisting that a fellow with a pick-up in Acapulco can't carry somebody else's motorcycle without a permit. It sounded like nonsense, but Ángel explained that Nambo's stamp left something to be desired. What was desired was a *mordida*, a bite, a pay-off. Otherwise the fine would be a thousand pesos.

Sad to say, the only money I had on me was from the ATM machine, and it was all in 200 peso notes. It was a big 'bite', but I didn't even bother to ask for change.

In tortured English, with great ceremony, the cop said, 'Thank you for the tip,' and immediately became my best friend, explaining where the motorcycle shop was and escorting us to it. Actually it turned out to be the wrong shop, but it also happened by chance to be the one where Ángel's cousin worked, so we stopped there instead. It was a Yamaha shop but they said they could do the job, and they'd start first thing in the morning.

It was time for Ángel to go. I gave him another twenty dollars and thanked him. I was giving away so much money that I wished I'd given some to Nambo as well. What can you do?

It was late. There was a thirty-five-dollar hotel nearby, an ugly place built round an asphalt parking lot. It was very hot, and I was definitely up the backside of Acapulco so I joined in with the mood of the place, bought some cheap take-away, drank beer and watched stupid television.

I was back at the shop early, drinking coffee from a paper cup until the workforce arrived. The guy who did the work did it well. The bolt had sheared off inside the alloy casing, and getting the broken-off stub out was difficult. He did it by welding a rod on to the broken end. I was afraid he might damage the casing, but after several failed attempts he got a fix, and was able to screw the thing out. Then we drilled right through the original BMW part and just put a plain bolt through the middle of it. The people in the shop were terrific. Their accountant, however, was unsentimental. All in all it was a 150-dollar breakdown. Coming from where I'd been, that was a lot. It was a sign that I was coming back to what we like to call civilisation.

While they were working on the job I went out to find a bank and an Internet shop, but the banks were either shut or uncooperative, and Acapulco was having an Internet blackout. I could see, walking down the main street, by the beach, how a person with a lot of money could have fun in Acapulco. The big Las Vegas names were there: Sands, Bali'hai, Flamingo. Personally I couldn't wait to get away from it. And at 2.30 p.m. I did.

About ten miles along the coast I came to a much cooler spot called Pie de la Cuesta, and found a great place, with beers for ten pesos and a nice room for not too much money. The hotel was called Roxana and so was the black lady who owned it, and they were both lovely.

Reflecting on my good fortune, I had to admit that life was a beach.

33

I was riding with a map that I bummed off my friend Dan in Antigua. He'd made some notes on it, and there was a circle inked around the road north of Zihuatanejo with the word 'dangerous' scribbled alongside it.

What was supposed to be dangerous about it? Could it be those damned elusive *bandidos* Americans are so scared of? People do get robbed on the roads, from time to time, I don't deny it, but the chances of it being me are so ridiculously low that I can't be bothered by them.

It was a lovely ride, even better than the day before. The road stayed much closer to the coast and wound up and down over bluffs and along beaches. There were very few villages, and little traffic. Coming away from one beach where I stopped to munch on a snack, a young woman saw me, made a nasty face and pretended to throw something at me. It was the first overt sign of dislike I'd met in thousands of miles. For the rest, it was a fabulous day.

Guadalajara was a long way off, though. I remembered that I had a note somewhere of a fellow called Roberto who had invited me to visit him in Guadalajara, and when I saw a phone set out on a table in a village I stopped and called him. He sounded enthusiastic, and said since Guadalajara was so far I should aim for Colima, where I could spend the night with his cousin. He said it would be fine, people on bikes were always coming through, and gave me the phone number to call. Then he asked, rather diffidently, where we had met.

I told him we had never met. He had simply emailed me suggesting I come by. I thought maybe he had found my website.

Then the penny dropped. 'Oh my God, it's you', and so on. I was tremendously impressed that he would have offered so much hospitality to someone he didn't even know, and when I met Roberto Lopez later, I understood that he was really the soul of generosity.

Meanwhile I headed for Colima, leaving the coast behind. I put a call in to Roberto's aunt, Alicia, and she gave me directions to her house, but my comprehension of Spanish on the phone is terrible. I thought I had understood her but I was hopelessly confused, ending up in the wrong suburb where, surprisingly, her phone number couldn't be reached. That I found her in the end was a miracle, but she was warmly welcoming and so was her husband, Rafael.

At least, I assumed he was her husband. He was a remarkable-looking man, with a majestic head and glossy hair, but his outstanding feature was his belly, outstanding not so much for volume, although it had that too, but for its pure sphericity. It was just hugely and geometrically round.

Tea and biscuits were served. Then they told me that Roberto's cousin had gone to Guadalajara and wouldn't be home that night. Well, I thought, never mind. Those you don't know you don't miss. But there was something else I didn't know that I did miss.

I went out for a walk and found a shopping mall with an enormous supermarket hardly distinguishable from the North American model. I bought Alicia some chocolates and myself some beer, but when I got back to the house I could feel there was something odd in the air. And then Roberto came on the phone. He was very embarrassed. Rafael and Alicia, it turned out, were divorced, so Rafael wouldn't be staying the night. And their son wouldn't be there either, because he was in Guadalajara, and that meant that I, a man, would be alone in the house with Alicia, a woman, and in Mexico . . .

Now I understood perfectly.

Rafael showed me to a funny little hotel on a very busy main road. It had theme rooms: Valley, Mountain, Forest, and so on. For

a mere eleven dollars I got a bed in the forest, with a bunch of
twigs and pine cones stuck to the wall above my head. The traffic in
the forest was deafening, but I managed to sleep in the end.

Colima to Guadalajara wasn't far, less than 125 miles. Roberto and
I agreed to meet at a BMW dealer's on the way into the city. The
highway was easy to find and after a while I came to a place where
I had to choose between staying on the toll road or going off on the
old road over the mountaintop, which was free. I stayed on the toll
road because it was the first I'd come to in Mexico and I was curious, but I soon regretted it.

The toll was an unbelievable eight dollars. They had cleverly
built the booth so far along that going back to the free road seemed
hardly worth the effort, but I would have made the effort if I had
known there was another eight dollars to pay at the other end.

Actually it is a spectacular road, carved through a range of
tumultuous mountains, and it must have cost a fortune to build. I
passed a smoking volcano on my left, and then, for a long time,
found myself riding across a completely flat sea of sand and salt.

The dealership was easy to find. Roberto arrived on an immac-
ulate old Beemer with his cousin on the back, and we rode through
the city to his place. Guadalajara is Mexico's second-largest city, and
it was an eye-opener to me: clean and orderly, with a strong cultural
core and much to admire. After two decades away from Mexico I
found the changes dramatic. I know there is still serious poverty, and
that but for the corruption and complacency of its rulers much
more could have been achieved. Even so, things have come a long
way.

Roberto was short, bald, cheerful and extremely nice. He
restored old BMW bikes for a living in the garage of his family
house, and he also imported Enfield Bullets from India, but he was
far from being just a mechanic. His father was a commercial airline
pilot. His grandfather was Mexico's most illustrious classical guitarist, and a disciple of Segovia. Roberto had a pile of his records,
and played them. It's such a rich world we live in.

As far back as Colombia I had noticed drops of oil collecting below the gear lever, and wondered where they came from. By the time I got to Guatemala the flow had increased, and the rim of my rear wheel was caked with oil and dust. I finally took the trouble to clean everything off and locate the source, and to my disbelief it seemed to be coming out of an electrical contact on the engine case.

It turned out to be the oil-pressure switch, which is famous for leaking. At the shop in Acapulco I'd tried to do something about it, and failed, but now I was losing too much oil. In pursuit of a new pressure switch Roberto took me downtown to an area where enthusiasts gathered. His friend Natcho thought he might have one. From the look of his shop, I thought he must have one of everything on the planet but, alas, the switch eluded him. Never mind. We had beer and conversation instead.

A young man threw an epileptic fit on the pavement opposite. There was blood on the froth. People called an ambulance. Cops came and looked on. Roberto said it was a drug thing, and not uncommon. The medics weren't long in coming, but by then the man had recovered and walked away. Still, an ambulance did come: a civilised response.

What we did in the end was take the old switch to a man who made exhaust pipes and get him to fill it in with brass. So it became a plug that would hold the oil until I found a new switch. What I really enjoyed most about my day with Roberto was being in a community of people who could get things done at a basic level.

From there to the border it was a straight shot. I aimed to be in Phoenix in three days. I've always thought of this stretch as a kind of dead zone, increasingly overwhelmed by gringos and their influence. It's not uninteresting, and I know there are nice places, but I wouldn't go to Mexico to meet gringos. I remember so well how tough it was in 1975, when the weather was extremely hot and dry, the Triumph was slowly burning up one of its exhaust valves, and I was in some doubt whether I could even make it to the border. It was along this road that I lost my flying-jacket, a traumatic event at the time.

The weather was much kinder now. I learned my lesson and stayed off the toll roads as much as I could, which was a good thing because most of the trucks stayed on them. I had a good ride to Mazatlán. The next night I was in Guaymas, and on the Saturday I arrived at the US border in Nogales, Arizona.

I was half expecting trouble here. After all, my passport still had all those Arabic stamps in them. It was only six months since 9/11, and I'd been hearing all sorts of grim stories about homeland security, but to my surprise I got through with hardly any formalities at all. When I flashed my green card and explained where I'd been for the last year, the US immigration agent said, 'Outstanding', and waved me through like a VIP. As for customs, there was no sign of them. I liked it then, but it was going to cause me a heap of trouble.

Three hours later I was in Phoenix, enjoying the hospitality of Al and Julie Jesse. They are old chums. They make terrific alloy boxes for bikes, and since my top box had taken a terrible beating in Robert Wanjiku's LandCruiser, in Africa, they gave me one of theirs to put on. They had the new tyres from Avon too, and while he was fitting them Jesse pointed to a fracture in the rim of the rear wheel and welded it up. Immediately my mind flew back to those three huge potholes in Malawi, and the mysteriously leaking tyre in Brazil was no longer a mystery.

So – halfway around the globe, and with five thousand more miles on the clock than last time. Very satisfying.

34

I had a date with Malú. Despite everything I had learned about life and travel, this rendezvous became an obsession. I imagined it as a vital junction in my life's story, from which all kinds of wonderful consequences would flow. I could not afford to miss it.

So far everything had followed the timetable I had set myself. Guadalajara, Mazatlán, Guaymas and Phoenix had all come and gone like clockwork. On 15 April I made a very enjoyable duty call on *Rider Magazine*, to thank Mark Tuttle for all the help he was giving me to stay on the road. On the 16th I enjoyed the hospitality of my friend Bob Sinclair, in Santa Barbara. On the morning of the 17th I set off up the 101 for San Rafael and the house of Isabel Allende, where Malú was expecting me.

The mornings were surprisingly cold. For the first time since Germany, I had pulled out my heated gloves and jacket and plugged them in, but otherwise conditions were just about perfect, and I was enjoying the ride as much as it is possible to enjoy any ride on a concrete slab. The Pacific slapped playfully at the sandy beaches on my left until the road turned away at San Luis Obispo and climbed a little to the dryer lands around Santa Ynez. I passed through Atascadero, and with only 250 miles or so to go I was confident of arriving at tea time.

Then the bike coughed, spluttered and stopped. I coasted to the side of the freeway. My heart was already sinking. On this day of all days, after all the attention we had given it in Phoenix, it just wasn't fair. I pressed the starter button and heard that dismal, futile clicking. A flat battery. My goose was cooked.

Hoping it was some kind of silly contact problem, I unpacked the bike and rummaged around, but without success. I got out the book to look for clues, but I was in despair. The electrics of this bike were still unfamiliar to me; I had never had to deal with them. Unlike the old Triumph which had forced me to delve into its famously fallible circuitry, the BMW's juice had flowed uninterrupted for thirty-five thousand miles. Indeed as I stood there lost in self-pity I remembered that on this very freeway, in 1975, I had been parked under an overpass, struggling for ages to find a broken spade connector.

The side of a freeway (and there was no way to get off it) is no place to take a course in electronics. In a hopeless gesture, I turned the ignition key one more time, pressed the button and . . . kaboom . . . she started right up. Unwilling to believe my luck, I packed everything together as fast as I could and got back on, knowing that the bike could stop again at any minute. It became an unbelievably tense ride. I figured that the electric jacket had drawn the battery right down, but with nothing plugged in and the lights off, it must have recovered just enough to get going. And now I noticed what I had missed before – the charge light was glowing. The bike wasn't making any juice. Could I possibly go another 250 miles on an almost empty battery?

Four hours later I was on the edge of San Francisco. Incredible. Any other day I would have gone straight to a bike shop, but I *had* to get to San Rafael on the other side of the city. The traffic on 19th Avenue was terrible, as always. The engine was not sounding good. Part of the time it was running on one cylinder. What if it stopped in the middle of the Golden Gate Bridge? What if it couldn't get up the hill on the other side? I willed it on through Mill Valley and Corte Madera, and with a sigh of relief went across the overpass, past the San Quentin turn-off and down into central San Rafael. Well, at least now I was within reach, but . . . I didn't know where I was going. Cursing myself for not having taken down directions earlier, I stopped at a petrol station. I would have to phone, but I dared not let the engine stop running.

Parked by the phone box, with the engine barely pumping through its cycles, I dialled the Allende number. Isabel's husband Willy (whom I had never met – indeed, I had never met either of them) answered the call, and just as I was introducing myself the engine stalled. I swallowed a silent four-letter word and, embarrassed, explained where I was and that I would have to get a jump-start before I went any further. Brisk but cheerful, he said, 'Wait there. I've got leads and I'll be along in a minute.'

Ten minutes later a big maroon Acura drove up and an energetic middle-aged man sprang out. Willy had the leads ready and we got the bike started. I followed him slowly off the forecourt, stopped for traffic . . . and the engine stalled again. There was nothing I could do but get off, roll the bike back out of the way, and wait while Willy drove round the block and came back. Under my tan and my helmet my face was burning.

He got the leads out again, the bike started again, and this time I followed him for about two miles on one cylinder, until ten yards from the Allende front gate the bike gave its last gasp, and finally and definitively expired.

From my point of view, coaxing the machine through all these vicissitudes to the very doorstep of the Allende mansion was a triumph of mind over matter, but Willy didn't see it like that. For him the whole thing had an air of comic ineptitude that reminded him of Peter Sellers in *The Pink Panther*. Next day a driver came with a pick-up to carry the paralysed bike off to the BMW shop in Marin, and he accidentally backed into the gatepost, destroying a rather fancy mailbox. My fate was sealed. I became Inspector Clouseau, a magnet for mishaps, and for the rest of my short stay I was stuck with it.

Isabel, a lovely tender woman, was very welcoming and caring, and I quickly developed a great affection for her. For the most part she made me completely at ease in her house. But I had only to tip over a salt cellar or drop a fork, and Willy's delighted voice would cry, 'Clouseau strikes again!' and Isabel and Malú would burst into laughter.

Of course I laughed along with the rest, like a good sport, but in my heart I was troubled by it. Right from the start of the journey I had been bothered by a wicked jester mocking me from the wings of my consciousness, because I could not rid myself of the suspicion that there was something faintly ridiculous about an elderly gentleman riding a white charger around the world. Wasn't one Don Quixote enough?

At times the jeering jester took a break. When I was in real trouble, lying in the mud in Kenya or on the asphalt in Colombia, or stuck in the wilderness of Bolivia, the clown was not around, but in the company of people who shared my language and background I often felt him whacking me on the head with his bladder. In part it was an image problem. After living with *Jupiter's Travels* for so long I had identified myself with that larger-than-life figure on the cover of my book: that lean, focused, tough, virile, resourceful, fiercely independent character with an almost limitless tenacity and endurance. A caricature, of course. A few of those qualities I did still possess to some degree, but others were woefully diminished, and in my more vulnerable moments I imagined that my deficiencies were all too obvious to everyone.

Happily, none of Willy's wisecracking ruined my reputation with Malú. She seemed to have complete confidence in me as an operator. It was my emotions that she distrusted. I knew I loved her, but that cut no ice with her.

'I don't believe in love,' she declared scornfully, convinced of it by the series of disastrous relationships that had filled her life. 'Never again do I want to be part of a couple, a *pareja*. It's horrible to contemplate.'

And yet we were behaving like lovers, as best we could. So we continued on a roller-coaster ride of emotional upheavals and I came to believe that she did love me. At any rate it seemed clear, in spite of her protestations, that she was willing to give it a try. Our problem of course was how to go about it, given that I was supposed to be riding around the world and had only got halfway.

'So now you will just go away for years, and I am supposed to play Penelope? Impossible. I suppose I will have to come out somewhere and travel with you for a while.'

Not that the thought hadn't occurred to me, but she was the first to put it into words, almost as a threat. I had to admit to myself that it *was* a bit threatening. I remembered from my first journey how difficult it had been to stick to my purpose when Carol had been riding with me. After a while I had refused to take her any further, but in the end had it really made that much difference? It was because of my obstinacy then that I lost Carol. I was determined not to lose Malú through the same pig-headedness.

It was remarkable, when I thought about it, how closely the two journeys were paralleling each other. It was almost as though after a certain amount of time on the road I *had* to fall in love, regardless of age or anything else, simply because the experience of travel so heightens the sensibilities and the joys of being alive that they have to express themselves, and for me at least it seems that love is the natural outlet.

A week from now I will be seventy-one years old. I had to keep telling myself, Ted, you're seventy-one. Be kind to yourself. You can't expect to perform like a forty-one-year-old.

What brought on this outburst of solicitude? Well, apart from the obvious, I had just had a very strange and disturbing experience. Down at the Marin BMW shop it was discovered that various electrical parts of the bike were defunct. The rotor was dead. So was the regulator. And the diode board, while it still worked, needed replacing. They managed to get the first bits done, but there was no time to replace the diode board, and since I had a spare, I thought it would be good for me to put that in myself and learn about the system as I went.

So they sent me to a specialist shop in San Francisco with the very appropriate name of Darwin Motors, so that I could evolve. And there they were kind enough to give me an excellent little book on electrics, and some floor space where I could work in peace. Squatting on the floor, alongside my motor, I really got into it. In fact I got so far into it that I went into a trance. I don't know how else to explain it. I finished the job, but I was in some kind of hallucinatory state. I knew the job was completed, but I felt I was in a dream and that I was far from finished, that there were crucial things left undone.

I asked the fellow working nearby if he'd seen anything odd about my behaviour, but he'd noticed nothing. I got the bike out on the road, and drove away. Everything worked well, but I was still in this weird state of mind, expecting to wake up at any moment and find . . .what?

I don't do drugs, ever, unless you include alcohol. I quite liked the idea that I might be open to paranormal experiences, but all the same, I thought, I needed a rest. Maybe a long rest. Malú has gone back to Santiago, I thought, and I'm going home, just three hours north of here, for my birthday. Home is where I first met Carol twenty-eight years ago, where I came with my wife and child, twenty-two years ago. I suppose it's where everything comes together. I shall go home and sleep.

Mundane matters kept me in California for several months. Malú and I were in constant touch by email. I visited her in Santiago and we made a brief journey together to the extreme south of Chile. Being a fierce environmentalist, she taught me about the unusual flora and fauna – and particularly the trees – that flourish down there in what she called Gondwana, a name given to all those cold southern lands, including the South Island of New Zealand and Tasmania. It made me all the more determined to see both this time.

We got on well together and it encouraged us, but I was still trying to get my mind around the idea of this high-born lady of a certain age, who had never been near a motorcycle in her life, perched on the back of my GS. I was helped by a memory from Australia in 1975 when, together with Carol, I rode down to visit Rupert Murdoch's mother, Dame Elizabeth, just south of Melbourne. She must have been in her sixties then too. I was prepared to meet a rather stuffy duchess, but she turned out to be delightfully unaffected, and curious about the world. She got on well with Carol, and something about the idea of travelling on the back of a bike fascinated her.

Outside on her gravel drive, as we were leaving, she said, 'Let me see what it's like', and without hesitation she hoisted her skirt and hopped on to the pillion, displaying old-fashioned stocking tops and suspenders as she did so. It is one of the most endearing memories I have of anyone. And I thought, if Malú wants to do it, why not? Maybe it won't all be martyrdom and sacrifice. Perhaps it could even be fun.

35

In the end the only way I could afford to get the bike to Australia was by boat in a crate from Long Beach. My freight person said it would take six weeks from the day I crated it to the day I got it back in Melbourne. I decided to take advantage of that time to see New Zealand.

I was in touch with a fellow called John Rains, who operated a bike rental business in Christchurch with a Maori name, Te Waipounamou, which he said means 'Greenstone Water' and is the native name for the South Island. He seemed enthusiastic to have me there: so keen, in fact, that he asked me if I'd like to explore New Zealand on an old Triumph, like the one I rode in the seventies. There happened to be one he could get hold of, and I fell for the idea.

Jacques's airline didn't fly to the Antipodes, but Air New Zealand gave me a discount on the ticket, hoping no doubt that tourists would throng in my wake. I spent a day with another email friend just outside Auckland, acclimatising myself, and landed in Christchurch on 12 September.

John Rains had his van there to meet me, driven by Rex, his helper, who gave me a little tour of Christchurch on the way to the shop. The similarity to a British provincial town of the fifties was very obvious, but the differences were clear too. In a way it was more like a story-book version. Cleaner. Less crowded. Orderly. Peaceful. One thing struck me as very strange, though. On top of a tall building, looming over the city, was an enormous sign saying POLICE in letters at least ten feet high. In most countries that would provoke paranoia, protests and mutterings about Big Brother. Here nobody could understand why I thought it odd. It seemed I was in a country where people thought the police were only there to help and keep the peace.

John Rains had a big rambling workshop with an office upstairs, which was where I found him. He was a tall, lanky man with a bushy moustache, thinning black hair and the friendly unemotional manner that I expect of New Zealanders. I guessed he was in his forties. He took me outside to show me the bike he had bought for me to ride. It was a 1970 Daytona with a purple tank, a slightly older cousin of the bike I had once ridden around the world. Standing out in the sun amongst his other more usual rentals, BMWs and Suzukis, it looked surprisingly small, and without a windscreen it seemed naked.

I should have wanted to leap on it and ride away rejoicing, but it seemed strange to me. It no longer felt like home, as it once had. I would have to learn it all over again.

I contented myself that afternoon with figuring out how to attach my luggage to it. John had had it equipped with two Givi bags, and I had straps that needed adjusting to fit on my tank bag. I didn't ride it at all that day, but went home with John in his van. I was feeling dull and unadventurous. Perhaps it was the long flight. I knew I wasn't ready.

John and Allison Rains live in a mud house they built overlooking Diamond Bay, about thirty miles from Christchurch. *They* called it a mud house. I wouldn't. It's a beautiful adobe structure, and they're justifiably proud of it. They gave me a delicious dinner, and a handsome bedroom with a lot of fine polished wood and brass in it. I slept very well and tried to gather my wits about me, without much success.

The next day was Friday the 13th, and for once the day lived up to its reputation. First there was a message from San Francisco. Customs. They wouldn't allow my bike to leave the USA because they had no record of it coming in. Well, of course not. At the Mexican border nobody had wanted to know. Now they wanted to see my *carnet de passage*. I spent all morning, and a good deal of money, sending it to them by courier, not knowing whether it would arrive in time for the bike to catch the boat.

And then, in the afternoon, I got on the Triumph and followed John's Kawasaki 400 back towards his house about twenty miles away. The weather was cool and looked a little rainy, and I had my Aerostich clothing on. The bike started well. I got back into the habit of changing gear with my right foot and braking well ahead of time. Then, as we started climbing, it seemed to me that the bike was losing power. Finally, near the top of a hill, I was forced to stop. There was so much smoke pouring out of the pipes, you'd have thought I was running on coal.

I tried parking at the side of the road, but the camber was too steep, the side-stand was too low and the bike began to fall. It was all I could do to hold it. In the position I was in I didn't have the strength to bring it up to vertical again. I felt ridiculous, but not nearly as ridiculous as I felt a few moments later.

John parked his bike and came over to help me raise mine, and then *his* bike fell over and smashed an indicator, the one that Rex had just spent hours repairing.

With admirable restraint, John stayed cool, and said, 'We're at the top of the hill now, and it's not far. Let's try to nurse it home.'

So I said, 'Right you are.' I raised my right leg to kick it over, and to my undying shame and embarrassment I couldn't pull my foot up high enough to get it on the kick-start.

I had a feeling of stark impotence. Until then I had not understood quite how much of me was invested in my history with that machine. Now, suddenly, I couldn't perform this simplest of actions. How would John Wayne have felt if he couldn't get up on his horse? It was the defining moment that so many other moments on this trip had been leading up to, and it was all over in a flash. Quite simply I was no longer the man I used to be. So obvious, and yet so difficult to accept. I had never before felt my age so painfully.

Of course I had explanations. My left foot was further down because of the steep camber. The rain gear was bulky and impeded my leg. Normally I would have stood on the pegs to start the bike. None of these excuses helped. When the ground beneath me refused to open and swallow me up, I said, feebly, 'You know John, I think it'd be better if you took it. You know it better than I do.'

There was still more humiliation to come. Sitting on his Kawasaki, I watched him as he effortlessly brought the Triumph spluttering into life, and a pint of dirty oil gushed out of the pipes. 'There's water pouring out,' I exclaimed, before I realised what an utterly stupid remark that was. It is to John's eternal credit that he didn't simply abandon me then and there as either a complete idiot or a rank impostor.

Of course *I* knew which of the two I was. That was Friday the 13th, that was.

The problem with the Triumph was easy to diagnose, but not so easy to cure. The sump was full of oil because it wasn't pumping out, even though John had just cleaned it and put in a good oil pump. And there were other baffling symptoms. So, displaying enormous courage, he decided to lend me one of his BMW 650s to run around on, while he went back into the Triumph.

Everybody knows that New Zealand is beautiful, so what can I say? The grass is green. The sheep are white. Lambs gambol. The coast is wild and unspoiled. The sea is full of seafood. You can eat crayfish for lunch (lobsters without claws) and roast lamb for dinner. People feel safe and are very hospitable. All these things I discovered in one day. I can't do justice to the pleasure of the experience. That run up the coast to Kaikoura and a night in Amberley, with strangers who became friends, soothed my battered soul.

The next day John had the Triumph going again, but he had qualms.

'It might not be the best bike for your purpose,' he said diplomatically, no doubt imagining the difficulties I might run into if I thought the bike was lubricated by water. 'Rex has to run down to Dunedin with the van, so you could ride down there on the

Triumph and he can carry the BMW. Then you can do a switch. Shame for you not to ride it now we've got it. Of course if you want to keep the Triumph, that's fine too . . . ?'

So that's what we did. It was a lovely day, but with a strong wind from the south that came right at me. I hadn't ridden a bike without a windscreen in over twenty years. I was amazed how hard I had to work. I felt that if I let go of the grips I'd be blown away. And I had gone round the world, through wind and rain, on a bike just like this? I began to form a healthy respect for that fellow Ted Simon who used to be me.

After fifty miles I was used to it and began to think about keeping the bike, but then common sense (to give it a nice name) got the better of me. I told myself that I really wanted to see these islands, that I might never get another chance, that I didn't want to spend my time on motorcycle maintenance. I just didn't have the Zen.

Sadly, and not without misgivings, I handed the Triumph over to Rex. I was so confused by my emotions that I forgot to take a picture of it until it was too late and Rex had driven off. I turned the F650 around and headed south to Invercargill. I never saw that Triumph again, but there was another one down the road, waiting to greet me.

What keeps the grass green is the rain, and the South Island gets a lot of it. It was early spring and I knew it would soon be time for me to get wet. The road surfaces in New Zealand are excellent, and so was my clothing, so I had no real worries, but rain is never very pleasant, and it obstructs the view. Christchurch to Invercargill is only 360 miles, but I took three days over it and by the time I got there the rain had started.

Graeme Howie had offered me a bed by email, and he came out on his old Triumph to fetch me from a petrol station. Graeme, Deborah and their two kids live in a house that gave me twinges of nostalgia for old England: a proper front door, a big hall, square rooms with high ceilings on two floors, and a cosy kitchen at the back with a coal-fired range, fairly standard for Invercargill. But Invercargill is not just quaint, it's really unusual. For example, the city runs the liquor business. They started doing this a long time ago, and the system works beautifully. All the profits have gone into improvements, like schools, and the huge and wonderful Queen's Park with sports fields, a brilliant hothouse, animal paddocks and so on.

Even the crime is idiosyncratic. Graeme told me about Owen McShane, who built the town's first prison back in the nineteenth century. Apparently McShane had a lucrative sideline, distilling illicit rum from the cabbage tree (really!), and wound up as the first inmate of his own prison.

My favourite crime, though, is house-stealing. It came up when Graeme was wondering whether to build a house on a piece of land he'd bought, or whether to move the house he already had. I was surprised to find that in New Zealand when people talk of moving house they often mean it literally. Going round town he pointed to a business and said, 'That rascal there stole a house.'

How do you steal a house? Well, he took a lease on some property somewhere with a wood-frame house on it, and one day he got some people in to pick up the house and hide it away. Apparently the owners could never prove that they'd had a house there in the first place. Strange things happen in far-flung places, and Invercargill is about as far south as you can get on land. I remember similar stories from Punta Arenas at the tip of Chile.

The rain kept me penned in for five days, and it was kind of the Howies to tolerate me, but I really enjoyed it and felt quite grounded by the time I could leave to go north into the mountains. Besides, Debbie taught me how to make apple jelly from windfalls, and they also introduced me to the mutton bird. Its real name is the sooty shearwater. It's a sea bird that flourishes in thousands out on the islands. They pluck it, gut it, split it down the middle, flatten it, salt it, and pack it in tins. It does taste vaguely like mutton, but I couldn't see the point, since mutton is cheaper.

Graeme rode up the hill with me when I left, and we stayed at his 'crib', which is an old English word they have kept for a place in the country. The cross-wind coming up there was incredibly strong, and I felt as though I was being blown all over the road. It worried me that Graeme, who was in front of me on his Triumph, seemed to be quite unmoved by it. How could that be, I asked myself. What am I doing wrong?

Graeme is a youngish man with a stolid outer shell that conceals a great deal of creativity and imagination, as I observed in his home, but he has that stiff upper lip the British were once famous for, so it was only a lot later that he admitted that he felt he was being blown all over the place too, and that it felt quite dangerous. I was relieved, but still puzzled that what you feel on the bike is often not visible to anyone else.

My next day in the mountains was astounding, and the day after that must have been one of the most beautiful days in New Zealand's history. The ride over Haast Pass, with a stop at the glaciers and then along the coast to Greymouth, was a biker's fantasy, and it led me straight into the past again when I found myself in Blackball.

In 1992, the managers of the Hilton hotel chain caught wind of a serious threat to their business. In the town of Blackball on the west coast of New Zealand's South Island it appeared that a hotel had dared to call itself The Blackball Hilton. A legal team was assembled to fight off this affront to Conrad's mighty legacy, and a stiff letter was sent demanding that the said hotel cease, desist, refrain, genuflect, pay damages and do all the other things lawyers require when they have billions of dollars behind them.

The letter is proudly displayed at the hotel. Of course none of the lawyers felt the need actually to inspect the place, or they would have known how remote and small Blackball was, and how small this hotel on Hilton Street was, and that they had made a laughing-stock of themselves. Wisely the Blackball lady who owns the hotel bowed to superior force, and changed the name. The hotel is now officially called Formerly The Blackball Hilton, a safer if more cumbersome title. I heard about it when I was in Christchurch, and determined to go there, but I wasn't prepared for anything quite so interesting. The place is steeped in radical traditions, and cocking a snook at Conrad Hilton came all too naturally.

Blackball is an old coal-mining town, and the similarities to the Rhondda Valley are startling. It has a history of strong union activity, pride in literacy and self-education, and a powerfully coherent culture all its own. There's a portrait of New Zealand's first Labour cabinet in the hotel dining-room, as well as a red banner across one corner that declares: 'United We Stand, Divided We Fall.' And the New Zealand Communist Party, knowing what it was about, moved its headquarters to Blackball in 1925.

Not what you expect to find in the vicinity of your average Hilton. But it's all treated with a good deal of humour as well as respect. The pit has been closed for some time, and the town is more famous for its salami than its black nuggets. The hotel itself has been through a great many hands, and at one time was left for derelict, but it was rescued and is now in fine shape. The food is great. There's beer to suit any palate, particularly pleasant for a visiting Englishman who likes his bitter and specialises in salami.

The atmosphere is very warm and comforting. Jane, the owner, runs the place like a mother hen, and I was very glad of it. Despite my wonderful day on the bike, I arrived with a very bad sore throat, and when the weather changed overnight to heavy rain I decided to stay and let Blackball take care of me. Dinner, bed, and breakfast for twenty quid? Hard to beat.

I had a duty call to make, not far from Blackball, at a coastal town called Westport. The rain had given way to lovely weather again, and the ride along the coast was a joy. I lingered over the incredible rock formations of Punakaiki, where the park people had created a marvellous display showing how the rocks had revealed themselves to the Maoris as a startling assortment of creatures and spirits.

In Westport I found Pete Lusk, who is a brother-in-arms to Malú. Pete is one of the rarest creatures on earth. Indeed, if he were under threat you would have to say he was an endangered species. He's an activist without an act. For many years he and a few others fought what most would have thought to be a losing battle against the big moneyed interests intent on cutting their way through all the native forests of these islands. Then, remarkably, both government and the public swung around.

A key moment must have been New Zealand's decision to oppose the movement of nuclear materials through its sphere of influence, separating itself off from the US–Australian axis. With this decision to go its own way and defy the conventional wisdom that would ally it to a superpower, it seems to have freed itself to make other independent decisions too. As a result, of all the countries I visited, New Zealand was far and away the most active in defending its environment, and virtually all of Pete Lusk's objectives in saving the forests are now fixed government policy.

It was very clear to me from the moment I met him that this was no ordinary man. He walks the earth with a tread so loose and light that I could almost imagine him floating over it. His piercing gaze, hawklike nose and thin, ascetic features mark him out to me as a man with the potential for fanaticism, and it is a good thing for us all that he has concentrated his energies and determination on a cause as beneficial as conservation. We had a tremendous amount to talk about, and a great deal in common in our backgrounds, and I hope and think that we understood each other well.

Almost as soon as I arrived, Pete took me for a walk to what Westport calls its 'domain', a term generally used in New Zealand to mean what we in England call a 'common'. In most towns it consists of open ground, or sometimes gardens, maybe with a bandstand. The Westport domain was once like that, planted by the colonialists with trees and flowers that reminded them of England. But many decades ago it was allowed to fall into disuse. Now it is completely overgrown, and Pete showed me with glee how the native vegetation had taken hold and flourished. For him the exotic imports are no match for the vibrant growth of the native trees like the matai and the rimu, the rata which climbs up and around them, and the numerous other plants that leapfrog over each other with such exuberance.

I was completely taken over by his enthusiasm.

It was appropriate to come to Pete from Blackball, because he too had a long history as a leftist radical, but I realised that there was something special about the reds of the Antipodes. It seemed to me that most of these old socialists and Communists were too far removed from the perversions of Stalinism to be infected by it, and they didn't seem to feel the stigma either. They were just people for whom the brotherhood of man was a shining ideal, the same ideal to which my mother devoted much of her life, and if capitalism has proved it to be a utopian dream, more's the pity.

36

I flew from Auckland to Melbourne on New Zealand Air. As I said, they gave me a good deal on the ticket, but I still have to say that it was one of the most enjoyable flights I can remember. An economy seat on that flight was like business class anywhere else. I'm not sure how they did it – leg room and real food with menus, I suppose, and free this and that certainly contributed.

I had a good lunch, and arrived in time for another one with a gang of journos, which is the name Australians use for journalists to make sure they don't get too self-important. It was another great meal – this one at a Vietnamese restaurant – and several of the people I met there are now friends for life. One of them was Dave Milligan, who had offered me a place to stay while I figured out what to do.

Because actually I had flown to Australia to ride a bike that wasn't there. My freight person made a muck of it, the US customs compounded the problem, the stevedores of Long Beach added the final touch by going on strike, and when I arrived in Melbourne my bike hadn't even left California. What was I going to do for the next month? Obviously I needed a bike.

So I turned to Phil Pilgrim. Decades ago we worked side by side in the venerable workshop of Frank Mussett on Sydney Road. He was a mechanic. I was working on my Triumph. For weeks we were steeped in the songs of David Essex, Rod Stewart, Dylan and Freddie Mercury on a local radio station called 3XY. It was a kind of baptism, and we became brothers in pop. So naturally I turned to Phil. He now has his own shop, Union Jack Motorcycles, on Lygon Street, a wonderful street that includes, at the city end, an entire neighbourhood of restaurants where I could happily spend all my days. Phil started ringing round, looking for someone to lend me a bike. These are the times when I discover just how many people there are in the bike world who have never heard of me. It didn't go well. Until finally, as a last resort, he thought of calling a bloke he knew vaguely at BMW, but he wasn't there.

The bloke who *was* there said, 'Sorry. Maybe I can help you?' and Phil, on the point of hanging up, said, 'Well, I don't know. We're looking for a bike for Ted Simon. He's halfway round the world—' and the bloke interrupted, 'Ted Simon? I think we should be able to do something for him.'

By sheer chance we'd stumbled on the one bloke in the whole outfit who *had* heard of Ted Simon. He was the parts manager and his name was Justin Hocevar. Who would ever have thought of calling him? But years ago he read *Jupiter's Travels* and as a result he and his wife got on a bike and rode to Europe. So, within an hour he had the authority to take a newly delivered bike out of its crate, run it in, service it and lend it to me. It was a big red beast, an 1100 RT, with lots of plastic fairing and clever accessories I wasn't used to, but for running around in southern Australia it was superb.

They used to call it the lucky country. When I was first there I thought it had a dreamy quality, like living in another age. Now it seems more like funny. I don't mean to be condescending. Australians like a good laugh, and so do I. I just kept running into things that made me laugh.

I took the coast road to Adelaide and stayed on the way with some elderly friends of Phil's. They asked me to tell them stories, and I obliged, but however startling my stories were all they ever said was, 'Oh yeah?' Not disbelieving. Just, 'Oh yeah?' I could have told them anything, like how I enjoy committing a murder or two before breakfast. I would have got the same 'Oh yeah?'

In Adelaide I visited a doctor called Ollie who at eighty-something was even older than me. He lived in a house full of birds, and that was funny. He didn't say, 'Oh yeah' because he never listened to anything I said. Instead he told me about all the amazing things he'd done in his life – and they *were* amazing, but funny too. Then he showed me around, and drove me down a twisty mountain road in his Volvo as if it were an Olympic bobsled. That was funny, but only afterwards.

Then there are the animals. Who couldn't laugh at kangaroos and koala bears and wombats? And all those lovely birds, dressed up and painted like clowns? Australian money was cheap at the time I was there, and Aussies are very generous, so all this amusement came at relatively little expense to me which also helped to lighten my mood.

Another friend in Sydney had fixed up for me to give a talk, so I rushed over there. Ollie helped me to sort out the quickest route. It ran 870 miles through Murray Bridge, Tailem Bend, Lameroo, Pinnaroo, Ouyen, Manangatang, Balranald, Hay, West Wyalong, Grenfell, Bathurst and Lithgow. I suppose that would have been an Australian history lesson right there, if I'd known how to interpret the names.

It was the sort of journey this BMW was made for, and in theory I could have done it in a day, but I had several things against me. First, the speed limits. They are low, at 100 k.p.h., and I still didn't know where the cops hung out, although I never saw one. Second, daylight saving started the day before, and I lost an hour and a half going east. Third, the kangaroos. I didn't want to ride after dark.

I hadn't seen a live kangaroo yet, but I saw plenty of dead ones and plenty of signs warning against them. What I did notice, though, was that the absence of kangaroos was most marked in those areas where the signs warned of their presence. In those stretches there were not even dead ones. Never. What I concluded from this was that kangaroos are not stupid. Ambling along the road they see the signs. 'Kangaroos?' they say to each other (probably in the voice of Peter Cook). 'Ho, ho, ho. Not blooming likely. I wouldn't be caught dead on a road like that. Oh dear, here comes a—' Splat!

On the first day I got as far as West Wyalong. That was about 560 miles. I enjoyed the journey a lot, though it's hard to say why. Endless paddocks, with old gum trees scattered around for shade. Cows, sheep, wheat. Enormous sheds and silos. Small settlements with modest houses. Railway lines that looked as if they hadn't seen a train this century. Occasional small forests (that's where the kangaroo signs were).

The wheat surprised me. It was barely twelve inches tall, and where it had been irrigated it was beginning to ripen. I remembered fields of wheat up to my waist. I knew they were breeding shorter stems – who needs straw? people don't even remember that that's what a straw means – but twelve inches is ridiculous. Some of the wheat was dry as stubble. That year the drought in Australia was terrible; the worst in twenty years, they said.

When I got into West Wyalong the sun was almost down, and I settled into the Palm Motel. It was clean but expensive. The owner told me I could get plenty of cheaper rooms in town, but the overnight trucks would be practically coming through my bedroom. I collapsed into acceptance. He was a German from Hamburg, where I was born, so we talked in German for a bit. He was short and jaunty, with a pot belly, and he was married to a Thai wife. He told me he wanted to sell the place and move to Thailand.

'Does your wife want to go back there?' I asked.

'She told me she is happy with me, or she would have gone long ago,' he said, which didn't really answer what was a stupid question in the first place.

I hadn't really liked Sydney much when I arrived there in the seventies, but I think now it had to do with the couple I was staying with. They were at each other's throats a lot, and I viewed Sydney through a prism of machismo and stifled resentment. I was much luckier this time. David McGonigal was an adventurer and a writer like me, who was making his own trip round the world, in stages, on a bike much like the one I was riding now. His home was in Sydney, and he and his wife Lyn offered me days of delightful hospitality.

But Australian society itself had changed. The tone was much closer to both Europe and America, and the different ethnic groups were better assimilated, although there were hold-outs of course, as there are everywhere. Sydney, Melbourne, and Adelaide too, seemed like attractive places to live in. As a favour, David had dragged a bunch of writers to a pub to listen to me ramble. I made new friends, and enjoyed the city much more than before, but the most memorable meeting was with an old friend.

In 1975, passing through Ecuador on my Triumph, I met an American couple, Bob and Annie, on a Norton in the streets of Quito. Bikes in those days were still pretty rare, so we stopped and talked. They told me they'd rented a hacienda near Otavalo, which was a big attraction, then and now, for its market. They invited me to come back there with them since it was on my way out to Colombia, and I stayed for a week or so.

'Hacienda' sounds rather grand. It was in fact a simple affair, but the way it was built made it look pretty nice. There were other travellers there, and one of them was a young Australian kid called Matt Handbury with tousled hair and a disposition that seemed both happy and troubled. He was on an old BMW and going south, vaguely, to Ushuaia.

There was plenty of pot and booze around, and we had a good time. Matt suggested that when I get to Australia I should visit his folks, who had a farm in Victoria. His mother Helen, as it turned out, was Rupert Murdoch's sister. Rupert wasn't quite the media monster he is today, but I knew a lot about him, of course, because of my years in newspapers in London, where he had bought the *News of the World* and the *Sun*.

When you travel the way we were travelling, all that glittering wealth and power doesn't seem terribly attractive, or even very interesting. In fact, I thought of it more as a pollutant, and the way it was generally used did nothing that I could see to improve the miserable conditions in the world around me, and particularly in South America at that time. So it didn't surprise me that Matt seemed pretty indifferent to his exalted connections, and unsure whether he wanted to take advantage of them. Well, a year later I did turn up at his home. Matt was still travelling, but I stayed for a week or so, with his parents, and that was how I came to meet his grandmother, Dame Elizabeth.

Now, a quarter of a century later, I found Matt Handbury again. A lot had happened. He did go to work for Rupert. He went through a lot, good and bad. He came out of the experience with his own magazine publishing company, but what really delighted me was to discover that success has not spoiled Matt Handbury. Not in the least. His hair is still tousled, and his disposition is much more happy than troubled. I spent an evening with him in Sydney, and then a day at his hugely beautiful place near Mittagong. What struck me again was the strength of the emotion that my reappearance evoked, as though I were somehow instrumental in bringing to the surface some cherished part of lives that lay buried.

After I'd left him, Matt sent me an email. 'Your journey is a great stimulation,' he wrote. 'It brought alive so much . . . not just from the past, but for the present and the future.' Of course that was what I always wanted to do for myself, but it's wonderful to find that it works for others too.

When I was ready to leave Sydney the obvious thing to do was to take a ferry to Tasmania, which I had missed in the seventies. The ferries sailed from Melbourne, so I went back there on the coast road from Sydney. That way I could revisit Eden, which had left a strong impression on me from my first visit, but when I got there it was hard to tell what the fuss had been about.

Maybe it had been more beautiful then. I heard it said that the place had been spoiled. More likely, though, it was to do with the people I'd met the first time. I remembered some students there doing voluntary work for the NGO, Habitat, who took us (I was with Carol at the time) under their wing and showed us wonderful things in the area. One of them had lost a leg earlier in life and was very cheerful about it. His best joke had been to go into the sea off a crowded beach, and then come hopping out of the water among the startled sunbathers shouting, 'Shark, shark!' Meeting someone like that can make a whole town seem happier.

I parked at the back of the Australasia Hotel (which is really a big pub) and went in to get a room. It's a long two-storey building with a wide white façade and a balcony, and fairly old as buildings go there.

The bloke behind the bar offered me a motel room for fifty-five Australian dollars, but I asked for a pub room. I'd just found out about pub rooms. They're inside the building and pretty cheap. Anyway he had one for twenty-five dollars, and he took me up to the first floor to look at it. He was a tall young bloke with a noisily nonchalant manner and a broad accent. He was quite efficient, and showed me where everything was, and called me 'mite' after every third word, but he never looked at me. He could have been leading a tour.

After I'd hauled my stuff up, I went down to the bar for a beer. My problem was to find a beer that didn't taste like Budweiser, which I don't care for. There were two groups of three taps on the bar, and three men sitting in front of each group. As I walked along to look at the labels, each man turned around and stared at me. I know I was supposed to say, 'How're ya goin' mite?' to each of them but I couldn't get it up somehow, and they all turned back to their drinks in disgust.

The only tap with a label I didn't know was Toohey. The others I knew I didn't like. The 'mite' man was pouring beer into a glass that looked like a pint glass.

'Is that a pint you're pouring?' I asked.

'No mite, it's a schooner,' he said with a trace of contempt in his voice.

'Then I'll have a schooner of Toohey.'

'Toohey's Old?' he asked. 'That's a dark beer. We don't have Toohey's New. Did they sell you on that up in Sydney? It's garbage.'

He was still addressing the crowd, and I didn't know what this New and Old business was about. 'Well just give me a bitter,' I said.

He poured me a schooner of the beer he thought I ought to have, and I took it away to a table. I thought it tasted like garbage, but consoled myself with the thought that if I had enough of it, maybe it would get better. I put my notebook down and it stuck to the table which had a thick layer of varnish or polymerised beer on it, and started to write. Behind me eight women were boozing and smoking, and shattering the atmosphere with frequent bursts of synchronised cackling. They might have been recording a laugh track.

I finished the beer and decided it wasn't good enough to go the distance on, so I prised my notebook off the table and went for a ride alongside Twofold Bay. I saw a lot of ocean, but the famous Killer Whale Museum was shut. There was a coffee place at the harbour, but it closed when it saw me coming.

I have to say dinner at the Australasia was very good but, as the Tyrolean landlord might have said, 'We are good in food, but not good in bed.' That is to say, the bed was OK, but the music downstairs in the bar was loud and relentless. Of course, had the beer been better I might have joined them. Well, that's why pub rooms are cheap.

I do have trouble with the language. Even though we all speak English, I am realising more and more that behind the use of quite common words and grammatical constructions lie very different ideas. This becomes obvious when you travel in India or Africa. Even the word 'yes' can mean many different things – like 'Yes, it's true' or 'Yes, if you think so', or 'Yes, it would be impolite to contradict you', or 'Yes, God will decide.'

So, for example, after the mite man had taken my money I'm pretty sure he said, 'Breakfast is between six thirty and eight in the morning, mite. So don't miss it, mite.' But he must have been saying something entirely different. I got out of bed earlier than I would have, to find every public room locked and the whole place sunk in a stupor (which was not surprising after the way the amplifiers had rocked into the night), and I was left hungry and mystified.

So, first to Tasmania, and luck seemed to be with me. I got a place on the ferry when there wasn't supposed to be room, and then, on the boat I met by pure chance a fellow I knew from Germany, also on a bike, with his girlfriend. Together we rode over to Bicheno, on the east coast.

It was Rob van Driesum, one of my 'journo' friends from Melbourne, who had sent me there, and I could see why. The place itself was a small, friendly and unpretentious village with a nice sandy beach and unusually dry weather for Tasmania.

And then there was Le Frog. That's Bertrand Cadart, a big,

big-hearted, bewhiskered Frenchman who started life on a family farm in the north of France, fertilised by the blood of more than a hundred thousand dead soldiers during the First World War. Since then he has followed an extraordinary career in radio, in cosmetics and in interior decorating. He has lived in Canada and the USA before reaching Australia, but what he does now pleases him most of all: he sells infuriatingly silly gadgets, mechanical jokes and souvenirs. His shop is stuffed with nonsense, like singing fish and puppets that drop their pants, and taps that pour water from nowhere, and anything he can find with frogs on.

Best of all he loves his big, metallic-blue trike with room on the back for two. In summer he takes tourists around on trike rides. I don't know what he does to *them*, but he frightened the life out of me. I could barely hang on as he flew round the corners. What I enjoyed most with Le Frog, though, was our visit to the oyster farm. I love oysters. Tasmanian oysters are great, but down there most restaurants, inexplicably, wash them. I couldn't believe it! The delicious natural taste of the liquid in the shell they just wash away. But Bertrand knew a place where you could buy them cheap in any quantity and open them yourself. With lemons and a bottle of Sauvignon Blanc we gorged ourselves. I can remember nothing better.

I went on down to the toe of Tasmania, and up the wet west side. It's a beautiful island savaged by greedy entrepreneurs who will dig up or chop down anything at all for a dollar. I saw mysterious temperate rain forests, and I also saw vast tracts of land stripped bare and still smouldering. The bitterest thing I heard was that since organic produce had become so profitable, big growers were cutting down native forest to give themselves instantly certifiable land. It seems there is no idea so good that it can't be trashed for money.

37

Dave Milligan and I got into his yellow van on a Friday morning about eight-thirty to get my bike out of the Melbourne docks. All the stories I'd heard from others foretold endless frustration, but Dave said it would be easy. He had been down there two days earlier, to make the appointment for a customs inspection, and two of the blokes he met had heard of *Jupiter's Travels* (though they hadn't read it). He thought that was a good sign. I thought I wished all the people who'd heard of it would read it. Buy it, even.

The bike was waiting for us in a bonded warehouse, inside the big wooden box that my friend John Conely and I had built back in early September. I thought the battery might be flat, after sitting there for three months. Maybe the tyres too. I was expecting the worst. After all, everything else to do with shipping this bike had gone wrong so far. Why shouldn't this?

The quarantine officers, who go by the acronym of AQIS, asked us if we'd brought tools to open the box. The way they asked, I was sure they knew we hadn't. It was like a piece of theatre. Dave said he'd been told there would be tools. They all rolled their eyes and went into a 'We-don't-do-tools' number.

The boss looked really pissed off. 'You're supposed to have a green piece of paper here which tells you to bring tools. Where is it?'

Dave and I looked blank. Things were not going well. 'Look,' I said. 'I know you're pissed—'

'No,' said the boss. 'I'm not pissed at you. It's those arseholes who are supposed to give you the green paper.'

There was a short period of suspense. Then somebody opened a drawer, and inside it there just happened to be a hammer and a jemmy.

It's amazing how two simple objects can make your day. Just a hammer with a broken claw, and a jemmy. All was not lost. We had surmounted the first hurdle.

We went into the warehouse with the AQIS guy and confronted the beast. The box looked very solid, almost impregnable. I remember how John Conely really enjoyed pounding those nails. Dave went at it. He likes to go at things, so I stood there and tried to entertain him. The banging and splintering went on for a while, and finally we got the top and one of the sides off. I remembered how long I'd taken washing the bike, but it still looked filthy. That's what AQIS can't stand. Dirt. I held my breath.

Our inspector looked inside. He asked a couple of questions. 'That looks all right to me,' he said, and signed me out. I heard my breath explode.

Then the customs guys turned up. They were very cheerful. They checked the numbers, and looked in one of my panniers. 'No worries,' they said, and that was that. Half an hour, and I was free to go.

When we got back to Dave's place I made a momentous decision. I took off the big metal boxes and put on some canvas bags that a friend of Dave's had designed. I had two good reasons. First, I thought it would be almost impossible for Malú to sit comfortably on the bike with those boxes there, because they were too long. Just as important, though, was my growing desire to lighten up. I felt as if I had never really given the bike a chance with all this weight on it. Andy White's bags were clever and convincing, and I went for them. Dave sent the boxes back to England, and I never regretted it.

I had an opportunity while I was there to do a lot of things to improve the bike, and Phil Pilgrim was an enormous help with many small details. I also thought it was time to service the Ohlins shock and took it to the dealer. He informed me that it was ruined. Somewhere, he said, I had smashed down on it so hard that the hydraulics were useless and I had been riding on the spring alone. Of course I knew immediately where that had happened: those same three potholes in Malawi. So I had come halfway round the world without a shock absorber, which shows how insensitive I am to the finer aspects of motorcycle technology, and how little it really matters. We replaced the broken parts, and instead of my yellow spring he gave me an even more potent red one.

At last I was free to follow my own designs, and after many rowdy farewells I set off northwards. First back to Sydney, then up the coast to Cairns, and finally across the much touted Outback to Darwin, something I'd been unable to do before because Darwin had been wiped off the map by a cyclone.

In the seventies, before email, friends would pass me on to their friends. I developed a chain of them, but they were relatively few and far apart. Things were a lot different in 2002. Now I was able to hop up the east coast of Australia from one email contact to another.

The McGonigals had left on their travels, so I stayed for a while with George Lockyer, in Sydney's Newtown. He and his wife Karen became good friends who helped me to know the city even better. From there I went a few hundred miles up the coast to drop in on friends of Rob van Driesum near Port Macquarie. Then on to Queensland to stay overnight with some other travellers, Ken and Carol Duval, in Brisbane. From there it was a skip and a jump to Bundaberg, famous for rum and whales, where Angus Hutchinson was waiting to show me the whaling wall and feed me roast leg of lamb.

Bundaberg to Airlie Beach is a long run, and I made it even longer by taking the old inland road from Marlborough to Sarina, a road with a spooky reputation earned by some unsolved murders. That's where I lived through one of the most enjoyable episodes of my first visit to these parts, when I was marooned between two flooded creeks with a party of Australian truckies.

Of course, I was careful to stifle my expectations, which is just as well. The first of the creeks, called Lotus Creek, was a long time appearing. There was an abandoned roadhouse on the south side of it, but a functioning BP station appeared soon after. I tried to talk to the proprietor. It was difficult. He was one of those people who treat every question with contempt. I explained that years ago I'd stopped at a place somewhere along here between two creeks.

'No way,' he said. 'Couldn'a done. Nothing there. Never was.'

We went on like this for a bit, before he admitted that there used to be a place 'down by Connor's'.

'On this side of Connor's?'

'Yeah.'

Enough said. I took off, but it was interesting, because he reminded me so much of the obnoxious Pole who had run that place down at Connor's Creek. It's all ancient history now. The place is a ruin, but I can still see the ghosts of the truckies playing cards on the highway, waiting for the water to go down. And the gum trees around here are white, and have a ghostly quality of their own. Beautiful, but at night, maybe just a little eerie . . . ?

Whitsun was my favourite bank holiday when I was very small. There was usually a fair to go to with sideshows and candy floss, and best of all a tower with a slide that corkscrewed round it. You slithered down on a doormat. Helter-skelter was one name for it, but for years I thought the slide itself was called a 'bank holiday'. So you can see I am disposed to have fun at Whitsun.

When I heard there were some islands coming my way called the Whitsundays I thought, Gee whiz, you could have fun there. That is certainly what they want you to believe at Airlie Beach, and they are quite good at making you believe things. For example, in spite of the name there is no beach. As it happens I was there in 1976, at almost exactly the same time, on Christmas Eve, and this is what I wrote in my notes then: 'This is a pleasant enough place, but the beach is useless.' Since then it has been obscenely overdeveloped, but I mustn't be too rude about it. It's still a seaside town, with lots of boats, and many of them will take you out to the islands and – ta-da! – the Great Barrier Reef.

I had two young email friends in Airlie, Rachel Skipsey, a joyful, attractive girl, and her ginger-haired husband 'Skip'. They were both travellers and fond of bikes, and very enthusiastic about having me to stay with them. And of course we had to go out to the reef. Rachel worked for the town tourism office, and she chose what she thought was a likely boat, so one morning we all three went out to board the good ship *Illusions*. The skipper was Malcolm, a seasoned fellow with crinkly eyes who looked the part. His helper was a young bloke with ropes of bleached hair hanging round his sunburned face who said, 'Hi, guys, my name is Rick and I'll be your diving instructor today.'

He tried to recruit me for diving lessons, but I declined. I got my certificate once in the Cayman Islands a long time ago. It was very beautiful down below, but my ears never did get accustomed to it. Snorkelling, on the other hand, had always been a brilliant success in the Caribbean, so I was looking forward to that.

The weather looked good enough. Some cloud, but plenty of sunshine. We were headed for Hayman Island. The whole island is owned by a five-star resort company, but apparently they would allow us a toehold on the edge, at Pearl Beach. The name has a nice ring to it, don't you think?

There were twelve of us on board, and we all went up to the bow where Rick told us what to do when the boat burned and sank. After that we were free to drink tea and coffee, and settle down for the two-and-a-quarter-hour cruise.

Two and a quarter hours can be a long time. The weather was going the wrong way. The waves were coming up. I was beginning to feel a little sick, but at long last we approached the islands and it was time to get fitted with flippers and masks, and to put on our 'stingies'. I forgot to tell you. You can't just snorkel out here, you have to wear a wetsuit to protect yourself from the lethal bite of the box jellyfish. I put mine on with difficulty. It seemed to have been made for a Gollum with several more limbs, but finally I zipped it up under my chin.

The skipper looked across at me. 'Skip,' he said, in the matter-of-fact manner that characterised this old salt's pronouncements, 'you've got that on back to front.'

I didn't bother to tell him that Skip was the other bloke over there, with Rachel. I assumed, wrongly, that he wouldn't have much reason to talk to me again. I went painfully into reverse with the suit, wondering as Rachel zipped up my back what you did when you needed to pee. Presumably, as Benny Hill once remarked, the P would be silent, as in pool.

We had just finished this manoeuvre when the boat rounded the point. It was a bit of a shock. Had we been the only boat, had the sun been out, had the beach been a beach, we might well have had the idyllic time forecast so effusively in the brochures. As it was, the water was the colour of sump oil, the beach was a two-hundred-foot bed of dead coral, and there were hundreds of people on it, all in black and blue neoprene, as thick as flies on a steak in New South Wales.

Rachel and Skip said they'd counted seventeen boats. Some of them were big. Magic forces had drawn them all to this same little bit of shore. The skipper was unperturbed. He prepared us to go ashore, and tossed a pair of black flip-flops my way. 'There you go, Skip', he said. It was too late to correct him now. I put on the flip-flops and they promptly fell apart.

He packed us all into a red rubber dinghy and as we floated offshore he flung a handful of food into the water and introduced us to 'his' fish. They flocked around the dinghy, flashing their fabulous coats at us, all working diligently for the tourist dollar. He played for a while with a large napoleon fish with a blue nose, and told us that there was a $2000 fine for taking any coral off the beach. Then he pointed out an area of water defined by some floating white buoys. 'Don't snorkel there,' he said. 'That's where we bring the boats in and out.'

We stumbled ashore as the great mass of walrus wannabes heaved and made way. With my flip-flops coming apart again I was even more of a clumsy amphibian.

'Can you bring another pair?' I asked the skipper. He said he would. I got into my flippers and mask, and fell into the water.

There was something wrong with my mask, or was it my nose? I couldn't stop the water trickling in. Distracted by this, I must have drifted into the shipping lane. As my head came up I heard a voice booming at me: 'Skip, don't swim over there. You need to keep looking out.'

But there was something else wrong. My snorkel was at the wrong angle. Water kept coming in. I struggled back to shore, to fix it. I found some new black flip-flops there waiting for me, and I put them on. They were fine. The skipper floated in with another pair. 'Here you are, Skip.'

'Thanks,' I said, 'I've already got some new ones.'

'They're the same ones, Skip. Maybe you've just found out how to use them.'

He gave a short laugh, and with an expert flip on the outboard, did a U-turn and zipped away. I knew they weren't the same ones. Later I saw someone else's black flip-flops fall apart, and I smiled secretly to myself.

Looking around me I saw crowds of earnest-looking men and women grouped in huddles in the shallow water with tanks on their backs. There were enough of them to mount a major commando raid on the five-star resort around the corner. I wished they would.

I managed to get the mask working better for a while and went out to look at the fish. They were lovely, and the whole thing could have been a bewitching experience. Unfortunately a lot of the time I was viewing them through a haze of fish food, and many colour-ful blue and yellow fish turned out to be rubber flippers. I did get over to the rocks for a bit and saw some amazing shapes and swirls of coral, but then I was back into trouble in the shipping lane – 'Skip, what did I tell you!' – and the water was getting up my nose again.

The boat ride back was even rougher, but there was a bit of lunch which helped with the sickness, and I learned to keep my eyes on the horizon. When you see sailors with their keen eyes fixed on the horizon, it doesn't mean they can perceive weather patterns invisible to you; it means they're trying not to get sick.

I was soon in trouble once more for wearing flip-flops on board – 'Skip, I'll get you to take those flip-flops off!' – but I scarcely noticed it now. For some reason the skipper never needed to speak to the real Skip, but with the reputation I've given him, he may never be allowed on a boat again.

*

There were things I had to do north of Cairns before I could head across to Darwin. In '76 this had been pretty wild country but I discovered that it had since been tamed and developed. Port Douglas, which used to be a small fishing village, was now a super-rich resort where President Clinton once holidayed. Tourism had taken hold all the way to Cape Tribulation, and maybe even beyond. It was sobering to see our species extending its habitat into these regions, sometimes with care and concern, sometimes recklessly.

I managed to celebrate Christmas, always a peculiar event in Australia, with some friends in Cairns, and finally began my journey across the Outback, the climax of my Australian experience, two days before New Year's Eve. It was the height of the Australian summer and not an ideal time to be going where the temperature can rise to 120 Fahrenheit, but it couldn't be helped, and the forecast for now was favourable.

Anyway, I could not afford to dawdle. I was warned that Darwin was entering the cyclone season, and somewhere just short of there the climate changed dramatically. If things got bad I might not be able to get through to Darwin on the final leg, and I would miss my boat to Singapore. For the same reason I chose to stay on asphalt. I wasn't afraid of dirt any more, but I thought it too risky to take the 'developmental road' alone at that time of year. It's 1772 miles to Darwin.

38

The first hundred miles west from Cairns are deceptively pleasant. They climb up over the Atherton Tableland, which is a great surprise. It's high, and green. You can grow coffee up here and run dairy farms. I know some lovely people here, the O'Sheas, and call in on their homestead for travel tips and a final cup of tea before diving down into the arid plains. At Mount Surprise the heat comes up to meet me.

They say it'll only be around 100 Fahrenheit for the next few days. The test for me is whether I can keep my jacket on. I've found that even in great heat it's best to keep it on. The moisture stays inside. It can be sweaty and disagreeable, but I have a theory that you don't lose so much to dehydration. I drink relatively little water, and carry only a couple of litres, but I've functioned very well on that so far. That way I don't risk losing the jacket, which is also my office, and I keep the protection. My right arm and both elbows have been hurt. I can't afford to hurt them any more.

Not that there's any reason to fall. The road here is sealed all the way across, and on some of the stretches there's no traffic. I mean, none. That emptiness is fine at first, but gradually it gets to you. By the time I come to Croydon I'm beginning to wonder if Australia is getting its own back.

I have joked about the Outback in the past. Many times. It made me laugh the way urban Australians would look you in the eye and say, in shuddering tones, 'You can perish in the Outback, mate.' As though they'd been there, when you knew they'd never been more than five miles from a pokie-machine in their lives. It went along with the endless talk of poisonous snakes (they have a lot, but hardly anyone gets bitten) and lethal jellyfish, and criminals on the lam. Australians must have a big investment in the legend of their perilous continent, I thought. Probably to do with beer. They think about how dangerous Australia is, and how lucky they are to survive it, and have another beer. Well, I was only having my fun.

Now it feels like the Outback is getting back at me. People *have* perished in it, of course, and today I get a good idea why. For hours I've been riding through land that stretches out flat and empty to the horizon and burned to a crisp. It's as dry as the kangaroo bones littering the side of the road. The sun's rays, UV-enriched for extra strength, hit like lasers to leave my skin tingling with incipient melanomas. And this is just the beginning. Ahead of me lie another 1400 miles, heading ever deeper into the fiery furnace.

This Croydon I've come to is no comfortable London suburb of shops, offices and semidetached villas. This Croydon is eighteen degrees south of the equator in the middle of Australia's worst drought in living memory, and it's as far as I'm going to get on my first day across the top. There's not much here: a crossroads baking and shimmering in the heat, a sprinkling of houses with nothing around them for a hundred miles, a BP station and, of course, the Great Australian Pub, which I enter very promptly.

A beautiful reddish blonde with a silver ring in her nose waits behind the counter, and speaks to me with an unmistakable Irish brogue.

'What would bring you here from Ireland?' I ask in astonishment.

'Well,' she says, thoughtfully. 'The weather's better.'

The Croydon pub has rooms with air, and good steaks. I treat myself, and go out at dusk to watch the kangaroo families enjoy the evening, because they are completely invisible during the heat of the day. They and a few starving cattle are the main reason, of course, why it's too dangerous to ride at night.

I'm off early in the morning but the sun is fierce as soon as it's up, and the next hundred miles are desolate. Some people, like the Irish girl, are drawn to these arid, empty spaces, but I don't understand it. Normanton, just below the Gulf of Carpentaria, is a bigger town which means there is more of not much. I look for a place to sit and have a cup of coffee. There are three café signs. Two lead nowhere. The third leads into a general store, where a girl is packing boxes.

'Is this a café?' I ask. 'Is there somewhere to sit?'

'No,' she says.

That's all, and she doesn't want to explain.

So I leave for the next sign of life, 120 miles away, known as the Burke & Wills Roadhouse. Burke and Wills were two explorers who perished in the Outback. Robert O'Hara Burke, who commanded an expedition to cross Australia from south to north in 1860, had courage and fortitude matched only by his stupidity. Like me, he started in the height of summer. He and the unfortunate Wills managed to get to the Gulf, but died on the way back.

Sometimes the landscape reminds me of the South African veldt, with the old-fashioned windmill pumps mooning over it. There must be some years when cows can survive here. Large areas have been cleared for them, but now the grass is tinder-dry and less nourishing than Astroturf. The few cattle I see are walking anatomy lessons in skin and bone.

The roadhouses are good, and I stop at every one. So would you. At Burke & Wills they do a good plate of eggs and bacon. The coffee's lousy, so I always drink tea. Next stop is another hundred miles, at Quamby (such names!). I drink a Coke on the porch, listening to the voices from inside. Out here they speak with long, rasping vowels but the people are pleasant and helpful. Then there's a short thirty-mile hop to Cloncurry, where I meet up with the main highway from Townsville. Cloncurry seems huge. Why, there must be at least a thousand people around here! I read that once in 1889 it got to 130 in the shade.

There's a street sign pointing to 'The Pool'. I'm roasting and I form a fantasy of falling into it. When I find it, the pool is 'Closed

Until Further Notice', but I can't let go of the idea. So I find a caravan park with a pool. It's called the Oasis.

'How much just to use your pool?' I ask.

'Now that's a very interesting question,' says this hairy bloke at the desk. 'I'll ask the boss.'

He comes back to tell me there's a public pool. I tell him it's closed. He's stymied, but I can see this is going nowhere.

'You don't want me in your pool, do you?' I say.

'Not really,' he says. Pleasant, but not helpful. It's a very small pool. I might use up all the water.

So I go to the Shell station, put some cold water inside me, and some fuel in the tank. The bike is only doing thirty-three miles to the gallon instead of the usual forty. I thought there was something very wrong, until it was explained to me. Australian fuel is terrible, and the further north you go the worse it gets. Up here it can cost $4 a gallon, but fortunately the Aussie dollar is worth only 55 cents in my money. Otherwise I'd be in real pain.

On to Mount Isa, another hour and a half, and now there's traffic. Road trains (trucks with three trailers, 166 feet long) whistle past, but the road is wide enough for us all. A lot of the ride recently has just been on bitumen strips, one lane wide. You get off on to the dirt when a road train comes through.

Now everything is changing. For the first time there's a break in the landscape, with big outcroppings of rock, and I can see rainclouds ahead. Then the huge mining complex of Mount Isa comes into view. It completely overshadows the town, with two towering smokestacks and sprawling plant raised high above the streets on a century's build-up of black tailings. All very grim and impressive. The biggest lead and silver producer in the West, so it's said, and this is where I'll stay the night.

I find a fairly cheap room at a good backpackers' hostel and I'm tipped to go to the Irish Club for a meal. Of course I imagine a small, cosy bar full of beer and blarney, so I have a hard time finding it. This Irish Club is built on a vast scale. At first I can't figure it out. I wander around in a small city of green motel units raised up

on stilts before I realise that the huge building on the other side of
the street, with a bottle shop buried in its side like a church crypt,
must be the club.

I find my way into the gaudy heart of it, where all the pokie-
machines are pinging away, and eventually detect Keane's Ranch 'n'
Reef Steak House. All the tables are neatly dressed with lacy paper.
Ropes of silver foil hang from the ceiling in memory of Christmas,
I suppose, but the place is almost empty. I order a salad and a pint
of this good beer I've found called Kilkenny.

A well dressed middle-aged gent comes in to slump at the bar,
with his grey-haired wife standing loyally by his side. Every now and
again he gazes at me with pure distaste, and mutters something to
his wife. I can't understand it, and keep checking around me. Once
I even stare him out. What is it? My helmet on the seat beside me?
My features? Something about me?

I construct an imaginary biography: middle-management mining
executive, passed over for promotion, drowning his frustration. But
what does he have against *me*? Only next morning, on the road, I
realise it must have been my T-shirt.

In Cairns a friend gave me a T-shirt. Normally I never wear
them (I'm sensitive about my narrow shoulders) so it didn't cross my
mind, but Australians who fancy themselves as having any class at
all have an obsession with dress rules. Anyone who crosses their
threshold after 7 p.m. in a T-shirt is regarded as a barbarian at the
gates. And yet, the restaurant staff would have ejected me ruthlessly
if T-shirts weren't permitted. The old man must have been simmering bitterly over some old defeat, when the club slipped even
further down the slope to anarchy.

Another early start. It's New Year's Eve and I'm a sucker for celebrations. Where am I going to toot my horn and sink the champers
tonight? The prospects are barren. It'll be two hours to Camooweal,
on the border between Queensland and the Northern Territory,
but there is still cloud cover and a bit of rain, so the beginning of
the ride is easy. The rain heralds the coming of the Wet. There are
two seasons in the Outback, the Dry and the Wet, and of course the
Wet has been a long time coming. I'm glad of the rain here, but I

hope it doesn't mean there's any chance of a cyclone forming further north. I'm very ignorant about these things. Long before my next stop, though, it's dry and hot again, and now the heat will really build up as I get closer to the centre of the continent.

Camooweal is nothing much, even by Outback standards. I get my breakfast – eggs and bacon again, but more expensive and less of it than yesterday. And the petrol is 20 per cent up in price too, so I pass. This is where my huge fuel tank really comes into its own.

I talk briefly to a trucker and his mate who've just come from Darwin. The trucker has big bushy white whiskers, and I can hardly hear anything he says through them, but I understand that in the evening the big red kangaroos come out on the road. They just stand there and look at you, he says, instead of getting out of the way. Then he tells me, 'Never let yer gear out of yer sight or they'll nick it.'

Who are 'they'? I'm pretty sure he means Aboriginals, but unlike in the seventies, you're not allowed to say that any more. I'm seeing more Aboriginals now around the fuel stops, strange wraithlike figures with black-putty faces, very thin, almost unreal, moving without apparent purpose. I hate to generalise. I know nothing about them still, but they don't look well.

Now it's 278 miles to where this Barkly Highway meets the Stuart Highway going north. Nothing to do but sit on the bike and absorb the heat. Sixty-five m.p.h. is the most comfortable speed, for me and for the bike. I'm looking around trying to think what I could say about this country, but what can you say about nothing?

About halfway along is another roadhouse called Barkly Homestead, and they're preparing it for a New Year's celebration. They are going to make it a Hawaiian Night, and women are pinning palm fronds and boogie boards up on the wall. A young bloke who obviously fancies himself is directing the proceedings, and telling the women what a good job they're doing. Apparently all the 'ringers' from the cattle stations around are coming here tonight. It's only midday and I haven't really gone far enough, but for a moment I think of making my New Year stand here.

There's one room left, for fifty dollars. I ask if I could use their phone line for my computer. The young man rejects the idea out of hand, with a good deal of self-importance. 'Can't do it, mate. I've told others. No way.'

He won't listen to argument. His ignorance offends me. What difference can a three-minute local call make to him? I give up the idea of staying, and get back on the road.

At the junction with Stuart Highway is another roadhouse called Three Corners. I drink a mug of tea, and sit for a while under the cool air from the fans. Then I fill up again, and ask the clerk how far north I have to go to find a bed. He nods the question across to an attractive woman standing next to us, and she says, 'Renner Springs has rooms, or you can go on to Elliot.'

Another 150 miles. That seems about right. Five-fifty miles for the day.

But when I go out to the bike, there's a man looking at it. 'Where you reckon to get to today, mate?' he asks.

I tell him Elliot.

'Don't go there, mate. It's a dump. Go to Dunmarra. That's a much better place. Clean. Decent. Only another hundred and ten kilometres.'

Another seventy miles or so. Might be stretching it, but still, I feel OK. I'll have a look at Elliot, and if I don't like it I can go on.

Before I can leave another motorbike arrives at the roadhouse from the north, the only other bike I've seen. The rider is a very tall, thin young man from Israel, on a small Yamaha with a huge amount of luggage. He's very excited about his journey around Australia, and tells me that he has just been through two scary lightning storms.

'Oh yeah,' I say.

I seem to have acquired the habit.

The land stretches out unbelievably far. A scattering of light cloud has formed above me, which helps to shield me a little. Somewhere north of Elliot, they told me, is where the tropics are reckoned to begin. I can see there are rainclouds in the far distant north. The land is different now, there are trees again, and amazing termite mounds that look like people, some single, some in small families.

It's five-thirty by the time I get to Elliot, and I ride slowly past the hotel.

There are aboriginal people flitting all around it. So that's what the man meant when he said it was a dump. But I have to admit it doesn't look inviting. If I hadn't come so far today maybe I would have the energy to involve myself in this as an experience, but it's New Year's Eve, and I want somewhere comfortable, clean and unchallenging. So I decide to ride on to Dunmarra. It shouldn't get dark before six-thirty.

When I arrive at the hotel there I see that it is indeed a good, well run establishment, and congratulate myself on my decision. Inside there's a man behind the counter.

'What can I do for you, mate?'

'I'd like a room.'

'No.'

That's all he says. Just 'No.'

My heart sinks. 'Why? Are you full?'

'We're not renting the rooms. We don't know how to run them.'

I can't understand what he's talking about. I start asking questions.

'Don't ask me, mate. I just work here.'

The guy is a stone wall, and refuses to explain. I'm really pissed off but I don't want to waste my energy on him. 'Well how far do I have to go now, to get a bed?'

'Another forty-four ks. To Daly Waters.'

So that's how I manage to ride more than 650 miles on New Year's Eve through the Outback. The tropical night is falling fast. I'm afraid of hitting the big red kangaroos that just stand there and look at you, but I don't see a single one.

When I get to Daly Waters it's good. I get the last free room. There's a swimming pool, and I fall into it as quickly as possible, feeling the heat drain out of me.

The woman I met at the Three Corners roadhouse is there at the bar, with a man who owns a pub nearby. She says she lived in London for a while, managing a pub called the Surrey Taverner, near a famous cricket ground. It seems to be something Aussies do when they go to London. She tells me about an elderly man from Jamaica who used to come into her pub every day, twice, and drank nothing but green Chartreuse. She meant to stay in London but she got homesick. Now she's a teacher. I think if anyone can explain the attraction of this territory, surely she can, and she tries really hard, but in the end she can't. But she does solve the mystery of Dunmarra – the owners went on holiday, and left caretakers behind who couldn't spare the breath to explain.

Her name is Robin, and we talk all evening. The fish dinner is delicious and so is the bottle of wine. I go to my room thinking I'm going to join her later at her friend's pub, but I fall asleep instead and wake up, fully clothed, at three in the morning with rain bucketing down and lightning all around. Happy New Year!

Next day I visit the pub. It's famous, and it's funny, but I won't describe it. Bill Bryson was there and I wouldn't dare compete.

According to the map I'm only 350 miles from Darwin. The rain has stopped and there's obviously no hurry, so I stop at a resort on the way with a lovely pool set in natural rock, beautiful grounds and good food. It's run by Aboriginals and they do a good job. It's certainly no dump, and I'm glad of that. What's more, nobody takes off with my kit.

Darwin, in a way, is more of a dump. Cyclone Tracy removed most of it on Christmas Eve 1974, and it's been replaced by utilitarian concrete buildings. The Poinciana Hotel is one of them. I'm there for a week, and through the TV I can reconnect with the ghastly world of geopolitics. I am quite sure now that Bush is going to invade Iraq, whatever he says. Since 9/11 I've been running a lively email debate on the subject. In principle I'm in favour of getting rid of Saddam, but I don't know enough about Iraq to make a judgement. I distrust completely the motives and the competence of Bush and his bunch of neo-Cons, and have the greatest difficulty explaining my own Prime Minister Blair's love affair with those people. I have lively arguments on both sides of the Atlantic, but I find the prospects very depressing, both for me and for the world in general. As against that, I have the rare pleasure of watching England defeat Australia at cricket.

Darwin is most interesting at night. I go people-watching on Mitchell Street, where most of the cafés and bars are. Outside a backpackers' hang-out is a big and beautiful tree that must have survived the cyclone, where a whole family of possums live. It's my memories of the possum tree and of a restaurant bar called Rorke's Drift that will linger the longest.

Perkins Shipping are as good as their word. Peter Hopkins, the boss, receives me kindly, and shakes my hand for the newspapers. They stuff my bike on to one of his boats for nothing and (which I appreciate even more) without having to put it in a crate, so I will be able to ride it away in Singapore with the minimum of hassle.

Australia, generous from top to toe.

39

By a wonderful stroke of timing I got an email, just before leaving for Singapore, from a man who said he had been an apprentice engineer at Meriden in 1973 and helped prepare my Triumph. He was the third person to claim that distinction, and I wonder how big was the army of people involved in getting that bike out of the Meriden factory, but anyway John Edwards was one of them.

Now he was the boss of a Dunlop factory in Singapore, and if there was one thing I lacked, it was a friend in Singapore. He met me at the airport, showed me around, introduced me to some excellent beer and a fabulous dish of spare ribs, and then gave me a bedroom in his apartment. And all the time we talked about everything that had happened to him, to me and to Singapore since those years in the seventies.

John likes Singapore. The city is really made for people like him. It is a highly evolved machine for doing business. It's clean. The traffic flows. Security is high.

For me, prepared though I was for change, it came as a shock. Nothing of what I had once found interesting in Singapore seemed to have survived. The sampans on the rivers, the washing hanging out to dry from the windows of the old Chinese houses, the weird and colourful transvestite scene on Boogi Street, all gone. As we drove around, the only building I wanted to photograph was the legendary Raffles Hotel, but the traffic defeated us and it was too much trouble to stop.

*

The bridge John Edwards sent me across into Malaysia was relatively new, and led to a brand-new inland motorway which runs
north from Singapore all the way to Thailand, but I was headed for
the older road that lies close to the west coast, and it was a while
before I found it. Now that I was back again on my original track, I
was hoping to reconnect with some of the most poignant moments
of the old journey, but sobered by past experience I was careful to
control my expectations, and it didn't surprise me that nothing was
familiar.

The air was humid but not too hot. Grey clouds billowed above
me, letting a silvery sun shine through occasionally, then releasing
showers. Riding in the rain was not the problem it had once been.
My clothing was completely waterproof, the roads were good and
my modern tyres clung to them, but visibility is always difficult
and it dampens one's view of the world. A particularly heavy
downpour caused me to stop outside a row of shops, and I managed to squeeze the bike in under an awning. The shops were all
raised above the road on a paved terrace to keep them clear of the
torrent of water rushing over the tarmac. One of them was a
coffee shop and I clumped over to it in my boots and clumsy
apparel.

It was an odd experience. Everything about the place was
extremely ugly, and so was everybody in it. The tin tables, no two
alike, wobbled precariously, the seats were moulded plastic, the floor
was cement, and very dirty, the area behind the counter looked like
a factory washroom, and the three young men who appeared to
work there obviously thought the job was beneath them. Perhaps
they were brothers. They all shared the same misshapen features.
Eventually one of them leered at me through moist, sagging lips and
said, 'What you want?'

He brought a cup of brown liquid made with condensed milk
and powdered coffee, most of which was in the saucer. But what
made the hilarious difference between something ordinarily awful
and something priceless was that all three of them wore the same
yellow T-shirts with the coffee shop logo printed on them: as though
that were enough to blind us to the squalor, enough to make them

Corporate, a Team, and cause us happy customers to exclaim, 'Ah, Fas' Food. Very good. Jus' like McDonal'.'

I got out as soon as I could and went on north to Pontian Kechil. I couldn't restrain myself from hoping that I might find some trace of Ambak Jaya and his wife who had given us, Carol and me, two of our best days together. It was in his little hotel that I had celebrated my forty-fifth birthday, and received from him as my present a little stuffed monkey which eventually made it all the way back to Europe.

Pontian, as I had known it, was a small village of one- and two-storey houses on both sides of the road. There had been a tourist lodge on the coast at the north end, with a pretty little pier that led out to a small trysting platform, where one could watch men fishing for shrimp at night with lights strapped to their foreheads.

As soon as I got past the first few houses my heart sank. The village had become a city. The buildings had three or four storeys. The main street was thick with traffic. The Jaya Hotel had disappeared, as had the lodge. The jetty had been swept away. I pulled some dollars out of a cash machine, recalling how much trouble it had been to get cash in 1976, and turned back.

There was another place I wanted to see a little way south at Kukup, a restaurant we had once visited, built out over the water on stilts, very peaceful, with delicious seafood. But I shouldn't have been surprised to find that Kukup had become a Coney Island. A man with a very drink-reddened face was touting a hotel, and I thought of staying there, at the Kukup Southern Lot Resort as it was called, but the planks leading out to it over the water looked too flimsy for my loaded bike, and I wasn't sufficiently tempted to take the risk.

I'd seen a sign for Tanjung Piai Resort a way back, and I made my way to this 'Destination of Enchantments'. It was far from the highway, and claimed to be the southernmost point of mainland Asia. This time I was not disappointed. There were many chalets set out over the sea on posts, but I was the only guest. An Indian family ran it, and the food was good. Monkeys patrolled the gangways and fished at the edge of the water, and in the distance I could see fleets of merchant ships standing out from Singapore, waiting for their numbers to come up.

Malaysia was where my first journey sank to its lowest ebb. It was where I abandoned Carol, although I loved her, believing that a journey like mine could only be made alone. What followed seemed like karmic punishment. A foolish accident almost cost me an eye. In hospital all my most precious documents were stolen from my bedside. It took six weeks to recover my health, my morale and my identity, and I spent much of that time in room number six of the Choong Thean Hotel on Rope Walk, in the predominantly Chinese city of George Town on the island of Penang, which they called the 'Pearl of the Orient'.

The life of Rope Walk enriched my own life enormously, and I have written a lot about that experience. My room was behind the top right-hand window three floors up. Opposite was an old roof of tiny scintillating handmade tiles, like fish scales, over a shop that arranged ceremonies for funerals. Next door you could buy elaborate paper houses, complete with furniture and fittings, to burn at the funeral so that the deceased could enter the hereafter in comfort and dignity. Most of Rope Walk was devoted to death and ceremony, but kung fu and the dragon dance were practised there too.

Of course I would have to revisit it, but with much trepidation. What if it had all gone, torn down by developers, as in Singapore.

I had been getting emails for a long time from someone called Lim Norton. I assumed he was Chinese. He invited me to stay at his house and we had a date to meet at a toll station on the mainland. It amazes me that so many people who are complete strangers can turn out to be such pleasant companions. I was ready to try my luck again, but first came a comic interlude.

After visiting Melaka and Ipoh, I rejoined the fine new freeway (free, that is, to motorcycles), still travelling north, when I observed menacing rainclouds ahead. So, planning to put on waterproofs I drew over to the shoulder, which was neatly bordered by well tended grass, came to a stop and leaned the bike over on to the side-stand. However, unfortunately, I had forgotten to put the side-stand down.

I blush, even as I write. Over we went on to the grass. Harmless enough, of course, except that my windshield lost another chunk of perspex, and I lost about half a litre of petrol before I could get all the various orifices blocked off.

At this point it started to rain heavily, so I put up my umbrella and stood there beside my prostrate motorcycle. It is unusual to see a motorcyclist standing over a recumbent motorbike holding a golfing umbrella. I myself have never seen such a sight, and nor I am sure had any of the hundred or so drivers who passed by before the rain stopped. I became quite interested in the expressions on their faces. I wondered whether it would occur to any of them to stop. I saw one older woman badger her husband into stopping, but not until they were about a hundred yards further along. Then another car stopped behind them. The driver got out. There was furious discussion. Then they all drove on.

Several riders on little Hondas went hurtling through the rain hardly a foot from me and never gave a thought to stopping, but I couldn't blame them. It was pissing down, and anyway I wasn't beckoning for help. Then, when the rain stopped, a nice young Malay man on a small Yamaha rode up with a puzzled expression. I explained that I was fine, and just needed a little help to raise the beast. With sixty-five pounds of petrol in my newly filled tank it was too much for me. He was pleased to assist, and I was on my way again.

But, oh boy. How did I ever come to do that?!

At 4 p.m., near the new bridge that connects the mainland to the island of Penang, Lim arrived on his sixties Triumph, lovingly restored, and took me to his house. He was indeed Chinese, with wife and child, and a neat unostentatious house on the mainland. He worked diligently as an engineer and reminded me often that it is every Chinese man's destiny to become a millionaire. We laughed a lot about that.

After a little time with him I crossed the bridge to George Town. It was a quick, easy crossing (a fact that was to cause me much anguish later), and after riding around a bit to regain my bearings, I finally found Rope Walk and made my way along it. I noticed that numbers of older buildings had been pulled down and replaced, and I began to fear the worst – but then, there it stood on the corner, a modest three-storey house with pale-blue windows and shutters that most people would pass without a glance. The Choong Thean Hotel.

A great wave of emotion swept over me at the sight of this building. Extraordinary that such a nondescript structure should have such a hold on my imagination. Many more beautiful buildings have been destroyed, I'm sure, but I went through a lot within its walls and I was so glad that it had survived. Much had changed, of course. The hotel itself had been closed and empty for five years and there was no knowing what would become of it.

The motherly prostitute who entertained her business clients on the ground floor was a Hindu but everybody else – the owners, the man who operated the mah-jong game, and T'an, the tongue-tied caretaker – was Chinese. T'an had been taken in by a hostel. The owners, whom I remembered very well, had retired to the country. The others were beyond my ken. Penang has had a preservation order on it for some years now. The old houses cannot be torn down any more, as they were in Singapore. The character of the city is saved. I felt a tremendous sense of relief.

After my eye injury in 1976 the retina had to reattach itself and recovery was slow. I was quite shaky for a while. I did a little trial run out to the beaches, and on Batu Ferringhi I met, quite by chance, a young German who was trying to choose what direction his life should take. I told him I planned to visit Thailand, and he suggested that I go to Phuket and maybe visit a woman he knew called Adrienne.

I wonder often about those chance meetings. In large measure my experiences during those four years were decided by them (to some extent they still are), and I can't remember one that went bad. Obviously it is not all a matter of chance. I can easily imagine following some stranger's suggestion and landing in disastrous trouble, and I have met other travellers to whom this has happened and who are dogged by violence and misfortune. But it seems that in some sense I choose my strangers, and my strangers choose me, which is another way of saying that who we are determines what will become of us, and that there are instincts at work which few of us recognise or understand.

In those days one could take a ship from Penang to India, and because of sailing dates I had not much time to see Thailand. Phuket was as far north as I went. It was already known as a vacation spot, but Adrienne lived on the far side of the peninsula, on Kata Beach, an unspoiled stretch of sand a mile or two long. Hers was the only house on it, and built of local materials it blended in well. The rest of the beach was lined with palm trees, and in the shade of the trees were a few fishermen's shacks and some water buffalo.

She welcomed me to stay a few days. One day I climbed over the next rise and looked down. The scene was so lovely that I tried to describe it. Here, I wrote, was 'another bay, smaller than Kata and uninhabited. I could encompass the whole picture in one glance: the long gentle slope of the beach, utterly smooth; an audience of palms respectfully inclined towards the sea, quite still in the hot afternoon lull; and the pale green water washing the sand and fading, with hypnotic regularity, to lay white lace ruffles of foam in unbroken arcs from one end of the beach to the other. It was an image of perfection, renewing itself with every fresh impulse from the sea.'

This was what I came back in 2003 to look for. The voice of reason told me it could not have survived, but I refused to listen. The ride to Phuket took me two days, through Hat Yai to Trang, and the next day through Krabi to Phuket. The riding was easy, the roads were good. It was nothing like 1976. I went through the heart of Phuket looking for the road to Kata Beach. In '76 it had been a dirt road, hard to find, but now it was asphalt and full of traffic. It reached the east coast eventually, though the sea was largely hidden behind developments, and I followed it south to Kata. I found myself on a busy commercial street with businesses, offices, shops and hotels on either side, and with occasional glimpses of a beach crowded with the usual paraphernalia. I wanted to believe I was mistaken, but I was not.

Where there had been palms and water buffalo there was now a complete urban infrastructure which continued uninterrupted through the second beach as well. Everything I had known and marvelled at was gone. Of all the disappointments of my second journey, this was probably the most shattering. To have known such natural perfection and to see it obliterated in so short a time was bad enough, but I think even worse was the knowledge that if I had tried to explain my feelings to any of these thousands of people pursuing their livelihoods and their packaged pleasures all I would have got, at best, would have been a shrug.

Since then, of course, nature has responded with a great tsunami that may have laid it all waste. And to be perfectly honest, I don't know where my sympathies lie. Do I care more for the world, or for the people on it? And what is the beauty of the world, except through the eyes of people? If I knew people who died there I would weep for them. Now I just weep for Kata Beach.

The political geography of this part of the world is quite extraordinary. How countries like Vietnam and Thailand can be expected to keep their territorial integrity is hard to see when they are almost split in two. The whole southern part of Thailand, mainly Muslim and about five hundred miles long, hangs by a thread from the rest of the country. On my way to Bangkok I passed through a corridor that was barely ten miles wide between Burma and the sea.

The going was pretty easy until I got near the capital. I had a map of Bangkok and studied it very carefully to make sure I could get where I needed without reading street directions, because they were completely meaningless to me. An Australian friend had recommended the Opera Hotel, and the Lonely Planet guide backed him up. It was near the big Siam Square, in the Pratunam area. I thought I had the problem licked because there was an overhead expressway which would have taken me very close to the hotel, but when I got to the ramp I discovered that motorcycles were prohibited. From that point on my efforts to find my way were a complete farce, and in the end I abandoned all my pride and paid a taxi to lead me there. It cost a pretty penny, but I can honestly say I didn't regret it.

40

Of all the various emotions I have experienced in seventy odd years, there is nothing more intense and more joyful than being in love. Hearts are trumps. Perhaps this is a truism. Maybe it's so obvious that it's not worth saying, but a person in love should be pardoned for wondering whether any other condition could possibly rival it.

The best discovery of all is that the sensation doesn't diminish with age. On the contrary, it seems to become purer and more exhilarating because there is less fear and uncertainty to cloud it. I already know it can't last for ever. There is also so much more to love than there used to be. I no longer fall for empty idealised images of teenage beauty. The women I have fallen in love with in these last decades of my life have been complex, interesting people with accomplishments, powerful opinions, and a life story to tell.

I know much better now how to revel in it for all it's worth, instead of worrying whether it will last, whether the one I love really loves me, whether practical difficulties will bring it down to earth, or 'spoil it all'. I knew Malú would probably put all this accumulated wisdom to the test, but I was in love with her, and nothing else mattered but that she would get off the plane at midnight and into my arms.

Of course I was at the airport much too early. It's what lovers, even ancient lovers, do. I had figured out a way to get there on public transport because I had all the time in the world, and taxis seemed very expensive. I took the pleasing and efficient Bangkok metro to the end of the line and started looking for buses. The choices were bewildering and difficult. So far as I could tell there were cheap ones, better ones, and expensive ones. Some had air-con, some stopped everywhere, some were expresses. They were in many different colours and went to many different destinations. I had no way of knowing which ones passed the airport. I just knew for certain that one of them did.

The night air was warm and pleasant. On an overpass leading from the metro station I looked down on the brightly lit chaos of people and vehicles below, trying to read bus numbers and discern some pattern or information, but nothing made much sense. I entertained myself for a while watching the shopgirls and office workers and all the other forms of Bangkok life rushing past below me.

In the end I went down to join the ever-shifting mass waiting by the roadside, picked a likely subject, and asked him, 'Pardon me, please. Which bus goes to the airport?'

He flung out his arm, dramatically pointing: 'This one. Blue. You can catch. Quick.'

A blue bus stood in the middle of the road amongst the others with its doors still open. I charged across and in. The doors shut.

Unbelieving, I said to nobody in particular, 'Airport?'

Heads nodded and said something like 'Aaaaanh.' With relief I sank into a seat.

We left a thinning suburbia behind and the dimly lit bus plunged far into the countryside, but it was too dark for a view. Time passed and I became nervous. Had I missed the stop? Then someone called 'Airport!', and I climbed out gratefully, expecting a long walk. Incredibly, an enclosed walkway began almost directly from the bus stop, and led in only a few minutes straight to the arrivals hall.

It couldn't have been simpler, and I was childishly pleased at having found a way around the knee-jerk tourist 'Taxi to the airport!' but we would certainly be taking a taxi back. When she came – if she came? can you ever be sure? – Malú would have been travelling for a staggering thirty-six hours, more than halfway round the globe, from Santiago to Dallas, to Tokyo, to Bangkok, and

I imagined her arriving with a twelve-hour jetlag, a shattered and bloodless wreck.

I had plenty of time to embellish this image. The plane wasn't due for an hour, but soon I became distracted by the people waiting with me. There were monks and nuns and mormons to goggle at. There was an impossibly heavy white guy in shorts whose over-loaded legs didn't look as though they would last the night. I was fascinated by an American woman in what was obviously a newly tailored cream silk business suit, because it was so badly made and she was so obviously unaware of it. One leg hung longer than the other, and ugly creases ran diagonally across the back of the jacket from shoulder to waist. Bangkok is a place to get clothes made quickly and cheaply and, I reflected wryly, she had probably got her money's worth.

I wondered what Malú might be carrying when she appeared. It was a major concern. I was very happy with the new soft luggage on the bike. I knew Malú would have been impossibly uncomfortable sitting astride the two alloy boxes, but luggage space was tight. I had cut down my own load to a small fraction of what I started out with, but there was an irreducible core. I hoped that her things would all fit into one of those black pannier bags.

I was nervous, no question. Imagine being introduced to motor-cycling in Bangkok traffic. Suddenly the idea seemed insane. What if we went round the block and she screamed, 'Stop! I will not go one more metre on this terrible machine!' What then? I swallowed my anxiety as best I could.

The airport announcer called out the plane arrivals, first in Thai and then in English, and I tried to use the endless repetitions to learn a few words in Thai, of which so far I knew nothing. By the time Malú's plane landed, late of course, I still knew nothing. The passengers took for ever to come through immigration and cus-toms. I had wanted to see what kind of person the girl in the cream suit was meeting, but lost sight of her. People streamed past, end-lessly. Then there was a lull. My heart sank. And then there she was, almost alone in the crowd, a slight, erect, vigorous, lovely person striding towards me with a happy smile.

She wore cotton trousers and a leather jacket. Her hair was swept back tightly, darker than I remembered it, emphasising the classic shape of her head. She carried one medium-sized soft black bag, a handbag, and a carton with two bottles of Chilean red. Her eyes sparkled, and she seemed hardly affected by the journey at all. We embraced and hugged and kissed and all the anxiety drained out of me right there.

Later, of course, the journey caught up with her, and happily our room at the Opera Hotel pleased her because she spent a good deal of time in it dealing with those twelve extra hours. Meanwhile, I was dispatched on a vital mission. I had to find an aesthetically pleasing but functionally effective helmet, and as I scurried around the stores and the back streets I was almost in despair. The Thai notion of beauty is special, and even though Malú is much attracted to Buddhism I didn't think she would want to ride around with a temple on her head. But in the end the joss was with me, and I found a sleek, silvery blue job that fitted her perfectly.

So on the second day we were ready for the moment of truth. I had already rehearsed the route, which embraced two city blocks and avoided all the one-way traps and cul-de-sacs that seemed to be a special feature of Bangkok. Outside the hotel, on the *soi*, or small alley, that led to the mechanised maelstrom of Thanon Phetburi, we practised. I stood across the bike trying to hold it like a rock, with the side-stand down, while she figured out how to get up on the seat between me and the top box. Then I lit the motor and we rumbled past the food stands and the taxi drivers to turn left into the traffic.

From that moment until we came back up to the hotel a mile or so later I drove more carefully than at any other time in my life. It was like taking my driving test all over again. Imagining it through her eyes and ears, the noise, the crush, the fumes all seemed horrendous. I had absolutely no idea whether she hated it or loved it until we stopped and Malú got down. I could see nothing through her visor. When she took off her helmet her hair fell all over the place, but all I could see was the broad smile on her face.

'I like it,' she said.

She liked it. She really liked it.

With new-found confidence we rode around Bangkok looking at the sights. Most of the city is built Western-style in huge blocks of offices, apartments, malls and stores. A grid of avenues carries a torrent of noisy traffic, and riding around is not much fun; but there are of course plenty of links to the traditional Thai culture, and we barely skimmed the surface of it. A boat ride on the river showed us how some working Thai families live, in picturesquely decrepit structures, some under scalloped and tiled roofs decorated with dragons, others under rusty tin, all decked out with a profusion of potted plants, all intimately connected to the water.

We went to Wat Pho to see the immense reclining Buddha, so enormous that I imagine the temple must have been built around it. And we both submitted, side by side, to the celebrated masseuses, where I suffered unspeakable agonies being torn limb from limb by a grade-one sadist, while Malú, to my chagrin, said she enjoyed every minute of it.

We walked around shops in back streets looking at oddities, and Malú suddenly cried, 'Look! Look at that. I want one. Come inside.'

She was pointing at wigs, but not ordinary wigs. These were made of long strands of nylon in garish blues and greens and reds. That night at the Opera she made me take a picture of her sitting cross-legged on the bed in this streaming luminescent blue wig, looking like an Indian witch goddess, and very beautiful besides.

But in spite of all this excitement we were both eager to leave the noise and pollution of the city, Malú even more than I. The route was up to me, and I wanted to go north to Chiang Mai. Malú was comfortable on the bike, but for how long? She is not a very well cushioned lady, and I wondered just how many miles she would be able to sit on the saddle before ecstasy gave way to agony. I had already agreed never to take her beyond her comfortable limit.

'You must promise,' she said fiercely. 'I trust you, but don't make me a victim.' With Malú you always knew where you were.

So we studied the maps together, and saw that we could make

Chiang Mai comfortably in two 150-mile days, stopping at Tak on the way. So far so good. Of course, it wasn't all plain sailing. We got into a heated exchange over the packing. We both had a lot to learn about packing for two. There were tears and recriminations and fearful threats, but we survived it. We ended up having to strap an extra Ortlieb bag alongside, but it didn't get in the way too much.

To my surprise most major roads north of the capital were dual-carriage, which is just as well since otherwise carnage would have reigned. On two-lane roads the Thais tended to drive as though there was nothing coming the other way. This was puzzling because I had not observed it coming up to Bangkok. At the same time I was tediously aware that these new roads had the same flattening effect on the environment that they have everywhere else in the world. It annoyed me that I should have come to Thailand to be absorbed in thoughts of traffic and road construction, and only gradually came to appreciate what a profound change had taken place there. When I was first in Thailand the American presence, due to the war in Vietnam, had been pervasive, and it seemed to me then that Thai culture already had a thick Western gloss laid over it. But now it was as though the Thai culture itself was the gloss.

Of course there were all the trappings of religion, just as there are in every society. Temples, shrines and monks abounded, and Malú revelled and gloried in them all. We stopped once by a road-side shrine shop – a 'Shrines 'R' Us', if you like. The forecourt was crowded with these gilded, glittering multicoloured mini-temples on pedestals, and Malú wandered among them, entranced.

'*Son casas de espíritus.* Houses of the spirits,' she murmured, think-ing of the book that had made her friend Isabel famous. '*Qué preciosas*, so adorable, where the ancestors live. It is so important to keep the past alive in the present,' and of course I agreed, but the underlying life of the country appeared to be much more driven by Western ideas of capital, growth and marketing. I could not forget the rape of Phuket, and it was in this part of the world that I came across by far the biggest billboards I have ever seen – towering erec-tions of scaffolding at least ten storeys high.

With her strong affinity to Buddhism, Malú rejoiced in the

peaceful atmosphere surrounding the saffron-robed monks and their temples. I suppose that of all the religions Buddhism is still the one that would appeal to me most, but I have a well developed cynicism, and I came to view the huge population of monks and their monasteries as a useful welfare programme for the unemployed.

Chiang Mai did not help much in this respect. It's true that we saw hill tribes in their colourful dress, we rode an elephant where there were many of these grand animals being worked and tended, and we wandered through markets where fried grubs were available for tasting among many other, and possibly more appealing, delicacies. So the Thai gloss was very thick, and enjoyable too, but all around us were American enterprises employing Thais to make textile items for export to the West, and I couldn't rid myself of the feeling that I was in some vast and elaborate theme park.

A friend of mine from Seattle, Dave Stafford, who had arrived in Chiang Mai with his own bike, introduced us to an American, originally of Dutch descent, who lived outside the city, and he invited us all to stay. He was a generous, balding retiree, once an engineer and very sure in his opinions, who liked to be known simply as Botter. He had lived for years in Bangkok where he opened what he said was the first riverboat restaurant there, but the experience had left his Americanness untarnished. He built his own house outside Chiang Mai, and the strange thing was that if you were to put it down on a tract in California you would not be able to distinguish it from its neighbours. He had married a young Thai woman, and she cooked bountifully for us all, but she was careful to keep everything bland for the American palate.

It was hardly the exotic environment Malú had come so far to experience, but I was glad to be somewhere neutral where I could do maintenance on the bike and above all work on my website. The website was a major commitment, and still took up at least a day out of every week on the journey. While I worked, Dave carried Malú off on sightseeing tours, but I caused us to stay just a day or two too long, as we discovered later to our mutual discomfort.

By now, in February 2003, it was obvious to everyone that George Bush was hell-bent on going to war in Iraq and that it could happen within weeks. Even worse, from my personal point of view, Tony Blair seemed incomprehensibly determined to go in there with him. So my British passport, which had always eased my passage, which had always identified me as one of the good guys, was now a stinking carcass tied around my neck. There was going to be trouble ahead, in Pakistan, in Iran, maybe even sooner than people thought. But the immediate consequence was the worst practical news I'd had for a long time. I could not fly the bike out of Bangkok.

How I mourned the passing of the *Chidambaram*, the ship that had once carried me and my Triumph across the Bay of Bengal from Penang to Madras. That would have been such a perfect way to proceed, but she had burned, and now there were no such sea crossings to be made. How sad, too, that we couldn't ride through Burma; that the disgusting military dictatorship that was sucking it dry and holding the world's most valiant lady, Aung San Suu Kyi, under house arrest because they did not dare to kill her, made crossing Burma impossible.

Air freight was now the only practicable method, and I had researched it thoroughly. There was a freight forwarder in Bangkok who could have flown the bike to Katmandu for a fairly reasonable price. He could have, but no more. 'I can't do it,' he told me on the phone. 'They have made it too difficult. With all the surcharges and restrictions and the rigmarole, it would cost you a fortune, and it's just not worth the effort.'

Fear of terrorism was spreading across the globe. Motorcycles were always classified as 'dangerous cargo', but that used to be routine. Now the terrorist threat was used as an excuse for all kinds of irrational behaviour. How else could you explain it? I found that I *could* fly the bike from Kuala Lumpur, in Malaysia. It would fly on the same airline. It would actually go back to Bangkok first, and then to Katmandu – but I couldn't put it on the plane in Bangkok.

For me the difference was having to ride almost a thousand miles further south, and with Malú on the bike that meant at least four more days. On top of that there was the cost of flying us and the bike those thousand miles back again. And there were other ticketing complications too banal and irritating to go into. For a few hours I wanted to smash everything in sight, then I got used to it.

For all her stated loathing of 'coupledom', Malú tried her best to be half a couple. She would slip her arm through mine walking along a market street, she liked me to watch her try things on, and asked for my opinion. We usually slept in the same bed even though she had always maintained that she preferred to sleep alone. 'Prefer', which she pronounced 'prefair', was a favourite word, a coolly aristocratic synonym for 'want', and Malú set aside many of her preferences on my account, though it was very clear that I could never take these concessions for granted.

For my part I was uneasily aware that somewhere I had lost my way. I ought really to be the perfect companion to a feminist. My instinct is to treat all women, desirable or not, with the same respect due to anyone, and while there is nothing wrong with that, I was finding it harder and harder, with age, to flick the switch from propriety to passion. It seemed to me that my behaviour must sometimes seem distant, even indifferent. I wondered now if it had always been, if maybe I had never known how to be emotionally comfortable with women, if perhaps I was afraid of them in some way, if maybe my mother had something to answer for.

I have always wanted a stable, loving relationship with a woman and yet I had never managed to make one last beyond a few years. Perhaps that Indian clairvoyant had, after all, seen something in me that I had always missed. So our journey became for me also an inquiry into my own psyche, which is what all the best journeys become.

On our way south we rode to Mae Sot, on the Burmese border, where I gazed in longing and frustration across the ironically named Friendship Bridge, which I could not cross. Malú bought a brocaded jacket, wondering how it would go down at presidential receptions back home, and added another important Buddhist temple to her collection. Four days later we crossed the border into Malaysia, on our way to Penang. We had been doing well. None of the rides had been too long for her. We had seen some interesting things. In Chumphon we had found ourselves at a festival where fabulous creatures in gaudy costumes and make-up proceeded through the streets carrying a red lacquered chair accompanied by loud music and firecrackers. Here and there groups of young men threw fits and fell writhing to the ground.

I asked the hotel receptionist what it was all about.

She tossed her head. 'Who knows?' she said. 'They're Chinese.'

There was a minor upset when Malú was perched on the bike for a photograph and the whole thing tipped over. I was helpless and horrified to see her go down, but she emerged from the mess smiling and unscathed.

We managed a beach experience at Hua Hin, smuggling ourselves into the confines of an expensive tourist hotel and enjoying its luxuries for a couple of hours. Malú had fun with her blue wig. We had nice, tender moments together, and all in all things were going splendidly. Now I was going to share with Malú some of my nostalgic pleasure in Penang. I told her about the Choong Thean Hotel and how relieved I had been to discover that the character of the town had been preserved. I described Penang's beaches, and the simple little hotels I remembered. I suppose I drew a rather idyllic picture of the island.

We were on our way from Krabi, a pleasant seaside town famous for the massive and unique pillars of limestone, tufted with vegetation, that erupt from the flat landscape as though punched out from below the earth's crust. We had avoided Bangkok on the way south, and Krabi was the only other place where we could sort out the tedious complexities of our ticket with the Thai airline. Malú already had a ticket from Bangkok to Katmandu for five days hence. Given the time I would need in Kuala Lumpur to crate and dispatch the bike, I knew we would have to reach Penang that day.

No problem, I thought. About 350 miles on fast roads. A long stretch for Malú, but it was time, not distance, that mattered to her. She shouldn't have to sit in the saddle for more than seven hours, max. We got to Hat Yai in time for lunch. The crossing into Malaysia was painless, as were the last hundred miles to Butterworth, where the ferry and the bridge to Penang began. We got there in the late afternoon. I could tell that Malú had had enough, but we were almost there. It's a doddle, I said to myself. We'll be on a beach before dark.

The new bridge to Penang is the longest in South-East Asia, a six-mile span. As we approached the tollbooths the heavy traffic from the south joined the road, and suddenly thickened. For a second I thought of turning back, but I'd seen nowhere to stay for a long time, so I ploughed on, and once through the tolls and on the bridge there was no longer any option. Then I knew I had made a terrible mistake. Container trucks, lorries, cars, taxis and a million two-strokes crowded in on us, and the whole mess set solid.

We were grinding along at walking pace in a thick haze of exhaust. The vehicles were too close together for my bulky bike to slip through like the nimble two-strokes. As far ahead as I could see there was no let-up, and I knew that if you were to ask Malú her definition of hell on earth, after imprisonment and torture this would be it. How often I had heard her describe the pollution in Santiago as though it were a poison-gas attack. Helplessly trapped in this smoggy gel, with Malú ticking behind me like a time-bomb, I was in a nightmare.

I was as shocked as she was. I'd given no thought to how much Penang must have swollen in twenty-five years. During the hour we were on the bridge dusk came and then nightfall. When at last we came out the other side I saw the same traffic jam stretching along the road to town, and I took what I hoped was a ring road to the coast. I was in open country, heading I knew not where. It went on and on.

'Stop!' screamed Malú.

'Where?' I shouted back.

'So this is your *maldición* paradise!' she spat. Imprecations poured out of her in Spanish. 'This is the end. I will go home. I won't go another mile with you. You must STOP!'

But there was nowhere to stop, for mile after mile. Then, like a trumpeting of angels, came a sign. Hotel Resort. It pointed left up a hill. We arrived on a dark, untidy parking area outside a sprawling, dilapidated house. Malú got down. She stood with her arms wrapped around her body in stony silence, the absolute embodiment of rage and hate. Various young people in cheap clothes stood about. To my jaundiced eye they all looked like drug addicts. I looked at the rooms. They were miserable. The bathrooms were worse. The prices were ridiculous.

I went back to Malú. 'We can stay if you like, but the place is awful.'

She shook her head. What she meant was, 'I don't give a fuck.'

'There are more hotels nearby, just down the road.'

Same response. I got on the bike. She got on too.

We rode half a mile down the road, and saw the sea on the right. We were on the beach at last, at Batu Ferringhi (Foreigners' Rock) as I had hoped, but it was not the Batu Ferringhi I remembered. Soon we were surrounded by high-rise luxury hotels. We took a room on the tenth floor of the Holiday Inn for $125 and for the next thirty-six hours we abandoned all thoughts of economy. Malú bought an amazing Malay-style evening dress in shimmering peacock-blue material that separated below the waist like flared trousers. It looked magnificent, though I couldn't imagine her wearing it anywhere else.

We went to George Town and visited the Kuan Ying Teng temple, where the celebrated Chinese goddess of mercy interceded for me. By the end of the day we were OK again. If we can come through that, I thought, then maybe there's hope for us after all.

The run to Kuala Lumpur was without stress. We stopped here and there – at one point for Malú to investigate a palm oil plantation – and once we got within range of the city there were always those immense Petronas Towers to guide us in. Near the central railway station we easily found a comfortable little backpackers' hostel called the Kameleon, just round the corner from a small intricately carved Hindu temple which glowed mysteriously at night. I had digested my bitterness at being forced to ship the bike out of KL, but I knew I was in for a hard day's work getting it crated and delivered in time. In fact it was twice as hard, and twice as costly, as my worst expectations, but I got the job done just as night fell, and nature saluted my achievement with an apocalyptic thunderstorm which crashed down over the whole city, converting the roads into rivers.

The next day we flew out to Katmandu, to wait for the bike to catch up with us.

41

How ironic that the one place where I would have welcomed progress was still stuck with the same grasping, reactionary regime. Not that I would have wanted Katmandu to lose even a single lacquered window or roof tile from those mysterious temples and palaces crowded around Durbar Square. But once outside the sacred heart of the city, conditions seemed, if anything, to be worse, and even within it some old and beautiful buildings were collapsing in decay.

I had many opportunities to observe Nepali misery. Our hotel was about a mile from the centre, an easy walk for a sure-footed pedestrian picking his way around broken pavements, puddles and heaps of rubbish. I passed many shops open to the weather. You can tell a lot about life from looking into shops, and I guessed from the prices and the goods that life here was hard.

The sky was generally clear, with occasional bouts of heavy rain. Because of the altitude and the cold air, as in Bolivia, the rubbish seemed inert and odourless. Halfway along, the road crossed the Vishnumati River, which was more like an open sewer – the kind of river where you might expect to look down and see a corpse spread-eagled amongst the rocks and the junk, though I never did. From our bedroom window I could look across into other courtyards, where I watched women scrubbing their clothes and linen by hand: a picturesque sight when you're not having to do it yourself. And these were the more prosperous Nepalis.

I recalled the big arguments of the seventies. There were so many foreign agencies there to do good, the Peace Corps, volunteer outfits from all the usual donor nations, the NGOs, and, of course, the UN. Purists like me feared that progress would bring roads and power into the mountains and that the world would lose for ever this extraordinary window into a pre-industrial world. We need not have worried. Despite the efforts of conscience-stricken Westerners, the people seemed to have made no progress at all.

I talked to people who were still trying to bring basic education and health services to the villages, and it seemed that nothing had changed. Where had all the money gone? Not just the aid money, but also the huge income from the mountaineering expeditions? By all accounts it had been scooped up by corrupt politicians and greedy royals. If I were a Nepali, I thought, I would probably be a Maoist rebel too.

However, there was nothing we could do about it, so we busied ourselves as good little tourists should with all the remarkable things there were to see, and since it was Malú's first visit she showed the way. One day in Durbar Square she found a tiny but exquisite young woman called Arita who sold woven shoulder bags, and made friends with her. Arita perched every day on one of the temple platforms with a pile of those colourful handmade artefacts. She was well under five feet, and almost doll-like in a long-sleeved scarlet blouse and tight ankle-length trousers, with a patterned red dress on top. It was a shock to see her dwarfed next to Malú, who is herself small, but Arita was in fact a strong woman with a very positive and resourceful spirit.

Her husband was unemployed, and she had children to feed. The bags were made in her village, and selling them supported her family. Despite the hardship, I never saw anything but tranquillity or joy on her beautiful face, and after a while I came to believe that her friendship with Malú was genuine.

As accidental tourists we were very fortunate. An important Hindu festival took place at the Pushpathinat temple while we were there, and devotees flocked in from all over India. It was all Malú could have dreamed of, with the extra bonus that marijuana could be smoked freely on the premises. In fact it was *de rigueur*, and as a non-smoker I felt quite out of it.

There were naked, ash-covered saddhus contorting themselves and hanging from branches in a haze of pot smoke. Right in front of us, pilgrims were performing impossible penances, dragging their limp bodies over the ground by their arms alone . There were more funeral pyres than usual burning on the banks of the Bagmati, and fascinating mini-ceremonies happening in little shrines wherever you looked. Immense colourful crowds flowed around the temples, and Arita found ways to get us to the heart of the event. Without her we would have been lost on the fringes, probably in a mile-long queue for a temple we would not have been allowed to enter anyway.

At one point I lost Malú briefly, then found her again surrounded by a curious crowd. She was squatting on the ground with an elderly bewhiskered holy man, apparently in a competition to see who could get the last drag out of their joint. For Malú it was a huge success, and being there with her overcame my unease at being a voyeur at these religious spectacles.

Nor was that all. Only four days later there was an equally significant Buddhist celebration at the Swayambhunat stupa. We clambered up below the huge white dome, and squatted behind the ornamental elephants to watch solemn Tibetans circling the stupa clockwise for the prescribed number of times. It seemed that Malú's spiritual needs were well served in Nepal. There remained only a visit to Buddha's birthplace at Lumbini, and we would pass by there on our way to India. For myself, I was happy to be with her, and I thought to myself, I'm really just along for the ride.

But there was a sad aspect to my thoughts that I tried unsuccessfully to stifle. Because Malú's time was limited, there could be no question of going back to Assam in the north-east corner of India, something I had been longing to do for years, and it opened up the whole dreary issue of my ambivalence. Even though I wanted to spend my life with Malú, I had to admit that her fear of 'coupledom' was solidly based. I knew I had compromised this journey to be with her, that it would be very different from the journey I had intended to make. She was another stake in my future to which I was now tethered.

Back in the seventies I had given up the girl for the journey. This time I was giving away the journey for the girl. But what if I ended up with neither?

The bike in its crate turned up in pretty good shape, and I enjoyed putting it together. We chose our hotel, which belonged to a dignified and friendly businessman called Amar, because it was quiet and comfortable and had a walled courtyard where there was room to rebuild the bike once it arrived. Malú went off on a solo trip to a mountain resort called Nagarkot while I worked alternately on the bike and my website. I had some trouble tuning the carbs, but finally the bike ran well enough.

There was a TV in our room, and I watched the mounting preparations for war in Iraq. It was inevitable now and could begin any day, and yet it was so distant, so unreal. I felt sure now that it was wrong, that Blair had been terribly misled, that it would have dreadful consequences; but viewed from Nepal it might have been happening on another planet.

We were very comfortable there. We even forgave the boy, one of Amar's servants, who would knock furiously on the door at our most intimate moments and insist on taking away the tea things. He didn't understand the phrase 'Go away', let alone 'Piss off!'

One morning, after nine days in Katmandu, we looked across at each other in our twin beds and agreed. 'It's time to go.' We took celebratory pictures and got on the road to Pokhara, and India.

I felt very good on the bike now. We worked well as a team, and I was scarcely aware of Malú's presence behind me. She had made herself pretty comfortable with padding across the front of the top box. Her biggest problem was keeping her helmet from flying up in front of her face, and I managed to fix that with a rubber band. It came from the same packet of outsize elastic bands that I had picked up from David Wyndham's stores back in Dorchester, and they turned out to be among the most valuable and versatile items I carried.

The climb out of the valley was steep and exhilarating and the views were sensational, but the traffic was bad. The road had been tarred over now, but was badly deformed in places, and with big trucks appearing suddenly around sharp bends, braking could be a little hairy. There were moments coming down on the other side when I felt uncomfortably close to disaster, but Malú said later that she hadn't noticed.

Unlike Katmandu, Pokhara had completely changed – from a few rustic shacks and tents beside the lake to a complete holiday town – although it had not, thank heavens, indulged in the excesses of Phuket. It retained an easy nonchalance that may be due to the Tibetan influence there, which is very strong. It captured us for a few days, before we took another deep breath and headed for India.

The road took us back the way we'd come for a while, and then went south into another giddy climb and descent. First there were great gorges and rivers, and then on the other side, coming down into the Terai, the heat began to hit us in waves; monkeys appeared at the roadside, forests enclosed us, and the villages were dry and dusty and looked like India.

Butwal was the last big town before the border and it was Indian in all but name. We tracked down the Hotel Kandara because according to the guide it had a garden where I could park the bike. A tall watchman, in full military regalia, saluted me and said that, alas, the garden had become a building site, but after some negotiation he said I could probably get in from the back. I rode around to the back gate and saw that the garden seemed to be full of newly laid wet cement. The owner of the hotel, a thick-set gentleman with white hair, was overseeing his workers from a deckchair and with their help I managed to squeeze the bike in somehow without it becoming cemented in overnight as a garden ornament.

When I removed my helmet the owner saw my greying hair and asked how old I was. This was not an uncommon question. In the old days they used to want to know only the cost of the bike. Now they wanted my age too.

I told him seventy-two, and he seized my hand with both of his and squeezed it fervently as if trying to extract the essence of longevity. 'I am only fifty-two,' he said, 'and I feel like an old man.'

I reflected that by the time they were my age, most Indian men were dead.

42

We came through the border crossing from Nepal to India on 10 March with remarkably little trouble. Gorakhpur was only a hundred miles away. I was quite relaxed. Malú was buoyed up by her time at the Buddha's birthplace, and I was excited to be back in India after so many years. My mind was full of the dramatic and astonishing things I had seen there in the past, and they obscured any memories I might have had of the hardships of day-to-day travelling.

On my first journey I spent nine months in India, Ceylon and Nepal. I started from Madras in the south. Maps were hard to find, but in Bangalore I managed to get a so-called 'road map', published by the Indian National Survey. It was printed on two large sections of bad paper and it was a terrible map, almost impossible to read, which was appropriate because the roads were terrible too. Afterwards I outlined the route I took in ink, and when I look at it now I am astonished at how much of India I saw.

Many years later, Lonely Planet published a road map in book form, and I got a copy when I was in Australia. It was beautifully done, on glossy paper. You could read the names of the towns, and the distances between them, and when we were in Nepal I spent a good deal of time studying this map, wondering how much of India I could show Malú before she had to be in Delhi.

We had three weeks left. Of course we would go to Varanasi, the holy city of Benares on the Ganges, only 250 miles south of the border and an experience of total Indian immersion. Then we would go east to Boddhgaya, another stop on the Buddhist trail, because it was important to both of us, though for different reasons. Then I thought we could circle south and west, see a magnificent bird sanctuary, take in Jaipur and other great sights in Rajasthan before coming up through Agra to see the Taj Mahal and then to Delhi.

'What do you think, Malú?' I kept asking, and she'd say, 'Whatever you like, Ted. You know these places. You decide. As long as I have time for Dharamsala and the Dalai Lama.'

Malú was devoted to the Dalai Lama. He had once spent some hours in her house at Santiago, and she longed to see him again. Apparently he was now at a monastery a day's journey north of Delhi, so she just needed a few days before flying home. I was confident that we could see a good deal in the time we had. We were in India soon after midday, and with only a hundred miles to go to the nearest town I thought we would have a pleasant afternoon's ride. But when we got on the road to Gorakhpur I realised that I had made the most elementary and stupid mistake. I had somehow let myself believe that because the map was better, the roads would be better too.

It might seem strange that there should be much difference in the state of the roads between India and Nepal, but I assume this is one area where foreign aid money produced a tangible result. The major roads in Nepal were generally constructed with grants from donor nations, and built to modern standards. Their problems are due mainly to maintenance. The road to Gorakhpur, on the other hand, was probably laid by the British under the Raj, then constantly refurbished. Normally when I think of a bad road, I think of surface damage, like potholes in asphalt or corrugations on dirt. How strange to discover, when we crossed the border, that the roads suffered from too much attention. It was obvious that every single pothole had been assiduously treated with its own overgenerous dose of tar – to produce, if you like, a reverse pothole, or pothill. After decades of this treatment, the entire surface consisted of little mounds of tar. It was not dangerous to ride on, it was just relentlessly, terminally jarring, and most of all for the passenger.

Anywhere else a good solution would have been to ride over it fast, but on Indian roads that could easily be a final solution. The roads are not broad. Two trucks side by side fill them completely. There were many trucks, and they slow down for no one. To survive on a bike it is necessary to anticipate, from some distance, where two trucks will pass and arrange not to be there when they do. This is aside from the possibility of hitting people, cows, camels and the occasional elephant.

But that's only the half of it. The other half is in the bazaars. Only the very biggest cities have bypasses. Most roads go through the middle of town, and the middle of town is the bazaar, which is the urban equivalent of a fly-trap. The road narrows, the traffic multiplies, shopkeepers and push-cart merchants spill out on to the tarmac (if there is any). Autorickshaws, Enfield Bullets, cows and water buffalo thread their way through the mêlée, and the temperature rises with the dust and the noise. At the heart of the bazaar it's as hot and dense and complex and aromatic as a good curry, and it defies progress.

We did the hundred miles to Gorakhpur in four hours, and arrived very tired. Since this was a railway town with nothing to recommend it but a reputation for flies and mosquitoes, we went on next day to Varanasi. Those 150 miles took us six gruelling hours and Malú came close to spontaneous combustion. By the time we arrived I knew that my earlier plan would put an impossible strain on her.

We could still ride the 160 miles to Boddhgaya; fortunately they were part of the Great Trunk Road, and should be much faster and smoother. Then we would come back to Varanasi and go straight on to Delhi. No birds, no Rajasthani palaces, just as little time on the road as possible. I tried to conceal my disappointment. Maybe I could do more on my own once she had left me, but that in itself was a sad thought. What sweetened the pill for both of us was the hotel we found in Varanasi.

We found it by the Malú Method, which consists in accepting the first thing that comes along. Luckily for her the part of town we hit first was the most habitable part of Varanasi, the cantonment area where the British rulers used to live and work, and as we trundled in over a bridge a man walked up and offered us the 'Surya Hotel, not far, very good'.

'We can go there, Ted,' she said, and it didn't sound like a suggestion.

Amazingly it was not far, and it was very good indeed. It was built round a pretty garden with a lawn. The food was excellent, the beer was cold, the people were invariably nice, and the rooms were pleasant. We were there for four days taking in the life and death of this city and the river, Mother Ganges, where all Hindus would most like to end their days. In the evenings we dined on the veranda, looking out over the roses and lilies, and then we went to our room to listen to the drumbeat on CNN as America and Britain prepared for war.

Indians of all persuasions were generally opposed to the war, but it was not important to them. Since they still quite like English people they were polite with me. For my part I was deeply perplexed. It became fashionable later to find all kinds of things wrong with Tony Blair, but at that time I had a very high opinion of his intelligence and ability, and I was unaware of his strong religious convictions. I simply could not understand what he was doing in this mess, and assumed he had some powerful but secret political motivation for clinging to George Bush and his gang.

Malú, who had even more reason to hate dictators than I did, was disgusted by the prospect of the war, believing (as turned out to be true) that it would kill many more people than it would save. Even so, like everyone around us, we just had to accept it as a fact of life. We were in a parallel universe. It didn't affect us, and it was easy to forget.

Early on 16 March we left for Boddhgaya and I soon found myself engaged in my own more personal war. Just getting out of the chaotic sprawl of Varanasi and on to the trunk route was an ordeal. The directions were very vague, and the feeder roads were all but destroyed by the heavy freight that passed over them. I took a number of wrong turns. Then we found ourselves jammed between lorries travelling at a snail's pace through a tunnel in complete darkness over a surface that was dangerously wet and rutted.

I was very nervous. I couldn't see what was coming under my wheels because the ground was hidden by the tailgate of the truck in front of me. I felt we would be lucky to come out the other end in one piece and I was expecting to hear screams of distress from Malú at any moment, but she never showed any fear, then or at any other time. Once I asked her about it and she said simply: 'I have confidence in you.'

More confidence than I had in myself.

We emerged finally to find ourselves on a very long bridge, and then among terrible slums, rubbish dumps, festering pools of slime, with cows wandering about, and finally on to the Great Trunk Road where it seemed for a while that our troubles were over. The surface was good and quite fast, there were few obstructions, and we had time to enjoy the lorries. For apart from the temples, the most beautiful objects in India – I would even say the only beautiful objects – are the lorries and trucks. They are not the businesslike articulated container-carrying semitrailers of the West, but older, traditional vehicles with slatted wooden sides usually topped with a tarp and painted in the most gorgeous colours.

Seeing India through Malú's eyes I realised again just how much ugliness there is. Someone, I forget who, once said that wherever you look in France you will always see a painting, and I daresay that outside the newest industrial suburbs this is still true. In India it is approximately the opposite. The houses and streets of India may be interesting, but they are a terrible ugly mess. Even the most sumptuous buildings are more ostentatious than attractive, and the squalor of the slums is legendary. Only the most traditional adobe farmhouses appealed to me, and we saw some on the road to Gorakhpur.

But the lorries of India are splendid, moveable feasts of colour and humour. For some reason the aesthetics that are such a disaster in domestic décor work wonderfully well on these vehicles. Like motorised baboons, their backsides are particularly colourful and provocative, covered with brightly painted geometrical designs and mysterious exhortations like 'Wait for Side' and 'Dip in Night' and 'Horn Please', which makes it almost a pleasure to be stuck behind them.

So we were doing well for a while and then, quite suddenly, our euphoria was shattered. We hit the biggest collection of stationary trucks I have ever encountered in my life.

Up to then my benchmark had always been the border of Iran and Turkey in 1977 where trucks were lined up for miles and the crews were camped along the roadside for days, but they caused me no problem then. I could simply ride past to the head of the line. Not this time. There were hundreds, maybe thousands, spread across the road as far as one could see, and although I could worm my way through for a while the gaps got narrower and narrower. It was hard work, and a bit nerve-racking. When there seemed to be no way through any more I was frustrated, but relieved at the same time.

'Maybe it's time for tea,' I said.

'*Por supuesto*,' she said, 'it is always tea time, no?'

She seemed quite cheerful, and brought out her digital Nikon.

On the dirt embankment beside us was a typical roadside *chai* shop, with charcoal-burning stoves made of baked mud. Mysterious substances steamed and bubbled in ancient blackened pots and kettles tended by men in a rich assortment of clothing, but what struck our eyes immediately was that much of the clothing was covered in vivid splashes of red, green and blue. Slowly it came to me. We had chosen to travel on the first day of the Holi festival, India's most joyful holiday, when the people, especially young ones, celebrate the end of winter by painting their faces and tossing coloured water and pigment at anyone in sight. This is not a time when very much else gets done.

Few people spoke English, but gradually bits of the story came together. We were close to the border between two states, Bihar and Uttar Pradesh. Truckers needed paperwork, but officials needed a holiday. Nothing looked like moving for a while, and nobody much cared either way. Some passengers from a bus had spent the night there. They seemed remarkably carefree.

A young man with a red and blue face and a toothy grin said, 'Ve are very happy. You are very happy. Ve are having chapati, puri, dal. You are wanting?'

We had tea and chapatis. Malú was chatting to a man behind the counter of a small kiosk, and taking pictures. She seemed to be enjoying herself, and that cheered me up. Absurdly, I felt responsible for her state of mind. I said, 'Maybe there's a way to get round this mess,' and crossed to the other side to look. The road was raised here, and the ground going down to some huts was dirt, with paths meandering through it. I thought I could see a way to get past this first bottleneck, so Malú walked past the trucks carrying her loose things and I rode the bike down and around the dirt until I could find my way back up to the road.

In three hours we had come thirty-five miles. For a while after that we were able to get through, slowly, before we were stopped by another horrendous jam, but this was different. We were approaching a river, which was also the state boundary. I could see in the distance that there were two bridges, both obviously old and not very wide. One was about ten feet higher than the other and the traffic was headed for both of them in separate streams.

I chose the wrong stream. I always do. At first it was moving faster, but the bridge it was aiming for was the narrower of the two. I was behind some buses and we got fairly near the bridge before they stopped. I tried getting past them but the bridge was too narrow. My lane was completely stuck, but traffic on the other bridge was moving. I asked Malú to walk up to the other bridge and painfully paddled myself backwards to where I could turn round. By now it was midday and hot. The dust and noise were exhausting. For a while I was stuck again, waiting for some trucks to move and open a gap, so I stopped my engine to save it from overheating. When a gap appeared I pressed the starter and nothing happened.

A hole opened in my stomach and my heart dropped into it, but I had to leave it there while I tried to get the bike started again. A feature of India is that there are always people around, and here too there were a few poor men standing about, though what they hoped to do there was beyond me. They saw my predicament and tried to help me with a push-start, but the run was too short. Then I saw that there was a longish path sloping down from the road, and managed to get myself on it. Near the bottom the engine came to life

and I brought the bike back up, eventually finding my way through
the tangle of vehicles and up to the higher level where Malú was
waiting.

As she got on a man came running and panting after me, carrying the black Ortlieb bag that had all Malú's possessions in it. I had
knocked it off coming round the back of a lorry. We were both overwhelmed by the honesty and kindness of these people. I was not
surprised because I had benefited from it in the past – just very glad
that this much had not changed.

This time there was room to fiddle my way past the line of lorries. I tried to stay calm. For one thing, I dared not let the engine
stall. As everyone knows, something that normally never happens
always seems to be on the verge of happening when it would be a
disaster. Finally we came out on to a fairly clear highway again,
and now we could see the beginnings of the 'Dream of Vajpayee'.

The Great Trunk Road from Pakistan to Calcutta is centuries
old. At one time a Mogal emperor lined it with trees and it was
shaded all the way. Later the British realigned part of it, and now
the dream of India's President Vajpayee, proclaimed from banners
across the road, was to make it a dual carriageway from end to
end. We passed great excavations and then two enormous
German machines laying beds of concrete for the second carriageway, but we were unable to stop and look so the romance of
progress was rather lost on us.

We halted once with the motor humming away to photograph a
particularly scrumptious truck in an edible shade of orange that had
come to the end of its days in the middle of the road while trying,
it seemed, to dive into the asphalt. Apart from that we ran non-stop
for the last four hours until we arrived at the Tourist Lodge in
Boddhgaya. We had spent nine hours covering some 150 miles,
without ever leaving the road.

It was too much for Malú. 'Tooooo much,' she said, in a joky
Spanish accent, but she meant it. 'I could not do this again. I will go
back to Varanasi by train.'

She was very kind to me. She kissed me and didn't blame me. I
couldn't blame her either. I didn't bother to suggest that we might

just have hit the worst day of the year at the worst part of the road. Anyway, I still didn't know what was wrong with the bike.

We were the only guests at the lodge, which was laid out in a very strange manner, in two buildings, one of them shut. A sad elderly gentleman behind the reception counter said it was owned by the state of Bihar, which refused to pay for anything, including salaries. I wasn't surprised. Bihar was the most populous and poverty-stricken state in India and I remembered its reputation for corruption. Eventually I found a kitchen and ordered onion pakora with beer. We curled up on the bed and switched on the telly to see that the war had still not started, though there was much talk of 'shock and awe'.

Later, I went to bring our things in and to look at the bike. It started perfectly, and the battery was charging. I couldn't make any sense of it. I decided to leave it all until the next day. The shower worked, so we washed, had more food and went to bed.

Malú's interest in Boddhgaya was very simple. It was where the Buddha was said to have attained enlightenment a very long time ago, and it was the last site of major importance that she would visit.

My interest was more personal. I came there in 1977, in need of a rest, and stayed for a month, except for a short break when I took a train to Delhi and back. Most travellers stayed at one or other of the retreats maintained for pilgrims by the different national branches of the Buddhist faith. There were many of these lodgings, or *vihars* as they were called, supported by Japan, Thailand, Nepal, Bangladesh, Bhutan and others. I stayed at the Burmese *vihar*, which was known to be very relaxed. A row of tiny brick cubicles ran down one side of an open garden, and I had one of them for two rupees a day, worth in those days about 20p.

I was able to cook for myself, so the cost to me was next to nothing. I took classes in meditation (at which I failed miserably) from a young Thai monk who was very popular, especially with the girls, and he also held yoga sessions (at which I was better) every morning on the roof. I wrote a lot, quietly, under a tree and remember it as one of the most peaceful periods of my life. How the place had fared in the last twenty-five years was of great interest to me.

After all my experiences of the last two years I naturally expected changes, but I was unprepared for what I saw. I had thought that given the very nature of Buddhism, the changes would be gentle and restrained, but I had forgotten that though this was a treasure of the Buddhist faith, it was located in a Hindu community. I was dismayed, and in the end revolted, by what had happened. The whole of the centre of the town, alongside the main temples, had been built up to become a huge bazaar trafficking in religion.

The streets were crowded. The biggest temple was decked out in fairy lights like a Christmas tree. Instead of the easy, understated atmosphere that I recalled, there was now evidence everywhere of determined organisation. Even the Burmese *vihar* was now built up to such an extent that there was little open space left. It was quite unrecognisable – yet, again, the buildings looked as though they had been there for centuries.

Malú, who had no preconceptions, was delighted with the place. While she was satisfying her curiosity I spent some of the time trying to fix up her train journey to Varanasi and ordering a taxi to take her to the station. I also took the bike off for a ride on the road to Gaya, curious to see what that city, reputed once to have been the filthiest in India, looked like today. I found it very congested and didn't penetrate very far before turning back. Everything on the bike worked well.

The one thing Malú and I did do together was to go inside the palace of the Maharajah of Boddghaya, which had been closed when I was there in '77 but had now been turned into a Hindu ashram. It was a relatively small and very attractive white structure, with two huge elephant stalls outside the gate. A canopy had been raised over a bed in the centre of the inner court, and a holy man squatted there. As we walked around examining the shrines I felt an air of disapproval, heightened, I expect, by my failure to leave a large donation as we left. I was in a sour mood.

'I don't understand what you are saying,' said Malú, quite

sharply. 'I think it is all *muy, muy precioso*. The atmosphere of Boddhgaya is very spiritual.'

That evening I was supposed to meet her in the illuminated temple to go to dinner. I took my shoes off at the main entrance, and walked all around what I felt was a Disneyfied version of Buddhism, but couldn't find her, so went on to the restaurant which was our fall-back rendezvous. Eventually she arrived, glowing with satisfaction.

'Why didn't you come into the temple? It was wonderful.'

I said I had, and tried to explain to her my feelings about the way things had changed, but I could see I wasn't making much headway. I began to realise just how personal and subjective all my judgements were about what had changed in the world, and what had been lost. It was a sad and lonely feeling.

Earlier that day there had been a ridiculous episode with the laundry. A tall, slightly officious young man had taken the place of the old receptionist, and I asked him to make sure that some laundry I had given them would be ready because we were leaving next morning.

'It will be coming tomorrow,' he said.

'But that will be too late. I must have it today.'

'Not possible, sir. It is with the *dhobiwalla*.'

'Well then we must get it back.'

'Sir, it is not possible for me to leave this place.'

'Well, I will get it then,' I said, already feeling annoyed. 'Tell me where it is.'

He explained. It was several miles up a back road. I got on the bike. It took me the best part of an hour to find the woman. She showed me what she had, but my shirts weren't there. When I got back to the hotel, in a state of fury after an hour and a half of fruitless running around, the young man had disappeared and the old man was there in his place.

'Look, you have to find my laundry,' I said, tight-lipped. 'I can't go without it.'

'But of course, dear sir,' he said, obviously surprised by my behaviour. 'Everything is ready,' and reaching behind him he pulled it out, neatly pressed and wrapped. I stifled my lust for revenge and walked away quietly. Next day I was glad that I had.

Malú's train left early on the third morning, and the taxi came to fetch her while it was still dark. As she left the bed and dressed she was quite brisk and happy. Early rising is a habit of hers anyway. She took my hand, and then disappeared, but when she had gone I felt rather bleak, as though something was draining away.

In northern India the nights are still frosty in March, and I waited for sunrise before I got up to pack the bike. When I had everything ready the bike wouldn't start. By now I was beyond surprise. Because the starter had been working fine I thought it was the battery. A family had arrived the day before and their car was parked near the bike, so I asked the old man if he would ask the father of the family to help me with a jump-start.

Apparently they had just ordered breakfast, and I had to wait a while before it seemed decent to get him down, but when he came he was very obliging and he had leads. We set everything up, he started his engine, I pressed the button, and nothing happened. So it was the starter after all. I was deeply embarrassed, but far from getting annoyed the car owner and the receptionist became keen to find a solution. So I said I was pretty sure it would start if we pushed it, but that it would be hard work because it was cold and the bike was heavy.

So they sent for the young man. With me sitting on the bike, all three of them pushed it from one end of the drive to the other three times, but it was the young man who did most of the work. Then it spluttered into life, and waving vigorously at them I wobbled out into the road, knowing I would have to get to Varanasi this time without ever stopping.

It was a hell of a ride. I had guessed right about the traffic: there was very little and I had a clear run, but as I went through the towns, marauding bands full of the Holi spirit saw me as the target of their dreams, and several balloons full of blue, green and red water burst over me. Unable to stop and wash the dye off, it became a permanent souvenir. I arrived at the Surya Hotel in very good time, like Joseph in his coat of many colours. Malú enjoyed the spectacle hugely, and it made her even more thankful that she had taken the train.

I got the starter off the bike quite quickly, and looked inside. It was the model made by Vallejo, in which the armature is stuck to the body with glue instead of being bolted on as it is in the Bosch version, and it had broken away in pieces. I found out from the front desk of the Surya where to find the mechanics in Varanasi, and got an autorickshaw to take me there. It is one of the wonderful things about India that you can find people in the street capable of repairing almost any device, and running up spare parts on the spot. It is a legacy of decades of import restrictions and high tariffs combined with poverty and great ingenuity, and this had not changed.

I found a man working out of a shed who said he could fix the starter, but what *had* changed was his appearance and the price. This was no longer the fellow in an oil-stained *dhoti* I might have met twenty-five years earlier who would do the job for twenty rupees. Now he wore a spotless blue-and-white-striped business shirt, sported a good watch and charged me in dollars. He said he would get an armature out of another starter and bring mine back to me, fixed, at the hotel next day. It was not cheap. I said I would want to put it on the bike and run it before I paid him, and he agreed.

So we had two more easy days at the Surya, exhausting the dinner menu, taking pictures, enjoying each other and taking care of business. I had not only the website to update, but three magazines to write for as well, and I was always behind with my chores.

The starter actually arrived the next day, confirming my suspicion that India might really be on the cusp of change. The man who brought it was not the same one I had handed it to, but he said it was fine. They had not been able to find a replacement armature, but they had reassembled enough of the broken one to make it work. I swallowed my doubts, fitted it to the bike, and it functioned without a hitch. I started the bike a dozen times, to be sure, and then handed over the money with gratitude. We packed that evening and left for Allahabad in the morning, on the road to Delhi. We didn't know, when we left, that the war had begun.

*

The ride to Allahabad was not very long or difficult, and the view of the old fort overlooking the Ganges when we crossed the river to the city was promising, but the streets offered nothing new. Since our devastating journey to Boddhgaya Malú was less comfortable on the back of the bike, and discomfort makes one much more vulnerable to environmental squalor. The hideous noise and pollution in the streets, the sheer ugliness of most buildings, the disfigurement and decay visible on most surfaces, whether vertical (walls) or horizontal (pavements), the heaps of refuse everywhere and the attendant scent of putrefaction all make for an aesthetic nightmare. In a few succinct Spanish words Malú let me know what she thought of it.

The Tourist Lodge, which again seemed like the best bet Lonely Planet had to offer, turned out to be a demoralising heap of cement, and the impression was not improved when a small rat ran over Malú's foot in the dining-room. I couldn't blame her for taking a depressed view of India. We had not seen the best of it. I recalled very well having much the same feelings myself on roughly the same route all those years ago.

One of my main reasons for travelling alone is that I find it much easier then to protect my morale or, if that is not possible, to draw something of value from the experience. As one half of a couple it isn't possible simply to cut out. We couldn't avoid the knowledge that this part of our journey together was just something to survive. We had had wonderful times, but now the important thing for Malú was to get to Dharamsala. In no sense did either of us regret our time together. It had been tremendously important for us both, and I was sure it would change my life, but I had to accept that at this particular moment it was not working well, and next day the ride to Kanpur started badly.

In the crowded streets I finally met the cycle rickshaw I couldn't avoid, and we fell. We were going very slowly and there was no damage to either party. Malú, always stoical in a crisis, showed no signs of dismay. A crowd rushed forward to raise the bike, and an English-speaker on an Enfield Bullet, with another man on his pillion, offered to guide us out of the city. He added, rather gratuitously, that he was a Christian, assuming I suppose that I would have more confidence in his sense of direction. Anyway we set off together, me following him with my self-image rather bruised. However, we were only a little way along when he also met his rickshaw from hell, and exactly the same thing happened to him as had happened to me. As he and his passenger toppled over I felt a shocking sense of satisfaction, but it didn't last.

There was long-term damage to Malú's confidence. It was a typically difficult day's riding, followed by a long and aggravating search for hotels. She was insisting that we had already passed them. I was sure we hadn't. For the first time I let some sharp words escape me, and Malú, who has all her life had to suffer macho insults from overbearing Latin males, was not having any of it from me.

Still, we tried to keep the lid on our simmering discontent.

The hotel we ultimately found was not bad, and the problem of where to put the bike was taken care of. There was a covered passageway alongside the hotel, closed by two iron gates chained together. Although the entrance to the passage was crowded with people selling tea and chapatis, they cleared a way for me to get through the gates, which were then locked behind me.

We ordered some food, and talked, and Malú said she wanted to go on to Delhi by train. I was expecting it, and didn't argue, and with that decision made we were able to hold on to our tempers, but the tinder was dry, and any spark could set it off. In the morning there was an explosion.

'You are not looking after me as you promised,' she said, with an edge of bitterness, and I blew up.

'You have absolutely no idea how hard it is to ride safely in these conditions,' I said loudly, 'and sniping at me from the back seat just makes it worse.'

'Don't shout at me,' she said, in a fury, and went on in Spanish. 'I will never tolerate to have a man shouting at me—'

'How can I help it when you criticise me like that?' I replied, and went on to say more unforgivable things about her expectations of men, until there was nothing to do but leave the room. While I was outside, busying myself unnecessarily with the bike, Malú escaped to the railway station in a rickshaw. When I came back in and found her gone I was devastated. I had been out for less than an hour, but at the desk they said she'd been gone some time.

I sped over to the station and rushed around the platforms trying to find out which trains were going where and thinking she must already have left, but in the end I found her sitting, very erect, at a table in a waiting-room. She had obviously been crying. Thank goodness I was able to repair some of the damage, but I didn't know until much later, in Delhi, that she had thought she would never see me again.

43

By the time I got going from Kanpur that day it was already early afternoon. I thought I might get as far as Agra and spend the night there. That's where the Taj Mahal is, of course, but I was in no mood to look at beautiful buildings. I wanted to move on to Delhi and catch up with Malú before she vanished again. She would be spending this night on the train, but we had picked out a hotel from the guidebook, the Namaskar, not far from the station in Delhi, and she had said she would spend the following night there before going on to Dharamsala. I was determined to be there with her.

The road to Agra was no easier than it ought to be. Averaging less than thirty miles an hour, I was well short of the city as night fell, and found myself in the teeming centre of a town called Firozabad. I knew it would be crazy to ride on at night, finding my way among hazards like water buffalo which are all but invisible in the dark, but there were no hotels to be seen and Lonely Planet didn't even mention Firozabad.

The town was very busy, very crowded, and not at all hospitable. I looked despairingly around, trying to imagine why anybody here should take any interest in me at all, and was struck immediately by the contrast with my first journey. In those years I was always the focus of attention. I had only to stop and people would crowd around eagerly. Getting help was easy. Today I felt none of that warm confidence.

Then, as I crept through the traffic a vision appeared before me. A tall white building, floodlit, sporting a driveway lined with palms and potted plants, guarded by *chowkidars* in resplendent white uniforms with cockades, rose up by the side of the road. The Hotel Monark announced itself. Physically weary and mentally exhausted by the day's events, I saw it as my salvation. The lobby was only a little less appealing than the exterior. The counter wasn't quite grand enough to match the edifice, and the two gentlemen behind it were a trifle scruffy. The cost of a room, unfortunately, was well up there with heads of state. On hearing the figure, 900 rupees, I displayed suitable shock and awe, so they asked me, politely, how much I wanted to pay.

'Six hundred,' I said, which was still too much.

This caused them to scurry into an office, from which then emerged, in a splendid striped shirt, the owner himself. In a hearty voice he explained that, as a hotelier, he took an interest in his patrons and was anxious to inspect the fish he had caught tonight. It seems he liked what he saw because he gave me the benefit of his ultimate, never-before-heard-of, huge discount, bringing the price down to a miserable 700 rupees.

'There is no other hotel?' I asked, knowing the answer already.

'No. No other.'

'Then I must take it.'

'Don't say it like that,' he said cheerfully, 'or you will be paying nothing,' but before I could say, 'Nothing's good for me' he had moved on to explain the burdens that afflict your modern Indian hotel owner. It seemed that here, as in the old Eastern Bloc, you needed a special permit to house foreign guests. This entailed providing them with drinking water suitable for their stomachs, and with toilet paper, as well as something to sit on when they used it. All of this, he explained, contributed to the exorbitant cost.

Grudgingly I agreed to pay the surcharge, so we went on to the trial by paperwork. India, surprisingly, is fearful that foreigners might want to stay there illegally. Every hotel required me to put all my details in its own ledger, and then fill out another form for the government, in triplicate. The only good news was that the Monark at least had carbon paper, but I was so parched by the ride that it was a major ordeal.

'Water,' I gasped, but no. First the papers. No water for the undocumented.

My room had marble floors, but the walls were covered with scuff marks and displayed batteries of switches unconnected to anything. An iron pipe of the kind that might release poison gas protruded from the ceiling, with two bare wires dangling from it. The window was sealed shut, and the air conditioning, which accounted partly for the high room charge, froze me at first, and then mercifully failed altogether. There was a foam mattress and a fan.

The staff slept on the floor on the landings. They were still sleeping when I stepped over them in the morning. They only *appeared* to be surly – it was just the peasant face at rest. Sad to say, in the end I could not recommend the Monark. I don't know what I would have done without it, but I hope never to need it again.

The next day could have been much worse if Agra were not blessed with a bypass. It got me on to the road to Delhi in good time and I found the Namaskar Hotel at about three in the afternoon. It was buried deep inside the labyrinthine bazaar of Pahar Ganj, a wonderful world of shops and stalls where you could do and buy almost anything your heart desired, but what my heart desired was to find Malú and she wasn't there.

The Namaskar is owned and managed, I found out later, by two brothers, Surinder and Rajinder, and one of them is always there. Rajinder, the one without the walrus moustache, was behind the counter when I arrived. He had never seen Malú but with remarkable prescience he told me exactly what had happened. An unscrupulous ricksaw driver had somehow persuaded her to go to another hotel, where he would get a commission. Meanwhile, if I wanted to find her, he knew where she would have to go to catch the buses to Dharamsala, and that they would be leaving at 4 p.m.

I rushed over on the bike and, sure enough, there she was at the bus stop, eating nuts from one of Arita's bags, and waiting. We were both overjoyed and hugged. She said the rickshaw driver at the station had told her the Namaskar no longer existed, and had taken her to a dirty place she was trying to forget. She had been sure we would never find each other again. It was something of a miracle, I felt, that we were together, and from then on I adopted Rajinder Budhraja as my godfather, although he never knew it.

The bus came and whisked her away, and I returned to the Namaskar to wait out her absence and investigate my new surroundings. The heart of Pahar Ganj is the Main Bazaar Road, approximately half a mile of extraordinary bustle. Actually I wouldn't really call it a road. It is more like a sclerotic artery. Several hundred businesses, mostly with shopfronts of no more than eight feet, reach out greedily into the street, attracting people like particles of cholesterol to choke the flow of carts, trolleys, rickshaws, cows, motorcycles, autorickshaws and wave upon wave of visitors.

When I first came in on my bike from the station end, I thought it might take me all afternoon to get halfway along it. For one thing, they were digging up what little was left of the road itself, and piling up large heaps of sludge, which had to be negotiated with considerable care. Then I saw how the residents, unhelmeted on their scooters and Hondas, dashed through the crowd, and I became a trifle bolder. I was looking for the third turning on the right. I might as well have been looking for Aladdin's cave. While the bazaar at its widest is perhaps fifteen feet across, the alleys are hardly five feet wide, and are so cluttered at their mouths with signs and vendors that they are virtually invisible.

For the most part this is a bazaar for clothing: saris, Punjabi dresses, kurtas and materials of all kinds. Then there's cheap luggage, leatherwork, belts, perfumes, metalwork and so on. But you can also make phone calls, have pots mended, keys cut, shoes repaired, hair cut, ears cleaned, fortunes told, anything. Moving through the crowd, men selling tablas tap out a rhythm; men selling popadums make a hollow clatter as they pass; men selling flutes make swirling patterns of sound. Trolleys of grapes, oranges and mangoes joust with the rickshaw men. Broad metal discs over charcoal fires move through the mob, frying potatoes in oil. Men in clean shirts dart out of crevices like moray eels, shouting, 'Excuse me, sir, you are from? Your country?', determined to shake your hand and drag you into their emporia.

Interspersed among the shops are hotel signs. The road boasts an almost impossible number of guest-houses. It would seem that practically all the living accommodation above the shops has been turned into cheap lodging for the swarms of backpackers that pour out of the station every day. The rubbish that accumulates in a day's work is monumental, laced with water, other unidentifiable liquids and long trails of cow manure, but early in the morning it is all swept and washed away, ready for a new day's pollution.

About fifty yards down the alley from the Namaskar was a crowded little Internet and phone shop, where I got my email and sent off my various articles and journals. After a few days, Malú let me know she was coming back. I found out where her bus would arrive and went there to wait. I waited a long time before I heard from passengers on a different bus that hers had broken down somewhere in the mountains. When it eventually came, six hours late, she was tired of course, but her stay in Dharamsala had reinvigorated her, and though she hadn't met the Dalai Lama she had obviously derived tremendous strength and tranquillity from the experience.

After that we stayed together at the Namaskar for almost a week before she flew home. I didn't try to entice her back on the bike. I tethered it to some iron bars outside the hotel, and we took a bus to Agra to see the Taj Mahal. Here, at last, was something that had lost none of its beauty in twenty-five years, and seeing this marbled vision of perfection floating apparently unchanged above the pools and terraces helped to shore up some of my crumbling faith in humanity.

We came closer during those days than ever before. The Namaskar defeated her preference for sleeping alone because the best room had only one big bed. Although she had accepted the compromise before, this was the first time since I'd known her that she actually seemed happy to find me in bed with her in the morning. In some relationships a small step can be a giant leap. I became certain that when the journey was over we would find a way to live together. We agreed to meet again in California in July. It couldn't possibly take me more than three months now to finish this journey. The prospect filled me with so much hope for the future that it helped me to deal with the aggravation and frustration I had to face as soon as Malú had flown away on 4 April.

44

The day after Malú left I began my hunt for visas. This took place in areas of Delhi where great houses commanded sweeping vistas of open space, in startling contrast to the bazaar, where every square foot was somebody's business. Pakistan was the next country I would have to cross, and I found the embassy eventually, a huge mosque-like building surrounded by high walls. I circled it and there seemed to be no way in or out, but at one point, on the caked mud between the wall and the pavement, was a surreal sight – like a scene from an experimental movie. A number of venerable white-whiskered gentlemen in robes and turbans were seated at trestle-tables behind mounds of paper. Then I saw three small barred windows in the wall, and beside one of them an alarming notice:

**FOREIGNERS MAY ONLY OBTAIN
VISAS IN THEIR
COUNTRIES OF RESIDENCE**

I felt a sharp stab of anxiety. Shit, I thought, it can't be true. How am I going to get out of here? I had really not faced the problem before, but now there was no avoiding it. If I couldn't go through Pakistan, getting out of India would be very difficult, and the last thing I wanted to confront. It was hard to admit, and I felt like a traitor to my own cause. I should have welcomed the challenge. It might lead to wonderful experiences. Hadn't I always proclaimed,

'The interruptions *are* the journey'? But to tell the truth, I just wanted this journey to end.

With the war in Iraq going full tilt, with the Taliban taking refuge more or less openly in the border areas of Pakistan, with the religious schools still churning out fighters for jihad and Al Qaeda, my British passport was not an asset. Her Majesty cut no ice here any more, but there was no other practicable route home.

I looked into the little window but it was too dark inside to see the man behind it. I pleaded and argued with a gruff, disembodied voice until finally it admitted that a ten-day transit visa could be had, but only if I could show a visa from Iran. So now everything hung on Iran.

That embassy was very different. I had no problem entering. It was a showplace of mosaics and images from Persepolis and Isfahan, a place of implications, rueful smiles and suave demurrals, where my future became even more obscure. I could apply for a visa, of course, but a normal visa might be very difficult. A seven-day transit visa would cost me sixty dollars, not refundable, but applications by British citizens would still have to be sent to Tehran. It would take at least two weeks, maybe much more, maybe much, much more.

I tried to sweet-talk the press attaché, a plump, affable but sly man who brought a bag of pistachio nuts to the meeting and picked his teeth thoughtfully as I told him of my undying respect for the Iranian people.

'Do you know anyone in Iran who could vouch for you? It could be helpful.'

To my own surprise I realised that Iran was probably the only large country where I knew nobody. I had known some people there once, but that was before the revolution.

'Aah,' he sighed, softly, sadly, and I came away with nothing sweeter than a bag of nuts.

I need hardly say how dispiriting this business of visas can be. Both the beginning and the end of my journey were bedevilled by it. The struggle to get into Libya was only exceeded by the desperate measures I had to take to be allowed into Sudan. Whether these regimes cared or not, the effect of all this paranoia is predictably negative. I went in feeling myself to be under a cloud of suspicion, and it is hard not to let this distort one's point of view. Now I was going through the whole thing again. There was no doubt in my mind that the Iranians were trying to discourage me, but I felt I had to put in my bid, pay my sixty dollars, hope for the best and think of other things.

For a few days I was occupied with the bike. The repair on the starter in Varanasi had worked well, but I didn't have a lot of faith in its longevity, and before I even left the Surya Hotel I had emailed Dave Wyndham to ask for another. Without blinking an eye (well, he was back in Dorchester, but I'm sure he didn't), Dave had it on the way. It was being sent to Kashyap Motors in an industrial part of Delhi called Okhla, where Avon had also sent a new set of tyres.

In my efforts to find the place I discovered how much Delhi had changed, and was still changing. The traffic had now become terrible, exaggerated by huge roadworks and excavations for a new metro. It was obvious that the Indian middle class was expanding rapidly, and enjoying its new-found freedom to consume and pollute. At the same time great efforts were apparently being made to clean up the pollution. Delhi was doing its best to go green.

I found Kashyap eventually on a trading estate, much like the older ones around London. It was a family-owned business and both father and son were remarkably warm and generous. The son, Anand, a tall, slender and sophisticated young man who had spent time in Europe, pretty much gave me the run of the place and even offered me a guest-room at the back, with meals, so that I could spend the night and get more done.

Although their business was with cars there was one genial mechanic, Dilip Singh, bulky, grease-stained and with an irrepressible grin, who knew about bikes, and between us we fitted the tyres and the starter, fixed the valve clearances and repaired a leaky exhaust. We tuned the carbs, put in new brake pads, tested the battery, found out why my neutral light wasn't coming on and gave the bike a shampoo. It felt like a new motorcycle, and in high spirits I took off for the mountains to wait for Iran.

A week earlier, while Malú's bus was making its slow and erratic way south from Dharamsala and I was cooling my heels in the bus station, I'd had a chance encounter with a man who ran a trekking business in the Himalayas. Usually I find that people express only a perfunctory interest in me before talking about themselves at length, and I'm a good listener, but Ravinder Sharma showed genuine and intelligent curiosity and I quickly came to like him. I asked him about his place in Himachal Pradesh and what he did there, and got him to write it all down. I had no thought then of going myself but now that the heat was building up in Delhi, it seemed like a perfect place to wait for news from Tehran.

I found his village, Naggar, on the map, and phoned him. He was overjoyed to hear that I was coming. It was a 350-mile trip, rather a lot for one day in India, and I stopped seventy-five miles short in Mandi, at the the Raj Mahal Hotel, which is part of the building that still houses the royal family of Mandi Riassat (long deposed). It's a wonderful, musty relic of times gone by, the kind where floors keep changing levels, but there was a TV in the room with BBC and movie channels. I'm ashamed to admit that I had dinner in my room and, in the absence of pork, pigged out on Iraq and De Niro.

The road to Naggar was slow but beautiful as it dipped and climbed. Already it was much cooler, although the sun was hot. Some of it was hard work. The road surface was not that good, and there was still a fair amount of traffic. I took it easy and arrived in the early afternoon. The last mile was a steep climb up from the Beas River to 'the Castle', a rather grand name for a large stone building with wooden balconies, where the nobility used to live. Then a narrow, plunging strip of concrete took me down to Ravi's Lodge.

His wife Neema was there to receive me with one of the sweetest smiles I'd seen in a while. She showed me where to park, and I settled into a room with a wood stove. It was early in the season. Generally I was the only guest. All around me were steep pine-covered slopes, snowy mountain peaks, streams and rivers rushing over polished granite boulders. There was fishing, and not far away, in

Manali, paragliding too. Up here the houses were wooden, traditional and often beautiful, some with shingled roofs, some still covered with stone slabs like those of my village in France. I spent most of my time on a balcony, writing and reading. Below me was Ravi's little restaurant terrace, a small temple to Vishnu and a tethered calf licking the tyres of my bike.

After a while I thought I could see a little deeper into the life of this village. I watched people come and go, bare-footed, to pray to Vishnu and ring the bell just inside the doorway. They had to reach in because most of the time an iron lattice gate barred the entrance, but in the morning a man came to open the temple and perform the necessary rites. Then there was prolonged bell-ringing and, on one occasion, a loud clashing like falling pots and pans, followed by a mournful series of very wobbly notes. I believe it was the sound of the conch shell, not a very reliable orchestral instrument.

The temple was ancient, a palpable focus of religious devotion, intended no doubt to bring out the best instincts in the people crowded around it, but this hope, I'm sorry to say, was dashed. Inexplicable hostilities within Ravi's family had led to all kinds of trouble. The family was quite large because his father had had four wives, and they and their progeny were all coagulated on this little plot of mountain village. Ravi was the first to offer trekking services in Naggar, but according to him his father did all he could to sabotage his efforts, and encouraged the others to set up businesses in competition with him.

The feud peaked the year before I came when stinking effluent from inadequate septic tanks came streaming down the path beside Ravi's restaurant and kitchen, and according to Ravi, his father had a significant part to play in that putrid affair. Finally a judge was found who couldn't be bribed, and the offenders were forced to pipe their foul waters further down the hill, where they now raised a stink outside other people's houses.

Hearsay, of course, is unreliable. The whole thing could have been fiction and one shouldn't judge by appearances, but from what I saw of the old man as he trudged past with a sour look on his walnut face, I thought he could have played the villain to perfection.

Anyway, I was on Ravi's side. I liked him and thought he did a good job. I'm happy to say that his hotel, the Poonam Mountain Lodge & Restaurant, was odour-free, and he cooked great food

All of this helped take my mind off my problems – more than that, it gave me some perspective. Would it really be so terrible if I were refused by Pakistan and Iran? After all, I had been that way before, and I knew enough now about this twenty-first-century world to guess at the changes. It annoyed me that even if I was granted those niggardly transit visas I would have to rush through both countries. Towards the end of my stay in Naggar I phoned the Iranians a few times, but always with the same inconclusive result, and the underlying hint that I would probably never hear anything. By the time I was ready to go back to Delhi I was in a mood to say, To hell with them.

45

I was in a large, untidy office, floored with bare boards, lined with mismatched and badly abused office cupboards and littered with broken chairs. I'd found one good chair, and was sitting beside a long, battered wooden table, waiting. It was the middle of the afternoon, and hot. I was in the New Customs House at Delhi airport and, among other things, I was trying to imagine what the Old Customs House must have been like.

Through the open door across the corridor I could see another door, which was closed. Behind it, sitting at his own desk, was Mr Noreng, the only man whose name I had been able to grasp. The door was closed because Mr Noreng was important. The fact that his door had no handles, but only a piece of cord threaded through plastic pipe, did not diminish his sense of importance. On the other hand, he seemed to be quite a decent fellow. We had met briefly some days earlier, and he listened courteously when I explained that I had my bike downstairs in a crate and needed to get it into the hands of Lufthansa.

'You want to do this today?' he asked in surprise. He looked at his watch. 'It is very late. It is already four p.m. Can't you come back tomorrow?'

'My plane leaves tomorrow,' I said sorrowfully. 'It would be very expensive if I missed it.'

He frowned deeply. 'Go to the other side,' he said, 'and see Mr . . .' and he uttered a long string of syllables. 'He will do it.'

I did as I was told, but the room was empty, so I returned to tell him so. He took me back to the room, said 'Sit!' and disappeared. So there I was, waiting. Then a young man in a blue shirt came in and balanced alongside me on a chair with a broken seat. I told him what I was doing.

'Does everything stop at four?' I asked.

'Oh no,' he said, 'they go on till six.'

So what's the problem? I asked myself, rhetorically. Actually I knew very well. In India time just passes. There's no need for a problem. After fifteen minutes the man with the impossible name appeared. I will call him Mr Krishna. We also had met before, and he interested me. With his smoothly handsome face, even white teeth, neat black moustache, carefully cut hair, spotless striped shirt and cream trousers he was something of a dandy – but not young, probably in his forties, and carrying the weight of a married man.

He came with a colleague who was never introduced to me, so I will call him Shiva. He was very different in appearance. His face was more rounded, with some red in the complexion, like a Burmese. His features were smaller, his lips pursed and sensual and his shirt a loud check pattern, but his manner was impassive and Buddha-like.

They sat opposite me across the table, and I began to bring out my papers. I had brought everything I thought they could conceivably ask for – carnet, title, licence, passport and various bits and pieces.

'Wait,' said Mr Krishna, with an avuncular smile (I had already forgotten that he was much younger than me). 'There is no hurry. First we take tea. You are taking tea?'

I assented. He barked out a command. A man appeared with a pot and I received a little paper cup of delicious sweet tea.

'Don't mind,' he said. 'It's a simple matter. It will be done in fifteen minutes.'

Several hours later, when we were still hard at it, I looked back in astonishment at that facile remark, but at the time I was encouraged. I finished my tea and then pushed the documents across to Mr Krishna. The carnet, a bulky document with many pages, seized his attention. Since I had not been asked for it on entry to India it should not have any part to play in my leaving, but he liked it. He fondled it and leafed back and forth through it in a way that made me fairly sure he didn't know what it was. Then he passed it over to Mr Shiva. They were talking in Hindi but his expression said, quite clearly, 'There. You see. It's a simple matter.'

Mr Shiva was not convinced. He examined it from every angle, and then just sat and stared at it, quite expressionless and immobile. As I waited for him to emerge from his reptilian repose I thought about all the events that had brought me here . . .

I hadn't actually given up on Iran until the end, but I'd started to think about shipping the bike even before I left Naggar. Ravi and I had parted with genuine declarations of gratitude and affection, and I made my way south through the awe-inspiring gorges of the Himalayas. By now I had mastered again the art of enjoying India's scenery while still watching the road like a hawk, and the drop down to Delhi was full of interest. There were mountain shrines to admire and markets to marvel at. I met a likeable Israeli couple on a bike near Mandi, who reminded me of the huge presence of Israelis in the travelling community and of my ambivalent feelings about them – lively, aggressive, intelligent, opportunistic, boisterous, intrusive – all adjectives which make nonsense of generalisations, and yet they *are* a distinctive group.

This time I spent the night at Chandigarh, a town planned by the French architect Le Corbusier, and found that I disliked it. It was a mess, and a contradiction between two immiscible views of urban life. I spent the evening in an underground pub devoted to British military history and was entertained by two drunken Indian gentlemen talking nonsense to each other at the bar.

Coming across the plain to Delhi the sky had turned to copper. Strange hot winds blew smatterings of rain at me, and for a while it was as though the world was coming to an end. I put it down to sandstorms from Rajasthan, but it was just a wild guess. After an hour things returned to normal, and I circled Delhi on a ring road and headed, not for the Namaskar Hotel, but for the town of Gurgaon.

My circumstances in Delhi were completely changed, thanks to
an email from an English woman called Lisa Roberts. She had been
riding around the world with her boyfriend when she broke her
ankle in Thailand. So she gave up being a biker babe in denim and
became a corporate sales manager in a business suit. These remarkable transformations no longer surprised me. Her boss at Xerox
gave her a marble apartment outside Delhi, with a cook and a
chauffeur, and having heard about me and feeling nostalgic for the
road, she emailed with the offer of her spare room for rest and
recuperation.

I missed the Namaskar, but Delhi was getting hot and I was glad
to find out how the other sixteenth lived. Without her help and the
use of her car I don't know how I would have managed.

A problem had developed with the hydraulics on my front brake,
and I had gone back to Kashyap Motors to clear it up. While I was
there Anand told me about a contact he had in the shipping business, and that was how I met K.C. Raju. The old English habit
among the professional classes of referring to each other by their
initials took hold in India under the Raj, and has lingered on. I
never knew Raju's first name though he was a major benefactor.

Like so many offices in the Unfinished World, his was reached
over an obstacle course of boulders, potholes, rubble and dirt, but
once inside it was like any office anywhere, a clutter of computers
and a claque of clerks. Raju was the boss and greeted me expan-
sively from behind a large desk. He was a young, handsome, athletic
man and obviously well off, which as it turned out was a good thing
for both of us. His interest in my journey and his eagerness to help
were a pleasant surprise. We had talked about various things,
including his trips to New York, before I introduced the problem.

'I've got to get this bike to Istanbul, somehow,' I said. 'Could it go
by boat, maybe, from Bombay?'

'Sure, why not?'

'I haven't got too much money,' I added. 'Air would be very expensive. I'm hoping it wouldn't cost more than six hundred dollars.'

I have no idea where I got that figure from. It seemed reasonable
at the time. He had brushed it aside.

'I'm sure that will be enough,' he said, airily. 'Don't worry. I will find out. Call my man here in a couple of days. We will take care of it.'

I left in a state of nervous euphoria. It seemed too easy.

When I called back, his man – another man whose name I lost – said it would have to go by air, and would I come in and do the paperwork. The euphoria was replaced by gloom. I knew now this would become very expensive, but I went in. Strangely, when I arrived neither Raju nor his man was there. It took hours to find the forms, but I got them filled out and in the afternoon Raju's assistant, a sombre, terse man, did turn up and said I should take the forms to the airport customs next day. The idea, it seemed, was that I should do the leg work, and they would do the technical stuff. Fair enough, I thought, but from that point on everything was total and surreal confusion.

At the airport I had found myself entrapped by one of the sleaziest-looking men who ever wore a turban. He insisted I should give up my crazy plan and pass the whole thing over to his friends at Golden Transport. I resisted. He got a man on the phone who, he said, was the Assistant Commissioner. In a silky, polite voice the man suggested we meet and discuss the matter.

'There are many considerations,' he said. 'Just now I am out of station, but tomorrow—'

'Ah, tomorrow I will be in Gurgaon.'

'That is far,' he said, sadly.

'Perhaps I can find someone else to help me here.'

'Perhaps,' he said, and I hung up. The sleazy Sikh gave up on me. I wandered off to find a telephone, but at the kiosk they sent me to the New Customs House and that was how I first found Mr Noreng, and then Mr Krishna who said, 'Don't worry. You can come back on Monday with the motorcycle. It is a simple matter. . .'

I was jerked from my reveries. Mr Shiva had moved. His face expressed concern. He spoke, and asked for my passport and driving licence. I passed them over, unwisely adding, 'You can have anything you want, though they aren't strictly relevant.'

This produced a bark of censure from Krishna. It was remarkable how his expression could switch so easily from benevolence to stern reproof and back again. I'm sure he thought of me as a child, despite my grey hair. He summoned a messenger, gave him the documents, and sent him off with instructions. Then they all left the room.

The bike, of course, had to be crated, and this was to be done by another of Anand's contacts, Mr A.P. Singh, who told me it would take two hours on Monday morning. He would crate the bike and deliver it to the airport for a hundred dollars. I arrived at Mr Singh's address early to find a number of small offices on two floors, crowded with Mr Singh's relations. The business was situated in a small yard, littered with offcuts of wood lying in muddy puddles. The crating itself would have to be done out in the street, but it was a while before the work could begin.

I enjoyed working with them, taking the bike down and fitting it to the pallet, but the job was obviously taking too long and I felt myself in the grip of fate. When it was finished the crate was a work of art, a beautiful latticework cage modelled on the Taj Mahal. Many hands loaded it into a van but it was already mid-afternoon. The traffic was predictably terrible. By the time we connected with another of Raju's men at the airport, it was plainly too late and the crate had to be locked away in a garage for the night.

But I had already booked a seat to Istanbul on Kazakhstan Airways for Wednesday night, so the bike would have to be got through customs to the freight terminal next day. Only one airline would take it, Lufthansa, and the charge was outrageous – well over $1200. Already the whole business had turned into a financial catastrophe, and now it was threatening to become even worse. I started phoning from Lisa's place early only to learn, to my horror, that the owner of the garage couldn't be found to open it. I sweated through the morning until, at last, I heard that the doors were open. Lisa's driver whisked me over there. I had to pay to reload the van and for overnight storage, and extra for the driver. At last I arrived, panting and flustered at Mr Noreng's door just before 4 p.m. But then you knew that already . . .

*

While I was waiting for Krishna and Shiva to come back, the other, younger, man came in and said, 'I don't think you will get your permission today.'

'Permission?' I asked. 'What permission?'

Slowly it dawned on me. We hadn't even started on the business of *exporting*. First I had to have permission to export my own bike? I was stunned. Incredulous. Nothing like this had come my way before.

I told him I *had* to get the bike out today.

He smiled sympathetically. 'You know Indian bureaucracy. You should talk to Noreng. Or even to Noreng's boss.'

This struck me as a dangerous policy. I didn't want to alienate Krishna and Shiva. I decided to wait, and soon they returned with the messenger. Now they had a thick sheaf of copies which all had to be shuffled many times. A hole was made through the top left-hand corner of each sheet and they were threaded one by one into a light-green cardboard folder.

Krishna's satisfaction as he held this file of paper was tangible. Then a shadow fell over his face. Something occurred to him, he brought out the carnet and sent it away again. Another ten-minute wait. Meanwhile, my anxiety was increasing by the minute. It was almost six o'clock, when everything stops. Would *they* stop? I faced a dreadful dilemma. They had all the authority. If I put too much pressure on them, they could simply wash their hands of the whole affair.

More copies came back and were laced into the file. It is not easy to convey the sense of reverence with which this folder was now being handled. From being a piece of rough card containing sheets of copy paper, in some way during the previous two hours of manipulation, discussion and ratiocination it had acquired status, an independent existence. Clearly it was still a work in progress and some way from perfection, but its creators could see its potential. Proudly the two of them carried it out of the room to Noreng's office. When they returned Krishna asked, 'What time is your flight tomorrow?'

This was the moment of truth. I decided to lie.

'Lunchtime,' I said. 'If I have to come back tomorrow I would have to cancel the flight. It would be very costly.'

He looked disappointed. They both sat down. Krishna shuffled through the papers for a long time, as though perplexed by them. Then a new man appeared on the scene.

He was thin, about thirty, and badly dressed. His trousers were made of a worn and shoddy navy-blue cotton, ragged at the cuffs. His shirt, too, was cheap and ugly, but the most prominent feature was the terrible acne that disfigured most of his narrow, hawk-like face. Yet despite his evident poverty he seemed to command respect. They started an intense discussion between them. Now the younger man I'd spoken to earlier also joined in. Of course I couldn't understand a word of it, but I knew my fate was being decided in front of me.

Finally, on the index page of the folder Krishna made some careful notes, signed them and beckoned to me. All five of us crossed the corridor to stand in front of Noreng's desk. There was more fierce discussion. Noreng seemed put out, but at last, with much pomp, he put his signature below Krishna's. Clearly, another crucial step.

With Noreng's blessing this artefact was now fit to be judged by an even more elevated connoisseur. I followed Krishna down the hall to a door that had not only a doorknob on it, but a brass plate. Here dwelled the Assistant Commissioner. Krishna knocked gently, poked his head around the door deferentially, then led me inside on to a carpet. I was struck immediately by the air of religious calm that pervaded the room. While the rest of the building was ramshackle, scruffy, soiled and broken, here there was order, harmony and perfection. The A.C. faced the door from behind his desk. In front of him was a fine carved lectern, lit by a lamp which cast a gentle glow over the room. We advanced across the carpet and Krishna made the offering of our file to a rather distinguished but severe gentleman with a full head of grey hair. Surely not the same man I'd spoken to on the phone?

I held my breath. He signed the file withut even looking at me. It seemed I now had India's permission to take my motorcycle out of the country. Now the real work could begin.

*

Incredibly, it took four more hours to get the bike from the New Customs House into the Lufthansa hangar three hundred yards away. I could fill a book with those four hours, but I'll concentrate on the highlights.

All four customs officials trotted down the stairs and out into the parking lot, pausing only to pay respects to Vishnu's shrine on the way. They gathered around the back of the van and glumly inspected the beast in its cage. The numbers had to be checked, of course, and while the chassis number was easily seen through the crate, the engine number was almost impossible to verify. At last, using lights and mirrors, they convinced themselves that it was indeed the bike I said it was. Then Shiva left us and the remaining three gathered together and began an argument. It seemed to be quite heated. Every now and then they would seem to come to a res- olution, but the thin ascetic with his piercing eyes would get them all going again like a Jesuit splitting hairs in a scholastic debate, and I came to hate him as though he had me on the rack of the Inquisition.

Twice they all trooped back up to Noreng to resolve some vital issue, only to come back and argue some more. Once I followed them up, climbing the stairs behind Krishna. I saw that he was not in good shape. His legs in the smart cream trousers moved heavily, and his sandalled feet were flat, belying his dapper appearance. My irritation gave way to sympathy. I felt sorry for him.

It was dark now outside, and occasionally it rained a little. Finally, after two more hours of this I insisted on knowing what was going on. Krishna was quite annoyed.

'You see, this crate is all holes. How can we sign it away? Afterwards anyone can put anything in through the openings before it goes into bond.'

I was flabbergasted. The problem was so ridiculous, and the remedy so obvious I could think of nothing to say. Krishna stalked off, and they argued some more, but finally the Jesuit said something in a triumphant tone of voice. They had come to a solution, and it was this: the whole crate would be tied up with string, and then the ends of the strings would be held together by red sealing-wax with the customs seal in it. At first there was no string, then no sealing-wax, but after another half-hour they were found and the ceremony was performed. It was purely symbolic. There were just as many holes in the crate as before, but at last it could be driven over to the hangar.

There were many more farcical moments at the hangar. At one point we were all driven out by guards and refused re-entry. My business with Lufthansa became very confusing, and for a while I couldn't work out who was paying what, but in the end it seemed Raju's agency was paying the bills and I would have to settle with him. At last I saw the crate, wobbling dangerously on a fork-lift, disappear behind Lufthansa's chain-link fence. At 10.30 p.m. it was done.

46

Kazakhstan Airways flew to Istanbul once a week, on Wednesdays. It was very cheap at $320, although there was a stop-over and they did take another $50 off me for excess luggage. I had to pay cash for the ticket, and while I was at it I bought a ten-pound note because my email friend in Istanbul, Derek Packham, said it would save me trouble at the other end when I got my visa. I tucked it into my passport.

Then I called K.C. Raju to learn the horrible truth about what I owed, wondering how I could get the money to him, but he was away in Bangalore. I went to his office and phoned him from there.

'Just leave the six hundred dollars on my desk,' he said.

'But it was more than twice that,' I gasped.

'Don't worry about it,' he said. 'I'm glad I could help.'

I thanked him profusely and decided to take his advice and stop worrying.

The plane left that night for Almaty, the capital of Kazakhstan. To my surprise the aircraft was a nice Boeing 737, it left on time, the service was good and the beer was free. Almaty is a lonely little airport lying under a range of snow-tipped Himalayan mountains. I couldn't imagine it had changed much since the Cold War.

The immigration officers all looked as though they had escaped from a cheap spy movie. They were all women, in khaki blouses and skirts and with lots of braid on their shoulders. Most of them had very bad hair – quite comically bad, in fact – and they also wore strange-looking shoes with immensely long, pointed toes and four-inch stiletto heels. To wear a stiletto takes a certain amount of style, which these women didn't have, and to watch them stumbling about on these ridiculous contraptions gave me some ironic amusement. But that was later. When I first encountered one of them it was just to hand over my passport and my plane ticket for her to look at.

'I am going on to Istanbul,' I said.

That meant nothing. No English.

'Transit,' I said. She got quite excited.

'Traanzeet,' she said, and rushed off to consult. After some time another woman came back, with my documents in her hand.

'You may sit here,' she said, waving autocratically at rows of metal seats in a large, bare space. 'I will keep your documents.'

She spoke quite decent, if stilted, English.

'Is there a toilet?' I asked. She pointed down the hall. I went, and came back. 'Can I get a drink of water?'

This request was not well received, but after a moment she said, 'You may go downstairs and purchase what you need.'

'With what money?' I asked.

'You can use dollars.'

I only had two hundred-dollar bills, and that was when I remembered the ten-pound note I had put in my passport to pay for the visa. I asked to see my passport. She showed it to me, and I saw that the money had disappeared.

I became unreasonably angry – with myself for letting it happen, and with them for making me so uncomfortable and then stealing from me. I told myself this would not be the best time to accuse them of theft, and then did it anyway.

'Where is the money I had in this passport?' I asked.

I won't bother to record the conversation. There was a lot of injured pride, protestation and barely concealed contempt. The English-speaking woman said she was the chief. She said I must have lost it somewhere else. I said I hadn't, and that I would write about this and tell the world what was the first thing that happened to me in Kazakhstan. Of course it did no good at all. I sat and read, and they clattered back and forth around me, treating me with stony indifference. I suppose if they'd been men, they might have beaten me up.

A man now came from below and talked to the chief. She said I had to go down with her and get my luggage. It was a lot to hump up three flights of marble stairs, seventy pounds altogether. 'Can I have help?' I asked, more to make trouble than with any hope of assistance.

'You are the man,' she said. 'You may carry it.'

The night dragged on for a couple more hours, and then surprisingly I saw through the open window that it was dawn. When the chief came out of her office again I asked her if she could tell me the time.

'No,' she said and walked on.

After another hour of silence I began to get agitated. This didn't make any sense at all. It occurred to me that maybe, in revenge, they were going to make sure I missed my plane. A woman in blue came in, walked up to me and said, 'Ticket.' I pointed to the chief's office. She came out with the flight coupons in her hand and, without a word to me, disappeared.

I waited another long time, and finally got fed up. So I went downstairs, where there were a few cleaners around, and asked to talk to someone from Air Kazakhstan. Another woman in blue appeared. She became quite agitated. The plane to Istanbul was already on the runway. 'Do you have luggage?' she asked. We went upstairs with a luggage handler following us. She got the passport and the rest of my ticket from the chief, who appeared to say nothing. The handler seized the lighter of the two bags, leaving me to puff across the tarmac with the big one and the two carry-ons, while everyone shouted, 'Quick, quick, come on.'

There was never an explanation, but I know that gang of girly cops was out to get me. I should never have had those bad thoughts about their hair.

Once I was on the plane, everything returned to normal. It was a big, beautiful jumbo Airbus. The flight attendants had the build of bouncers, but they were attentive. The food was fine. The flight was on time. Kazakhstan became a Kafkaesque dream, but I was still pissed off about that ten-pound note.

Derek Packham, the English biker who lived just outside Istanbul, rescued me from the airport and gave me shelter until Lufthansa were pleased to relinquish my crated bike, having first taken it to Cologne and back again. I tried to hold on to the Indian customs seal as a souvenir of ultimate futility, but it fell apart in my hands.

Meanwhile, emailing Dave in Dorchester to tell him I was on my way, we discovered we had a problem. I had already promised to meet Malú in California at the end of July. Now, for all kinds of reasons it turned out that I needed to arrive in England on 20 June, which put some pressure on. I was determined to have some quiet days in France before it all ended, and the way it worked out I had to choose between seeing nothing of Turkey or rushing home through the Balkans.

I chose Turkey, and whirled around that big country, doing about three thousand miles in eight days of riding. It was only a superficial glimpse, perhaps, but enough to see that Turkey and Europe were obviously moving closer together. In 1977 I would have said that Europe ended in Istanbul, but now the cultural border seems much further east. I enjoyed it enormously, became familiar with its geography and determined once again that I must come back and see a lot more.

Erzerum in the far east was a particular target. It was there that I entered Turkey from Iran in 1977, having almost frozen to death on the passes, and I had powerful memories of a rather cloistered, backward town with steep cobbled streets, and of the intimate atmosphere in a bakery that produced the most delicious savoury bread I had ever tasted. My impression on returning was quite different. No cobbles, no mystery, just a busy, ordinary town. The only signs of backwardness were the corrupt cops I met on the way out and, to my Western eyes, the women hidden inside their black burkas.

Most surprising of all was the beauty of the Black Sea coast, where some of the fishing villages and bays have the lazy, undemanding charm that was once such a seductive feature of the French Mediterranean. Other than that, the sweetest of my Turkish delights was finding Paolo Volpara and his peach of a wife, Serap, on the Mediterranean coast at Gocek in a gorgeous house which she designed and built. He's a passionate motorcyclist, larger than life, with a great appetite for enjoyment, and they are both people I will surely meet again.

Back in Istanbul for a last day with Derek, I scored. The thing I had brought back with me on the bike on my first journey that I prized the most was a beautiful Kashmiri carpet. Later I lost it in bizarre circumstances and had hoped to find another on my way through Iran. Now, serendipitously, a man turned up with some Afghan carpets he had brought from Mazar-i-Sharif, and the most beautiful of them was within my means. It is impossible to account for the joy it gave me. Perhaps, in part, it made up for missing that whole stretch of the Middle East, but those shimmering shades of red silk bathed my heart in a warm glow. Packed in a sturdy plastic bag, the carpet sat behind me as I set off on the final three thousand miles.

Bulgaria, Yugoslavia, Bosnia, Croatia, Slovenia and Italy in four days. It was absurd, of course, but still I managed to extract a great deal from it. I slept in Sofia, and in Sarajevo and Ljubljana. Ten years after the war, the aftermath of destruction in the Bosnian countryside was still obvious, but Sarajevo, which we used to watch nightly being shelled and where people suffered for so long, appeared remarkably free of scars, and the city seemed so busy and consumed with its own growing prosperity that it was almost alienating.

What I had not appreciated before was how tumultuous and fascinating the landscape is in that part of the world, and how any small part of it could exert such a strong hold on its peasant proprietors. Then as I emerged from those ghost-ridden mountains to the flatter land of Slovenia it began already to feel as though the journey was ended.

47

The closer I got to home the more I thought about the book I was going to write, and the more depressed I became. It seemed to me impossible to say anything upbeat and optimistic about the changes I had seen. Even if many people were materially better off than they had been, they didn't know it, and were no happier because of it. On the contrary, the little they had convinced them that they needed much more.

For this reason alone, I thought, overpopulation must lead the human race to disaster. I had no doubt that this overcrowding of the planet, which made us all part of one global society, would produce the same systemic problems of rage and aggression that rats exhibit when they're packed too closely together. Indeed it was already happening, and I saw the wars in the Middle East as among the first efforts of rich nations to defend themselves from the consequences of unsustainable growth.

So much of what had fascinated me on my first voyage through the world was disappearing – cultures, customs, animals, whole ecologies, all diluted, muddied or driven to extinction.

It didn't help that my own personal deterioration seemed to be running in parallel. A farcical episode in Ljubljana reminded me of that. I arrived in the capital of Slovenia in the afternoon, looking for somewhere to change the banknotes I'd bought in Yugoslavia, but at the usual money-changing places they were considered worthless. Someone said, 'Try the railway station.' I went there and parked alongside a large and populated outdoor concourse. As soon as I got off the bike I had to pee. Not just that, I knew I would have to pee very soon. Try as I could to hold it, to bear down on it, I knew it was out of control. There was nowhere to go, and only one thing I could do – run, run anywhere. For some reason running holds it back.

I was wearing the whole cumbersome outfit, jacket, heavy rain-proof pants and so on, and I felt absurdly conspicuous puffing over the pavement through the crowds, though most probably nobody even noticed or cared. But I knew I dared not stop. I ran to one end of the concourse, and then to the other. There was no sign of a toilet, not even a suitable wall, and if there had been, I couldn't afford the time to dig through the layers of clothing. I would be undone before I was undone.

I was panting and sweating and ready to accept the inevitable when, glory be, the urge diminished and I was saved. I could stop running, feign indifference, ask someone where the loo was and, with the few minutes of grace I had won, find it.

Of course mortality can't be denied or stopped in its relentless attrition, I know that. But philosophical resignation is no help when joints lock up for no apparent reason, muscles go into inconvenient spasm, valves declare their right to open and shut regardless of my intentions, pumps behave erratically or not at all, and the whole marvellous mechanism of life, which for seven decades has operated beautifully out of sight and mind, now demands maintenance and supervision and threatens to run amok. Meanwhile my motorcycle functions perfectly and makes a mockery of me.

There are days when I feel like some antiquated factory, patched and riveted and scarred by welds, spurting steam and smoke from split pipes and burst gaskets, leaking and dribbling and rustily squeaking away its last days before the scrapyard. Well, at least the factory still produces something. I'm far from wanting to go gentle into that good night, and a certain amount of rage is appropriate, but then I have to appreciate also how fortunate I am. I have con-temporaries who are envious of my good health, and it's true that all the really vital components do their job and show no sign of giving up. If I put my mind to it and make the effort I could probably even turn my body clock back a year or two. I wish I could say the same about the human race. It is, to my mind, the overwhelming tragedy of our time that as individuals we are capable of making great changes in our lives, while as a species we stumble wide-eyed and irrevocably towards disaster. When the end of oil, wood and coal finally halts global warming, how many of us will be left alive on this barren planet, and what sort of people will those survivors be?

When I recorded my first journey I devoted myself to a certain kind of truth. I believed that if I came as close as I could to describing exactly how things looked, tasted, felt, smelled and sounded, it would carry conviction. I wanted to counter the waves of self-serving disinformation – call it bullshit – that I thought were washing over the world, but equally important was my desire to convey how 'the world' was receiving me, how it responded to the unexpected arrival of one individual, largely ignorant of the history, culture, political circumstances and even language of the societies I was passing through.

Because my reception was generally so welcoming and benign, I see now that I projected some of my newborn optimism on the world at large. Looking back, I cannot help but see in the world of the seventies a kind of innocence, but I think this is really just a reflection of my own delight at finding my place in it.

Clearly that perception of innocence cannot be sustained. Perhaps I described the threat best when I came to Kenya in 1974. As it appeared to me then, the impact of the modern world on Kenya was limited to the commercial interests of Nairobi. 'London and Nairobi,' I said, referring to the airline connection, 'are joined by a silver tube, and the same stuff pours out at each end', stuff that I called 'bankers' baloney'. I saw it as a pollutant that breaks everything down into money. In those days it was confined to major cities with airports. Now the world is drowning in it. Idealism has been discredited. All that remains is money, and yet there are more people starving in Kenya today.

The most obvious evidence is the proliferation of gambling casinos and slot-machines, and everyone is into plastic now, and cash machines are worldwide, so bankers' baloney, like AIDS and chicken, has spread everywhere.

Chicken? Yes, everybody eats chicken, from London to Cape Town, from Alaska to Tierra del Fuego, from Sydney to Istanbul and, by all accounts, from Moscow to Beijing. This one-time luxury has become the basic protein of the poor, and before I even arrived in Singapore, before anyone had ever heard of 'bird flu', I was wondering whether some disease might not strike the chicken population. Monocrops are susceptible to ravaging diseases, and the way chickens are raised now certainly puts them into that category. It could be like the Irish potato blight on a global scale.

Since the seventies vast amounts of money have flowed into the Unfinished World, in the efforts of Cold War combatants to hold on to strategic bases and materials, but only a fraction has found its way into the pockets of the people. Most of it appears to have gone into sustaining avaricious tyrants who have used it to secure their power and send even more money to Switzerland.

Following the example of my deckhand on the *Zoë. G* all those years ago, people everywhere are now absorbing information. They may not have computers or Internet services or even televisions, but everybody now knows somebody who does. People in remote tribal and rural areas have been introduced to the concept of 'growth', but are denied the means to apply it. In fact these places are no longer really 'remote', but they can't sustain their increased populations. People turn to the cities for work, and lacking work some turn to crime. Meanwhile the West's appetite for raw materials increases constantly, making it profitable to cut down forests and to cover the land with monocultures like sugar, maize and pine.

So what I am seeing now is not so much how it is – but how it differs from what it was. And if the world delighted me in the seventies because I delighted in myself, you might ask whether my disappointment with the world today reflects some dissatisfaction with myself? Of course I have given this a lot of thought, but I think not. It is true that on my first journey I was in love twice, whereas this time I only managed it once, but love is love, and not to be measured by numbers.

I have broken bones on this trip, but in a way I find that very satisfying. There was something a bit wrong about coming through it all unscathed. It's about time my body bore some evidence of my life passage, something a bit more dramatic than a few grey hairs and a lazy bladder. Nor does the slow but inevitable deterioration of my faculties dull my pleasure in living. So far, thank goodness, I can take pleasure in the fact that it *is* slow, and gives me plenty of time to make peace with my condition, however much I may resent it.

I think my disappointment arises out of a genuine sense of loss. Obviously I can't regret the passing of South American dictators, or the end of apartheid, or the unseating of Haile Selassie, or even the independence of Zimbabwe. But I do regret that my son will never be able to dance with the Turkana as I once did, that China has lost its mystery, that it is possible to travel from one end of Africa to the other without seeing a wild animal that isn't protected, and that all the empty beaches I once loved are full.

I regret that one culture has become so powerful that it has made all the others slaves or tributaries to it, even though it is my culture.

The paradox is built into me. In essence I am an optimist. Amongst the pleasures of life, I can't sustain these gloomy thoughts of the future. Near Ljubljana I found a cosy inn where I ate and drank too much for very little. Next day I completed the circle by meeting up with Franco Panzanini in Milan and having the dinner I missed back in 2001. He rode his Harley with me halfway to the border in the morning, and then I cut into the French Alps through a series of spectacular tunnels and emerged to see those stupendous mountains looming above me, quite as grand in their way as anything I had seen in the Andes or the Himalayas. I arrived exactly as I had twenty-six years earlier, at the small chateau of my friends at Arboras near Montpellier, and a few days later I rode north to Paris

I love France, but Paris is even more than France. From within the walls of Paris I think of France as another country. I lived in Paris for two years as a young man, it changed me for ever, and no happy thing could happen to me anywhere that would not make me even happier if it occurred in Paris. Through a mutual friend I was invited by a university professor to stay briefly in his small top-floor apartment a short walk away from the river and the Eiffel Tower. It was early June, and the weather was wonderful. I was able to tuck the bike away in a corner at the back of the cobbled courtyard, and walked out a little later into the warmth of the early evening down the Rue de Bourgogne to the riverbank, then down towards St-Germain.

It was the part of the Left Bank where the tour and dinner boats tie up. There are the *bateaux mouches*, these days more like scaled-down cruise ships, which each transport hundreds of day-trippers up and down the Seine under glass. Then there are the rather select boats that wine and dine you as you float gently through the heart of Paris. In my youth these were wildly beyond my means, and I scorned them as bourgeois frivolities. Since then I had got into the habit of ignoring them as an extravagance, but Paris and the weather worked their magic on me that evening, and opened my eyes.

One of the boats in particular caught my fancy. It was fairly small and painted mostly black, with glittering brasswork, and handsome lamps strung out over the sides. It had a small black funnel ringed in gold at the top, like a Russian Sobranie cigarette. The tables on the deck were laid very attractively, and everything about the boat looked exquisite. It was called *Le Calife*, and it advertised a two-hour cruise with dinner for thirty-five euros, and maybe half as much again for a bottle of wine. The price seemed too low. I was afraid the food would be ordinary. I walked past it a couple of times, but it was irresistible.

The sixty euros I spent on *Le Calife* count among the best investments I have ever made. I suppose I have had more than my share of moments of pure happiness in my life. None that I recall had anything much to do with money. Some of them were on this journey – at the *Costa do Sol* in Mozambique, sitting in a café in Rio, on the road to Bariloche, that morning in bed with Malú at the Namaskar, just a few examples. They usually take me completely by surprise, just as this did. In fact, surprise is a precondition.

I took the eight o'clock cruise, and soon after we started to move

I got a bottle of Merlot. We chugged down towards Notre Dame past the Île de la Cité. I had never seen those immense government buildings and lawcourts from the river. The scale of them is astonishing, with their mansard roofs, turrets, crenelations and huge chimney-stacks stretched out along the riverbank like stranded leviathans.

A delicious smoked salmon salad with chopped peppers and mustard sauce appeared before me. We rounded Notre Dame and for the first time I noticed the modern clock at the back of it. Then the Île St-Louis, where I once met the writer James Jones outside his house in his cowboy boots. All along the quais were groups of young people out in the setting sun picnicking, playing guitars, singing, and waving gaily at *me*, the plutocrat. I felt like tossing them a crust.

The waiter brought couscous with grilled fish and cumin as we turned around and headed downriver to the ultramodern buildings of La Défense, where I was dazzled by the last rays of the sun bouncing off their glass curtain walls. In the warmth, the pleasure and the inspiration of Paris I thought about this book again and saw that what was going to happen to the world in ten, twenty or fifty years from now was only half the story – the next half, if you like.

The first half, which ended now, had produced this marvellously civilised city and my ecstasy at being alive in it. Just to be able to experience this joy, to have lived the life I have, to have done what I've done, was something to write home about. I would do all I could to demonstrate what wonderful things there are still to do and what fine people there are to meet in the world, that a man can still be in love at the age of seventy-two, and that it doesn't matter if my body doesn't always do what I want it to. Adjustments can be made, love-making doesn't have to be a contest, and besides, a lot of it is very funny.

I don't mean to abandon the future, but where societies are concerned I have been a pessimist since my twenties. I put my faith in individuals, in their genius, their beauty, their feelings, and the splendid things they have accomplished in the past, and can accomplish in the present. The future will be what it will be.

My elation stayed with me through northern France, and on the boat overnight to Southampton I slept like a prince. More by accident than design Stephen Burgess and I encountered each other on the road outside the port, had breakfast, and rode off towards Dorchester. He said thirty-five bikers were waiting at Bere Regis to join the procession. I didn't know where Bere Regis was, but Steve said it didn't matter. There were some motorcycle police waiting too, he said, and once they'd checked out my lapsed tax disc and MOT and issued the appropriate tickets, they'd take care of things.

Fortunately, he was joking. The police were there, the same ones that had seen me off two and a half years earlier. They turned a blind eye to the tax disc, easily done since it was invisible under a thick cake of mud, and waved me on. I looked around for the thirty-five bikers, wondering what to do, when they all suddenly emerged from a slip road. Out there in the sunshine. I wanted to stop and watch them all go past, but that would have spoilt it for them. A lovely sight.

Anyway, we arrived safely and someone handed me a pint of bitter, which I must have drunk with stunning expertise because the crowd applauded. Everyone said I looked younger than when I'd left, which was very nice of them. And that, believe it or not, was the end of a journey around the world – 59,000 miles of riding, forty-eight countries, all that time passed. But I had a hard job believing that I'd been anywhere. Standing there in Dorset I couldn't find anything to connect me with the Sudanese desert or the music of Brazil, or the Andes, or the Outback.

It was all very peculiar. As though I hadn't really been anywhere at all.

EPILOGUE

I learned some things in 1977. I learned that the journey doesn't stop just because I do. The sense of travelling continues as a mind trip, and the memories and feelings do come back. I also learned that even though the book may be very important, it's better not to neglect human relationships, and I was determined this time not to sacrifice my relationship with Malú. So I devoted my first months at home in California to making our life together in Chile a possibility and – what do you know? – I got it wrong and it didn't work.

Not that I wasn't thinking about the book. It was always floating there, in embryo, but I couldn't see how to make it grow. My problem was to identify its significance. What was the point of it? For a year I struggled in vain. In desperation I went back to France, to the same place where I had written much of *Jupiter's Travels*; and finally, delving ever deeper into the past, I rediscovered the deckhand on the *Zoë. G.* Just how or why that figure should spark the engine that drove this book remains a mystery, but suddenly I felt I had some way of giving form and purpose to an otherwise rambling diary of events. Even so, it took more than a year to carry through.

In the two and a half years since I returned, the world's prospects have gone from bad to worse and look like continuing that way. In the hands of wiser men 9/11 might just possibly have offered an opportunity to reach across ethnic and religious frontiers and bring together the best of us. Instead we are launched on a path that promises more conflict, death and physical degradation. Just when we should be doing all we can to protect our environment, we are threatening to extinguish another sixteen thousand species (not to mention our own) and heat the world up to intolerable levels. In the seventies I came back with a fanciful vision of the human race as a cancer on the face of the earth. There is nothing fanciful about that comparison today.

So much for people in their billions.

What about you and me? Can we do anything about it?

I was raised to do good in a rather militant way. The battle was always about ends and means, and became dispiriting. Then, almost thirty years ago I discovered that choosing good over bad is the best thing to do regardless of the likely outcome. It makes me happier and, coincidentally, seems to work in my favour in the long run. I hope this doesn't sound simplistic and smug. I don't mean to imply that I used to choose bad, or that others do so routinely. It's a question of motivation. I try to do the right thing for its own sake, and not for a purpose. The choice is remarkably liberating and makes it easier to live in a world that seems to be drifting toward destruction. Of course the idea is close to the heart of all great religions, but it is more effective, I believe, when you discover it for yourself and learn that the reward comes here rather than in heaven.

Finding the good thing to do is not always easy, but it comes with practice. In the end it seems to boil down to two precepts: do the least possible harm to the world around you, and make the best possible use of the gifts you were born with.

Naturally I believe that if everyone behaved accordingly we wouldn't be in such a mess, but it's a good approach to life anyway, so those of us lucky enough to know it have nothing to lose. It is also a wonderful way to travel. It causes splendid things to happen along the way. If I have one hope for this book, it is my hope that it will encourage others to travel the world in that way and, by looking for the good in it, have wonderful adventures and do some good in return. That may be the least, and the best, we can do.

*

When the book was written, I was looking idly through some old photographs and came across a roll of scratched black-and-white negatives. There was a picture of the deckhand I'd forgotten I had. It was similar to my memory of him, but his special quality doesn't shine through. Alongside it was a picture he must have taken of me. For me this really is the stuff of dreams.

ACKNOWLEDGEMENTS

My journey would have been almost impossible but for the help of countless good-hearted people and a number of equally generous companies. Many have already been mentioned in these pages. I hope I have made my appreciation clear to them, but some bear repetition and there were many more. First the companies. Pride of place must obviously go to CW Motorcycles, of Dorchester. Dave Wyndham and his enthusiastic team were with me in spirit all the way. www.cwmotorcycles.co.uk

My sincere thanks also to:

Avon Tyres, who shod my wheels on both journeys. Great performance, and I still consider it miraculous that on this trip their Distanzia tyres suffered not a single puncture in all those 59,000 miles. www.avontyres.com

Maybe Seal-a-Wheel had something to do with, too. I used their goo all the way round. www.seal-a-wheel.co.uk

Andy Goldfine at Aerostich, whose jacket saved me from worse injury in Colombia, and who has persistently offered more help than I could accept. www.aerostich.com

Bernd Tesch, an irrepressible campaigner for long-distance motorcycling who ekes out a living supplying tips and equipment to his brothers and sisters on wheels. He gave me his boxes at cost. www.berndtesch.de

David Gerbing for his very effective electrically-heated clothing. www.gerbing.com

And Mike Coan for the clever Heat-Troller that regulated it. www.warmnsafe.com

Tony Hickey of Village Ethiopia whose passion for his adopted country is inspiring, and through him the Goha Hotel in Gondar and the Sheraton in Addis Ababa, who offered much-needed rest and recuperation. www.village-ethiopia.net

Christoph Handschuh, an intrepid traveller himself, who was working for Mashariki's BMW in Nairobi when I was holed up there over a month with a broken leg. He gave me shelter and valuable access to Mashariki's service department.

Walter Nosiglias, a great enthusiast, whose Honda dealership outside La Paz is a tremendous resource for passing adventurers.

Phil Pilgrim, an old Australian mate from my first trip, who now owns Union Jack Motorcycles on Lygon street, Melbourne and did just about everything a man could do to look after me and my bike. www.unionjack.com.au

Andy White practically donated his workshop for a day to build the prototype soft bags that were such a success on the return half of the trip. www.andystrapz.com

Anand Kashyap, of Kashyap Motors, New Delhi, who was remarkably generous with help, accommodation, and introductions. And K.C. Raju, of OPT Services in New Delhi, who was unbelievably supportive in getting my bike out of India.

Then come the media: Mark Tuttle and Ken Freund at *Rider Magazine*; Reiner Nitschke of *Touren-Fahrer*, and Markus Biebricher who had the task of translating me into German; Bill Golden at *Classic Bike*; Brian Halton at San Francisco's *CityBike*; they all helped in their various ways to keep me going. And while the job lasted it was a great pleasure to write for the *Independent on Sunday*.

Finally, but most important of all, were the people who helped me along the way, wrote to me, encouraged me, sent small contributions and made it all seem worthwhile. Many of them I have never met, and it would be impossible to name them all here, but I have to take the obvious risk of mentioning some of them, in the hope that others won't feel excluded.

So thanks first and foremost, to Stephen Burgess, and to Jo

Sandilands, Franco Panzanini, Stuart Larman, Lorraine Chittock, Alex Hooper, Yoav, Dr Robert Faccin, Professor Mbyindi, Elmarie Theron, Paul Moody, Amin and Jacira, the Grise family, Anniken and Dan O'Connell, the Wesleys, the Viale family, Ricardo Rocco, Tiberio Jaramillo, Mauricio and Macky, Colin Goodwin, Al and Julie Jesse, John Conely, Ty Pink, John Rains, Graeme Howe, Pete Lusk, Dave Milligan, Rob van Driesum, Guy Allen, Dave McGonigal, George Lockyer, Martin Belson, John Edwards, the O'Sheas, David Stafford, Botter, Lisa Roberts, Derek Packham, and of course all 350 members of the Order of PSJ who appear on my website at www.jupitalia.com/dec3_txt_31.html.

FACTS AND FIGURES, NUTS & BOLTS, BAGS AND BOXES

Distance ridden on the bike: 59,000 miles (First journey – 64,000 miles)

Time on the bike: 29 months (First journey – 44 months)

Countries visited: 47 (First journey – 45)

Tyres used: six sets, fitted in UK, Nairobi, Chile, Arizona, Australia and India. Not a single puncture.

The Bike: BMW 1997 R80 GS 'Basic' fitted with Avon Distanzia tyres.

Modifications carried out by CW Motorcycles of Dorchester:
> 1000cc cylinders: Brembo front disc brakes: White Power front springs: Ohlins rear shock absorber: UK Police spec. alternator and battery: Three independent 12v sockets: Garmin GPS: Renthal handlebars with 50mm risers: Acerbis 43-litre tank: Acerbis brush guards: Heated grips: 'Sure Foot' side-stand with desert pad: Tesch TT4 49-litre Aluminium panniers on square section tubular frame: Zega 33-litre top box: Kick and electric start

CW did everything brilliantly, down to the smallest detail – like tying the spokes together where they crossed to avoid a broken spoke puncturing a tyre. The major problem I had was with the panniers. They were a new design when Bernd Tesch offered them to me. I liked them for their slim profile – deep rather than wide – but there was no time to build the proper frame for them. As a result they sat too far forward on the old frame. This certainly contributed to my breaking a leg in Kenya, but the fault was entirely mine. I wanted them. CW did the best they could.

There was also a mystery surrounding the alternator. CW insist they fitted the most powerful one going, but right at the start, in France, it failed to supply enough current for all the stuff I had plugged in. In Germany, courtesy of Reiner Nitschke and *Touren-Fahrer*, I fitted a new 20-amp alternator and from then on everything ran well. What caused the problem in France will never be known, but I'm willing to bet it was something I did.

In addition to the hard luggage I started out with a tank bag and two Ortlieb bags. Apart from personal items and camping gear I also carried a Macintosh laptop in a Pelican case, a Nikon N90s film camera, a Coolpix digital, two mobile phones (for the film project), a battery charger, many spare parts, inner tubes for emergencies, and of course my trademark umbrella. Much of this changed over time. I found the Mac was tough enough to cope without the bulky Pelican case. After Africa I cut 50lb off my load. In Arizona I replaced the battered Zega box with one of Al Jesse's top boxes. In Australia I finally abandoned the Tesch boxes and sent them home with all the camping gear I wasn't using. Instead, I fitted soft bags designed for me by Andy White, took another 50lb off the weight and transformed the biking experience. I have been a fan of soft luggage ever since.

Useful things to take that you might not think of: big rubber bands, soft wire, and more rubber bands.